Goat Production and Health Management

NIPA® GENX ELECTRONIC RESOURCES & SOLUTIONS P. LTD.
New Delhi-110 034

Goat Production and Health Management

S.K. JINDAL
Principal Scientist and Head
Division of Physiology, Reproduction and Shelter Management
Central Institute for Research on Goats
Makhdoom, Mathura, Uttar Pradesh

NIPA® GENX ELECTRONIC RESOURCES & SOLUTIONS P. LTD.
New Delhi-110 034

NIPA® GENX ELECTRONIC
RESOURCES & SOLUTIONS P. LTD.

101,103, Vikas Surya Plaza, CU Block
L.S.C. Market, Pitam Pura, New Delhi-110 034
Ph : +91 11 27341616, 27341717, 27341718
E-mail: newindiapublishingagency@gmail.com
web: www.nipabooks.com

For customer assistance, please contact
Phone: + 91-11-27 34 17 17
Fax: + 91-11- 27 34 16 16
E-Mail: feedbacks@nipabooks.com

ISBN: 978-81-19215-08-9

Composed and Designed by NIPA®.

Preface

The food production system is being challenged by a number of threats including changes in the climate, competition for resources (land, water supply and energy), and changing consumption patterns. This increasing demand for livestock products cannot be met by higher livestock numbers alone as natural resources to produce these livestock has a ceiling. Since, goat is an important source of meat, milk, fiber, skin and manure especially in the subsistant agriculture in arid and semi-arid zones of Asia and Africa, it can contribute substantially to fulfilling the increasing demand for livestock products in developing and developed countries of the world. Goats have a bright future as a domestic animal because of its continued usefulness and generation of new information to maintain this species in a more sustainable and profitable manner. Goat farming requires less capital to start and maintain than cattle or buffalo farming. Goat also has a higher reproductive rate as compared to cattle or buffaloes. Goat can sustain itself on marginal lands where other species of livestock may not even survive. Zero input goat production system is changing to a more intensive commercial goat production system. Decreasing common property resources are driving farmers to take up intensive system more seriously. There exists a great diversity in types of goats which provides a great scope for natural and artificial selection. Goat improvement programmes are at the forefront in the agenda of governments for poverty alleviation and for ensuring nutritional and food security to the ever growing population. Livestock production is fast changing and goat has a great future. Newer technologies in the area of breeding, feeding, management and disease control are changing the goat production scenario. In India and other developing countries, increasing production and efficiency of the goat production system through improved animal health, fertility, longevity and nutrition hold the most potential for enhancing nutrient use efficiency in food chains and for ensuring nutritional and food security which hold the key to transform the goat production system from subsistent to sustainable and viable. Technology support is imperative not only for enhancement of productivity but also reduction of per unit cost. Strategies to facilitate sustainable livestock production in different agro-climatic zones include evaluation of alternative forage and feed resources and augment the supply of forages and feeds with better nutritional attributes through treatments, enhancing bio availability of nutrients and precision nutrition for maximizing efficient utilization of feeds and feed processing technologies, rumen modulation through manipulation of the ruminal microfauna to improve utilization of low quality feeds, identification of mineral imbalances and their ameliorations, enhancing efficiency of AI, improvement in reproduction efficiency using suitable assisted reproductive technologies, climate change-vulnerability and impact assessment studies and identification of genes related to production and reproduction function are some of the upcoming areas in which important contributions are being made and new discoveries added. Similarly newer disease control and prevention strategies are becoming available and useful.

These newer developments need to be collated and synthesized and this small book is a humble effort in this direction. In this book, I have tried to put emphasis on goat production in India but lot of information from world over is mentioned. Goats have been a major part of the research and development programmes aimed at poverty alleviation via the use of small ruminants. Research is of little use if its results are not disseminated and this book is part of the strategy for the dissemination and promotion of the research results to ensure that poor and under-resourced farmers benefit. The publication is expected to provide a useful reference source for all those who are interested in goats.

I thank profusely to all my colleagues at Central Institute for Research on Goats, Makhdoom for much assistance, discussion and guidance in writing this book. Acknowledgement to individuals is listed separately. It is hoped that this book will be of help not only to students but also to goat keepers. There is no claim of originality as much of the information has been obtained from books and journals and internet resources. I am grateful to my wife Mrs.Sadhana Jindal and my son Mr. Nishant and daughter Dr. Nitasha for their help and support.

S.K. Jindal

Acknowledgements

- Dr. Devendra Swarup, Director, Central Institute for Research on Goats, for kind encouragement and support.
- Dr. G.F.W.Haenlein, for his support over the past many many years.
- Dr. Naveen Kumar for writing part of the chapter on goat diseases especially bacterial and viral diseases.
- Dr. A.K. Goel, Dr. N. Ramachandran, Dr. Priyadharshini Raju, Dr. Ravinder Kumar, Dr. M.K.Tripathi, Dr. T.K.Dutta, Dr. P.K.Rout, Dr. A.K. Verma, Dr.B. Rai , Dr. A.K. Dixit, Dr. Vasan , Dr. Souvik Pal, Dr. G.B. Manjunath Reddy, for reading some of the chapters and for useful suggestions.
- Director, CIRG and Dr. M.K.Singh for some of the photographs.

Contents

1

Introduction

Over the past 12,000 years *Homo sapiens* have moved from the hunter–gatherer life-style to settled agriculture to advanced civilization in urban society with improved quality of life. Livestock has played an important role as an instrument of bringing out this change. Farmers all over the world, attach great importance to livestock ownership as a source of nutrition, as a mechanism for capital accumulation, and concomitantly, as a symbol of wealth and status in the community. Just as in today's society, money is used to exchange goods and services, livestock including goats used to play the same role in times gone by. Most farmers consider livestock as a important resource for income generation. Livestock sector plays a significant role in supplementing family income and generating gainful employment in the rural sector, particularly among the landless, marginal and small farmers and women, besides providing cheap nutritional food to millions of people. History indicates that livestock has been not only a resource, but also an instrument of dominance and a source of conflict in the society. Livestock especially small ruminants have often served as a means for exchange of goods and services and thus becoming increasingly important in the growth of agriculture in developing economies.

Livestock species which man domesticated for improving the quality of human life include goat, sheep, cattle, buffalo, pig, poultry, horses and camels. Among these goats were the first among livestock species domesticated by man. Goats are among the smallest domesticated ruminants and have served mankind longer than cattle or sheep. Goat is an important source of meat, milk, skin, fiber and manure since then. Traditionally goats have been an important source of income generation among small households. Goats have been used to buy salt, cloth and groceries in many communities. Goats provide a large part of the cash income for smallholder farmers. Goats are friendly animals; with proper attention they maintain good health and can be managed easily even by children.

Sailors and other explorers out on the high seas kept goats as a ready stock of meat & milk on long voyages. Captain Cook's goat had already sailed around the world before it entered on its first voyage with Cook, and helped save everyone on board the ship from scurvy. Goats are some times kept as pet or companion animal. Their use as pet is common in European countries especially U.K. Some owners keep goats for purpose of goat shows.

Goats play an important role in the agriculture all over the world especially in subsistent agriculture of developing countries where over 90% of the world goat populations are raised. Underprivileged families account for about one-fourth of the population and contribute 70-80 % of the total livestock produce. Two-third of the world's poor live in Asia and are below nationally defined poverty lines and 65 % of them are poor livestock keepers who derive a large part of their household income from domesticated animals. Goats are the lifeline of millions of small/marginal/landless farmers in India, the middle and Far East, Africa and countries of North, South and Central America. Goats are the key to survival of millions of poor and underprivileged people around the world who strive to make a living from livestock. Goats are valuable even in developed countries of Europe, Australia, and New Zealand. Goats were brought to the New World countries by early settlers who carried goats to sustain themselves during the long journey through sea routes. Goats were a common sight on early European sailing ships. They were desirable because of their relatively small size.

Goat farming in India has been practiced using traditional and conventional methods for centuries. Goat Farming has history as old as human civilization. The archaeological evidence traces goat domestication as far back as ca. 10,500 calibrated Before Present (cal. B.P.) in the high Euphrates valleys, in Southeastern Anatolia and 9900 to 9500 cal. B.P. in the Zagros Mountains in Iran and Iraq. Unlike sheep, goats easily revert to feral or wild condition given a chance.

All over the world, landholdings are becoming increasingly small and fragmented because of population pressure. Consequently there has been a restructuring of land and labour use which has more often than not favoured goat production. Unavailability of community pasture previously available for livestock production and need to devote adult household labor to more intensive off-farm employment has also favoured increasing emphasis on goat production. Common property resources (CPRs), though neglected by policy makers and planners, play a significant role in the life of the rural poor as goat production under extensive system is greatly or entirely dependent on common property resources. Large-scale privatisation of CPR has taken place mainly during the last three decades with the consequence that such resources are less and not available to poor goat keepers. Thus, the rural poor collectively lost a significant part of the source of their sustenance through the decline of CPRs.

Goats have been used for centuries, to carry loads, starting in places like Iran and Tibet. Goats can easily carry 1/4 of their total body weight. Goats require very little extra food to be transported for them, unlike llamas and horses.Goats of any breed make excellent land-clearers. Goats are natural climbers and enjoy steep or rough terrain. They can go places where clearing machinery cannot. Goats can quietly clear the vegetation from such land and leave a clear open space. Goats are far more sure-footed, especially in mountainous terrain and loose rocks.

The effectiveness of a mountain goat's hoof in providing that animal with sure footing on diverse and extreme ground conditions has been recognized. Footwear intended primarily for outdoor use, wherein a variety of ground conditions are likely to be encountered , has a sole with traction elements inspired by the hoof of a mountain goat (United states Patent assigned to Nike, Inc., Oreg No 08/785,666. Dated Jul 27, 1999).

Migration of goats from different parts of the world

Goats migrated from central Asia where they originated to all parts of Europe, Africa, East and Middle East Asia. Domesticated goats migrated from the Western Asia to the eastern region. The other route is the northern route via Afghanistan and Turkistan to Mongolia and Northern China. Yet another route exists through the Khyber Pass to the Indian sub-continent and then to the south East Asia. besides a sea route.

The most recent and possibly greatest migration of goat and sheep took place 200-300 years ago, when the Europeans settled in the Southern Hemisphere i.e. South America, South Africa, Australia, and New Zealand.

Goats as an instrument to ensure nutritional and food security

Goats are a source of food and nutritional security for those teeming millions in the poorest parts of the world. Goat is an important livestock species for sustenance of rural poor in India as well as other countries of the world.Goats significantly contribute to the agrarian economy and play a very vital role in the livelihood security of the small and marginal farmers and landless laborers especially in arid, semi-arid and mountainous regions of the country. Rearing of sheep and goats plays an important role in the economy of India in general and sustainable livelihood of poor people of rainfed agro-ecosystem in particular, because of inherent risk involved in the crop farming due to uncertainty of rainfall and occurrence of recurrent droughts. Goats are hardy, disease resistant and widely adapted. They thrive well and reproduce well in tropical, cold, humid as well as dry regions.

Their small size compared to cattle and buffaloes permit them to be maintained on a limited area Goats consume a wide variety of grasses, weeds, forbs, bushes, shrubs, tree leaves and crop residues that would otherwise go waste and cause pollution. Goat is an efficient converter of the sparse vegetation available in wastelands, community grazing lands of arid, semi-arid and mountainous regions into milk, meat, skin, fiber and manure while utilizing traditional and under employed manpower. They are gentle and easy to control. Their small size makes them suitable for backyard slaughter and the meat can be consumed by the family. The goats can be milked any time of the day and are therefore named as the moving refrigerators. Goat milk is prescribed for children, old and sick people as it is easily digestible and has possible medicinal value. Goat meat (chevon) is preferred over other meats because it is leaner and there are no religious taboos against its consumption. The vast population and large genetic resource are the strengths of the goat production programme.

Not only goat has served for a longer period, the ways by which it has served are also varied. Goats are potential source of meat, milk, skin, fiber and are valued as a laboratory as well as pet animals. The wide range of utility combined with its docile, intelligent, graceful and frugal nature, perhaps contributed much to its earliest domestication. With the advent of civilization, goats were relegated to the oblivion, being surpassed by cattle and buffalo, in several important characteristics,but goat proliferated and survived in genetic isolation. The destructive habit of goats detracted many and more were detracted by the strong odor emanated by the male. But the advantages of goat far outweigh these disadvantages. Goats proved to be a great boon to the poor and landless or marginal farmers. Goat has been described as a poor man's cow, a befitting description of their immense contribution to the poor people's economy.

Of all the domestic animals, the goat doubtless has the greatest range of adaptations. Goats have been described in Encyclopedia Britannica as mountain dwellers. But they have equally adapted themselves to be widely known as desert dwellers. No other animal has been known to withstand the vagaries of the harsh environments as goats on both the extremes. The early domestication process along with certain definite physiological characteristics is perhaps responsible for its better adaptability. Its flexible integration into dissimilar socio-economic situations is associated with its high economic viability. Goats thrive well on poor agricultural lands, where they browse on incidental vegetation. In arid areas where vegetation is sparse and land is too steep for cultivation, goats roam more widely than other herbivores and meet their requirements from browsing on weeds neglected by others. They have a higher tolerance to feed deficient in crude protein and certain minerals. The goat is characterized by its ability for higher digestion of raw fibers as compared to other species of livestock. The nutrient supply of the goat is favored by

- it's tough mouth which is undeterred by thorns, bristles etc.
- its relatively high capacity to take up dry matter to make up the deficiency by poor quality forages.
- It's ability to consume a surprisingly wide variety of plants, grasses, bushes, tree leaves, industrial wastes which if fed to other classes of livestock will make them starve.
- Goats are also reputed to have bitter taste receptors which may be the probable reason for higher intake of bitter forages like neem leaves.
- Goats, because of their difference in feeding habits from the cow and sheep, serve as complementary rather than competitive, in the utilization of rangelands. Goats travel longer distances than sheep and cattle in search of food. The mobile upper lips of goats enable them to select discriminately favored parts of plants.

Land use in the Indian arid zone has been both thoughtless and nonscientific. The forces of desertification have gathered momentum within this zone. If this trend is to be reversed a suitable system of mixed farming with emphasis on animal husbandry has to be evolved and practiced. In evolving such a programme the choice of appropriate livestock becomes crucial. Where feed is scarce and of low nutritive value, larger animals are at a disadvantage because of their greater maintenance requirements. Smaller animals like goat with lower maintenance needs can cover large areas to gather sufficient nutrients for survival and minimum production of meat and milk. There are two conflicting views about the goat's role in land use. One view holds that the goat is the major cause of rangeland destruction and soil erosion, and its propagation should be checked. On the contrary the goat is after all a major supplier of animal protein and that since it usually consumes the scrub left-over from the overgrazing by cattle and sheep, it is unrealistic to blame the goat for environmental destruction.

Rapidly increasing goat populations in developing countries, point to the goat assisting in solving some of the needs created by the rising human populations. Consumer's acceptance of high quality goat products coupled to longstanding cultural traditions sets a positive outlook for the goat sector in the developed and developing countries.

The poor man's cow- goat has tremendous potential to be projected as the 'Future Animal' for rural prosperity under the changing agro-geo-climatic conditions and depleting resources for crop-based livelihood. Goat husbandry in India is essentially an endeavor of millions of small holders who rear animals on "Crop Residues" and "Common Property Resources". The small holders produce milk, meat, fiber, skin etc. for the community with virtually no capital, resource, training. There are around 920 million goats in the world out of which India has over 154 million goats (16.7%) of 23 defined breeds adapted efficiently in climatic conditions all over the country. The goats in India are reared primarily for meat and also for milk. The goat meat production in India has doubled (9.3% to 18.3%) and goat milk production has shown a growth rate of 31.53% during the last decade. The country stands first in goat milk production and is the second largest meat producer in the world sharing 26.31% goat milk, 10.41% goat meat and 13.14% of the goat skin production. Besides meat and milk, goats also produce good quality skin, valuable Pashmina fiber and around 400 TMT manure. The goat sector contributes Rs 14,453 crores to the agricultural economy of the country through meat (Rs 6851 crores), milk (Rs 4588 crores), skin (Rs 648 crores), etc. which accounts for around 8 per cent of the Gross Domestic Product (GDP) from livestock sector. In addition, the goat sector generates about 4% rural employment and about 20 million small and marginal farmers' and landless laborers' families depend on goats for their livelihood partially or completely. Current availability of animal proteins (10.8gms/day/capita) is just half of the daily requirement of (20 gms/day /capita and it is targeted to achieve this by the year 2020.The demand for livestock including goat products is a function of income, and sustained growth in per capita income, rising urban populations and changes in diet and lifestyle are fuelling growth in livestock production in general and goat production in particular.

Worldwide 100 million people in arid areas, have only possible source of livelihood by grazing small ruminants. Grazing goats can improve soil and vegetation cover and plant and animal biodiversity, for example by removing biomass, which otherwise might provide the fuel for bush fires, by controlling shrub growth and by dispersing seeds through their hoofs and manure, which can improve plant species composition. Other major benefits are the improved productivity of small farms by the incorporation of manure and the use of other farming practices such as the planting of trees and forages controlling soil erosion. Goats are easy to rear and serve as a ready source of income. Further, goats are intelligent, agile and resistant to many diseases including certain toxic chemicals and can look after themselves much better than other livestock species.

The chief difference between the goat and the sheep are in their ecological requirements. The sheep is essentially a grass-feeder whereas the goat is a browser. The goat is content with even sparser food than the sheep. It is therefore supplementary to sheep rather than a competitor. In particular, it eats aromatic herbs despised by sheep and other ruminants. Goat furnishes more milk than sheep and it has been speculated that the use of milk and its derivatives was first established with the goat before the cattle were domesticated (Randhava, 1980).It can therefore, be safely concluded that goat served a useful purpose to people of India since times immemorial and today it is an important source of meat and milk, fibre and skin to the poor, landless and marginal farmers of this country. It is rightly stated as Poor Man's Cow and is walking bank for many of the goat keepers who sell or kill one or more of their goats during periods of dire need. Not only goat serves mankind in many varied ways but has also served it for much longer period of history.

However, importance of this valuable genetic resource is often neglected due to many social and environmental biases and misconceptions.The advantages of goat rearing are:

- The initial investment needed for goat farming is low.
- Goats are more economical than sheep on free range grazing under semi-arid conditions.
- Goat creates employment to the rural poor besides effectively utilizing unpaid family labor. There is ample scope for establishing cottage industries based on goat meat and milk products and value addition to skin and fiber.
- Goats are a valuable asset for families and communities around the world
- Goats are friendly animals and enjoy being with the people.
- In drought prone areas risk of goat farming is very much less as compared to other livestock species.
- Goats are ideal for mixed species grazing. The animal can thrive well on wide variety of thorny bushes, weeds, crop residues, agricultural by-products unsuitable for human consumption.
- Under proper management, goats can improve and maintain grazing land and reduce bush encroachment (biological control) without causing harm to the environment.
- Unlike large animals in commercial farm conditions both male and female goats have equal value.
- Due to small body size and docile nature, housing requirements and manage mental problems with goats are less.
- Goats are prolific breeders and achieve sexual maturity at the age of 10-12 months, gestation period is short and at the age of 16-17 months it starts giving milk. Twinning is very common and triplets and quadruplets are low.
- Goats often have two or three kids a year, enabling families to start small dairies.
- The goat meat is more lean (low cholesterol) and relatively good for people who prefer low energy diet especially in summer and sometimes goat meat (chevon) is preferred over mutton because of its "chewability"
- Slaughter and dressing operation and meat disposal can be carried without much environmental problems.

- No religious taboo against goat slaughter and meat consumption prevalent in the country.
- Goat milk is easy to digest than cow milk because of small fat globules and is naturally homogenized. Goat milk is said to play a role in improving appetite and digestive efficiency. Goat milk is non-allergic as compared to cow milk and it has anti-fungal and anti-bacterial properties and can be used for treating urogenital diseases of fungal origin.
- Goat is termed as moving refrigerator for the storage of milk and can be milked number of times in a day.
- Goats can supply a family with plenty of milk each day — important nutrition for undernourished children.
- Extra milk can be made into paneer.
- Goats can graze even on poor, dry land unsuitable for other livestock.
- Goat manure is a good fertilizer for agriculture land.
- With their earnings from goat keeping, families can afford food, education and health care.

In recent years, due to the ongoing problems with Avian flu, poultry production has become increasingly difficult for the farmers and more attention has therefore been paid to small ruminants especially goat.

Distribution of goats in the world

India has the largest population of goats in the world.F.A.0. (2010) estimates that there are around 920 million goats in the world out of which 154 million goats are found in India and 150.7 million goats in China. Although goat is present in most parts of the world, over 90% of the goat population of the world is distributed in the two continents of Asia and Africa (Fig 1). The continents of Europe and USA possess a much smaller population of goats than Asia and Africa. The world goat population has increased 66% during the last 20 years as compared to only 9% for cattle.

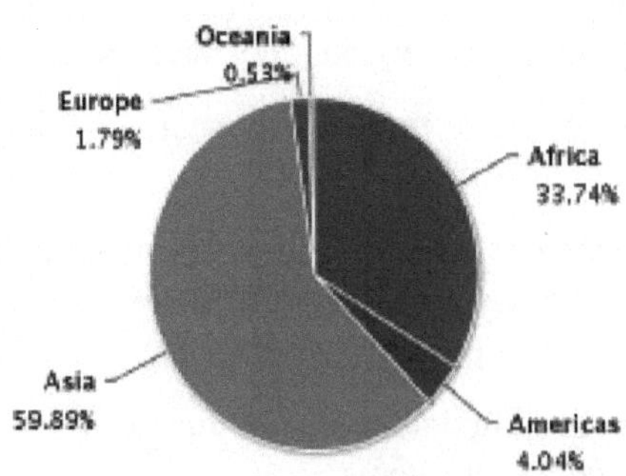

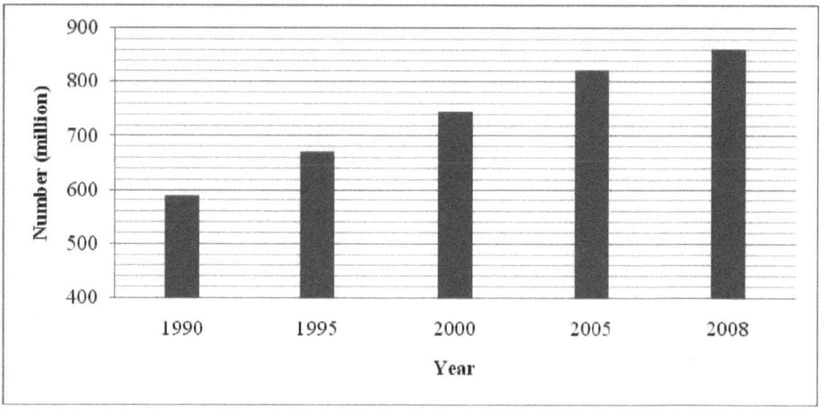

Fig.: Number of goats in the world during the period from 1990 to 2008 (FAOSTAT, 2008)

Most goats kept in developing countries are inaccurately estimated in number. Cattle are likely to be counted while goat number are most often approximated.In India, the population of goats is increasing.

Although Europe has only 1.7% of total goat population of the world, almost all the dairy breeds of goats had their origin in Europe. In the Oceania, goats are a recent introduction, with Angora and the European milch breeds. Originally, a good number of Feral goats have existed in these countries which were used predominantly for meat purpose. In the North and Central America, most of the goats introduced are either the European Milch breeds (Saanen, Alpine, Toggenburg) or the Spanish goats. Great variation in terms of the ratio of goat to

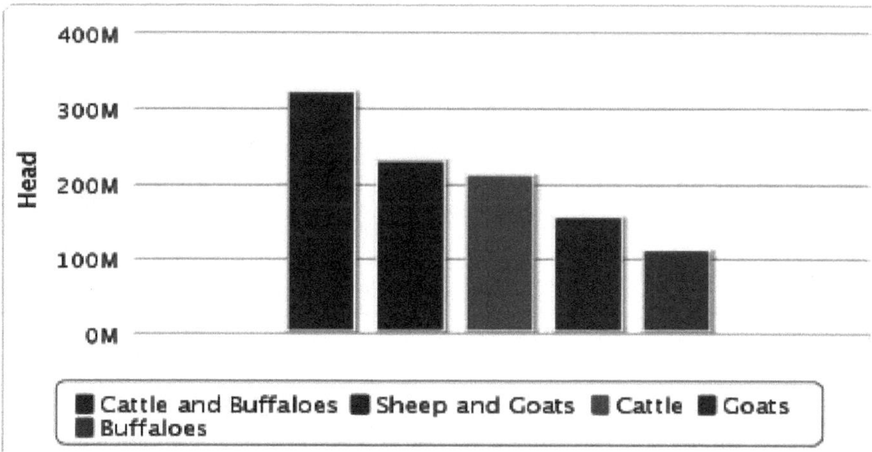

Fig : Number of animals in India (number of heads) (2010)

sheep exists among them, ranging between 1 goat to 0.02 sheep in Bangladesh to 1 goat to 2.13 sheep in Iran.

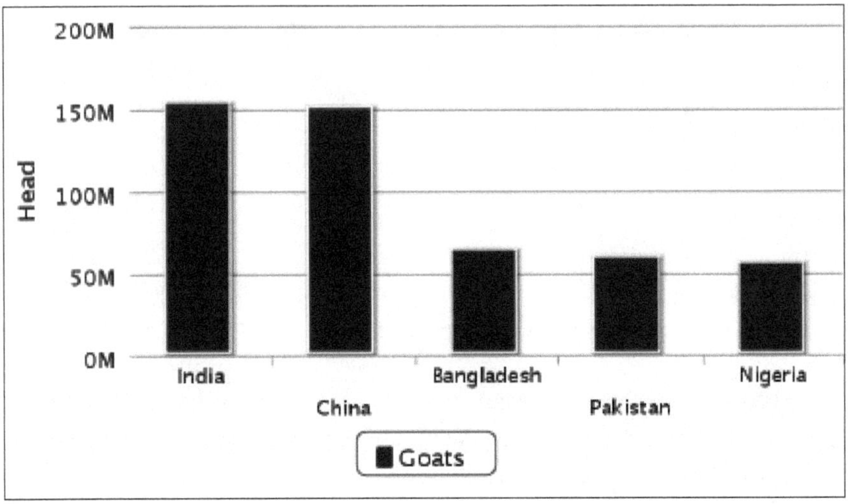

Fig : Top 5 countries in goat population (number of heads) (2010)

Table 2: Livestock Population

(In Million Nos.)

S.No.	Species	Livestock Census		Growth Rate (%)	
		2003	2007$	2007 over 2003	Annual
1.	Cattle	185.2	199.1	7.50	1.83
2.	Buffalo	97.9	105.3	7.58	1.84
3.	Goat	124.4	140.5	13.01	3.10
4.	Sheep	61.5	71.6	16.41	3.87
	Total Livestock	485.0	529.7	9.22	2.23

The number of goats has increased at a rate of 3.10 % as per the Livestock Census of India data for 2003 and 2007. This is in spite of the lack of' a developmental program for this species. The population growth rate of goats in India was higher than that of total livestock for the same period (Table 2)

Table 3: Population of goats in India (FAOSTAT 2012)

	year	Goats
Stocks (Head)	2001	123805000
Stocks (Head)	2002	124077000
Stocks (Head)	2003	124358000
Stocks (Head)	2004	128213000
Stocks (Head)	2005	132188000
Stocks (Head)	2006	136286000
Stocks (Head)	2007	140540000
Stocks (Head)	2008	145000000
Stocks (Head)	2009	149000000
Stocks (Head)	2010	154000000

FAOSTAT | © FAO Statistics Division 2012 | 18 February 2012

Population statistics of goats in the past in various parts of the world have been influenced by war, famine etc. However, still most countries have shown an increase in the population of goats. Thus, goats are the predominant livestock species in the third world countries especially in arid and semi-arid regions, the sub-tropics and the humid tropics. In some countries they are numerically more important than sheep. Goats are concentrated in dry tropical and subtropical areas of poor agricultural potential and on marginal lands. In many marginal areas, the seasonality of pasture growth affects both the quantity and the quality of herbage available and can limit the level of nutrition to livestock. There is a difficulty in ensuring annual regularity of food supply to small ruminants and this is one of the major constraints for the extensive systems of goat production. The relatively small investment required generally makes goat farming a good choice or an incentive for farmers of rural areas.

Goat for meat

Traditionally, sacrificing a goat has a strong religious meaning in Islam because it symbolizes Abraham´s son being saved by God (and a goat being sacrificed instead of him). For instance, the end of Ramadan is celebrated by slaughtering a goat. Goat meat is sold at a higher price as compared to beef in many countries. For example, the consumer price of goat meat in Surinam was 7.5-9.0 Euro/kg whereas beef was sold at 4.0-5.0 Euro /kg in 2008 (http://edepot.wur.nl/199).

Goat meat is perceived to be of higher quality than beef having about 50–60% lower fat percentage. Goat meat also contains 40% less saturated fatty acids compared to broiler meat. Goat's meat is in high demand which far outweighs its supply in many countries. Although limited interest has been taken in exploiting meat production from goats, possibilities exist. There is growing demand for goat meat in the export market due to its lean characters and near organic meat production. Value addition of goat meat is an area which is fast catching up with

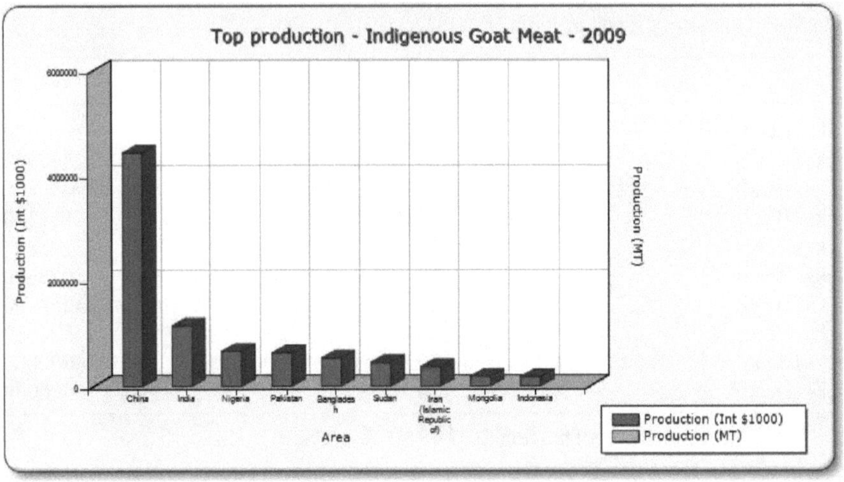

http://faostat.fao.org/site/339/default.aspx

Fig. : Goat meat production by top ten countries

the farmers as well as entrepreneurs. Rapid socio-economic shifts and fast changing food habits provide new opportunities for processed goat meat products, both for exports and domestic consumption, adopting good manufacturing practices and quality concepts. In this endeavor, close interaction of farmers, meat entrepreneurs and researchers have become necessary to understand the needs under changed international trade regime. There is a need for strengthening the infra-structural facilities for hygienic meat production, processing, storage and marketing including cold chain systems of transport.

Table 4: Goat Meat production in India during the last ten years (tonnes)

Year	Production of goat meat (tonnes)
2000	469000
2001	470000
2002	471400
2003	472500
2004	487000
2005	502000
2006	517800
2007	533800
2008	550000
2009	567500
2010	586500

FAOSTAT | © FAO Statistics Division 2012 | 18 February 2012

A number of value added products from goat meat can be prepared. Use of spent goat meat for value added products is a new development which can be harnessed for profit.

Recipe and processing technique for manufacture of value added products from spent goat meat such as chevon pickle, sausages, cubes/nuggets, Shami kebab, Samosa, meat rolls /slices, meat balls, cutlets, patties, croquettes, warm and serve meat curry, Chevonette, crisp snack from goat stomach are available . In the Asian and African countries, goat meat is preferred over that of sheep, cattle or buffalo. In India, where beef and pork is taboo with many communities, goat meat is highly preferred.

Goat for milk

Dairy goats are special to farmers because they provide nutritious milk to the struggling population during difficult times. Goats produce approximately 2% of the world's total annual milk supply. Milk has been used over a very long time as a natural, complete food source to provide fat, protein, vitamin and minerals especially calcium. Although meat can be produced from a number of domestic and wild animals, the production of milk is limited to a very few species of animals selectively bred and domesticated by man so that they produce milk in quantities far in excess of the needs of their young and which is harvested by man for his own and his children's nurture. The main producers of milk are cow, followed by the water buffalo and the goat. Although goat's contribution to the world's production of milk is low, nevertheless it is important for a variety of reasons.

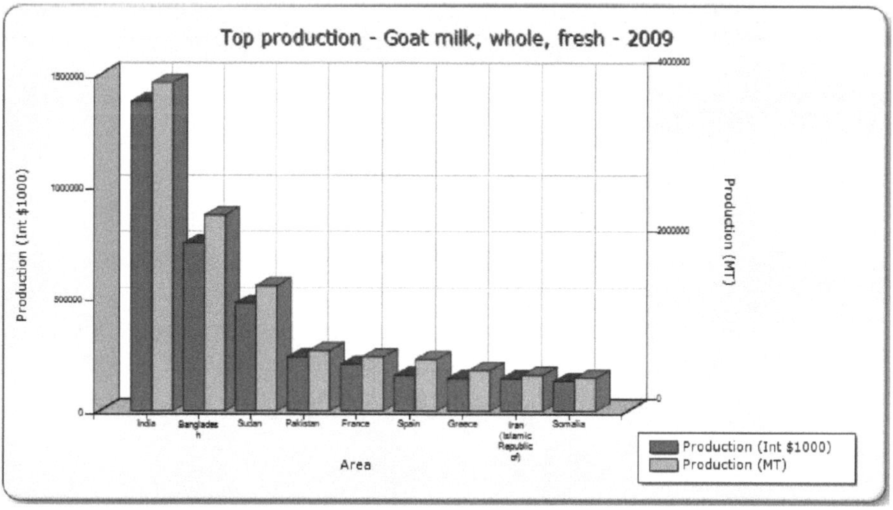

Fig. 4 : Goat milk production by top ten countries

Goat milk is having high nutritive value, wholesome, easily digestible and possesses medicinal value. Hence goat is called as the "poor man's cow" in India and "wet nurse of infants" in Europe. Goat is more efficient as a milk producer in areas where the available fodder is of such low quality that a cow can barely survive. Also it is an important source of milk to the poor landless or marginal farmer who cannot afford to keep a cow or buffalo, or to city dwellers that do not have space to keep a big cow and wants to produce milk only for the family consumption. In addition, goat's milk offers several advantages over cow's milk. Due to the alkaline reaction and absence of gamma globulins in goat's milk, it is useful for certain patients suffering from peptic ulcer, allergic eczema and infantile diarrhea, which usually develop from the intolerance to cow's milk. Goat's milk has much smaller size of fat globules and the absence of a fat globule clustering agent facilitates easy digestion. Goat milk also contains more of the essential fatty acids, linoleic and arachidonic acids, as compared to the cow's milk. Tuberculosis bacilli are also rare in goat's milk. The curd tension of goat's milk is much lower than that of cow's milk which may account for the better digestibility of the former.

India produces more goat milk than any other country in the world. However, goat milk contributes less than 4 % of the total milk produced in the country. India produced 112.1 million metric tonnes of milk during 2009 out of which 62.86 was contributed by buffalo,45.14 by cow and 4.1 by goat (FAOSTAT 2011). India, Bangladesh, Sudan and Pakistan are the largest goat milk producing countries in the world in that order.

Table 5: Goat milk vis-a-vis cattle, buffalo and sheep milk production (million mt)

	Cattle	Buffalo	Sheep	Goat
World	580.0	89.35	9.1	15.4
Africa	28.42	2.64	1.9	3.3
America	169.5	-	0.04	0.56
Asia	148.0	86.5	4.02	8.95
Europe	209.9	0.22	3.1	2.57
Oceania	24.50	-	-	-
India	44.1	60.90	-	4.0

(FAOSTAT, 2008)

In India, several breeds are good milk producers namely Jamunapari, Jakhrana, Barbari, Malabari, Surti and Beetal. However, Black Bengal is a poor milk producer breed. An average goat produces around one kg milk per day.

Table 6: List of top twenty countries producing goat milk and their production in 2009

Rank	Area	Production (Int $1000)	Production (MT)
1.	India	1380673	3910000
2.	Bangladesh	747303	2328000
3.	Sudan	480131	1493120
4.	Pakistan	241282	719000
5.	France	208885	645176
6.	Spain	158729	615000
7.	Greece	146178	484000
8.	Iran (Islamic Republic of)	143991	429082
9.	Somalia	132511	394873
10.	Niger	92650	276091
11.	Indonesia	92620	276000
12.	China	87147	272443
13.	Russian Federation	78819	238475
14.	Mali	75108	330500
15.	Algeria	74074	220736
16.	Jamaica	68241	203353
17.	Turkey	64501	192210
18.	Mexico	56947	164756
19.	Brazil	48245	143768
20.	Kenya	43266	128930

Goat milk composition is similar to other domestic animals in that it contains fat, carbohydrate (lactose), protein (casein), minerals and vitamins (Table 7). Goat milk is often used by those who are young, ill, or have a low tolerance to cow's milk. The goat milk resembles the human milk composition in most chemical attributes and therefore considered a suitable substitute. Goat milk is actually very similar to that of human breast milk. The main objection to goat milk is its typical goaty flavor. If the milking does are maintained separately from the buck, the goaty flavor in milk can be considerably reduced. The flavor can also be masked using elaichi (cinnamon) etc.

Table 7: Composition of milk of goat, cow and human

Species	Water %	Fat %	Sugar %	Protein %	Ash %
Goat	85.2	4.9	5.1	4.00	0.76
Cow	86.0	4.7	4.8	3.77	0.72
Human	87.4	3.0	6.5	0.74	0.25

The composition of goat milk varies with breeds, stage of lactation and feeding regimes. In addition to its use as fluid milk, goat milk is also suitable for preparing various milk products. Goat milk is suitable for production of paneer from goat's milk which has found good acceptability with the farmers. In China, most of the goat milk is converted into powdered milk, some of which is exported to other Asian countries (http://www.sheepandgoat.com/articles/China.htm).

Goat cheese has been made for thousands of years, and was probably one of the earliest made dairy products. Although cow's milk and goat's milk have similar overall fat contents, the higher proportion of medium-chain fatty acids such as caproic, caprylic and capric acid in goat's milk contributes to the characteristic tart flavor of goat's milk cheese. In France, goat milk is often intended for cheese making as 75-80% of goat milk is transformed into cheese. When compared with cow and buffalo milk products, judges did not find any 'goaty' flavor in the products prepared from goat milk.

History of goat production and animal husbandry

Goats have a long history of its existence and usefulness for mankind.The association of animals with man is as old as civilization itself. Our common domestic animals were domesticated much before the beginning of written history and the advent of agriculture. Animal remains found in the Belan Valley of Mirzapur district in Uttar Pradesh show that goats, sheep and cattle were exploited by the hunters during Paleolithic period (Old Stone Age). In this period man barely managed to gather his food and lived by hunting. It is speculated that animals were hunted for food before they were domesticated by human beings to cater to their demand for meat and milk. It was in the Neolithic or New Stone age that men first practiced agriculture, which included the raising of domestic animals. This phase generally continued till 9000 BC. Neolithic settlements in South India are not older than 2500 BC and in some parts of Southern and Eastern Indiathey are as late as 1000 BC. It is believed that people in India resorted to animal husbandry some 2000 years BC. MAHABHARATA mentions that lion, tiger, boar, buffalo, elephant, bear and ape are the seven wild animals (aranyah) and cow , goat , sheep , horse, mule and ass are the domestic animals (Randhava, 1980). Cow, buffalo, goat and sheep were reared for dairy (gorasam) as well as for meat supply and skin.Goat is also mentioned in the Jatakas. In the Dhumakari Jataka (III, 401) several high caste people are mentioned as goat keepers (Randhava, 1980 pp 117). The greatest artistic creations of the Harappan culture are the seals. About 2000 seals have been found and of these a great majority carries short inscriptions and pictures of bulls, buffalo and goat and elephant. These excavations from Indus valley civilization support the view that animal husbandry was popular in the Indian peninsula in very old times. Some of the seals of Indus Valley civilization have engravings which resemble the goat.The Harappan toys included goats, which suggested that goats were domesticated in India as early as 2000 B.C.Neolithic people of South India, south of Godawari River were reputed to possess cattle, sheep and goats.Goat found mentions not only in scriptures and mythology, but also in Indian art & literature, painting & folklore. It has been estimated that goats and sheep were domesticated some eight thousand seven hundred years ago. The place where goats and sheep were first domesticated is supposed to be near Iraq and United Arab Emirates. Goat is one of the earliest animals domesticated by man. Adamgarh in MP and Bagor in Rajasthan provide the earliest evidence of domestication of animals in India – around 5000 BC. The people living in the Chalcolithic age in South Eastern Rajasthan, Western Madhya Pradesh, Western Maharashtra, and elsewhere were known to keep goats, pigs, and buffaloes.

The domestic goat evolved from the the wild goat (*Capra hircus*) which still exists in the barren hills of Baluchistan and Western Sind. It is the chief ancestral stock from which the various breeds of domestic goats have been derived. In the north east of Quetta, it is replaced by Markhor (*Capra falconeri*) and is found in Turkistan, Afghanistan, Baluchistan and Kashmir. The Circassian goat is said to be the descendent of the markhor. By far the most important is the Bezoar goat (*Capra hircus aegagrus*) which ranges from Sind in the east through Iran and Asia Minor to Crete and Cyclades in the west. In many parts of this area, it has disappeared. From Iran, it extends into Russian Turkestan and the Caucasus and into the west of Asia Minor. In the late Pleistocene, the bezoar extended south into Lebanon where its remains were found in an upper paleolithic context in the Antelias cave near Beirut. This goat is a true Bezoar. In addition, the bezoar was recorded from the cave called Mugharet-el-wad on Mount Carmel in Plestine.In addition it was found in the natufian cave of El Khiam in Israel.Domestic goats existed in Iran about 6000 BC.

Animal Husbandry in India made great progress during the Mauryan Age. As a milch animal, the goat is mentioned in the Arthasastra and seems to have become fairly important also, as the outturn of butter from goats milk has been considered worthy of being reckoned in comparison with that of the cow or buffalo. Arthasastra states that " One drone of cow's milk when churned will yield one prasthas of butter, the same quantity of buffalo milk yield one seventh parastha more and the same quantity of goat and sheep milk will produce one half more". The assumption is incorrect as we know that buffalo milk has lot more fat than cow or goat milk.

In modern times, during droughts in Africa, goat and sheep have shown greater resistance to stress and has made up for shortages caused by cattle losses. Thus goats act as an insurance against natural calamities whereas cattle and buffaloes perish under such circumstances.

Goats and common property resources and forests

Issues of ecological degradation, soil erosion and desertification

Goat farming plays a key environmental role that includes the natural upkeep of less fertile areas, the maintenance of biodiversity, sensitive ecosystems and water quality, the fight against erosion, floods, avalanches and fires. Typically, goat farming takes place in less favoured areas, where such farming is very often the only agricultural option and which therefore makes a crucial contribution to the economy in rural areas.

Goats have been wrongly implicated in ecological degradation, soil erosion and desertification. Acharya and Singh (1992) conclude that goat farming is not a threat to ecology, and indeed, the role of goat is well documented in regeneration of vegetation (Harsh and Shankar Narayana, 1982), in weed control and prevention of forest fire. Government of India in the year 1987 constituted a task force under the chairmanship of Prof. K.H. Rao one of the leading economists of India. This task force observed that there was no definite evidence to prove that goat posed threat to the ecology as was generally believed. They further recommended that sheep and goat should not be categorized as animals responsible for the destruction of ecology. Goats actually act as regenerators of vegetation through dispersal of seeds in their droppings and vegetative propagation through browsing.Many hard coated seeds that normally require acid treatment before sowing get precisely the same acid treatment while passing through the goat's alimentary tract and get broadcasted encapsulated in the fecal droppings. The grazing habit of sheep and goats is complementary and not competitive.

Goat is usually called the "scape goat". It is generally blamed for things for which it is not responsible. Goats in particular have been held responsible for causing ecological degradation and desertification because of over grazing and producing methane as an end product of digestion. However, expansion of shifting cultivation and human population growth are the prime contributors to deforestation, and contribution of livestock to the greenhouse effect has been exaggerated. Ruminant livestock contribute only 2.5 percent of the total greenhouse gases.

A conflicting view is that goats act as regenerator of vegetation through dispersal of seeds in their droppings and vegetative propagation through browsing. It is undoubtedly true that an uncontrolled population of goats, like any ruminants, roaming in open can be extremely harmful to the growth and development of vegetation. However, indiscriminate felling of trees and deforestation, removal of shrubs, bushes and roots for fuel purposes, use of machines for cultivation and continuous neglect of the grazing lands are the real reasons causing damage to the ecology. Moreover, the scrub vegetation left behind after such activities could only be utilized by goats, and goats may have stayed in such degraded ecologies when other species have left.

Agriculture operations, especially on arid and semi-arid lands cause more soil erosion than livestock grazing (Shankarnarayana et al. 1985). Unlike cattle and sheep, goats are mainly browsers and would seldom go for mature trees. In several behavioral studies, goats have been found to defoliate only the smallest branches of trees without damaging the twigs. Their browsing habit tends to reclaim saline soils as they consume the salt laden leaves of the range plants and contribute fertility to soil and seed dispersal by even distribution of essential manure on the lands they graze. Such seeds germinate in large number as soon as soil moisture conditions are favorable, and it would take only 3-4 years' protection from grazing for areas grazed by goats to develop into a high class three tier silvipasture for livestock grazing. Sharma and Ogra (1987), reported that vegetative regeneration was found to be 27 percent greater in goat paddocks comprising *Cenchrus ciliaris*, *Dichrostachys nutans* and *Leucaena leucocephala* as compared to sheep paddocks. Moreover, cattle exploit 3–5 times more phytomass than goats.

In India, the National Commission on Agriculture in 1976 recommended a reduction in goat numbers from the then 67million to 40 million. The population has since doubled. A task force to evaluate the impact of goat rearing in ecologically fragile zones was established by the Government of India in 1987. It observed that there was no definite evidence to prove that goats pose a threat to the ecology and that within the desired grazing pressure, sheep and goats are more economical and less harmful than large ruminants (GOI 1987).

What is needed, however is to maintain a balance between the number of goats and other livestock species and the quantity and type of feed resources, which are available for the combined population? In a developed three tier silvi pasture system, the goats should be introduced first followed by cattle and then sheep. After the sheep are out of the grazing area, the land should be given a rest for regeneration/reseeding. This way the goat will go for bush, shrub and low set tree branches, cattle would utilize taller grasses and the sheep eat shorter and closer to the surface vegetation resulting is most efficient and judicious utilization of the available feed resources.

Role of women in goat production

Goat farming play a great role in women empowerment as most of the activities related to goat rearing are carried out by women and children. Menfolk are mostly involved in marketing and play some role in disease control decisions. Goats used to be an important factor in deciding dowries. Women played (and still play) a major role in rearing the goats as well as taking decisions with regard to this wealth.

Animal husbandry is a labor intensive vocation where men, women and children contribute maximally as per their ability. Animal husbandry unlike agriculture is not seasonal and labour requirement has to be worked out and met on daily basis. Since outside labor is costly and difficult to come by, family labor which is cheap, reliable and available round the year is most often the only source of managing the goat husbandry operations. Men often get employment outside or at far away places like military or industry, it is often the women and children who invariably manage the goats.

Animal husbandry sector almost entirely dependent upon women and children is goat rearing. Goats because of their small size are amenable for handling by the women and children. Even operations like kidding which generally are managed by menfolk in case of larger animals (cattle, buffalo, camel etc) can be easily handled by women in case of goat. Thus goat rearing provides safe, reliable and year round employment to women in the rural and semi urban areas. Most operations like grazing, feeding, milking, kidding, vaccinations, inseminations, treatment, and housing are invariably or mostly handled by women and children of the household. In general, the contribution of women in goat rearing has been underestimated.

A large number of women in developing countries are engaged in goat rearing. They make significant contributions to the rural economy in all developing country regions. Their roles differ across regions, yet they consistently have less access than men to the resources and opportunities they need to be more productive. Increasing women's access to land, livestock, education, financial services, extension, technology and rural employment would boost their productivity and generate gains in terms of agricultural production, food security, economic growth and social welfare. Closing the gender gap in agricultural inputs alone could lift 100–150 million people out of hunger.

No blueprint exists for closing the gender gap, but some basic principles are universal: governments, the international community and civil society should work together to eliminate discrimination under the law, to promote equal access to resources and opportunities, to ensure that agricultural policies and programmes are gender-aware, and to make women's voices heard as equal partners for sustainable development. Achieving gender equality and empowering women in agriculture is not only the right thing to do. It is also crucial for agricultural development and food security. One method suggested is to give goats to women, who have lost their husbands during civil wars. That allows them to come back to active life and feed their children.

One example of increasing the role of women in goat farming is the formation of women self help groups promoted by NGOs in Kerala. The Self help groups (SHGs) are small informal groups those enable women to come together, discuss and analyze their issues and problems and reap economic benefit out of mutual help, solidarity and joint responsibility. The group approach helps them do away with the social limitations and inculcates a greater confidence in the minds of rural women. Kudumbashree is a multifaceted programme organized by Government of Kerala and NABARD in cooperation with Panchayat Raj institutions through Community Based Organizations (CBOs) of poor women based on self-help strategy backed by thrift-linked credit. Kudumbashree aims at the empowerment of women, by giving them the central place in the programmes meant for their benefit. The micro enterprises in Animal Husbandry sector have considerable potential as sustainable income generating activities for the rural women in SHGs. Especially, goat farming as a micro enterprise has special advantage for women since the management of goats needs comparatively less labour.

Future perspectives

Development of goat production in the past has been besieged with several contraints. High mortality is one of the factors responsible for huge economic losses in goat farming. However, scientific methods of goat farming including management and health care have shown that mortality can be contained below 5 % per annum. Another constraint is that majority of goat farmers are poor, landless and by and large illiterate. Several studies have clearly pointed out that goat production is more economical as compared to sheep and buffalo.

The rise in the prices of animal feed and production inputs in general constitutes a particular threat to goat farming, increasing costs and bringing further pressure to bear on a sector which is already at the limit of its competitiveness.

There is a need for ensuring price transparency within the goat sector so that producers get remunerative price for their produce. Marketing of goats and goat milk and meat products is one of the most neglected areas which need urgent attention. There is a need to include goat in the 'Community Action Programme for public health' in order to promote the health and protein benefits of goat products to consumers.The existing import quota management regimes by the European Union countries puts Indian goat products exposed to unfair competition.

The jungle fire has been a great threat to goats under extensive or transhumant management but generally never mentioned. Constraints to goat husbandry include the scarcity of good breeding stock, inadequate veterinary and extension services, lack of credit and access to markets. Focusing more assistance on small holder farmers would improve impact on the poor. Value-based holistic community development with self-help groups may create a foundation for increasing farmer incomes by providing a forum for education, mutual support and developing markets. Constraints faced in the introduction and spread of goats and increasing their benefit to the small scale producers as well as success factors and best practices will be worked out and suitable frame work will be employed. The goat products are among the foods available with human health promoting characteristics.

Lack of awareness to adopt improved technologies due to poverty, illiteracy and little or no say in decision making process is the weakness of the goat owners. Lesser availability of elite breeding males, effective vaccines, grazing lands and feed resources are the other weaknesses. The goat farmers are exploited by the middlemen in marketing of surplus animals for meat markets. Sufficient modern abattoirs for hygienic slaughter are not available and a large number of goats are slaughtered in unauthorized places. There is ample scope for rearing goats for meat production under semi-intensive and intensive systems of management. The reproduction rate, multiple births, growth, slaughter - weight, dressing percentage, bone: meat ratio and survivability can be significantly improved which in turn will provide higher returns to the goat owners. Scope for value addition in milk, meat, skin fiber and manure is tremendous. Opportunities for employment generation and foreign exchange earnings are very high. Increase in population, shrinkage in grazing lands, slaughter of elite breeding males, emerging diseases and shortage of trained manpower are posing threat to development of goat industry in the country.

Despite the least attention from the planners, goat population in India has increased at the fastest rate among all major livestock species during last two decades. However, instead of increasing the goat population, emphasis should be laid on productivity per goat, organized marketing and prevention of emergence of new diseases like Peste des petits ruminants (PPR) which has led to higher mortality and abortion in goats. The goat improvement programme is to be given a push through extending credit to the poor landless farmers. Due to progressive fall in the forest cover (currently less than 20%), the administrators and planners are highly critical about the development of goats, dependent on extensive grazing in areas defined as fragile zone. On the contrary, the demand for reclamation of low capability soil to more productive agricultural land is ever increasing with the phenomenal growth in human population over years in India. Although, it is hard to overestimate the importance of goat in the tropics, there is ample scope for further improvement in growth and milk production in goat. Some of the threats to maintain the sustainability of goat enterprises in the agricultural economy of India include shrinkage of grazing land, poor scientific information about scientific management, new emerging goat diseases and lesser returns per animal etc. Goat production for value added goat milk, meat and skin products should further pave the way for continued sustainability of goat enterprises. Pashmina and goat skin has international market. Adequate thrust is needed to improve pashmina production per animal possibly by crossbreeding. Some of the value added goat meat and milk products have international acceptability. These are kabab, meat pickle, sausage and goat milk cheese. Further efforts should be made to improve these products. The process technology for preparation of better quality leather from goat skin also needs to be improved.

Therefore, some of the important issues which need to be taken up to maintain sustainability of goat production enterprise include genetic characterization and evaluation of goat breeds, enhancing chevon production, improvement of goat productivity through reproductive biotechnology, improved feeding practices for economic production, control of diseases and their surveillance, meat and milk technology to produce value added products, human resource development etc. Similarly, work also needs to be further consolidated and strengthened in the area of environmental physiology and reproduction of goats, emerging biotechnologies like in vitro maturation and fertilization, micro-manipulation of embryos, gene injection, sexing, cloning and transgenic goat production, shelter engineering and appliances, management techniques for goats, land and labor, feed and fodder availability with respect to environment, welfare measures and transfer of known/ developed improved technologies.

The goat excellently fits the definition of sustainable animal production in the Indian context. It is expected to be of immense help in devising most suitable exploitation and management of natural resources of the arid regions of this country and is non competitive with other forms of agriculture and animal production on such lands and is rather complimentary. Rearing of goats is environmentally non polluting and non-degrading. In fact it helps in conserving and even enhancing environmental quality by providing valuable fertilizer to the arid soil where it is kept. Goat keeping is also in consonance with the social needs of a large section of our society and thus ensures the attainment and continued satisfaction of large section of human society for the present and future. Goat keeping is economically viable, technically and technologically appropriate in the parts of the world and in India where it is kept and is socially the most acceptable species. Thus role of goats in sustainable animal production of the present and future generations of the country is assured.

The rapidly changing patterns of demand for livestock and livestock products point to livestock production being an increasing component of the agricultural economy in India. The extent to which the rural poor will benefit from these changes depends on how livestock can be integrated into developing markets and whether cheaper livestock products benefit the rural poor as consumers as well as producers. There is scope for small ruminant's viz. goats and sheep to play an important role for smallholder farmers in accessing these new markets. Their significance, which is now being exploited in several countries, is that they are small livestock in high demand and can thrive on low inputs and local resources. Goat production in practical terms consists of birth of young ones at regular interval, milk and meat production, fiber, skin and other by-products.

The poor man's cow- goat has tremendous potential to be projected as the 'Future Animal' for rural prosperity under the changing agro-geo-climatic conditions and depleting resources for crop-based livelihood.

References

Acharya, R.M. and Singh, N.P. (1992). Pre-conference Proceedings and plenary papers and invited lectures. 5 th International Conference on Goats.

Faostat, (2011). FAOSTAT | © FAO Statistics Division.

Govt. of India, (1987). The report of the task force to evaluate the impact of sheep and goat rearing in ecologically fragile zone. Ministry of Agriculture, Govt. of India, New Delhi.

Harsh, L.N. and Shankar Narayana, K.A. (1982). Performance of sheep and goats under different intensities of grazing on *Cenchurs* pasture dominated by *Zizyphus numularia*. Paper presented in the Seminar on Problems and Prospects of Livestock Development, held at CAZRI, Jodhpur.

Randhawa, M.S. (1980). A History of Agriculture in India. Volume 1. Indian Council of Agricultural Research, New Delhi, India. 541 pp.

Shankarnarayana, K.A., Bohra, H.C. and Ghosh, P.K. (1985). The goat an appropriate animal for arid and semi-arid regioms. Economic and Political Weekly, **20:**1965-72.

Sharma, K. and Ogra, J.L. (1987). Reaction of component plant species of synthesized pausture under three-tire system to high intensity of grazing by goats and sheep in semi-arid zone. Proceedings of 4th International Confrence on Goats, Brazil.

2

Breeds

Worldwide, almost 90% of the human food supply is provided by only 15 crop species and eight livestock species. The eight livestock species useful to man include cattle, buffalo, sheep, goat, pig, poultry, camel and horses. All or some of these species provide milk, meat, skin, fiber and manure for use of mankind. Whereas, milk and meat are important component of human food supply, skin, fiber and manure are also useful in different manner. Goats are important food-producing animals especially in tropical and subtropical regions. Goats are the most adaptable and geographically wide spread livestock species.

A breed of livestock is a group of animals that, through selection and breeding, have distinguishable characteristics and resemble one another and pass those traits uniformly to their offspring. Or A breed is defined as a group of animals that has been selected by humans to possess a set of inherited characteristics that distinguishes it from other animals within the same species. A cluster of domestic animals of a species where individuals are homogeneous in certain distinguishable characters which differ from one to the other group of animals constitute the breeds. Breeds are primarily distinguished by visual characteristics: color pattern, polled or horned condition, or extreme differences in form and shape. Breed is indicative of the perception of the breeders and the livestock industry which decides when a group of individuals constitutes a "breed". Livestock breeds have evolved over time through genetic changes that are both natural and selected by man.

Primarily breeds have been developed to provide increased production of meat, milk and/or wool, pashmina within a certain environmental area. This breed development is a process of continuous selection over a number of generations so as to stabilize the characters in the animals for the selected traits. The distinguishable characters are quite often color markings, size, and shape, hair pattern which may have little economic significance in terms of meat, wool or pashmina production. Breed development may have begun soon after animals were first domesticated. Breed is a group of animals related by descent and similar in most characteristics like general appearance, features, size, configuration, etc. In most cases, selection has been practiced for many generations in order to fix certain characteristics in the breed. The goat breeds have since long been described primarily in terms of physical conformation (chiefly, ear, nose, face and horn), body coat/colour characteristics and body measurements with subtle reference to production traits. Today there are more than 300 breeds of goats, and they live in climates ranging from high altitude mountains to deserts. Some breeds are known by the same name in different places, but are phenotypically different from one place to another. Conversely, there are breeds that look alike but have different names in different places.

Indigenous goats are valuable reservoirs of genes for adaptive and economic traits. Indigenous goat breeds can be useful in providing diversified genetic pool, which can help in meeting future challenges resulting from possible changes in production systems and consumer requirements. In the tropics, indigenous goat breeds are better able to utilise low quality feeds and can walk for longer distances, in search for water and food, than the imported breeds. Inspite of this, several breeds have been introduced by different countries of the world eg Boer breed has been introduced in several tropical countries.

Origin and classification of goats

Goats belong to the class Mammalia, Order- Artiodactyla, Sub order-Ruminantia Family Bovidae. Most authors have a further sub-division of sub-family- Caprini. The sub-family or tribe caprini includes five fossil and five existing genera which include sheep and goat.

The members of this tribe are fossil in Europe and Asia in the Pliocene and Pleistocene and in northern Africa and Western Northern America in the Pleistocene and still occurs mostly in mountains, scattered throughout this range, but only one genus of this tribe has reached western northern America. Together with sheep, cattle, and pigs, goats were one of the first domesticated ungulates.Zeuner (1963) based on archeological evidence believes that goat was the earliest ruminant and probably the first animal after dog to be domesticated by man. The archaeological evidence traces goat domestication as far back as ca. 10,500 calibrated Before Present (cal. B.P.) in the high Euphrates valleys, in Southeastern Anatolia and 9900 to 9500 cal. B.P. in the Zagros mountains (Zagros mountains are largest mountain range of Iran and Iraq). The domestic goat is probably derived from the existing Mediterranean. The wild goat was domesticated by the seventh century B.C. This is quite earlier than cattle, just when farming began in South

West Asia. The wild goat was found in Asia Minor (the western most extension of the Asian Landmass, forming the greater part of the modern Turkey, Persia and nearby countries. Asia Minor is one of the world's oldest regions of settled habitation. In the chalcolithic period of about the 4th millenium B.C. there is evidence of a widely distributed agricultural life of uniform character.

The five existing genera of this tribe have nine species. They are described as under:

1. Goats (Capra)
2. Barberry sheep (Ammotragus)
3. Tahrs (Hemitragus)
4. Blue sheep (Pseudois)
5. Sheep (Ovis)

The wild goats have four species as follows:

1. Ibex (Capra ibex)
2. Spanish Ibex (Capra pyrenacia)
3. Markhor (Capra falconeri)
4. Wild goat (Capra aegagrus)

Most of the today's breeds of domestic goat are believed to have descended from the wild Bezoar or psang (*Capra hircus aegagrus*), one of the two living races of wild goats; the other race is the Sind wild goat (*Capra hircus blythi*) of Pakistan. The Bezoar which may reach 36 inches in height (91 cm) at the withers and has horns 53 inches (1.3 meters) long, 119 still found in the mountains of South-western Asia. The Kashmir and Chegu goats are reputed to have derived from Markhor (*Capra falconeri*): the Angora goat from a cross between the Markhor (*Capra falconeri*) and the Bezoar or Psang (*Capra aegagrus*).

Goat breeds in the World

The Global Data Bank in Rome contains information on 255 breeds or breed varieties of goat in the world. The detailed breakup is as below.

USSR *(formerly)*	20
Africa	59
N & C America	12
South America	11
Asia	147
Oceania	6
Total	255

The book, World Dictionary of Livestock Breeds by (Mason, 1988) was used as the primary source of information on breeds and breed varieties for the data bank.Inadequate description, classification and evaluation of goats have resulted in a poor understanding of the potential of most tropical breeds. Information about description of the breeds is to be found in the publication of Mason (1951) for the West African breeds, Mason and Maule (1960) for the eastern and southern African breeds, Epstein (1969)and Cheng (1984) for the Chinese breeds, Kaura (1952) for the Indian and Pakistani breeds, Devendra (1966) for the Malaysian breeds and Gall (1996) for goat breeds of the world although sporadic attempts have been made to describe some individual breeds in more detail by several authors.

The goats, *Capra hircus* is an ungulate mammal belonging to the order Artiodactyla, suborder Ruminanta, family Bovidae. It is an agreed fact that the goat was the first animals to be domesticated by man for the direct satisfaction of his need for food, whereas the dog, domesticated earlier, was only used in hunting. Goat is a very prolific animal and useful for human being from horn to hoof.

Goats (*Capra hircus*) were among the first domesticated animals, adapted from the wild version Capra aegargus. Beginning about 10,000-11,000 years ago, Neolithic farmers in the Near East began keeping small herds of goats for their milk and meat, and for their dung for fuel, as well as for materials for clothing and building: hair, bone, skin and sinew. Recent mtDNA research suggests that all goats today are descended from a handful of animals and may have been domesticated in a handful of different places. Archaeological data suggest two distinct places of domestication: the Euphrates river valley at Nevali Çori, Turkey (11,000 bp), and the Zagros Mountains of Iran at Ganj Dareh (10,000). Other possible sites of domestication include the Indus Basin in Pakistan at (Mehrgarh, 9,000 bp) and perhaps central Anatolia and the southern Levant. Other important archaeological sites with evidence for the initial process of goat domestication include Cayönü, Turkey (8500-8000 BC), Tell Abu Hureyra, Syria (8000-7400 BC), Jericho, Israel (7500 BC), and Ain Ghazal, Jordan 7600-7500 BC) (http://archaeology.about.com/od/domestications/qt/goats.htm.)

Animal	Where Domesticated	Date
Dog	undetermined	~14-30,000 BC?
Sheep	Western Asia	8500 BC
Goats	Western Asia	8000 BC
Pigs	Western Asia	7000 BC
Cattle	Eastern Sahara	7000 BC
Chicken	Thailand	6000 BC
Donkey	Northeast Africa	4000 BC
Horse	Kazakhstan	3600 BC
Dromedary camel	Saudi Arabia	3000 BC
Water buffalo	India/Pakistan	2500 BC

Though breeds have certain distinguishable characteristics, there is also much variation within each breed which is partly genetic and partly due to environmental causes. It is argued that some genetic variation is essential in order to make progress by selection. A large population of the world's population of goats is an amorphous collection that is not easily categorized or characterized easily. However, within this number some well defined types have been developed or have evolved, to serve specific function or adaptation to specific production or environmental conditions.

More than 90% of the world population is concentrated in two continents of Asia and Africa. Rest of the world which includes North and Central America, South America, Europe and USSR contains only 10% of the world's goat population. Thus goats are important mainly for the less developed or developing countries of Asia and Africa. There are more than 300 different breeds and types of goats in the world, many of which have been bred to specific purposes, i.e. milk, meat or fiber production. Majority of these breeds are in the tropics but someof the best dairy breeds come from the temperate climate. By comparison with such breeds as the Saanen and the Anglo-Nubian, selected and bred for high milk production in temperate regions, only limited progress is evident in respect of the more prominent breeds of goats in the tropics.

Goat production in India

Goats are among the major economically important livestock inIndia. The play an important role in ensuring the livelihood of resource-poor farmers. They provide their owners with a vast range of products and services such as meat, milk, skin, hair, horns, bones, manure and urine for cash, security, gifts, religious rituals, medicine, etc. Goat breeds in India are widely adapted to different climates and are found in all production systems. Goats are relatively cheap and are often the first asset acquired, through purchase or customary means, by a poor family recovering from a disaster such as drought.

Goats are distributed in all the agro-climatic regions of India from cold desert (-40 °C) of Ladakh in North to saline water of Andaman in South and from dry desert (48 °C) of Rajasthan in West to humid climate of Bengal in Eastern regions of India (Singh *et al.,* 2009). Goats are found all over India and range from the large, well proportioned long haired breeds of Himalayas to the non-descript but hardy varieties south of the peninsula.India is endowed with around 20 descript breeds which constitute nearly 20 % of the total goat population and remaining goats are non-descript with mixed features. Most of them have low production potential since they were subject to artificial as well as natural selection in the past for adaptability to the climatic stress and enzootic diseases of the tropics, rather than improving the production potential. However, their optimum production potential has not been expressed due to subsistence production system. Formation of goat breeder's cooperative societies is utmost important for the development of the goat sector. Low adoption of improved technologies and package of practices is one of main reasons of low productivity of Indian goats.

The goat population in India has increased at the fastest rate among all major livestock species during last couple of decades. Goat population of India has increased from 47.14 (1951) to 125.5 millions (2007) with an over all growth rate of 3.05 % being highest among all ruminant species. Steady growth of goat population in all the regions of India has made this species as animal of future. Higher growth rate of goat is due to more preference by small and marginal farmers and land less labour due to less initial investment, low maintenance, less risk, early return, easy liquidity, high prolificacy, rising market demand and no taboos for rearing/eating goat meat against any religion.

The population of goats is more than sheep in high rain- fall than in dry areas. There are about 5 to 8 times more goats than sheep in all the North Eastern states where the rainfall is high and plenty of plant material available for grazing. In coastal area of Kerala with a rainfall of about 120 inches, there are 140 goats to one sheep. On the other hand, in the dry areas of Haryana and Rajasthan the ratio of goat to sheep is 1: 1. There is a distinct zonal distribution of goats for meat or milk or both or pashmina. While small pockets of pashmina goats exist in Ladakh and Himachal Pradesh, important milk breeds are found in north western zone, dual purpose breeds are to be found in the dry southern zone and highly prolific meat breeds are to be found in the north eastern zone.

The goats of hircus species reached undivided Indian sub–continent from the western Asia by north-western and north eastern routes between 7500–7000 BC. But it is strongly believed that the present breeds have evolved from the crossings of hircus species brought to India along with Muslim invasions up to the 14th Century.

The Harappa toys contain representations of a goat. Two seals from Mohanjo-daro show a wild bezoar goat with enormous curled horns, and a bearded domestic male goat with side-spreading horns (Acharya, 1982).

A number of breeds of goats are available in the country. In the strict sense, there are no specific breeds, since the majority of them do not have specified defined characters. Neither are there breeding societies or agencies to register animals of particular breeds, maintain flock books and ensure the purity of the breed. Few of the goat breeds are maintained at ICAR research institute, AICRP centres and state owned organized farms where information on growth, production and reproduction parameters is recorded and maintained. Information on some of the breeds has also been collected through field surveys. However, there are still some breeds which neither have neither any organized farm nor any systematic survey has been conducted (eg Kutchi, Surti, Gohilwadi, Ganjam, Sangamneri,Malabari,Changthangi) (ftp://ftp.fao.org/docrep/fao/010/a1250e/annexes/CountryReports/India.pdf). Most of the breeds have been identified on the basis of morphological characters while the information on genetic architecture is available for few breeds. The crossbreeding with the European breeds has been sporadically admitted in different pockets of India and claims have been made for the development of breeds or strains. But the population of these crosses was so limited that sooner or later it got lost in the genetic mosaic already existing in the Indian goats. The breeds maintained by the farmers are selected on the basis of their suitability for their socio-economic environment.

Lall (1947), Khan and Rai (2000), Khan and Bhatt (1981) & Acharya (1984), Ahlawat *et al.* (2009) have summarized the animal genetic resources available in Indian breeds of goats. India possesses 20 well established breeds of goats apart from many non-descript local goats. The origin of goat breeds of Indian sub-continent is not clearly known (Khan and Bhatt, 1981). They are believed to have been derived from wild goats which inhabited the Asian mountain regions in antiquity. It is believed that they were domesticated around 7th century B.C. much earlier than cattle. Some of the Indian breeds are famous for their high prolificacy and can be used as an improver breed to introduce high production potential with high prolificacy.

Acharya (1982) has listed 20 different breeds of goats in India and Handbook of Animal Husbandry (ICAR) lists 23 breeds of goats in India. The advent of new era of national sovereignty over genetic resources under Convention on Biological Diversity (CBD) requires a new approach to describe and catalogue livestock and poultry breeds (http://www.nbagr.res.in/Accessionbreed.html). Trade-Related aspects of Intellectual Property Rights (TRIPS) under General Agreement on Tariff and Trade (GATT) of the World Trade Organisation (WTO) through Article 27, "patents shall be available for any invention". It implies member countries to provide protection to its livestock and poultry genetic resources by an effective sui generis system. This in turn demands an authentic national documentation system of valuable sovereign genetic resources with well defined characteristics. Towards this end a mechanism for "Registration of Animal Germplasm" is being initiated at National Bureau of Animal Genetic Resources (NBAGR), Karnal under the aegis of the Indian Council of Agricultural Research (ICAR). This would provide identity and protection to the valuable animal genetic resources and facilitate its access for genetic improvement and economic utilisation. NBAGR (2011) has assigned accession number to following twenty breeds of goat in India(http://www.nbagr.res.in/Accessionbreed.html).

S.N.	Breed	Home Tract	Accession number
1.	Attapady	Kerala	INDIA_GOAT_0900_ATTAPADYBLACK_06001
2.	Barbari	Uttar Pradesh and Rajasthan	INDIA_GOAT_2017_BARBARI_06002
3.	Beetal	Punjab	INDIA_GOAT_1600_BEETAL_06003
4.	Black Bengal	West Bengal	INDIA_GOAT_2100_BLACKBENGAL_06004
5.	Changthangi	Jammu and Kashmir	NDIA_GOAT_0700_CHANGTHANGI_06005
6.	Chegu	Himachal Pradesh	INDIA_GOAT_0600_CHEGU_06006
7.	Gaddi	Himachal Pradesh	INDIA_GOAT_0600_GADDI_06007
8.	Ganjam	Orissa	INDIA_GOAT_1500_GANJAM_06008
9.	Gohilwadi	Gujarat	INDIA_GOAT_0400_GOHILWADI_06009
10.	Jakhrana	Rajasthan	INDIA_GOAT_1700_JAKHRANA_06010
11.	Jamunapari	Uttar Pradesh	INDIA_GOAT_2000_JAMUNAPARI_06011
12.	KanniAdu	Tamilnadu	INDIA_GOAT_1800_KANNIADU_06012
13.	Kutchi	Gujarat	INDIA_GOAT_0400_KUTCHI_06013
14.	Malabari	Kerala	INDIA_GOAT_0900_MALABARI_06014
15.	Marwari	Rajasthan	INDIA_GOAT_1700_MARWARI_06015
16.	Mehsana	Gujarat	INDIA_GOAT_0400_MEHSANA_06016
17.	Osmanabadi	Maharashtra	INDIA_GOAT_1100_ OSMANABADI _06017
18.	Sangamneri	Maharashtra	INDIA_GOAT_1100_ SANGAMNERI _06018
19.	Sirohi	Rajasthan and Gujarat	INDIA_GOAT_1704_SIROHI _06019
20.	Surti	Gujarat	INDIA_GOAT_0400_SURTI_06020
21.	Zalawadi	Gujarat	INDIA_GOAT_0400_ZALAWADI _06021

There has been a very great amount of inter-mixture among indigenous breeds. Some breeds like Lohi, Beetal, Marwari, Sirohi, Surti and Osmanabadi do well in semi-arid, arid and desert conditions of the North Western part of India; other types like Gaddi, Chegu and Changthangi live only in cold and mountainous areas. Other important breeds like Jamunapari and Barbari are found in Central India; Black Bengal, White Bengal and Assam Hill in the eastern part; and Sangamneri, Malabari and Kani Adu and Deccani in coastal areas. The Jamunapari breed of the chambal ravines in the Etah district (UP) has been extensively used for improvement of native breeds in India and many other countries. The dwarf breeds of goats like Black Bengal, Barbari, Malabari and

Assam Hill are famous for high prolificacy (multiple births), early sexual maturity and generally produce two crops in a period of 14 months. The Pashmina (Cashmere) goats of Leh-ladakh produce the fine quality Pashmina fibre which has no substitute so far.

Several breeds like Jamunapari have been exported to many countries and used to improve the local goat population in the importing countries like Indonesia, Malaysia. Similarly the famous Anglo-Nubian breed was evolved in Britain, apparently from a cross between the Jamunapari and some of the native British goats.

The goat breeds have since long been described primarily in terms of physical conformation (chiefly, ear, nose, face and horn), body coat/colour characteristics and body measurements with subtle reference to production traits. There are as many as 23 well-defined breeds of goats in India, though a few others are being identified/claimed in different agro-climatic regions.The preservation of the biodiversity of animal breeds is an important condition to maintain the ability of animal production to adapt to the changing conditions of breeding and production systems in the future.

The milk production potential of most of the indigenous breeds is low. There is no breed in India, which is exclusively reared for milk Jamunapari, Beetal, Kutchi and Jakhrana are important milch breeds of goat besides good meat production potential. In addition, Surti, Malabari, Sangamneri, Osmanabadi and Barbari breeds are also reputed to have good milk production potential.

Total Goat population in India according to 18th livestock census is about 140.53 million. There is remarkable 13 % growth (124.35 millions according to 2003 census). Authentic breed-wise population data is not available for the country as a whole. However, some states have initiated breed–wise census in recent years. Analysis of livestock production in North East India shows that goat is a potential animal, secondary to pigs, for economic meat production in most states of the northeastern region of India. Goat population of India registered an il'lcrease of 21% during 1982 to 1992.Among major states, Punjab and Andhra Pradesh have shown decline in goats by 23.29 and 22.32%, respectively. The increase was observed in most of other major states. The population almost doubled in Assam whereas Jammu and Kashmir, Bihar and Uttar Pradesh registered increase of 55.90, 42.88 and 35.35% respectively (Tantia and Vij, 2000).

Breedwise estimates of Goat breeds ('000)

Breed	Total Population (2007)
Bengal	20928
Marwari	7575
Barbari	3156
Sirohi	2909
Kannaidu	2094
Jhakrana	1953
Osmanabadi	1553
Jamunapari	1057
Zalawadi	823
Malabari	711
Surti	674
Kutchi	662
Mehsana	597
Gaddi	472
Gohilwadi	322
Beetal	304
Sangamneri	211
Changthangi	206
Ganjam	148
Chegu	10

2007 Livestock Census data

As per 1987 census data, Bengal, Marwari, Sangamneri, Gaddi and Ganjam were the most populous goat breeds in India in that order.

Top five states (goat population) are

1.	Rajasthan	21.5 millions
2.	West Bengal	15.06 millions
3.	Uttar Pradesh	14.79 millions
4.	Maharastra	10.39millions
5.	Bihar	10.16 millions

States like Andhra Pradesh, Manipur and Assam have shown the highest growth rates during 2003 to 2007 livestock census data whereas maximum negative growth has been recorded for Sikkim and West Bengal. It was reported that number of goats per 1000 total in urban areas decreased from 55 to 51 during 2003-2007. Among the various states, Rajasthan accounted for 15.3%, West Bengal for 10.7 %, Uttar Pradesh 10.5 %. Maharashtra for 7.4 % and Bihar for 7.2 % , which together accounted for 51.1 % of the total goat population in the country.

State Wise Goat Population in India (2007) in Thousands.

Sr.No	States/Union Territories	Total Population (in Thousands)
1.	Andhra Pradesh	9626
2.	Arunachal Pradesh	292
3.	Asom(Assam)	4320
4.	Bihar	10167
5.	Chattisgarh	2768
6.	Goa	11
7.	Gujarat	4640
8.	Haryana	538
9.	Himachal Pradesh	1241
10.	Jammu & Kashmir	2068
11.	Jharkhand	6592
12.	Karnataka	6153
13.	Kerala	1729
14.	Madhya Pradesh	9014
15.	Maharashtra	10391
16.	Manipur	51
17.	Meghalaya	365
18.	Mizoram	16
19.	Nagaland	178
20.	Orissa	7127
21.	Punjab	290
22.	Rajasthan	21503
23.	Sikkim	92
24.	Tamil Nadu	9275

Contd.

Sr.No	States/Union Territories	Total Population (in Thousands)
25.	Tripura	633
26.	Uttar Pradesh	14793
27.	Uttarakhand	1335
28.	West Bengal	15069
	Union Territories	
29.	Andaman & Nicobar Islands	67
30.	Chandigarh	1
31.	Dadra & N Haveli	25
32.	Daman & Diu	3
33.	Delhi	21
34.	Lakshadweep	76
34.	Pudducherry	69
	All INDIA	140537

Source: 18th Livestock census, Department of Animal Husbandry, Dairying and Fisheries, M/O Agriculture

Table: Goat Population Distribution in different state and agro-climatic regions

State	Goat population	Goat population/sq. km	% total goat population	Goat/ human
Northern Temperate Region				
Himachal Pradesh	1125000	20.98	0.950	0.192
Jammu & Kashmir	2055000	8.14	1.472	0.180
Uttaranchal	1158000	20.30	0.883	0.128
Northern plains				
Gujarat	4541000	22.37	3.568	0.087
Rajasthan	16809000	0.70	13.780	0.300
Haryana	460000	18.05	0.649	0.038
Madhya Pradesh	8142000	13.11	4.729	0.096
Punjab	278000	8.22	0.337	0.017
Uttar Pradesh	12941000	40.01	9.585	0.071
Chandigarh	1000	-	-	-
Delhi	17000	16.86	0.020	0.002
Eastern Region				
Bihar	9490000	116.63	2.178	0.101
Assam	2987000	34.13	4.203	0.068
Daman & Diu	21000	4.93	0.003	0.025
Chhattisgarh	2336000	16.08	1.769	0.105
Orissa	5803000	37.07	4.696	0.157
West Bengal	18774000	176.32	12.731	0.195
North-eastern Hilly Zone				
Manipur	33000	1.48	0.027	0.014
Meghalaya	327000	12.48	0.228	0.121
Nagaland	175000	9.70	0.131	0.081

Contd.

State	Goat population	Goat population/sq. km	% total goat population	Goat/ human
Mizoram	17000	0.71	0.012	0.017
Tripura	472000	60.91	0.520	0.200
Sikkim	124000	12.12	0.070	0.159
Arunachal Pradesh	231000	2.20	0.150	0.168
Southern Region				
Andhra Pradesh	6277000	18.78	4.203	0.068
Goa	11000	3.42	0.010	0.009
Karnataka	4484000	25.42	3.966	0.092
Kerala	1213000	47.87	1.514	0.058
Tamilnadu	8177000	48.63	5.146	0.102
Pondicherry	48000	83.33	0.033	0.042
Maharashtra	10684000	37.16	9.303	0.118
Lakshadweep	47000	812.50	0.021	0.374
Andaman & Nicobar	64000	8.61	0.058	0.199
India	124358000	37.39	100.000	0.120

Source: Livestock Census 2003

India can be divided into four regions on the basis of agro-climatic conditions viz. North-Western and Central Arid/Semi-Arid Region, Southern Peninsular Region, Eastern Region and Northern Temperate Region (Acharya, 1982). The highest concentration of goats is found in North Western Region (39%), followed by Eastern Region (32%), Southern Peninsular Region (26%) and Northern Temperate Region (2%).

North Western Region: The climatic condition in this region is arid/semi-arid. The states of Haryana, Punjab, Rajasthan, Gujarat, Uttar Pradesh, and Madhya Pradesh belong to this region. Maximum numbers of goat breeds are found in this region, as the dry climatic condition is conducive for growth, reproduction and survival. The breeds found in this region are Jamanapari, Barbari, Beetal, Jhakhrana, Sirohi, Marwari, Kutchi, Mehsana, Zalawadi, Gohilwadi, and Surti. Most of these breeds are reared for milk and meat. An additional crop of hair is also harvested once in a year from some of the breeds.

Southern Peninsular Region: The climatic condition of this region is semi-arid in the central peninsula and hot-humid along the west-coast. The States of Maharashtra, Karnataka, Andhra Pradesh, Tamil Nadu and Kerala belong to this region. The breeds of goats found in this region are Osmanabadi, Sangamneri, Kannai Adu and Malabari.

Eastern Region: It comprises states of Bihar, West Bengal, Orissa and the north eastern hill states. The climatic condition is warm and humid in the Lower Gangetic Basin, Coastal Plains and Plateau region, while it is sub-temperate in the hills. The breeds of goats found in this region are Black Bengal, Ganjam and Khasi (Assam Hill Goat).

Northern Temperate Region: It includes the states of Jammu & Kashmir, Himachal Pradesh and Uttaranchal. The goat breeds of this region are Changthangi, Chegu and Gaddi. They are found at a high altitude in the Himalayan/ Trans-Himalayan terrain. The climatic condition of this region is extremely cold with heavy downpour in monsoon and moderate to heavy snowfall in the winter. The goats, which produce precious pashmina fibres, are found in the cold mountain deserts in this region.

The state of goat production in different states of India is given below.

Andhra Pradesh

A.P. has a small ruminant population of 276.53 lakhs- Sheep (213.76 lakh) and Goats (62.77 lakh).Andhra Pradesh, with 6.27 million goats in India. Mahabubnagar district in Andhra Pradesh tops in goat population with 5.09 lakhs local goats (Livestock Census, 2003).

Eastern and North East States (Assam, Arunachal Pradesh, Manipur, Meghalaya, Mizoram, Nagaland, Tripura).

The pace of agricultural growth in the Eastern and North Eastern regions has been slower than in the rest of the country. In terms of development indices, the Eastern and North Eastern States are among the most backward in the country. Livestock rearing is an important enterprise in the North Eastern region. Livestock in this region comprises of cattle (3.2m), buffalo (0.21m), sheep (0.9m), goat (1.07m) and pig (1.43m). Goats can play an important role in amerlioration of this situation. Eastern and north eastern part of India is proud of prevailing very good quality goat breeds like Black Bengal, Assam hills, Ganjam etc (http://www.lrrd.org/lrrd19/8/zesh19114.htm). Black Bengal is a famous breed known for high prolificacy, superior chevon quality, best quality skin, early sexual maturity, low kidding interval and very good adaptability. The home tract of the breed is throughout West Bengal although it is distributed in the adjoining part of Jharkhand, Orrisa, Bihar, Tripura states of India and also available in Bangladesh. Assam Hill Goat breed is found in Assam and its adjoining areas. The body coat is black and sometimes white and the breed is famous for meat production. It is a poor milk yielder. This breed was utilized by the poor farmers of Assam and its adjoining areas for their economic upliftment. Local non-descriptive goats at Imphal, Manipur is also preferred by the rural farmers at this area as there livelihood. Basic problem of livestock rearing in North East States is low productivity of animals, inadequate veterinary services, non-availability of improved breeds, shortage of feed and fodder, poor dissemination of technical know-how, absence of backward and forward linkages for processing andmarketing. Despite the high potential of goat rearing in the Eastern and North Eastern regions the opportunities are largely untapped. Goat rearing can also bring a major boost in women empowerment, as most of goat rearing is carried out by women.

Bihar

Being the 5th largest goat population state (9489830 in numbers), Bihar contributes about 7.63% of India's total goat population (Department of Animal Husbandry and Dairying 2005). As per an estimate (1999-2000) by the Department of Animal Husbandry, Government of Bihar, around 574000 goats are slaughtered annually in recognized slaughterhouses in Bihar, which accounts for some percentage of the total production as most of the goat meat production industry is under unorganized sector. However, monthly per capita consumption of goat meat/ mutton is limited only to 0.04 kg; consumption is limited to 16.6% of households in rural Bihar. In urban areas, 25.6% households reported consumption of goat meat/ mutton of 0.08 kg per month per capita (NSSO 2001).

Village goat is mostly of Bengal breed. However, crosses with other breeds like Jamunapari, Barberi, Sirohi and Jakharna are also available. Even though, there is no definite government policy to improve the breed of goat but due to non-systemic and unscientific crossing has been done at farmer's level (Dey *et al.,* 2007).

Table: District wise goat population density in Bihar

District*	Density of goat population (numbers/sq km)
Kaimur (Bhabua), Jahanabad, Buxer, Rohtas, Bhojpur, West Champaran, Saran, Patna, Aurangabad and Nalanda	30–75
Lakhisarai, Begusarai, Sheikhpura, Gaya, Madhubani, Darbhanga, Siwan, Jamui, Samastipur and Munger	75–100
Gopalganj, Banka, Vaishali, Khagaria, Nawada, East Champaran, Purnia, Bhagalpur, Muzaffarpur and Katihar	100–150
Kishanganj, Sitamarhi, Madhepura, Saharsa, Araria, Supaul and Sheohar	> 150

*Districts are listed as per increasing density category wise

Source: Based on Livestock Census (2003), Department of Animal Husbandry and Dairying, Government. of India

Chattisgarh

The state of Chhattisgarh came in to existence on November 1, 2000. This land locked state was carved out of Madhya Pradesh. The total area of the state is 1, 35,000 Sq. km and has a total of 18 districts; with Raipur is the State capital. Chhattisgarh has a rich livestock wealth of 1.4 crore animals, as per the 2007 livestock census, of which the maximum of 65% is the cattle population followed by 20% of goat population. Goat rearers across Chhattisgarh are increasingly turning to goats as a meansof survival and a way of boosting their incomes. It has shown remarkably over 18% growths (during 2003 to 2007) in spite of high slaughter rate (over 39% annual). It may be noticed that the goat population is predominantly higher in the tribal dominated districts like Sarguja, Dantewada, Bastar and Jashpurnagar districts. There is no recognized breed of goat in Chhattisgarh. There is one government goat breeding farm in chattisgarh at Pakariya.

Goa

A small population of goats (10711) are available in Goa.

Gujarat

Gujarat has about 4.54 million goats (Livestock census 2003) consisting of five goat breeds namely Kutchi, Zalawadi, Gohilwadi, Surati, Mehsana. Goats have contributed to the livelihood of Maldharis and other weaker sections of the society (Singh *et al,* 2008)

Haryana

As per livestock census 2007, there were 5,38,320 goats in Haryana with maximum number of goats in Bhiwani, Mewat and Mohindergarh districts of the state.As per the breeding policy of the State, the department is striving hard to upgrade the local breeds of goat by natural mating with bucks of A.B.J.Cross, A.J.Cross and Alpine cross with Beetal breed. Buck of superior quality are produced at Goat Farm, Hisar and given to farmers for cross breeding in the State.Milk production data from goats in Haryana is given below (Source : Department of Agriculture, Govt. of Haryana.)

District	Goat		
	No. of Animal in Milk	Av. Daily Milk Yield	Annual Milk Production (In Litre)
Ambala	1871	0.723	494035
Bhiwani	25043	0.778	7114136
Faridabad	8302	0.776	2351997
Fatehabad	4877	0.743	1323384
Gurgaon	26687	0.774	7543317
Hisar	9474	0.796	2742746
Jhajjar	3797	0.777	1076597
Jind	2883	0.712	749797
Kaithal	1534	0.727	407146
Karnal	2793	0.749	763456
Krukshetra	1276	0.776	361426
Mahender Garh	25154	0.789	7242490

Contd.

District	Goat		
	No. of Animal in Milk	Av. Daily Milk Yield	Annual Milk Production (In Litre)
Panipat	3292	0.777	933041
Panchkula	1576	0.776	446400
Rewari	12885	0.786	3697571
Rohtak	2840	0.776	804427
Sirsa	18076	0.778	5133860
Sonipat	2131	0.743	578052
Yamuna Nagar	3305	0.776	936041
Haryana	157796	0.776	44699919

Himachal Pradesh

Livestock keeping is very common in Himachal Pradesh. Nearly one fourth of the households keep goat. Kangra, Mandi and Chamba districts have the highest concentration of goats in the state. Together these districts share more than half of the goat population of the state. The population of goats in the state is increasing while those of cattle, sheep and horses are decreasing.

Jammu and Kashmir

The distribution of livestock differs in different zones. For example, the goat ismainly distributed in Ladakh, Gurez, Karnath and hills of Baramulla. The most important challenge for the animal and goat husbandry sector is theproblem of fodder in the winter season, particularly for the Valley. Pashmina or Changra goat produces softest and warmest animal fibre used for high quality fabric (Pashmina wool). This pastoral farming is confined to the highest belt called 'Changthang' area of Ladakh around 4300 meters above sea level. Goat hair is used for making ropes, coarse blankets and namdas.

Jharkhand

Goat, pig, backyard poultry are preferred animal husbandry activities in the rural areas especially in tribal areas. These need to be promoted for increasing the income of rural population. Most of the goats in the state are non descript and need to be upgraded. The state government intends to use Black Bengal and Beetal breeds as improver goat breeds.

Karnataka

The important goat breeds in south India including Karnataka are Osmanabadi, Kannai adu, and Malabari.The major portion of the goat population is found in the rural areas and raised by the poorer socioeconomic sections of the community.

Most of the flocks consist of two to five goats grazed on marginal lands and consuming agricultural by-products and kitchen waste.

Kerala

The major proportion of the goat population in Kerala belongs to Malabari breed and is well adapted to the agro-climatic conditions of the State. Malabari is the only recognized breed of goat native to the state, known for their prolificacy and weight gain even under adverse management conditions. Among the schemes for the welfare and upliftment of weaker sections of society goat distribution has great importance as it encourages them to take up goat rearing as a profession and earn a livelihood. Production and distribution of good quality breeds of goats is indispensable for the successful implementation of these schemes. To meet this, three goat breeding farms were established in the state at Parassala of Thiruvanathapuram district, Kommeri of Kannur District and Attappadi of Palakkad district. Besides these, there are goat rearing units attached to the District Livestock Farm, Thiruvanathapuram; Buffalo Breeding Farm, Kuriottumala, Kollam; Jersey Farm Vithura, Thiruvanathapuram. All these farms are mandated to produce good quality Malabari goats for distribution and demonstration.

Madhya Pradesh

As per Seventeenth Livestock Census, Madhya Pradesh has 8.1 million goats in the state. The agro climatic conditions are conducive to development of goat rearing in the state. Approx. 25.84% growth of caprine during the period of 16th and 17th Livestock Census establishes the potential in the sector. Jamnapari and Barberi breeds of caprine have been introduced in different part of the state.

Maharashtra

As per livestock census of 2008, there are 10.98 million goats are reared in the State. The top two districts as far as goat production is concerned are Ahmadnagar and Solapur respectively.

Sr. No.	Name of the Division	No. of goats	Goat milk production during 2008-09 (000 Mts)
1	Mumbai (Konkon)	352112	10.186
2.	Nasik	3173555	77.692
3.	Pune	2369037	63.887
4.	Aurangabad	1185165	46.795
5.	Latur	919395	19.258
6.	Amravati	1440810	39.163
7.	Nagpur	1541107	20.269
	Total	10981181	277.250

Orissa

There are 5973919 goats as per livestock census 2003.The goat breeds in the state like Black Bengal, Ghumusur, Ganjam, Raighar, Maraguda are famous for meat purpose (http://orissaahvs.com/File/perspective%20plan.pdf).In Western Orissa, mostly Black Bengal breed is reared, which is well known for its superior meat and skin quality and higher twinning percentage. In Odisha, goats are reared mainly for meat purpose. Goat produces about 43.544 TMT meat per year (2008-09), which is about 70% of the total animal meat production (62.139TMT). Small ruminant production is perceived as having the greatest potential to meet the growing demand for meat and meat products. There are 6 goat breeding farms and one sheep breeding farm in the state.The sheep and goat graze mainly on the common property resources and the production cost is almost negligible.

Punjab

The total goat population in Punjab in the year 1977 was 722.1 thousand while it was 278.2 thousand in the year 2003 showing a decline of 61.47%. Thus the goat population in Punjab has shown a progressive decline over the years. Beetal is a breed of goats used for meat and milk production found throughout the states of Punjab and Haryana. True-bred animals are, however, found in the districts of Gurdaspur, Amritsar and Ferozepur in Punjab. The Beetal is usually black or red with pendulous ears. The males have long twisting horns. It is considered a good dairy breed, second to Jamnapari in size but is superior to it in that it is more prolific and more easily adaptable to different agro-ecological conditions and to some extent to stall-feeding. Beetal (Amritsari) with primarily black, tan or spotted colour, long, drooping ears and roman nose are some important characteristics.In Punjab Stall-feeding (Intensive) and semi-intensive system which includes partial grazing and partial stall-feeding is suitable.

Rajasthan

In Rajasthan, goat husbandry is not merely a supplement to agriculture or cattle /buffalo production but is a major economic activity, especially in the arid and semi-arid areas. Goat production has highest potential for employment generation and for income enhancement with low investment. The main goat breeds are Jamunapari, Jakhrana, Sirohi, Marwari, Barbari. The state government has one goat farm at Ramsar in Ajmer District for the development of Sirohi breed. There are about 21.5 million goats as per livestock census 2007. The state produced 850 thousand tons of goat milk in 2002-03. Goat development programme is aimed to develop Sirohi goats in ten districts of South-Western regions of the State viz.: Ajmer, Pali, Sirohi, Bhilwara, Rajasmand, Chittorgarh, Dungarpur, Banswara, Nagaur and Udaipur. Sirohi breed kids of about 4-6 months age are selected from the home tract and are reared at Ramsar farm Ajmer and Cattle Breeding farm, Nagaur. The bucks of Jamunapari breed of goat are being reared at Cattle Breeding farm, Kumher, in Bharatpur District. These bucks are distributed in Bharatpur, Dholpur, Karauli, Alwar and Sawai Madhopur Districts.

These elite Sirohi bucks after attaining breeding age are distributed to goat breeders @ Rs.600 to BPL families and to others @ Rs. 800 per Buck. The Jamunapari bucks are distributed to SC/ST/BPL families @ Rs. 1200 per buck and for general category Rs. 1500 per buck and for other institutions @ Rs.3000 per buck (http://www.animalhusbandrytest.rajasthan.gov.in/activities.aspx).

Tamil Nadu

The eighteenth livestock census has indicated 92.75 lakh goats in the state with 13 % increase over the seventeenth livestock census. The predominant goat breeds in Tamil Nadu are Kanni adu, Kodi adu and Salem black. Besides District Livestock Farms in Tamil Nadu maintains Jamunapari, Kodivalli, Kanni, Telichery (http://www.tn.gov.in/policynotes/pdf/animal_husbandry.pdf).Utmost care is given to prevent economic loss to the farmers by mortality and morbidity of goats by periodical deworming, vaccination and treatment in all veterinary institutions, Kalnadai Padhukappu Thittam camps and under Assistance to States for Control of Animal Diseases programme by the state animal husbandry department.Prabaharan and Thirunavakkarasu (1994) studied the constraints in goat farming in seven agro-climatic zones of Tamil Nadu. They found inadequate fodder and grazing lands, exploitation by middlemen was the major constraints of goat farming.

Uttar Pradesh

Uttar Pradesh has 129.50 lakh goats and 47% of them are females (Livestock Census, 2003).

Uttarakhand

The number of goats reported from Uttarakhand is 13.35 lakh (2007). The number of goats in the state are increasing at the rate of 3.62% per annum.In Uttarakhand, particularly in the hillyregions, to cater to the need of quality and quantity production of meat ingoat, it is essential to provide good quality germplasm for breed improvement and animal health services to these rural populations.

West Bengal

The only goat of the state is Bengal goat. The core of the breeding tract is West Bengal and the neighbouring Bangladesh. Very close variants of the breed are widely distributed all over eastern India. Among three major coat colour varieties, viz., black, brown and white, prevalence of black is highest and hence is also popular as Black Bengal. However relative ratio of different coat colours is variable over the breeding tract. Jamunapari, Beetal, Barbari, Sirohi and their crosses with Bengal goat are also occasionally seen. As per seventeenth livestock census there are 1,17,56,690 goats in West Bengal.

Table: Goat breeds and their distribution in different agro-climatic region of India.

Temperate	North-western	Southern	Eastern
Gaddi	Jamunapari	Sangamneri	Ganjam
Chegu	Beetal	Osmanabadi	Black Bengal
Changthangi	Jakhrana	Kanni Adu	
	Barbari	Malabari	
	Sirohi		
	Kutchi		
	Marwari		
	Mehsana		
	Zalawadi		
	Gohilwadi		
	Surti		

Classification of Indian Goat Breeds

Goat breeds of the country can be classified on the basis of their body size and body weight into the three categories:

1. **Large Size** : Jamunapari, Beetal, Jakhrana, Sirohi
2. **Medium Size**: Marwari, Kutchi, Surti, Barbari, Mehsana, Gohilwadi, Kanni Adu, Malabari, Sangamneri, Osmanabadi, Ganjam, Changthangi, Chegu, Gaddi.
3. **Small Size**: Black Bengal.

Goat breeds can also be classified on the basis of their productivity and production type. Numerically, Marwari in the western dry region of Rajasthan, Kutchi in the Gujarat plains and Black Bengal in the lower Gangetic plains of West Bengal are the important breeds for the purpose of the meat production. Black Bengal, Barbari (in the upper Gangetic plains) and Surti have, of course, more market demand for the quality meat. The Jamunapari in upper Gangetic, Beetal in Trans-Gangetic, Jhakhrana in the central plateau and Osmanabadi in the western plateau, and hill regions, have been the breeds of choice for higher milk production.

1. **Milk/Meat**: Jakhrana, Jamunapari, Beetal, Barbari, Sirohi.
2. **Meat and Milk**: Sangamneri, Kutchi, Zalawadi, Gohilwadi, Mehsana, Osmanabadi
3. **Meat**: Black Bengal, Ganjam, Malabari, Kanni Adu.
4. **Fiber and Meat**: Gaddi, Marwari, Changthangi, Chegu.

1. Attapady Black

The 'Attappady Black' goat, reared in the hill tracts of the district by tribal people, is under serious threat of extinction. The breed, known as the 'poor man's cow,' is highly resistant to diseases and can adapt to extreme climatic conditions. This goat is found only in the remote hamlets of Pudur, Agali and Sholayur panchayats, which have scanty vegetation. When food is limited, these animals are good at adapting to the available fodder. The animals are black in colour with bronze-coloured eyes. The goat has cultural values too. The wealth of a tribal family is measured by the number of goats reared in the house. Many times, they are gifted to newly married couples. They believe that milk and meat of these goats possess medicinal values. The ears are black and pendulous and the tail is curved and bunchy. These black goats are poor milk producers but reared mainly by women and old people for meat and manure purpose. The birth weight of males and females is around 1.73 Kg and 1.60 Kg respectively. The average live weight of males at 6th, 9th and 12th month of age are 14.61 Kg, 18.0 Kg and 20.8 Kg respectively. The estimated total population of Attappady black goats in their breeding tract is as low as 9351, putting this breed of goats under the insecure category listed by the FAO. Hence it is inevitable to adopt conservation efforts for this genetic resource (http://www.vechur.org/info/attappady.htm).

2. Barbari

This is also known as dwarf guinea goat and the animals are smaller than, Jamunapari and Beetal. The breed is supposed to have had its origin in East Africa where it was found in the area around Nile, Mauritius, Madagascar and Bourlon and Barbara city in Somaliland. In India it is found around Mathura, Agra, Aligarh,

Etah in UP and Gurgaon and Karnal districts in Haryana. The colour is usually white or red with a few red or tan spots. The adult male weighs around 30-40 kg while the female weighs around 25 to 35 kg. The doe measures 90 cm in body length, 60 cm in body height. The buck measures 95 and 65 cm respectively. The animals adapt well to stall feeding and are quite popular in cities on this account. Highest milk yield of 2.7 kg/day with 350 day lactation has been reported although the breed is generally used for meat because of the high fecundity. The animals of this breed can breed two times in a year. The average birth weight of the kid is around 1.0 kg. The average kidding rate under farm conditions is 1.7.

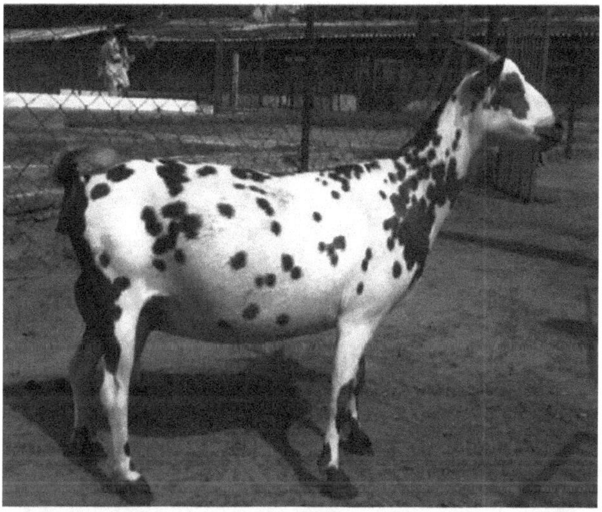

3. Beetal

Beetal goat is large in size, tall and popular among the farmers of Haryana and Punjab.The animals of this breed are found in Gurdaspur and Amritsar districts of Punjab. The animals have a roman nose and long cars with a beard in the male only. Common colours are black, red or tan heavily spotted in white. The weight of adult is about 70 kg in the male and 45 kg in the female. Adult buck is about 125 cms in body length and 90 cm in body weight while the corresponding values for females are 105 and 75 cm respectively. The ears are long and pendulous and hang like betel leaf at sides covering the ears. Horns are carried horizontally with somewhat backward and outward twisting. The animals are a good source of quality meat as well as milk.

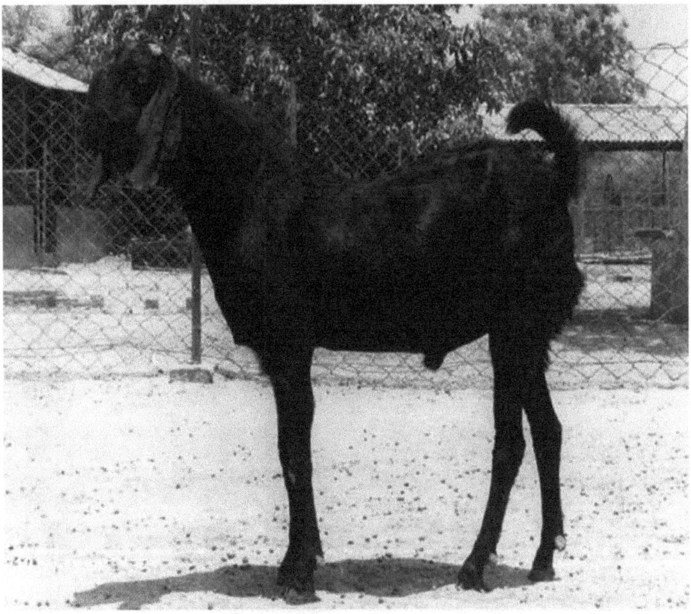

4. Bengal goats

Black Bengal is one of the two most important goat breeds inhabitating the Eastern part of India, the other one being Ganjam. There are three different types of Bengal goat namely Black Bengal, Brown Bengal and White Bengal. Black Bengal is the most popular, being jet black in colour. Native habitat of these goats is in West Bengal in India and it is found in central and south parts of West Bengal and distributed in adjoining states of Bihar, Jharkhand, Odisha,Tripura and Asom but is found in most pure form in the district of Murshidabad and surrounding places in West Bengal and Bangladesh. It is one of the most important meat breed of goats. Small legged Bengal weighing over 15 kg yields excellent quality meat.

The skin is of superior quality and is in demand both in India and abroad. The quality Black Bengal goat skins known as Calcuttias are used for shoe uppers. Except for nourishing the kids for a brief period, the she goats do not yield any appreciable quantity of milk. The shoulders and hips are of equal height, chest is wide and ears are nearly upright. The animal possesses short but soft hair. Multiple births are common, twins or triplets are born to 12 to 14 months old. The mortality in Black Bengal goats particularly in young kid is high as compared to other breeds which is due to smaller birth weight of the litter and low milk yield of the dams.These goats have typically been raised as scavengers, but now the traditional rearing system is under threat.

Black Bengal is a small sized breed which is primarily meat purpose breed. The breed is well adapted to the hot humid climatic conditions. This is the most prolific breed of goat. The breed is famous for excellent chevon and morocco leather production (Sahoo *et al.,* 2004, NBAGR, 2012). The population of this breed in India during 2004 has been estimated as 1,87,36,721 (NBAGR 2012).

5. Changthangi

Changthangi is a medium size breed of goat found in the cold, arid Changthang region of Jammu and Kashmir in India at an altitude of 3000 m. Changthangi goats are reared by a nomadic race.

These goats are found in high hills of Kashmir and Tibet. The breed is also popular in Himachal Pradesh and Punjab. They do not thrive on damp hot climate of other parts of India. They are large, hardy goats, average weight reaches upto

68 kg. The goats generally have white fleece but grey and brown animals are not uncommon. In many places the goats are used for transport particularly at high altitudes. The body is covered with a fine silky hair, about 10 to 12 cm long beneath which is a fur like undercoat of great fineness and warmth and called pashmina. This valuable hair grows from October to February and is shed in the spring. It is used for making Kashmir ring shawl. Both the males and females have horns and beards. The goats are combed for 8 to 1 0 days and the undercoat collected, leaving the long silky hair to be clipped latter. The average outturn of pashmina is about 100-120 gms from each goat. The goats are very hardy and can stand very cold weather. These goats are not bred for milk production and their milk yield is rather low. The hair of these goats is commonly used for making ropes, numdahs etc. The skins are largely used by hillmen to make sacks for transporting grain from one place to another. They are used as a beast of burden and meat.

Pashmina goat produces a double coat consisting of finer undercoat and outer course coat called guard hair. These goats are medium in height ranging from 60-80 cm. The body colour of goat varies from white to light brown, white being more dominant over other shades. These goats tend to be alert and cautious, rather than docile and placid. They also tend to be very easy kidders and good moms. The face and muzzle are devoid of hairs. Ear are small, erect and stumpy while horn possess a typical character. The horn curved first upward then backward, downward and onwards.

6. Chegu

The home of this breed of goats is the high mountain ranges of Spiti, Yaksar and Kashmir and Tibet. They are smaller than the Gaddi goats in size, but the weight of male and female is 31.5 kg to 36 kg and 13.5 to 18 kg respectively. The colour is usually white but greyish red and mixed colours can also be seen. The face and muzzle are tapering. Horns bend backwards and outwards. They possess long hair below which a second coat of fine hair or pashmina grows. Pashmina is graded into different classes according to fineness and sold in Kulu and markets of Kangra districts. Fine chaddars and mufflers are manufactured from the fine hair. The Chegu if brought to lower altitudes lose its second coat and cannot stand the heat very well. As the high hills are devoid of scrub forest, the animals subsist on shrub and leaves, but chiefly on grass locally known as neru. In addition to use as slaughter animals, they are used as pack animals to carry salt and similar small loads. The body measurements of adult male chegu goat are 108.32 cm length, 72.33 cm height and 89.38 cm heart girth.

7. Gaddi

This breed is found in Kangra and Kulu valleys, Chamba and Simla in Himachal Pradesh and parts of Jammu hills. During winter, the herds graze in valleys, while in summer they move to higher altitudes where the lush green grass springs up. The breed can thrive well on leaves of bushes and trees. General colour is white. Horns are pointed at the apex, bending upwards and backwards. Skin is very tough, covered with coarse long hairs measuring 17 to 25 cms. One clip weighs

about 0.5 to 1 kg. Gaddi goats are very firm footed. Each animal can transport about 8 kg of merchandise. The head possesses tapering muzzle, prominent, with alert eyes and Roman nose. Ears are drooping and pointed about 12 cm in length. The male weighs about 30 kg while female 18 kg. They kid once a year, with a rare twin. Litter size 1.2. Average age at first kidding is 18-19 month. Meat is coarse and devoid of fat. Breed is widely used for sacrificial purposes. Udder is small with well set pointed teats. The average milk yield is 0.5 kg per day. The hairs are used for ropes, snow boots and coarse rug making.

The Gaddi goat, which greatly resembles the ancestral wild goat, was used as a beast of burden in the mountains and is still used in the Himalayan region of India for carrying salt and food grains (Acharya, 1982).

8. Ganjam

The breed derives its name from the name of the place "Ganjam" in Orissa. These goats are mainly found in the southern region (Ganjam and Puri districts) of Orissa. The breed is distributed in Chatrapur, Rambha, Bhanjanagar, Khallikote, and Digaphandi areas of the Ganjam district. It is widely distributed in south Orissa and adjoining areas of coastal Andhra Pradesh and Jagdalpur in Madhya Pradesh. Goats are mainly raised by the tribals and also people living in rural areas. They are well adapted to heavy rainfall and meagre feeding. Ganjam is predominantly black in colour but black with brown crest and white patches and brown are also seen. Some have wattle and beard. Horns grow parallel, curve backward and downward. Legs are long. Body weight of adult buck and doe is about 35 and 30 kg respectively. Ganjam goats are poor milker and the daily milk yield ranges from 300 to 400 gm under village conditions. Animals are kept on extensive grazing. The goat moves mostly along with the nomadic tribals who mostly rear goats. This is a hardy breed and known for its disease resistance.

9. Gohilwadi

The animals of this breed are found in Bhavnagar, Amrah and Junagarh districts of Gujarat. Gohilwadi is a medium size, well built and dual-purpose goat. The animals of this breed are generally black with long hairs. Adult male and females weigh 48 and 37 kg, respectively. The milk yield is around 1.2kg. Average of 52% multiple births have been reported. The animals of this breed are maintained for meat. Gohilwadi goats are locally known as Gohil or Gola Bakari and native of the then Gohilwad province of Kathiawad presently known as Bhavnagar district of Gujarat (Singh *et al.*, 2008). Estimated population of these goats is about 3 lakhs predominantly in Bhavnagar, Amreli, Junagarh and Ahmedabad districts. Member of Rabaries and Bharwad communities keep Gohilwadi goats.

10. Jakhrana

The animals of this breed are found in Behror tehsil of Alwar district of Rajasthan. The animals are predominantly black in color with white spots on ears and forehead.

The females of this breed are good milkers. Adult male and females weight 51 and 44 kg, respectively. These animals have very good potential as an improver breed for milk. Jakhrana is a large sized breed and is known for both milk and meat production (Rai *et al.*, 2001).

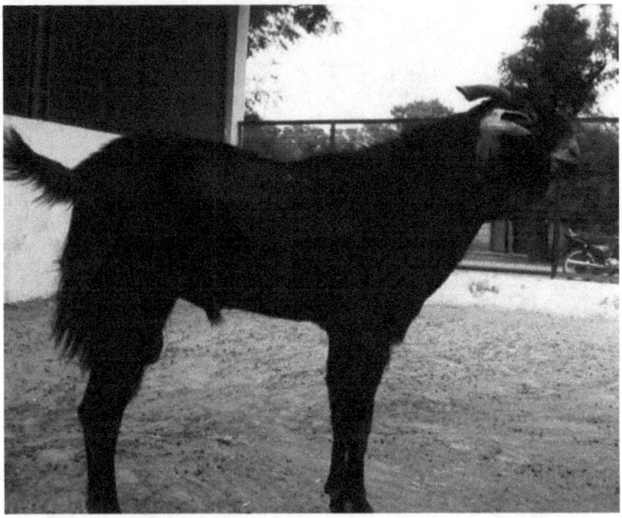

11. Jamunapari

Jamunapari is one of the largest and most majestic breed of goats in India; it has been extensively utilized to upgrade indigenous breeds for meat and milk, and has been taken to neighboring countries for the same purpose. The name is derived from the location of the breed beyond the river Jamuna (Jamuna Par) in Uttar Pradesh. Its home is between Jamuna, Ganges and Chambal rivers. Distributed in Agra, Mathura and Etawah districts in UP and Bhind and Morena districts in MP. They are found in most pure form in the Chakkarnagar tehsil of Etawah district (UP). Now this breed is also available in Tamilnadu, Karnataka and Andhra Pradesh states in India.

They are dual purpose goats, combining meat and milk qualities, constitute a good source of income for the poor sections of the people. The typical character of the breed is a highly convex nose line with a tuft of hair, yielding a parrot mouth appearance. The breed has no uniform color, but the animals having a white coat with tan markings are common. The ears are very long, flat and drooping pendulous ears (10-12 cm in length). Both sexes are horned; horn length: 8.69 ± 0.27 cm. Tail is thin and short. A thick growth of hair on the buttocks, obscures the udder when observed from behind. The udder is well developed, round, with large conical teats.. The female kids once a year and one kid at a time. The mature body weight of males varies from 68 to 91 kg. The average kidding rate under farm conditions reaches upto 1.4.

The home tract of Jamunapari goat is drained by Chambal river .The agriculture consists of thorny scrub. Jamunapari goat survives in this difficult terrain and negotiates the ravines easily.Jamunapari is undoubtedly the most exported breed from India. It was exported to United Kingom and helped develop the Anglo-Nubian Breed. The breed was exported to Vietnam and Indonesia. Peranakan Etawah goats of India descend from crossings between the Kacang with Etawah (from India) goats.

	Length	Height at withers	Body weight
Male	50-54 in	36-40 in	68-91 kg
Female	46-50 in	30-34 in	36-63 kg

12.Kannai Adu

This breed is present in Ramanathpuram and Tirunelveli districts in Tamil Nadu.The animals of this breed are tall. The predominant color is black or white with black spots. Ears are of medium length. Adult males and females weigh 35 and 28 kg, respectively. This is a predominantly meat breed.

13. Kutchi (Gujrati, Cuthi)

Kutchi goats are found in a comparatively pure form throughout Cutch (Ahmedabad and adjoining districts). They are medium sized black goats, with cork screw horns and long black hairs. Their ears are of medium length and usually white or speckled white. They may also have white markings on the face. They are good milkers. Their average daily milk yield is 1.25 to 1.5 kg, though does with higher milk yield are not infrequent. On account of their size, the male kids after castration can be profitably reared for meat. They have a roman nose. The animals are kept for milk, meat and fibre.

The Bhuj goat breed from northeastern Brazil also known as Bhuj Brasileirais, are derived from the Kutchi goat of India. Bhuj goats are usually black with white or spotted lop ears and a Roman nose. The name Bhuj apparently comes from an area in the Western part of India from which goats were imported to a Brazilian island called "Fernando de Noronha".

14. Malabari (Tellicherry)

This type is found mostly in north Kerala in the taluks of Kurumbranad, Kottayam and Chirakkal and also in Calicut and Ponani. Tellicherry breed of goats are being preferred by lot of farmers in in Tamil Nadu for its better kidding percentage and better overall performances. The goat population is heavy in and around towns of Calicut, Tellicherry, Cannanore and Mangalore and it becomes gradually less from the coast to the Ghat on the eastern side. There are many trees in this area which provide plenty of fodder. The staple food is jack tree leaves. Malabar is not a pure breed but a mixture of 2 or more types with a preponderance of Surti breed, which owes its origin to Arabian and Mesopotamian goats. They have no uniform colour. It may be white, black, and brown, black and white, black and brown, but the white and white with coloured patches are common. Both the long and short haired varieties are found. The average length of goat is 65 cm. height 60 cm. and girth 70 cm. The face is about 20 cm. long and the horns are bent backwards and are about 15 to 20cm. long. The female kids attain sexual maturity at 6 months, take the buck at the 7 or 8th month and kid when 14 month old. They usually give birth to one to four kids. The milk yield varies from 1 to 3. 5 kg per day. Male goats are kept for slaughter.

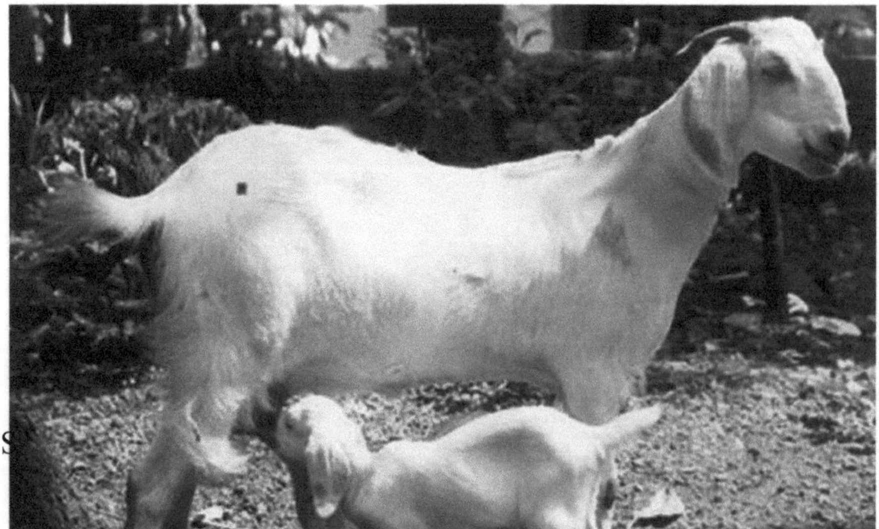

15. Marwari

Marwari is a medium-sized and dual-purpose (meat/milk) goat breed of the northwestern arid region of Rajasthan (India). The name Marwari is after the "Marwar" region of Rajasthan, which is the natural habitat of this breed. The breed is distributed mainly across Barmer, Jaisalmer, Jalore, Jodhpur, Nagaur and Pali districts of Rajasthan. The breed is well adapted to the arid environment, grows faster, breeds efficiently, can tolerate higher salt loads, and requires less water than many other species of the region.Marwari goat have small muzzle and a beard. The skin is greyish red in colour covered with black hair of 10-15, cm length. They are medium milkers and possess long teats.

16. Mehsana

This breed is found in the Mehsana district and adjoiningareas of Kankrej and a part of Vidhiri in Gujarat and spread up to the southern parts of Palanpur in the north and Nadiad in south. Goats of this breed are medium sized with roman-nose. The colour is greyish black and ears are white with black spots. Usually a small beard is present. Hairs on the body are black and a mixture of grey. The length of the hair is about 10 cm. Udder is well developed. Animals of this breed are good milkers.

17. Osmanabadi

The breed is spread over the greater part of the central peninsular region, comprising the semi-arid areas of Maharashtra, Andhra Pradesh and Karnataka. It covers the Major part of Southern Maharashtra (especially Osmanabad, Beed, Sholapur, Latur, Parbani and Ahmed Nagar Districts) Western Andra Pradesh and North Eastern Karnataka. The most common color is black although a mixture of white and black or red is often noticed. The goats are divided into long and short haired types; the latter weighs about 45 kg. Twinning is quite common in this breed. Kidding percentage and twinning ability in this breed was found to be 55.87 % and 10.52 % respectively (Sahare *et al.,* 2009).

18: Sangamneri

The breed is a native of Rahuri, Poona and Ahmednagar districts of Maharashtra. Sangamneri is spread over the adjoining places of Sangamner tehsil, viz Sinnar from Nasik districts, Junnar from Pune district and Sangamner, Rahuri, Shrirampur, Nagar and Parner from Ahemdnagar districts of Maharashtra, India (Deokar *et al.,* 2007). This is a medium sized breed. This is a dual purpose breed ie used for meat as well as milk.

19. Sirohi

The Sirohibreed is a native of Sirohi district in Rajasthan and is spread over wide areas of Rajasthan and in adjoining areas of Gujarat. They are medium sized and compact goats of black or brown colour. A mixture of these two types is, however, not uncommon. They are good milkers and easily adapt to stall feeding. They kid once a year and twins are common. Body length, height and heart girth of an adult Sirohi goat is 67, 71 and 68 cms, respectively.

20. Surti

It is also known as Khandeshi. The breed is mostly found in Surat (Gujarat) and Nasik (Maharashtra). Short statured animals are generally reared in towns by the artisan class. The breed is unable to walk long distances and is stall fed. They are most economic to rear because they can thrive on leaves or on food waste and are good milk producers yielding 1 to 2 kg of milk per day.

21. Zalawadi

Zalawadi is a promising dual purpose goat breed of India (Singh *et al.,* 2008). This breed is found in Surendranagar district (formerly known as Zalawad district) of Saurashtra region (Kathiawad (Gujarat). These goats are also distributed in pockets of Mehsana, Ahmedabad and Bhavnagar districts adjoining to Surendranagar. It is also found in western Mehsana and Radhanpur districts of Gujarat. Zalawadi are generally large sized goats, with straight screw type horns. Usually two lobular appendages are found in the throat region. The skin colour is pinkish blue with black lusterous hair on the body measuring about 15 cm long. The goat is a good milker and kids only once a year. Daily milk yield is 1.17kg (range 1.02-1.57).Traditional Zalawadi goat keepers mostly belong to Rabari and Bharwad communities who are mostly pastoralists and semi-nomadic. The breed is well adapted to the harsh climatic conditions and can consume a wide range of vegetation. Estimated population in India is 2,60,000.

List of Nucleus goat herds in the country

The purebred animals of different breeds of goats are being maintained at some of the government farms. However, some progressive farmers may be maintaining small number of pure bred animals.

1. Central Institute for Research on Goats, Makhdoom, Farah , Mathura ---- Barbari

2. Central Institute for Research on Goats, Makhdoom, Farah , Mathura ---- Jamunapari
3. Central Institute for Research on Goats, Makhdoom, Farah , Mathura ---- Jakhrana
4. Central Sheep and Wool Research Institute, Avikanagar, Via Jaipur -------- Sirohi
5. Central Sheep Breeding Farm, Post Box No 10, Hisar, Haryana --------- Beetal

Some lesser known goat breeds of India

Biodiversity is important. Genetic diversity should be maintained to help meet the potential challenge resulting from changes in production resources and market requirements. Trust for advancement in Agricultural Sciences (TAAS) list the following breeds as part of the domestic goat biodiversity in India (http://www.taas.in/documents/pub17.pdf)

Local :	Andaman Feral Goat, Assamese Hill, Attapady Black, Baigani , Barren goat, Bidari, Changthangi, Chegu, Dalua, Ganjam, Gohilwadi, Himalayan Ibex, Himalayan Tahr, Indian Mohair, Jhakrana, Kannai Adu, Kutchi, Malabari, Marwari, Mehsana, Nilgiri Tahr, Osmanabadi, Ramdhan, Sangamneri, Sirohi, Surti, Teressa, Zalawadi.
Regional Transboundary :	Bengal, Gaddi, Tibetan.
International Transboundary :	Barbari, Beetal, Jamunapari

Following is a selected list of lesser known breed of goats found in India.

1. **Andaman goats** : Breeds of goats (Local Andama and Teressa and Andaman Feral goats) belonging to Andaman and Nicobar islands have been phenotypically characterized recently. A sustained effort by scientists of the Animal Science Division at CARI has resulted in the successful production of cross breeds of goats (Andaman local goat x Boer goat). The Andaman local goats are known to be salt tolerant.Andaman feral goats have survived the volcano's eruptions by migrating to the unaffected side of the island, feeding on its sparse foliage and survivingand thriving, on seawater. Few other animals have been known to withstand the vagaries of such harsh environment.The Andaman feral goat could be the answer to the livestock problems of drought-affected regions, where fresh water is in short supply.

2. **Assamese or Assam Hill (syn Khasi)** The animals of this breed are found in the Khasi, Naga and Lushi hills of Assam. The animals are bearded, long haired, and usually pure white in colour but grey colour has also been reported in some animals. The animals are short legged and long bodied. The adult male weighs about 30 kg and female 25 kg. The body length, height and heart girth of this goat is 69, 54 and 69 cm respectively. Majority of goat's kid twice yearly and twins are common. This is a predominantly meat breed of goats and the animals are not generally milked. The kids at birth weigh 0.8 to 1.2 kg. The ears are short (13-14 cm) and erect. The horns are curved backwards from head.
3. **Baigani**
4. **Bakharwal**: This breed is found in hilly tracts of Himachal Pradesh. The breed is characterized by long hair which are used for making ropes. Animals are good meat producers. (ICAR Handbook of Animal Husbandry, 2002 3rd Edition pp 127). Essentially, the name "Bakarwal" implies "high-altitude goatherds/shepherds".
5. **Baltistani**
6. **Berari goats:** This breed is found in Nagpur and Wardha districts of Maharashtra and Nimar district of Madhya Pradesh. It is tall and dark black coloured goat. The average yield is about 0.6 kg per day. The animals are used for both meat and milk.
7. **Bezoar**
8. **Bundelkhandi**
9. **Dalua**
10. **Dorangi Goat Nayagarh** (http://orissaahvs.com/website/bio-diversity-in-orissa/goat.htm
11. **Gua Chheli Of Gajapati District** (http://orissaahvs.com/website/bio-diversity-in-orissa/goat.htm)
12. **Kagani**
13. **Kangra/Chamba/Kangan** : This breed is reported from Hills of Himachal Pradesh.
14. **Kodi adu**
15. **Ladakhi pashmina**
16. **Mahabubnagar goats**-Mahabubnagar local goats, though yet to berecognized as a breed, are well known for their production potential and prolificacy.

17. **Malkangiri Goat**: Early maturing, prolific, kidding twice in 14 months, mostly twins, heavy chevon goats. Found in Odisha (Orissa)
18. **Raighar Goat**: Early maturing, prolific, kidding twice in 14 months, mostly twins some triplets, can be a good milk goat used for chevon.Found in Odisha (Orissa) (http://orissaahvs.com/website/bio-diversity-in-orissa/goat.htm)
19. **Narayanapatna breed**: A mutton type prolific, twin kidding, 14 to 15 month two kiddings, large goat with good udder and teats.Found in Odisha (Orissa) (http://orissaahvs.com/website/bio-diversity-in-orissa/goat.htm)
20. **Koraput Hill Goat**: Early maturity, prolific, kidding twice 14 months, mostly twinning, fastest growing goats for chevon production.Found in Odisha (Orissa) (http://orissaahvs.com/website/bio-diversity-in-orissa/goat.htm)
21. **Ganjam Hill Goat**: Very similar to Koraput Hill Goat, but slightly compact (Gua Chelli) with good Udder.(http://orissaahvs.com/website/bio-diversity-in-orissa/goat.htm)
22. **Markhor**
23. **Parbatsar goat :** Parbatsari goats are light brown or dark brown colour with no patches.Parbatsarigoats have bodysize and bodyweights lower thanSirohi goats.

1. **Pateri**
2. **Phulbani Goats**
3. **Ramdan**
4. **Sojat goats** (Rajasthan)
5. **Tellichery goat**-Tellichery goat is reared for milk and chevon in most of the south Indian states.

Conservation and Improvement of threatened breed

Of the more than 7 600 breeds in FAO's global database of farm animal genetic resources, 190 have become extinct in the past 15 years and a further 1 500 are considered at risk of extinction.

Table 1: The habitat and projected population size (2004) of different breeds based on the actual population size extrapolated from the Livestock Census Report- 1977, Volume- II.

Breed	Broad Habitat	Population (In Lakh)
Dual Purpose Breeds (Milk & Meat)		
Barbari	Agra, Mathura, Etah and Aligarh districts in U.P.	5.10
Barbari	Agra, Mathura, Etah and Aligarh districts in U.P.	5.10
Beetal	Gurdaspur, Amritsar and Firozpur districts in Punjab.	1.19
Gohilwadi*	Bhavnagar, Amreli and Junagarh districts.	5.19
Jhakhrana	Jhakhrana village in Alwar district of Rajasthan.	0.02
Jamunapari	Chakarnagar Block in Etawah district of U.P.	0.08
Kutchi*	Kutch district in Gujarat.	4.69
Malabari	Calicut, Cannanore and Malapuram district in Kerala.	5.24
Marwari*	Western Rajasthan.	74.29
Mehsana*	Mehsana and Banaskantha districts in Gujarat.	6.26
Sirohi	Sirohi and Ajmer districts in Rajasthan.	7.20
Surti	Surat and Vadodara districts in Gujarat.	3.80
Zalawadi*	Surendranagar and Rajkot districts in Gujarat.	4.10
Meat Breeds		
Bakharwal*	Hill regions in Kashmir	-
Black Bengal	West Bengal, Jharkhand, Orissa, Bihar and Assam.	629.64
Gaddi*	Chamba, Kangra, Kulu, Bilaspur, Kinnanaur and Lahul-Spiti districts in Himachal Pradesh.	5.33
Ganjam	Ganjam district in Orissa.	3.70
Kannai Adu	Ramanathpuram and Tirunelveli districts in T.N.	9.74
Khasi*	Khasi, Jayantia and Garo hills in Meghalaya.	2.02
Osmanabadi	Osmanabad district in Maharashtra.	4.52
Sangamneri	Ahmednagar district in Maharashtra.	9.08
Pashmina Breeds		
Changthangi*	Ladakh district in Jammu & Kashmir.	3.02
Chegu*	Uttarkashi, Chamoli and Pithoragarh districts in Uttarakhand	4.84

* Hair is an additional attribute in these breeds.

A breed is considered as endangered, when the effective population size is too small to prevent genetic loss through inbreeding leading to infertility and lack of survivability resulting in ultimate loss of the population. According to FAO, a breed with a population size of 5000 breeding females or less can be declared as endangered. A breed is vulnerable, when the population is rapidly declining numerically or its security is under threat. The recognized breeds of Indian goat population are facing a greater threat of endangeredness due to various problems. Lack of enforcement of proper breeding policy, inadequate number of bucks of recognized breed in the breeding tract, indiscriminate cross breeding and intermixing amongst breeds with local animals are the major factors for pushing Indian goats to the path of vulnerability and extinction.

The purebred Jamunapari population has declined seriously and it is less than 8,500 in its habitat due to different reasons. Beetal is drawing attention for conservation as the number is declining due to changing agricultural patterns in Punjab. Barbari is facing dilution in breed characteristics due to cross breeding with Sirohi and Jamunapari breeds in its home tract. Due to decrease in natural browse and geographical restriction, Surti and Jhakhrana are decreasing in number. The changthangi breed of the Ladakh region is the subject for special concern as they are declining both in number and in performance. More weightage on improvement of some breeds and extensive use of these breeds such as Beetal, Barbari and Jamunapari could result in the elimination of other distinctive breeds by cross breeding. Generally two approaches viz. Ex-situ and In-situ methods of conservation may be adopted for the goat breeds in India.

Endangered Breeds of Goats

The last few decades have witnessed serious erosion of native germ plasm and even extinction of a number of indigenous animal breeds in the world. Many existing breeds are facing varying degrees of threat, endangerment and are heading towards eventual extinction. It has been globally recognized that conservation and improvement of native animal genetic resources are essential for sustainable development in agriculture and animal husbandry. The need to preserve farm animal diversity is increasingly urgent. Livestock hold critical keys for our survival and with each extinction, genetic traits of potentially vital importance to our agricultural future and progress are forever lost.Global concerns towards loss of livestock biodiversity is reflected in the FAO sponsored "State of the World Animal Genetic Resources (SoWAnGR)" process culminating in Interlaken Declaration in 2007. Having been a participant in the process and signatory to the Declaration, India has international obligations to fulfill, besides addressing national priorities concerning livestock breeds.

Definition of endangered breed according to FAO is a breed where the total number of breeding females is between 100 and 1 000 or the total number of breeding males is less than or equal to 20 and greater than five; or the overall population size is close to, but slightly above 100 and increasing, and the percentage of pure-bred females is above 80%; or the overall population size is close to, but slightly above, 1 000 and decreasing, and the percentage of pure-bred females is below 80%. (Source: FAO, 1999).Each country has its own system for assessing the state of endangerment (risk status) of farm animal breeds.It has been reported that some Indian goat breeds with valuable genetic traits are declining numerically {for example the Barbari, present population 30 000, and Jamunapari 5000), conservation of these breeds is needed (http://www.fao.org/docrep/010/ah806e/AH806E03.htm). Surti breed is also among the endangered breeds of Indian goats.

Conservation efforts generally include i) Establishment of nucleus breeding units., iii) Support to breeders association and its formation, ex situ and in situ conseration efforts.Enumeration/survey needs to be carried out for existing breeds. Breeds with characteristics and defects not yet defined will be candidates for characterization. Quantitative data and analysis of breed population as well as distribution should constitute scientific basis for setting priorities for conservation action.

Foreign breeds introduced in India

Although there are a number of indigenous breeds well adapted to Indian conditions, there have been several attempts to introduce foreign breeds in India. The prominent foreign breed introductions include Saanen, Alpine, Boer and Angora.

Boer goats are considered far superior to any other goats for meat production. It is known for rapid weight gain and heavy muscling and has high fertility. Boers typically give birth to twins. Crosses of local goats with Boers have proved to be a suitable genotype for the goat production system and well adapted to all types of climate. Considering the potentials of Boer goats and the necessity for improving the productivity of goats in the Kerala by genetic improvement, the Kerala Livestock Development Board introduced Boer goats. As a first step 50 selected Boer goats and 10 selected Boer bucks were imported from Australia during 2001 under the National buck Production Programme.

In order to improve the milk yielding ability of Indian goats, Alpine and Saanen breeds were introduced in India and crossed with Beetal to produce Saanen x Beetal and Alpine x Beetal crosses at National Dairy Research Institute.

In order to improve the mohair production in India, Angora goats were imported in Maharashtra but the imported goats could not sustain the hot climate of India. Recently some farmers from Kerala have imported Damascus (Shami) goats from Cyprus.

Synthetic breeds of goats

Kenya dual purpose goat breed is an example of a synthetic goat breed developed in recent times after more than 14 years of efforts since the local east African breed had limited scope for improvement through selection and temperate breeds could not survive under Kenyan conditions.Four breeds–two temperate (Toggenburg and Anglo Nubian) and two tropical (Small east African and Somali) were chosen to make the synthetic breed (Peacock, 1996).

Goat production in Asia

Yemen : Yemen's livestock appear to comprise at least 5 breeds of goat.

Nepal:Goat rearing is an important aspect of the Nepali farming system and provides an important source of cash income for most households in Nepal; animals are reared under traditional management systems - sedentary or migratory

- without many external inputs.The native Kage breed of goat is reported to have greater resistance to *Haemonchus contortus* infection.

Pakistan: Pakistan at present supports 56.7 millions head of goats consisting of about 25 well-recognized breeds found in different regions of the country. The indigenous milch breeds include Beetal, Dera Din Panah (DDP), Naachi, Damani, and Kamori.

Iran : In Iran, there are more than 27 million goats, with about 10–15 breeds, with the Markhoz goat being one of the most important indigenous breeds. This breed is raised in a wide range of forest mountain habitats in region of Kurdistan. Markhoz and Raini are the important goat breeds.

Laos:Laos is a developing country with good potentials for goat production. However, so far goat production has been still extensive , mainly exploiting natural feed resources and the indigenous breed (Lat goat) , which has a small size and low meat yield in spite of being well adapted to the local conditions (Phengsavanh, 2003 - http: / /www.nfnyxb.com).

Vietnam: Goat milk production is not traditional in Vietnam, with nearly all the country's 780000 goats being raised for meat production purposes. However one local goat breed, the Bach Thao breed, has been improved in order to produce both meat and milk; there are approximately 15 000 goats of this breed in Vietnam. Goat farming is largely carried out in small peasant farms, using locally produced feed resources. An important function of goat production is to produce manure that can be used as a fertilizer for crop production. Total goat meat production is estimated at 35700 tonnes, of which 75% is consumed in cities, while goat milk production amounts to 8100 tonnes, of which 75% is consumed by peasant families. In order to develop goat production in Vietnam, the Ministry of Agriculture and Rural Development has established a Centre for Research into Goats and Rabbits. This centre's objectives include evaluating the production potential of local breeds with regard to both meat and milk. In 1994, goats of the Barbary, Jumnapary and Beetal breeds were imported from India with the aim of assessing their potential for use in mountainous regions. In January 2002, the Vietnamese government established a programme to develop goat production with the introduction of two new dairy breeds (Saanen and Alpine) and one meat breed (Boer) from the USA.

Indonesia: The major breeds of goats in Indonesia are the Kacang and Peranakan Etawah goat. Kacang is an indigenous breed of goat found in Indonesia. Peranakan Etawah goats descend from crossings between the Kacang with Etawah (Jamunapari from India) goats.Goats are important for a large part of the Indonesian rural population.Nearly ninety nine percent of small ruminants in Indonesia are found in the hands of smallholders. Goats in Indonesia are kept primarily for meat production.

Kacang goats are relatively small with a compact body frame, have erect ears and short horns in both sexes.Peranakan Etawah goats descended from crossings between the Kacang with Etawah (Jamnapari) goats. Generally known simply as PE goat, animals of this population are distinctly different from the Kacang goats. They have a larger body frame, long hanging ears, a convex face and larger horns.Other breeds of goat found in Indonesia are Gembrong and the Kosta.

Lao PDR

Goats in Lao PDR are small in size and are used only for meat. Lao native goats are morphologically and genetically similar to the north Vietnamese native goats. Their body size is similar to the Southeast Asian dwarf goats ("Kambing-Katjang"-typed goats).

Bangladesh

The population of goats in Bangladesh currently includes about 18 million animals, which are dispersed throughout the country. The average number of goats per household is 2.3 and they are mostly reared by landless, small and medium farmers. Goats are used primarily for meat production, but their skin is a valuable by-product.Bangladesh has a native goat breed commonly known as the Black Bengal goat, exotic breeds such as the Sirohi, Beetal and Jamnapari, and crossbreds between the Black Bengal goat and exotics. Black Bengal goats are found all over the country. They can be classified into 3 sub populations; Bangladesh West (BBW), Bangladesh Central (BBC) and Bangladesh East (BBH); according to their geographical distribution. The exotic breeds and crossbreds are concentrated in the western part of the country and in some specific areas of central and eastern Bangladesh. Sirohi and Beetal bucks are imported by the farmers privately and used mainly for crossbreeding purposes (http://www-naweb.iaea.org/nafa/aph/stories/2006-goat-genetic.html).

Goats in Bangladesh are typically reared as scavengers. They are used like a cash crop and farmers usually sell them at the time of particular financial need or during festivals of Muslim and Hindu people. With the growing human population and demand for cereal food, the fallow lands used for natural grazing of goats are reducing day by day. Therefore, the traditional goat rearing system in Bangladesh is under threat. Farmers are now trying to adapt and rear goats under intensive management systems.

Pakistan

Pakistan has nearly 50 million goats. Goats are kept for milk and meat production and contribute significantly to the income of the rural farmers. Dairy goats are commonly kept by the farmers belonging to the poor socio-economic class of the society, most of which are landless. They prefer goats as an initial investment in agriculture as capital costs and fodder requirements are small. Thirty-six recognized breeds of goats can be found in Pakistan (http://www-naweb.iaea.org/nafa/aph/stories/2006-goat-genetic-pakistan.html).

Baluchi, Baltistani (Baltistand District), Bari, Chaper, Damani, Dera Din Panah, Jattan, Kaghani, Kamori, Leri, Salt Range (Salt Range Area), Sirli, Teddy Goats, Tharki (Thar Desert),Thori.

Dera din Panah : This is a milch breed of Pakistan which is found in Muzaffargarh & Multan districts of Pakistan.Characteristics include Large head with Roman nose, hair on the chin, long broad ears; cartilaginous appendages on sides of neck, long and thick spiralled horns; hairy body; tail medium covered with rough hair; udder and teats welldeveloped, milk yield 160 litres in a 150-day lactation; twin births common.

Hairy goat is a milch breed of goat found in Dera ghazi Khan area of Pakistan.

Kajli (Pahari) is breed found in D.G. Khan in Punjab & Loralai district in Balochistan.Head small, ears erect, horns thin, white or brown hair streaks run from base of horns to muzzle; udder medium, 120 litres milk in 120 days; twins rare.

Teddy is a meat breed found in Sargodha, Jhelum & Rawalpindi districts. Yields 65 litres milk in 130 days;

Bari is a meat breed.

Bugri (Bagitoori) is also a meat breed.

Jattan breed of goats, which derives its name from camel-raising tribe of jats in sindh is a milch breed.

Kamori is a milch breed found in Sindh.

Pateri is a milch breed of Pakistan with milk yield of 170 litres in 120 days;

Tapri is a meat breed.

Middle East Asia (Syria, Jordan, Lebanon)

Sheep and goat production contributes to the livelihoods of a large numbers of small scale resource-poor farmers in Middle Eastern countries, particularly Syria, Jordan and Lebanon, and accounts for 28–58% of agricultural output in the Middle East (Iñiguez, 2005). Various breeds of goats are widely distributed in different agro-ecological zones (Iñiguez, 2005). Shami and Jabali goats are the main breeds in Syria and Lebanon, the latter being important in the economically underdeveloped mountainous regions (Wurzinger *et al.,* 2008). Shami and Baladi are the main goat breeds in Jordan (Iñiguez, 2005).

Myanmar

The population of Sheep and Goats in Myanmar amounted to million. There are 2 types of goats in Myanmar, one is characterized by black and white color with drooping ears commonly found in Nyaung Oo, Kyaukpadaung, Meiktila, Ma Hlaing townships and the another is red breed prevalent in Myingyan, Nahtoe Gyi and Taungthar areas of Upper Myanmar. Black Bengal and Dwarf types are also found in northern Shan State and coastal region in the country respectively. Jumunapuri breed was a breed that was introduced long time ago under colonial period.

Goat

1. Nyaung Oo
2. Jade Ni
3. Hkway Seik

Oman

The Dhofari breed of goats contributes about 44 % of the total goats in Oman. They are sabre-horned, with short erect ears, short hair and of a variety of colors with the white color more prominent. Dhofari goats are kept in large flocks of about 50-300 by Jaballi herdsman who live on the hilly area in Dhofar.

Philippines

Goats provide livelihood to about 15 million Filipinos. As its productionrequires low initial investment with small risks, it is an attractive undertaking among rural farm households and a sound option to augment the country's programmes on livelihood development. At present, the goat population is estimated at 3.5 million, with 99 percent in the hands of backyard raisers and a meager 0.4 percent in commercial farms. Basically, the goat genetic resources in the country consist of the native, the exotic breeds (most notably the Anglo Nubian and the Boer), and the "upgrades": crossbred among the native and exotic breeds (Villar 2006)

Afganistan

Vatani and Asmari are the important breeds of goat of Afghanistan and produce fibre from the undercoat.

Malaysia

Current stocks of goats are made up from Katjang (native), Boer, Jamnapari, Anglo ubian and Feral (Australian) breeds and their crosses.The current goat population is about 250,000 heads, having risen from 190,000 in 1999.

Mongolian

All goats throughout Mongolia belong to one primitive type. The live weight is 30.41 kg, the height at withers 59-63 cm. The goats are usually horned. The colour is variable, mostly grey.

Nepal

Khari (Hill) Goats of Nepal

Khari (Capra hircus) goats are the principal goat breed of Nepal and are found across the hills and inner valleys in the country. They are quite widespread and can be found in the mid hills and immediate south of high mountains. They represent 56 % of the total goat population. They are prolific and good for meat production. They are hardy and well adapted to local environments, and occur in 6 different colour types namely, Seti (White), Kali (Black), Khairi (Brown), Ghorli (Brown mixed with other colours), Singari (Black with white markings) and Dhobini (White with black markings) (Oli, 1987; Neopane, 1997).

Saudi Arabia

The three local breeds of goats distributed in different regions of the Kingdom of Saudi Arabia with varying numbers namely the Aardi, Hipsi and Zumri, are raised mainly for meat production.

Sri Lanka

Small ruminant population represents 23.5% of the total ruminant population of Sri Lanka, where goats and sheep contribute 23.0% (500,000) and 0.5% (8,900), respectively. The majority of these goats are non-descript-type indigenous animals.

The only identified native breed, known as "Kottukachchiya", is currently endangered, in part due to the lack of a properly organized breeding program (http://www-naweb.iaea.org/nafa/aph/stories/2006-small-ruminants.html). Akyab (JAFNA. CEYLON)

Kacang

The breed is indigenous to Indonesia. It is a small goat, with males weighing 35 kg and the female 30 kg. There is no uniformity in colour, but is usually black, brown or white with various combinations of all the three colours. They have small ears and short horns which are backwards sloping with tips bent outwards.

Peranakan Ettawah

These goats are also found in Indonesia. It is the result of crossing the native Kacang goats with Jamnapari breed of India. The goats are brown with black and white spots. These goats are weighing about 60 kg in male and 50 kg in female and have madium to long pendulous ears and large horns.

Kambing Gembrong

This goat is also found in the eastern coast of Bali Island and is intermediate in size between the Kacang goats and grade Etawah. The mature weight is 45 and 38 kg in males and females respectively. The colour is usually white.

Raeini

Raeini goat is an Iranian Cashmere goat which is raised in large numbers in Kerman province of Iran where goat production contributes significantly to the agricultural economy. Raeini goat is one of the most famous Cashmere breeds in Iran.Iran has more than 5,000,000 Cashmere producing goats, which produce approximately 1500 metric tones of raw Cashmere. Raeini goat is an Iranian Cashmere goat which is raised in large numbers in Kerman province of Iran where goat production contributes significantly to the agricultural economy (Radfar *et al.,* 2011).

Japanese Native

They are small sized native goats reared as meat animals. Their number is very small (25,000) and they represent the domestic goat brought from the Asian continent 1500 years ago. Rests of the goats in Japan are Saanen, a dairy breed.

Korean Native

The body weight of male ranges from 30-40 kg and those of females from 25 to 30 kg. The colour is usually black. The horns are about 20.3 cm long in males and 11 cm in females which are curved backwards. The diameter of the horn is 13.8 cm in males and 8.3 cm in females and the average distance between the horns is 2.3 cm. These goats are used as meat animals. Their number is around 1.5 million. Age at weaning is 2.3 months. The females are kept upto the age of five.

Kambing Katjang

This breed is native to Malaysia and numerically the most important coat breed there. This breed is also found in Thailand. The adult female weighs 23 kg and the height at withers is 55-65 cm. The ears are short and upright. The horns are scimitar shaped curved upwards and backwards. Udder is well developed with small teats but very little milk is produced. The goats are highly resistant to heat, direct solar radiations, parasites and diseases. The age at first use in males is 365 days and in females is 575 days. There is no seasonality in estrous and birth. The colour is usually white in male and brown in females but great variation is seen.

Taiwan Native

The goats resemble those of southern part of mainland China. They are of small size with a moderately long neck, long back, broad and muscular loin, muscular thigh and short, strong and straight legs. The body weight is about 50 kg in males and 42 kg in females. The body height is 58 and 49 cm, body length 63 and 57 cm and heart girth 72 and 69cm in males and females, respectively. The head has a concave profile, prominent forehead and narrow erect ears are approximately 8cm long. Both sexes have a beard, which is particularly profuse in the buck and strong conical horns, which project upwards, backwards and outwards to reach a length of about 150cm. The coat is usually short. Most goats are completely black, some are completely brown and a few are brown with a mingling of black hair. Adult buck develops a mane. The native goats are considered seasonal breeders. The gestation period varies from 138 to 156 days. The native goat is used for meat production.

Sinhal

This breed is found in high hills of Nepal, generally at an elevation of 1500 to 3000 m. The male goat weighs about 40 to 50 kg and female about 30 to 40 kg. The estrous behaviour is non-seasonal and generally one kid is produced in a year, although twinning sometimes occurs. Both males and females have horns and medium sized ears. The goats are generally black in colour, but white and brown patches are not uncommon.

Nepal Hill

This type of goat is found between the terai (low land) and high Mountain regions. The hill goat is smaller than Sinhal, weighing about 25 to 30 kg. Two kid crops can be obtained easily from the breed in 14 months. Both sexes have horns and the body is multicoloured.

Kilis

These goats are found in Turkey. Usually black with lop ears. They are dairy animals, which originated from Damascus X Anatolian black.

Angora

The native home of the Angora is the district of Angora in Asia Minor (Turkey). Angora, the principal city, is about 220 miles south by southeast of Constantinople, Turkey. This is a mountainous region, 2000 to 4000 feet high, lying south of the Black Sea. The climate has wide extremes of heat and cold. The goat has inhabited this region for many centuries, dating back to days before the Christian era. Plumb has described five varieties of Angora. The Angora goat is smaller than the ordinary goat. The back should be straight with shoulders and hips of equal height. The chest should be broad, indicating good constitution and the body round, legs short and strong. The horns are greyish, never black, in the buck they are heavy, with an inward twist, inclining backward and to the outside. The does horns rise immediately upwards and backward, slightly outward, with very little inclination to twist. In most animals the ears are pendant and from 6 to 9 inches long, with an average width of about 2 inches and well pointed. The fleece of the animals should be pure white, although there are coloured Angoras. The fleece should cover the entire body as dense on the belly and neck as on the back and sides; they should extend to the ears and jaws. The mohair should grow to the length of about 10 inches during a year and hang in tight ringlets or wavy curls. The curl should extend entirely up to the skin. The Angora shed its fleece each spring if not shorn. Angora has no strong musky odour, like the common goat, excepting in the case of male during the breeding season. The Angoras are very widepread especially in Asia Minor, South Africa and the United States. The prolificacy is not marked. Rarely more than one kid is dropped a year, though twins occur

Goat production of Africa

Asia and Africa represent nearly 94 % of the total goat population of the world. Asia represents nearly 60 % and Africa represents 34 % of the world total.Tropical Africa is an important area of goat production with one third of world goat population. Among the African countries Sudan, Nigeria and Ethiopia are the most populous as regards goats. Most of the goat owners in these countries are in the nomadic sector with flocks ranging from 20 to 100 being kept per family. Organized goat dairying is almost non-existing in these countries. They have a key socio-economic role through meat, milk and skin production. West Africa mainly is characterised by a great genetic diversity with two types of goat:

the long-legged and trypanosusceptible type found in tsetse free area and the dwarf and trypanotolerant type which lives in humid zone. The West African Dwarf (WAD) goat is kept by crop farmers as a secondary enterprise in the subhumid zone.

Goats play a vital role in the rural economy of many countries in central and eastern Africa (Rwanda, Burundi, Uganda, Tanzania, Kenya, DRC, Congo, Cameroon, CAR, Sudan, Ethiopia, Nigeria, Chad, Gabon, and Somalia. Eastern Africa Region (Kenya, Uganda, Tanzania, Sudan, Ethiopia, and Somalia) holds the largest ruminant livestock population in sub-Saharan Africa.This abundant resource has not been exploited optimally to generate wealth and improve the welfare of the people, especially the poorer rural communities which are in the majority.

Tanzania has an estimated 8.5 million goats(http://www.nda.agric.za/docs/AAPS/Articles/Goats/Production/Project%20R5499.pdf) .They are kept primarily by small-scale farmers and pastoralists under traditional systems of management. These goats are very important to the livelihoods of their owners, particularly women.

The main meat goat breeds in Kenya include: Galla; East African; Boer and crosses of these three with local goats.

Ethiopia : According to recent estimates, the goat population in Ethiopia is about 23.3 million. A large proportion is found in the lowlands of the country, raised in large flocks by pastoralists. Nearly 10 million goats (42% of the total) are found in the highlands.

Namibia: Namibia's goat export to South Africa is estimated to be around 250 000 animals annually, generating approximately N$6 million in revenue. Currently Namibia's on-the-hoof goat population stands at two million. Namibia's local consumption of goat meat is on a lesser scale, with the bulk of the goats or close to 100 percent goats being reared mainly for the export market in South Africa.

Main local and exotic breeds of Africa

Country	Indigenous (local breeds)	Exotic (imported) breeds
Rwanda	Common local goat	Boer, Galla, Anglo-nubian, Alpine, Saanen, Toggenburg,,Spanish, and crossbred with exotic and local breeds
Burundi	Common local goat	
DRC	West African Dwarf	
Uganda	Mubende, Small East African, Kigezi, Karamoja,	
Tanzania	East African small goat	
Kenya	Galla and East African small goat	
CAR	West african Dwarf	
Cameroon	West african Dwarf, sahelian goat, pygmy goat,	

Contd.

Country	Indigenous (local breeds)	Exotic (imported) breeds
Sudan	Nubian, sudan desert, nilotic dwarf, Tegri	
Ethiopia	Abergelle goats, Begait, Afar, Arsi-Bale, Woy to-Guji, Central Highland goats,Hararghe Highland goats,Keffa goats, Somali goats	
Congo	West african Dwarf, Sahelian goat	
Nigeria	Sahel or desert goat (West African long-legged , Red Sokoto (Maradi), West African Dwarf goat	
Chad	West african Dwarf, Sahelian goat	
Gabon	West African dwarf goat	
South Africa	Boer (Syn Afrikander: Afrikaner)	
Egypt	Zairabi	
Syria, Lebanon. Israel, Jordan, Iraq	Syrian Mountain , Damascus (Shami)	
Somalia: Ogaden: Kenya	Somali	
	Maltese	

Anatolian Black (Syn Turkish Native)

This is most common breed in Turkey, mainly bred for milk, meat and hair. It is usually found in hills and forest areas and has poor yields. The animals have long hair and the usual colour is black but also brown, grey or pied. The percentage of single born kids averages 85, twins 15 and triplets nil.

Begayit (Barka) goats

It is believed that the Begayit, also known as Barka in Eritrea, was derived from Nubian type goats. These goats are mainly found in western Tigray. Begayit goats have a predominantly Roman type facial profile. They are tall with mean height at the shoulders being 74.3 cm for adult bucks and 67.9 cm for does.

The coat color of Begayit goats is mainly white with brown patches. Their hair is particularly long around the thighs. Both sexes have horns that are straight or curved and oriented backwards. Males have beards and ruffs. Begayit goats have relatively large udders and are milked.

Boer

The breed of the Boer goat actually originated from South Africa wherein the animals are being developed to produce meat as early as the 1990s. Boer is actually a word of the Afrikaans and Dutch which means farmer. This goat breed is said to have been derived from the indigenous goats herded by Bantu tribes and Namaqua Bushmen. The successive cross breeding from the goat breeds from India and Europe was the reason why they are what they are today.This is a milk and meat breed of goat. The Boer goat is a hardy breed with great capacity for adaptation and an exceptional ability to withstand and resist diseases. The Boer goat is highly fertile, conception rate is about 90%, kidding rate about 189% and fecundity rate 210%. Colour is usually white with red head markings. The meat of boer goat is coarse grained and palatable, the flavour closely resembling that of mutton. The animals have convex noses and lop ears. Twin or triplet births are usual. These goats seemed to have resulted from crossing long legged African goat with goats of Indian origin. Perhaps the breed which has received the most development of meat production is the Boer goat of South Africa (Shelton, 1978). The animal is large weighing upto 90 kg (bucks) and 60 kg (does). Numerous countries had imported Boer goats from South Africa including USA, New Zealand, Australia, Germany, Israel, France and more recently India and China.Boer goats were imported into China in the 1998 from New Zealand and Germany (http://www.sheepandgoat.com/articles/China.htm).Boer goats were imported into the United States in 1993.

Damascus (Baladi or Shami)

Largest number of goats are found in Suhag and Minia provinces of upper Egypt while they are least numerous in the delta (lower Egypt). Such differences between lower and upper Egypt could be attributed either to scarcity of animal feeds during a great part of the year or to neglect by big landowners (Ahmed and Tantawy, 1960). The animals of this breed have evolved by a cross between the ancient Syrian and the Nubian. The colour is usually reddish brown with long straight hair smoother and shorter on neck and head. The animals have a convex profile with large and pendulous udders with unshapely teats. Average milk yield of Damascus is 450 to 500 kg. The outline of the face is straight and the head which is beardless is long and possesses two tassels. Some animals have horns which are small and curl back on the head but others are hornless. The sex ratio is 59% male and 41% female. Twinning percentage is 53 while 9% produce triplets.

Maltese

These goats are especially bred on the island of Malta in the Mediterranean Sea. The Maltese goats are usually hornless. The body is compact and legs short. The ears are carried rather horizontally and are fairly long. In colour they are usually white, with some red marking and have long hair. The udders are very large and of much capacity and come near to the ground. This is one of the best milking breeds of goats.

Red Sokoto Goat

This goat is found in Maradi in Niger and Sokoto province in northern Nigeria. It is famous for its skin, which is marketed under the name of sokoto. In fact the best goat leather in the world is obtained from Red Sokoto goat. The breed is also a good meat animal. It is about 65 cm in height and weight ranges from 20-25 kg. The usual colour is red and goats are short haired and horned in both the sexes. These goats kid three to four times in two years. Milk yield is 0.5 kg in dry season and 1.5 kg in the wet season. Lactation length is 100 days with an annual production of 150 kg. They are common village goats in the Northern part of Nigeria. Red glossy coat colour and fine bones. Skin is light , thin and supple due to very fine pattern of hair follicles. Best leather from well fed young ones of about one years of age. Kept mainly for skin.

Somali

This breed is found in East Africa especially in Somalia, Ogadon and Kenya. The colour is white and skin short haired. The animals are kept for meat and skin production. The animals are intermediate in size between the desert goats of the north and the small goats of East Africa. The males are horned while the females are either horned or polled. The Short- and Long-eared Somali goats are related. The Short-eared Somali goats are widely distributed in northern and eastern Ogaden, Dire Dawa. The Long-eared Somali goats are found in all parts of the Ogaden, lowlands of Bale and Borana zones of Oromia and in some parts of Sidama zone of the Southern Region.

The Short-eared Somali goats are smaller than the Long-eared ones. Mean height at shoulders for adult Short-eared Somali bucks and does is 64.9 cm and 61.8 cm, respectively. The corresponding figures for Long-eared Somali adult male and female goats are 75.8 cm and 69.4 cm, respectively.

Syrian Mountain (Iraqi, Mamber, Palestinian, Djelab)

This breed is common in Syria, Israel, Jordan, Iraq, Lebanon, Anatolia countries of Middle East. The colour is usually black and the animals are long haired. The breed is kept for meat, milk and fleece. Devendra and Burn (1970) have reported that female's weight anywhere from 20 to 40 kg and give milk about 1.5 kg/day with yields upto 500 kg per lactation in the best herds. Annual kidding is usual and twinnings fairly frequent in the larger types.

West African Dwarf–(syn-African Dwarf, Djallonke, Dwarf West African, Forest goat, Fouta Djallon, Grassland Dwarf, Chevre naine de Savanes, Guinean, Guinean Dwarf, Pygmy, Tibetana, Cameroon Dwarf, Chevre de Casamance, Diougry, Chevre naine de l'est, Kosi, Nigerian Dwarf).

It is about 40-50 cm in height and weighs about 18-20 kg. The horns are fairly large in the male and small in the female. They are curved and directed backwards. Ears are long and horizontal. Beard and mane are small. Common colours are brown with black extremities and dorsal strips, white with coloured markings or tricolor. It is very hardy and resistant to trypnosomiosis. The females are poor milkers. It occurs in whole area of West Africa and in the coastal area it is the only breed. Other names for this breed are miniature goat, African Pygmy and the Cameroon goat and are widely advocated as a research animal in the United States. The WAD goat is a prolific and hardy breed. The overall mean litter sizes at birth and at weaning were put at 1.82 and 1.56 respectively

West African long legged (Sahel also called Desert goat)

Occurs along the entire northern border of Nigeria, particularly Borno State. It is large leggy animal; the male is 80-85 cm tall and the female 70-75 cm. Its weight varies between 25 and 35 kg. The male has long horns directed backwards; those of the female are thinner and shorter. The ears are short and horizontal, sometimes drooping. The male is maned and beard and wattles are common. The coat is short and fine; its colour is very variable, often with two or three colours. The goat of the Sahel breed is a good milk and meat animal. Kidding interval is 11.3 months. Litter size is 1.4. Marked foraging and browsing abilities that enable them to survive and multiply when available vegetation cover would be inadequate for cattle maintenance.

Yemen Mountain

The Yemen Mountain breed is a long haired goat that is usually black found in the mountains of northern Yemen.

Zaraibi

This is a milch breed is found in Egypt. The animals are short haired and the colour is variable.

Goat production in China

China has far more goats than any country in the world: over 197 million, according to the FAO (2007). Majority of goats in China are meat goats. There is also a large population of Cashmere goats. Boer goats were imported into China in the 1998 from New Zealand and Germany (http://www.sheepandgoat.com/articles/China.htm). Meat goats are slaughtered when they are approximately 10 to 12 months of age and weigh over 35 kg. Most of the kids are born from December through March. Dairy goats are special to farmers in China because during difficult times, dairy goats provide nutritious milk to the struggling population. Millions of people starved to death during the Great Leap Forward and Cultural Revolution (http://www.sheepandgoat.com/articles/China.htm). Prices are similar for goat and cow milk. The following goat breeds are known to be found in China. The goat breeds of China have been described by Epstein (1969), (Cheng (1984) and Mason (1996).

Cashmere goats

Haimen

The Haimen breed is found in Zhejiang, China. It is a white coated meat breed known for its prolific reproduction.

Huaitoutala

The Huaitoutala is a cashmere breed found in Qinghai, China.

Huaipi

The Huaipi is a prolific meat breed found in the region of Henan in China. They are white in color and both horned and polled individuals are seen.

Ma t'ou goats

South china dwarf goat

Xinjiang

The Xinjiang is used for milk, cashmere and meat production. This breed is found in the mountains of Xinjiang in China and its coloration is white, black or brown.

Xuhai: The Xuhai is a varity of Huanghuai found in Jiangsu, China. The breed is kept primarily for meat production.

Zhiwulin Black: The Zhiwulin Black is found in northern Shaanxi region of China and is kept for cashmere and meat production.

Zhongwei: Zhongwei goats are produced only in the arid desert steppes of some counties in the Ningxia Hui Autonomous Region and Gansu Province. They live chiefly, if not solely, on salty or sandy plants or shrubs. The kids are slaughtered at 35 days of age for their pelts, which have white, lustrous staples and attractive curls.

Goat production in Europe

There are about 18 million goats in Europe which represent nearly 2.1 % of the world total. In Europe, goat breeding is strongly oriented towards milk production, with only 2.1 % of the world goat population producing about 15 % of the world's goat milk, which is mostly used for cheese production. There are three European countries in the list of top ten goat milk producers of the world, producing a considerable amount of goat milk: Spain, France and Greece. Although goat production systems in North European countries are under strong climatic influence, namely low temperature and high precipitation, there is considerable variation.Housing and indoor feeding is required throughout the winter in all Nordic and Alpine regions due to snow and frost, for several months of the year in most cases. Such systems depend largely on upland and mountain grazing in summer under marginal conditions while the lowland systems are more intensive and in many cases they share land resources with other agricultural enterprises. Goat production in Europe is characterized by milk as the main product while meat is secondary in most cases followed by skins and hair. In Greenland and on the Faroe Islands of northern Europe there are no goats at all. In some of the countries there is a strong tradition of goat keeping, mainly for milk production, for example, in Norway, Switzerland and Austria. The main reason why there are so many goats in Greece is because there is a strong tradition of cheese consumption in the Greek gastronomy. For the Greeks, cheese is not a food supplement, it is food.The major milking breeds of goats originated primarily in the Europe. These breeds include Saanen, Toggenburg, Anglo-Nubian and Alpine. The use of goat milk to produce cheese is an important industry in France, Spain and other European Countries.In Croatia, goats are primarily bred for meat production.

The size of UK goat population has been variously estimated at about 75,000 -100,000 with most of the dairy animals being in small herds averaging less than ten.Goats in the UK are mainly of the Saanen, Anglo-Nubian, Toggenburg and Alpine breeds, kept for milk production.

Major goat Breeds of Europe

U.K.

Anglo Nubian (Great Britain), British Alpine: British Saanen.: British Toggenburg:

France

French Alpine (France), French Toggenburg, French Saanen, Poitou

Netherland

Dutch Toggenburg (Netherland): Dutch White (Netherland)

Germany

Greman Improved Fawn(Germany): German Improved White

Switzerland

Appenzell (Switzerland):Chamois Colored (Switzerland):Grissons Stripped (Switzerland):Saanen (Switzerland Toggenburg (Switzerland). Valais Black Neck (Switzerland): Verzasca (Switzerland).

Italy

Agrigento (Sicily: Italy): Syn Girgenti :Apulian (Apulia: Italy) :

Spain

Granada (Spain).: Malaga (Spain): Murcian (Spain: Poitou (France) - Verata

Norway

Dole (Norway):Telemark (Norway)

Belgium

Belgian Fawn: Campine (North Belgium):

Portugal

Alen- Tejo (Portugal):

Yugoslavia

Red Bosnia (Yugoslavia),

1. **Agrigento (Syn. Girgenti, Girgentana):** This breed is found in the purest form in north and east of Agrigento province (Sicily). Average adult weight for male is 64 kg and 45 kg for female. Adult heightis about 72 cm at withers. The head is short and tapering-19 cm long and 12 cm broad at the orbits. The horns are almost vertical and spirally twisted. Mean length is 45 cm in female and 55 cm in male. Ears are dark brown, rather small and always erect. Tassels are normally present in both the sexes. The normal colour is white with irregular brown patches or roan spots on the head. The male carries a beard. Adult animals give 95% twins, 5% triplets. The daily milk yield is 2.14 kg. Fat per cent ranges from 3.20 to 4.65. The breed is used for both meat and milk.

2. **Anglo Nubian:** Anglo Nubian has its origin in late nineteenth century in Great Britain when domestic stock and goats of Swiss origin were mated to bucks imported from Africa and India. The distinctive features owe to many breeds including Jamunapari, Chitral, Zaraibi, Toggenburg and old English type goats. It is one of the most important milk breeds of western hemisphere. The average mature doe weighs 64 kg or more and usually tends to be meatier than the Swiss breeds. Anglo Nubian may be of any colour varying from roan to white and include a uniquely spotted type - similar to the appaloosa horse. The Nubian looks different from all breeds, having short sleek hair, long drooping ears and a roman nose. The legs are long, thus giving the udder a better ground clearance. The facial line is convex and the animals are generally polled. Nublan generally does not give as much milk as the Swiss breeds; however, it is of the highest butterfat content. They are constant milkers with 5% fat and 10-11% SNF and are usually called 'Jersey' of the goat world. On an average they yield one kg milk per day. Anglo Nubian goats are present in Australia, Malaysia, America, India, Trinidad and Mauritius. Nubians in America today all trace to English imports. According to the British Goat Society Yearbook (1940) the two Jamunapari bucks viz., 'Sedgemere Chancellor' and 'Brachest cross' (the first imported in 1896 and the second in 1904) used for breeding have greatly influenced the building up of the Anglo-Nubian breed.

3. **Appenzell:** Appenzell is a breed found in the Toggenburg valley of Switzerland. The colour is usually white, though some are dark or spotted.

The animals of this breed weigh about 70-75 kg and are good milker next only to Saanen and Toggenburg breed of goats.

4. **Apulian:** This goat is found in Apulia (Italy). The usual colour is pied and animals are short haired and kept for milk. It has two varieties-Murge, which is usually pied, horned and polled, short haired, and Gargane, which is brown with V shaped screw horns (Cagnanese) or short backward curving horns (Conoechiola).

5. **Belgium Fawn:** These goats are found in Belgium. The colour is fawn and the animals are short haired and kept for milk. The breed is polled.

6. **Alpine:** A breed of goat native to Swiss Alps mountains. Animals of this breed are known for their milking ability. Alpine goats include French, Italian, Spanish and Swiss Alpines. These were originally found throughout the Alps. It is large breed multicoloured that may or may not bear horns. The goats of Alpine type that were brought to the United States from France where they had been selected for much greater uniformity, size, and production than was true of the goats that were taken from Switzerland to France.The British Alpine colour is usually black with light points and face strips. The average doe should weigh a minimum of 55 kg. The eye is alert and ears are erect and the nose is usually straight.This breed was imported in India and bred with Beetal to produce Alpine x Beetal crossbred at National Dairy Research Institute, Karnal. The another name for an alpine or mountain goat is IBEX.

French Alpine

The colour is usually white. The males weigh from 80 to 100 kg and the females about 55 to 80 kg. The height at withers is 90 to 100 cm in males and 70-80 cm in females. The length is about 110-130 cm in males and 80-100 cm in females. The udders are large and well developed.

7. **Campine (Syn. Belgian White):** This breed is found in Belgium and is white coloured. The animals are short haired and usually kept for milk. The animals are polled. This breed originates from Saanen x Local (H.B. 1931).

8. **Chamois Coloured :** This breed is found in Austrian alps (Switzerland). It is a strongly built animal with males weighing 70 to 100 kg and females 40-60 kg. The chamois coloured goat excels in hardiness, thriftiness and fertility. Twinning is usual. Goats are kept for both milk and meat. Lactation period is 6 months. Milk production is 350-450 kg and 3.5 to 4% butterfat. The colour is usually brown with black face, str.ips, back stripes, on belly and legs.

9. **Dole:** Dole is one of the principal goat breeds of Norway. The usual colour is blue pied or brown. The milk yield is 375 kg with a fat percent of 3.9. This is a polled breed.

10. **Dutch White:** This breed is found in Netherland. The animals are white coloured, short haired and kept for milk. The breed originated from Saanen x Local.

12. **German Improved Fawn:** It is fawn or reddish brown in colour with either black limbs and belly and a black dorsal stripe or pale coloured belly. This comprises 22.73% of total goats in Germany. The animals of this breed are short haired and are kept for milk. This breed originated from Chamois coloured x native.

13. **German Improved White:** It constitute's about 63.76% of the total number of goats in Germany. The colour is white and hairs are short. The animals are generally kept for milk. The animals originated from Saanen X native.

14. **Granada:** The granada breed originates from the Spanish province of that name, but is now found throughout the Andulasia. Two varieties can be distinguished; the low-land and the mountain. Height at withers is 81 & 68 cm in male and female respectively. Live weight is 68 and 45 kg in lowland variety and 73 and 55.5 kg respectively in the mountain varieties. The coat which is rougher in the mountain variety is usually black but may be spotted with white. The dressing percentage is 42.5 to 45. Age at first breeding is 1 to 2 years in males and 1 to 1.5 years in females although estrus commences at 5 to 7 months of age.

15. **Crissons Striped:** This goat is found in Switzerland. The colour is black with pale face stripes. The animals are short haired and kept for milk and meat.

16. **Maloga:** The breed is found in Spain. The colour is red and the animals are long haired. The breed is a milch one.

17. **Murcian:** The murcian goat which regularly produces twins and triplets, and often 4 or 5 kids at a time is found in the Mediterranean region of Spain, mainly near the Segura River, but also in the coastal districts of Alicante. Barcelona is the trading centre for this breed. Both the varieties, domestic and mountain, are small, well proportioned with well strong ribs. The head is biggish and ears are straight and outspread. Only the mountain variety has horns. The coat is fine, silky and glossy and while the mountain goats are of mahogany red, black is the commonest colour among the domestic variety. The males have capacious, well attached udders although those of the mountain does are smaller and show less tendency to be pendulous. The mountain goats are used for their meat and the skins for wine bottles. The domestic goats are primarily a dairy animal. The weightof castrated male and female average 70 and 60 kg, respectively.

18. **Saanen:** Saanen from the Saanen valley in Switzerland is one of the larger

breeds and a good milk producer. It is white or cream coloured and horned or hornless, both sexes may have beards. The Saanen has declined in popularity and now ranks third in number of registrations in the United States. The yield is about 2180 litres in a lactation with 4.3% fat and 8.5% SNF. In 1890 several thousand herds were taken out of Assnen valley and spread throughout Europe. Adult does weigh 64 kg or more and stand from 75 cm av. at withers. Bucks are much heavier and at least 90 cm at the withers. The ears are erect and alert, the nose is straight or dished slightly. Both bucks and doe may have beards, but the bucks have a fuller one.

19. **Toggenburg:** Toggenburg from the Toggenburg valley in Switzerland is one of the smaller of the European breeds. It is light fawn to dark brown in colour and has characteristic white markings on each side of face, on the edge of the ears, on each side of the tail and below the knee and hock joints. Horns may or may not occur, though it is registered as a breed. The ears are of moderate size and are usually carried somewhat erect. The males have a coarse beard and are rather freer of offensive odour than male animals of other breeds. The milk production average is 1450 litres per lactation. This is the oldest officially recognised breed of dairy goats. Many of the Toggenburg does can milk for two years without being bred. Adult does weigh 56 to 90 kg.

20. **Poitou:** This breed is found in France. The male animals weigh about 60 to 80 kg. The height at withers is 75 to 90 cms in male 70 to 80 cms in females. The length is 80 to 110 cm in males and 75 to 95 cm in females. The colour is black to brown. The males have a beard.

21. **Red Bosnian:** The breed is found in Yugoslavia. The colour is red, grey, black, brown or pied. The animals are good milkers.

22. **Telemark:** This goat is found in Norway. The usual colour is white. The hairs are long. The milk yield is 439 kg with a fat percentages of 3.30.

23. **Valais Blackneck:** Valais Blackneck is especially found is the Canton Valais, Switzerland and in the Rhone valley. It is also known as, Glaxier goat. This is a rather large breed of striking appearance with horns and tufts of long hair on the forehead and slender legs; the front part of the body to back of the shoulders is black while the rest of the body is white. The front hoofs are black and hind ones are yellow. This is an extremely hardy breed.

24. **Verata:** A meat and dairy breed found in Vera, Caceres, Spain. Chestnut, black or grey in coloration and the Verata has twisted horns.

25. **Verzasea:** These goats are found in Ticine (Switzerland) and are used for dairy and meat. The colour is black. This is Swiss mountain type.

26. **Skopelos:** These goats are found in Skopelos,Alonissos,Skiathos, North

Sporades province of Greece. Breed is characterized by smooth glossy hair coat. Main use: (1) milk, (2) meat, (3) hair production.

27. **Vlahiki, Eghoria, Paggaio:** (greek): This is a Indigenous breed of goat in Greece with Capra Prisca origin. Milk is useful for preparation of various types of cheece.

Goat production in Former USSR

Goats are raised in practically all climatic zones of the former USSR. Due to their unique biological features, goats can be successfully raised in zones with poor grass vegetation such as highlands, mountains, deserts, semi-deserts and steppes. The most famous product of goat husbandry is cashmere, whose lightness, softness, relative strength, low heat conductivity and uniformity make it one of the most valuable wool fibres. The cashmere, either pure or mixed with Merino wool, is used for production of high-quality light shawls, fine knitted goods and the best kinds of felt. Orenburg cashmere shawls, which together with Palekh boxes and Vologda lace are masterpieces of folk art, are well known far outside Russia. "Gossamer" cashmere shawls were shown, as unique works of art in International Exhibitions, and awarded top prizes (Orekhovhttp://www.fao.org/docrep/009/ah759e/AH759E14.htm). In Central Asian countries such as Kyrgyzstan and Tajikistan, centralized, state-run breeding programs that supported sheep and goat production collapsed after the breakdown of the Soviet Union and were never replaced by breeding programs for small, private producers. Recognised as one of the centres of goat domestication in Central Asia, Kyrgyzstan is a major genetic resource of cashmere goats. The indigenous goats, known locally as Jaidari, produce a fine warm undercoat in various colours, including black, white, and red, with the finest white fibre fetching the highest prices on international markets.Goat breeds of former USSR has been described by Dmitriez and Ernst (1989)

Altai Mountain

This breed originated from Don and Local goats. Body weight is 65-70 kg in males and 41-44 kg in the females. Under coat yield is 0.60-0.90 kg in females. Fibre length is 8-9 cm in both males and females. The usual tolour is black with grey undercoat. This breed was recognised in 1968.

Azerbaijan (Syn South Caucasian)

These goats are found in Armenia and Azerbaijan provinces. This is a meat as well as dairy breed. The colour is usually black dappled with red, also black, red, pied or grey.

Don

These breed animals are concentrated along the shores of river Don. Don goats are bred in the Stalingrad Voronezh provinces and have been introduced into the Kirghiz, Kazakh and Bashkir republics, where they acclimatized well and are used for improving indigenous goats. This breed of animals have black, pied, white or grey coat colour. The average weight of the female is 32 to 40 kg and of male 43 to 52 kg. The body length is 64.8 cm. This breed yields 400 to 600 gm of down. The fibre length is 9.6 cm, dog hair 5.74 cm and fibre fineness 18.96μ. The average milk yield is 170 litres with 4.3% fat. The breed is very fertile with 50% twins and 3-6% triplets.

Improved North Russian

The colour is white and the animals are short haired. This is a milch breed. This breed originated from Saanen X North Russian (origin 1905 onwards). The animals are distributed in the North West and European USSR.

Kirghiz (Jaidari)

These goats are found in Kirgyhzstan (USSR). Kyrgyzstan is home to the jaidari goat, which produces ultra-fine cashmere.The colour of the coat is variable, dark colours being predominant. The goats are kept for milk, wool and meat. As spring blossoms across the temperate region in the northern hemisphere, high up in the remote Pamir Mountains of Central Asia, Kyrgyz women comb their indigenous goats to harvest the soft downy undercoat, known as cashmere. The mean fleece weight of adult female was found to be 0.47 kg. The relative proportion of down: dog hair was 19.7% Vs. 80.22%. The lactation period is 8 months. Annual milk yields are 79.26 litres. Dressing out percentage is 42.5. The varieties include Kazakh, Orenburg and Uzbak. There is substantial scope to increase the production and commercial value of cashmere produced by Kyrgyz goats.

Mingrelian

Mingrelian goat is a local breed of Western Georgia (USSR). It is about 65cm high at withers and weighs 37 to 48 kg. It is usually light coloured (white, roan or grey) and horned. Milk production is good, the average yield varying from 200 to 300 kg. There is considerable individual variation, some animals giving upto 600 kg. in one lactation. The animals are kept on pastures all year round.

North Russian

This is also a short haired white breed kept for milk.

Soviet Mohair Syn Askanian Mohair

This breed is found in Uzbek, Tadzbik, Turkmen and Dazukh republics and have been developed by crossing Angora males with local coarse haired goats. These goats have a strong constitution and are well developed. They have a long white lustrous coat. The body weight of bucks is 55-60 kg and of 3-5 year females 36-42 kg. The other production figures are : Birth weight 2.6 kg, body weight of yearling 15.4 kg and at 1.5 year of age 25.1 kg. Mohair yield as about 1.01 kg and staple length 17,7 cm. Kemp percentage in fleece 7.1 0% . The carcass yield is 17.0-20.0 kg and the dressing percentage is 42-50%.

Goat production in North America

Goats were among the first arrivals with the early European settlers to the United States. The total number of goats in North America was 3099350 head in 2009 (FAOSTAT). For the three major goat-producing states (Arizona, New Mexico, and Texas) there were 1,200,000 goats at the end of 2002.The most common breeds of goats in United States include Saanen, Alpine, Toggenburg, Nubian and Pygmy. ADGA currently has herd books for the following breeds of dairy goats: Alpine, LaMancha, Nigerian Dwarf, Nubian, Oberhasli, Saanen, Sable and Toggenburg. Toggenburg goats which originated in Switzerland are by far the most common goat breed in USA. Toggenburg goats resemble a deer in its alert expression and active temperament. Top meat goat producing states in the USA include Texas, Tennessee, Oklahoma, and California in that order.When Coronado, DeSoto and other Spanish explorers came to America they brought goats as a meat source. Some of these goats either escaped or were released when alternate meat sources were discovered.That would have placed the first goats in Oklahoma and Texas in the early 1540s. Pockets of wild goats, decended from these animals, developed for over 400 years before developing this livestock became profitable. These feral goats became known as "Spanish" or "brush goat".Recently,new and larger breeding animals, such as the Boer goat, have been imported in the United States.

LaMancha

American Lamancha, or more commonly, simply Lamancha or LaMancha, is a formally recognized breed of dairy goat, first bred in Oregon by Mrs. Eula Fay Frey. Lamancha goats are perhaps the most distinctive goat breed; easily recognizable by their very short ear pinnae.La Mancha breed registry started in 1952. They are also known for their high milk production, and the comparatively high butterfat content in their milk.

Goat production in South America

Goat production in México since the beginning has been associated with poverty because only low income families who live in rural areas were the only ones that raise goats with the purpose to make a profit or to obtain food from them (meat, milk, skins, etc.(Tovar-Luna, 2009).Goat population in México was integrated for centuries by the offspring of those animals brought by Spaniards 500 years ago without introducing new blood, which became the native or "Criollo" goat, although very few and isolated importations were made by particular producers with no significant effect on changing the genetics of Mexican goat population.Although goat production contributed with only 1.25% of the total value of animal production in México in 2007 (SGARPA,, 2008), it is estimated that around 400 thousand families (one million and a half people) depend from goats, whose primary or complementary activityis raising goats (SGARPA,, 2008).Argentina has about four million goats, mostly in amorphous herds.The goat population of Argentina is mostly located in smallholder farming areas, and their function is the production of meat. The traditional production system is extensive, with grazing on natural grassland with shrubs and forest and with little or no feed supplementation.The Creole Argentine goat is a descendant of the Iberian introduced in Argentina from Peru by the Spanish conquerors in the sixteenth century.

Goat Breeds of South America

Moxoto and Marota

The most traditional Brazilian naturalized standard goat breed is the Moxotó breed, originally developed in the Brazilian state of Pernambuco (Machado, 2000) and characterized by desirable traits such as disease resistance, fecundity and the ability to produce high quality leather, although this breed produces only small amounts of milk and meat. Most animals are small and compact with erect or hori- zontal ears, short, curved horns in the male and short sleek coats (Mason, 1988). The age at puberty in this breed is 12.4 months, and average litter sizeis 1.4.

Goat production in Australia

The lowest number of goats is found in Oceania, accounting for 0.1% out of the world total number. Goats arrived in Australia with the First Fleet in 1788 and spread with settlers throughout the country. The original goats were a varied and hardy herd capable of utilising harsh Australian pastures to produce milk and meat.

Some of the first herd escaped into the wild and have evolved into the unique Australian rangeland goat. These goats have since contributed to the development of the modern Australian Cashmere and Angora breeds which have been invaluable to many farmers as they diversify their income. More recently these rangeland goats have become the mainstay of a growing goat meat industry.

Goats in Australia include dairy, feral and rangeland and meat breeds. The common dairy goat breeds in Australia are Saanen, Toggenberg, British Alpine and Anglo-Nubian (http://www.aphca.org/index.php).Meat is produced from three production systems based on feral goats (domestic breeds that have escaped and thrive in the wild), rangeland goats that graze extensively, and specialist meat breeds (including Boer, other meat breeds and their crossbreds) that are managed more intensively.The Boer goat descends from the nomadic goats of South Africa and was introduced to Australia in the late 1980s, but not released from quarantine until 1993.

Feral Goats of Australia

These are wild goats of Australia. The meat of feral goats is exported to US and Middle-east countries. These goats vary considerably in appearance, with a wide range of colours and coat lengths; they are a mixture of many breeds. The body weight at 5 months is 27 and 22 kg in male and females respectively.

References

Acharya, R.M. (1982). Sheep and goat breeds of India. FAO Production and Health paper no. 30. FAO of the United Nations, Rome, Italy.

Acharya, R.M., Bhat, P.N. (1984). Livestock and poultry genetic resources in India. Indian Veterinary Research Institute, Izatnagar, India. 76 pp.

Ahlawat, S.P.S., Gupta, S.C. and Dinesh Kumar (2009) Atlas Animal Genetic Resources of India, Today and Tomorrow's Printers and Publishers, New Delhi

Ahmed, F.A. and Tantawy, A.O. (1960) Studies on Egyptian Baladi goats ll Some factors affecting mortality rate. Emp. J. Exp. Agric. 28: 104-108.

Cheng. P. (1984) Livestock breeds of China. Animal Production and Health Paper 46 (E, F, S). Publ. by FAO, Rome, 217 pp.

Deokar, D.K.,V.S., Lawar, B.K. Pawar, and R.R. Andhale (2007).Breed characterization of Sangamneri goat. . Indian Journal of Small Ruminants.13 (2): 213-215.

Devendra, C. and Burns, M. (1970). Goat production in the tropics C.A.B. , U.K.

Devendra, C.(1966) Goat breeding in Malaysia. Malay. Agric. J. 45:268-274.

Dey A, Barari S K and Yadav B P S (2007): Goat production scenario in Bihar, India. Livestock Research for Rural Development. Volume 19, Article #123. Retrieved February 17, 2012, from http://www.lrrd.org/lrrd19/9/dey19123.htm

Diez-Tascón C, Littlejohn RP, Almeida PAR and Crawford AM (2000) - Genetic variation within the Merino sheep breed: Analysis of closely related populations using microsatellites. Anim Genet 31:243-251.

Dmitriez, N.G and Ernst, L.K. (1989) Animal Genetic Resources of the USSR. Animal Production and Health Paper Publ. by FAO, Rome, 517 pp.

Epstein, H. (1969) Domestic animals of China. CAB 166 pp. Scotland.

FAOSTAT (2007,2008)faostat.fao.org/

Gall, C. (1996): Goat breeds around the world. CTA, Margraf/FAO. Weikersheim, Germany, 186 pp.

Iniguez, L. (2005a). Characterization of small ruminant breeds in West Asia and North Africa.Vol.1. North Africa. International Center for Agricultural Research in the Dry Areas(ICARDA), Aleppo, Syria, 462 pp. ISBN:92-9127-164-9

Iniguez, L. (2005b). Characterization of small ruminant breeds in West Asia and North Africa.Vol.2. North Africa. International Center for Agricultural Research in the Dry Areas(ICARDA), Aleppo, Syria, pp.196

Kaura, R.L. (1952). Indian breeds of livestock. Prem Publ., Lucknow

Khan, B.U. and Bhat, P.N. (1981) -, Animal genetic resources in India, NDRI.

Khan, B.U. and Rai, B. (2000) Goat Breeds of India. Central Sheep and Wool Research Institute,

Avikangar

Lall, H.K. (1947) Some common breeds of goats in India. 111. Indian Fmg 8:322-327 .

Machado, T.M.M., (2000). The native populations of Brazil: identification, standardization and preservation.. In: Proceedings of the 7th InternationalConference on Goats, vol. 1, Institut de l'élevage et INRA,Ivry-sur-Seine, pp. 941–943.

Mason IL (1988)A world dictionary of livestock breeds, types and varieties: CAB International, Wallingford, Oxon. OX10 8DE, UK, , 348 pp

Mason, I. L., and V. Porter. (2002). Mason's World Dictionary of Livestock Breeds, Types, and Varieties. 5th ed. CAB Int., Wallingford, U.K.

Mason, I.L. (1951) -. The classification of West African Livestock, C.A.B., U.K.

Mason, I.L. & Maule, J.P. (1960)-. The indigenous livestock of Eastern & Western Africa, C.A.B.

Mason, I.L. (1996). A World Dictionary of Livestock Breeds, Types and Varieties. Fourth Edition. C.A.B International. 273 pp.

Moioli B, Georgoudis A, Napolitano F, Catillo G, Giubilei E, Ligda CH and Hassanane M (2001) - Genetic diversity between Italian, Greek and Egyptian buffalo populations. Livest Product Sci 70:203-211.

NBAGR (2012) Breed descriptor of goats. Indian Journal of Animal Sciences 82(2) 223-230

Neopane, S.P. (1997)The Genetics of Productivity Traits in a Nepalese Hill Goat Herd, Thesis, London University, U.K.

Oli, K.P. (1987)Goat breed comparison study in Hattikharka Panchayat [hill areas, Nepal,agris.fao.org

Peacock, C.P. (1996): Improving Goat Production in the Tropics. A manual for development workers. FARM-Africa/Oxfam,Oxford.

Porter, Valerie (2002) Mason's world dictionary of livestock breeds, types and varieties/, 5th Ed, CABI

Radfar, M. H.; Sakhaee, E.; Shamsaddini Bafti, M. and Haj Mohammadi, H. (2011) Study on gastrointestinal parasitic infections of Raeini goats Iranian Journal of Veterinary Research, Shiraz University, Vol. 12, No. 1, 76-81.

Rai, B., Tiwari, S. and Khan, B.U. (2001) The Jakhrana goat in India. Animal Genetic Resource Information, FAO, Rome 29:41-48

Rubino, R. (1993) Goat breeds of Italy Animal Genetic Resources Information 11:47-62.

Sahare, M.G,A.D.Sawaimul, A.D. , Aliz, S.Z. and KolteAli,B.R.Kolte (2009)Kidding Percentage and Twinning Ability inOsmanabadi goat in Vidarbha Climatic Condition,Veterinary World, Vol.2(2): 60-61

Sahoo, A.K., Pan, S., Tantia, M.S. and Ahlawat, S.P.S.(2004) Bengal goat. WBUA&FS, West Bengal

Scherf, B.D. (ed.)(2000) World watch list for domestic animal diversity, 3rd edn, FAO, Rome 726 pp

SGARPA, (2008). Secretaría de Agricultura, Ganadería, Desarrollo Rural, Pesca y Alimentación. Ganadería http://www.sagarpa.gob.mx/ganaderia/estadisticas.

Shelton, M.(1978) Reproduction and breeding of goats. J. Dairy Sci. 61:994-1010.

Singh, M.K., Ashok Kumar, M.C.Sharma, S.K.Jindal and B.Rai (2009) Goat production status in different agro-climatic regions of India. Central Institute for Research on Gaots, Makhdoom, Farah, Mathura

Singh, M.K., Ashok Kumar, M.C.Sharma, S.K.Jindal, A.K.Goel and B.Rai (2009) Queen of goat : Jamunapari, Central Institute for Research on Gaots, Makhdoom, Farah, Mathura

Singh, M.K., B.Rai, Ashok Kuamr, H.S.Sisodiya, M.B.Simaria and N.P.Singh (2008) A Pride of Saurashtra : Zalawadi goat.Central Institute for Research on Gaots, Makhdoom, Farah, Mathura

Takezaki N and Nei M (1996) Genetic distances and reconstruction of phylogenetic trees from microsatellite DNA. Genetics 144:389-399.

Tantia, M.S. and P.K.Vijh (2000)population estimates of sheep and goat breeds of indiaIndian J. Anim. Res., 34(1): 60·63,

Tovar-Luna,Ignacio (2009)Dairy Goat Production in Mexico, Proc. 24th Annual Goat Field Day of the E (Kika) de la Garza American Institute for Goat Research of Langston University.

Villar (2006) Goats - Undervalued assets in asiaProceedings of the aphca-ilri regional workshop on goat production systems and markets,Luang Prabang, Lao PDR, 24 – 25 October 2006,International Livestock Research Institute, Kenya

Wurzinger, M., L. Iniguez, M. Zaklouta, M. Hilaliand J. Sölkner, (2008). The Syrian Jabali goat andits production system. Journal of Arid Environments,72: 384-391.

Zeuner, F.E.(1963) A history of domesticated animals. Hutchinson, London. 560pp

3

Improvement Through Breeding and Genetics

Mostly goats are reared in extensive small holder systems in developing countries. Goat breeding programmes in these environments have been limited, amongst other factors, by the non availability of pedigree and performance records for traits of economic importance. Cross-breeding and selection play an important role in increasing production in the goats.The development of breeding strategy for the improvement of goats should be based on genetic parameter estimates of economically important traits. Biological, cultural, statistical, socio-economical and management aspects should also be an important component of the selection process.

Goats were domesticated for the triple purpose of milk, meat and hair. Although the development of milk and hair producing animals did not go together, the development of meat and hair together worked very well and there are several breeds like Angora which in addition to providing fiber, are excellent meat animals too. The development of meat breeds was favored by natural selection. The characters which aided to this aspect were high fertility rates and the relatively more active life which goats were forced to lead in order to get enough of nutrition in poor agricultural lands, deserts etc. where these animals were domesticated. These animals were exposed to the vagaries of the environment resulting in decline in production traits such as milk, meat etc. But meat production was not. Most of the breeds of Asia and Africa are thus predominant meat breeds which have been improved little by conscious effort of breeders. Some of them still have slow growth rate and feed conversion efficiency. The preference for goat meat had eroded the dairy potential of Indian goats, as the fastest growing males are slaughtered for meat purposes and only poor animals are retained for breeding purposes. Careful selection and utilisation of breeding males can alleviate this problem to a large measure and animals for both milk and meat production can be developed.There are several goat breeds that have good potential for meat production. Generally, there have been limited planned selection and breeding programs carried out by animal scientists to improve rate of growth and carcass composition of goats. As a result, many goat breeds deposit less intramuscular and subcutaneous fat. In the past, domesticated meat animals were selected for heavier mature weight and greater rate of gain. Selection for such parameters usually resulted in undesirable characteristics because some of the animals had not only gained weight faster and were heavier at maturity, but also had more subcutaneous and intramascular fat. Since consumers currently prefer leaner red meat, the livestock industry is making significant changes to satisfy these demands. Goat meat has unique attributes which will be beneficial to the present day consumer. Goat meat has 10% more lean carcass than cattle. At the same time the fat content is lower by 47% than beef. These qualities of the goat meat need to be emphasized so that the general public can become aware of this useful product.

Inbreeding in goats though present in some of the small flocks where bucks from external sources are not available or used. Inbreeding leads to low productivity of inbred animals, higher kid mortality, slow growth rate and low fertility. Birth defects are also more in inbred population. This reduction in productivity and viability is called inbreeding depression.Careful planning of a breeding programme can help achieve substantial genetic progress while maintaining inbreeding at acceptable levels.

Breeds of goat for meat production

Genetic parameter estimates for reproduction and growth assembled from numerous studies offer theoretical promise in direct selection for improvement of the efficiency of meat goat production (Shrestha and Fahmy, 2007). A production programme for goat meat would begin with the choice of breed that could be adapted to the climatic and topographic environment, or that is suitable for a particular production system. The breed must have the characteristics of a meat-producing animal. Important meat producing breeds exist in the tropical Asia and Far East as well as in Africa. Black Bengal, Kanai adu and Assam Hill are reported as good meat breeds in India whereas several other breeds are good as both meat and milk breeds. Most other breeds which are used for milk, fibre etc is also equally good as meat breeds. Jamunapari, Barbari, Beetal, Malabari, Jakhrana, Sirohi, Kutchi, Gaddi and Osmanabadi are examples of dual purpose goat breeds. In India, Barbari and Jamunapari have been rated as the improved breeds of goats for meat production. Boer from South Africa appears to hold a great potential as improver breed for meat production in the tropics. Barbari, Jamunapari, Ma Tou, Kambling Katzang,Sudan desert goats and Fijian are some of the improver breeds of goats for meat production in the tropics. Boer goat, which is excellent meat breed developed in Southern Africa, has been used for upgrading the indigenous stock in several countries in Asia and Africa, to improve the meat production capabilities of these goats. Characters associated with carcass yield, which are not so closely linked with survival, tend to have high heritability in comparison with those associated with reproductive fitness (i.e. mothering ability and prolificacy). There is thus considerable scope for use of breeds such as Boer and Jamunapari, which appear to be genetically superior with regard to carcass characteristics. Other goat breeds, suitable for meat production include, Angora, Black Bengal, Barbari, Malawi (West African Dwarf) etc.

The strategies to manipulate reproduction for increased meat production, includes induction of puberty, out-of-season breeding, hormonal manipulation of oestrus cycle, improvement of litter size, assisted reproductive technologies (artificial insemination, embryo transfer), and genetic improvement of reproductive traits.

There are few scientific studies to determine growth and fattening propensities under different condition of management and feeding ranging from poor pasturage to intensive system utilizingfodder and concentrates, in spite of the empirical evidence that goats can maintain good condition even when only coarse fodder is available. Few data are available on the daily weight gain, feed conversion efficiency and carcass yield of various breeds of goats. Efficiency of meat production is influenced by many factors which include relative fertility, liveweight and conformation of types and breeds, birth weight and growth rate etc. Live weight and growth rate of definite breeds are most important indicators of meat production potential. The variations in size and weight of types, breeds and individuals indicate the possibilities of selection of breeding stock for meat production.Better feeding and management can go a long way in improving the growth rate and meat production potential of existing stock. The introduction and extension of simple management techniques, such as castration could improve this already valuable animal as meat producer.

Animal growth is the consequence of complex interactions between the genetic potential of the animal and several hormones, the nutrient supply and the environment. This complexity is beneficial in terms of manipulating growth and development because it provides the possibility for many different ways of manipulating growth. The most significant means of manipulating growth and development in goats include genetic selection, castration and intensive fattening. Selection pressure on different production characteristics has resulted in the development of different types of goat for different purposes.

External linear measurements of live meat producing animal have attracted attention as possible predictors of parameters such as live weights, carcass weights and dressing percentage. Such measurements can also provide information on the physical characters of the animal body and on its growth pattern. Best predictor of live weight and carcass weight is chest circumference or the girth to be the best predictor of live weight.Live weight is a useful measurement for assessing growth; however, it does not accurately predict the amount of meat on the carcass.Dressing percentage, although considered to be more reliable, is also influenced by variables such as age, sex, diet, stress, amount of noncarcass parts and method of dissection.

Breeds of goat for milk production

Primarily breeds have been developed to provide increased production of meat, milk and/or wool, pashmina within a certain environmental area. In the west, where goat meat is not much preferred as compared to beef, mutton or pork, goats have been developed solely as a dairy animal; as a result most of the high yielding dairy breeds of goats have been developed there. Saanen, Toggenburg, Alpine, Anglo-Nubian and La Mancha are all superb dairy breeds with milk production of 600 to 1200 kg per lactation. Out of approximately 300 breed in the world, the majority is found in the tropics and these are mainly meat breeds. Only a few dairy breeds are identifiable in the tropics, consistent with limited progress in breeding and selection for high milk production. Among the African breeds, only Damascus and the Nubians are rated as dairy breeds although they are also important as a meat producer. The Jamunapari, Jakhrana and Barbari of India also compare with the Damascus and the Nubians in being both dairy and meat breeds. However, the milk yield of local goats is dismally poor.

Animals of many a breed are not milked at all and the milk produced is just enough to raise the kids which are allowed to suckle as long as they wish. The Black Bengal breed is a good example of such type of breed.

Several factors such as nutrition, management, and environment are known to affect milk production.

Breeding practices in goats

Selection

Animals vary between breeds and within breeds in their capacity to provide food, fibre and work. Selection consists in choosing the parents of next generation so that they excel the parent generation in the average production characteristics. While selecting animals for breeding, the aim is to select the ones which will pass on good genes to their offspring. Selection in goats can be directed towards increased milk production, meat production or fiber production. Since these traits are controlledby so many factors, compilation of uniform data for efficient selection is important.

Variations are the basis of selection. Ronningen (1967) analyzed the relative importance of age and weight sources of variation of milk yield and found that age had a predominant effect. The common influence of weight and age on milk and fat production were 5.7%, 27.9%, 5% and 23.4%, respectively. Gall (1969) showed about 60% of the variation in milk yield was attributable to body weight, rumen volume, skeletal size, muscle volume and body fat. Milk yield in goat increases linearly with age until about the third to fifth lactation when it tends to decrease.

Selection is based on the phenotypes of the breeding animals and sometimes on those of their relatives. Therefore, the accuracy of the phenotype as an indication of genotype deserves careful attention. The relative agreement between phenotype and genotype is measured by heritability. The heritability of a trait is the ratio of its genetic variance and total variance. Heritability in the broad sense estimates the proportion of phenotypic variation caused by differences in the whole genotype. Estimates of heritability are thus of great importance in predicting whether or not selection will be effective. A high level of heritability means selection can be based on the measurement of individual animals without the need for repeated measurements on the animal, or for measurement of relatives. That means progeny tests are not desired when selection is practiced for characters having high heritabilities like birth weight etc. However, a medium level of heritability may mean that additional observation needs to be taken either on the same animal or on relatives, before predicting whether or not the selection will be effective. A low level of heritability will mean that selection will not be effective. The heritability estimates are normally, effective only for that particular group of animals in the same environmental and other conditions. Heritabilities have been reported for most traits for goats. These data suggest that desirable traits for goats are at least moderately high in heritability and closely approach that expected from work with other species. These data show heritability of dairy traits to be of the order of 0.3. The heritability of milk yield in goats is much higher than the average reported for cattle (around 0.25). Thus selection of goats with high milk producing ability should be expected to increase the herd average more quickly.

The term repeatability signifies correlation among repeated expressions of a given trait for the same individual. Repeatability is the superiority or inferiority of a given record on an individual, as compared with the herd average, which may be expected in future performance of that individual. Repeatability estimates are useful in selection and future planning of improvement of goat breeds.The ability of an individual to repeat any trait is sum of genetic and environmental factors. The low estimate indicates that temporary environmental conditions have a marked influence on weaning weight. Thus in any selection programme to improve weaning weight emphasis should be given to multiple records because the selection/culling on the basis of single record will not be effective. Comparatively low repetability estimates have been reported in goats for birth weight, weaning weights and other production parameters like litter size.

The simple Mendelian schemes that are used to explain the inheritance of qualitative traits like coat colour and blood group have not been successful in accounting for the inheritance of quantitative traits such as milk yield and growth rate. Such traits are called polygenic traits. The application of population genetics, however, has proved much useful to explain the inheritance of quantitative traits. The objectives of goat breeder varies according to his requirement as to what type of animals he wants to raise but in general he is to make animals whose offspring will be as close as possible to the ideals in production and reproduction characteristics as well as body type. Selection of animals for breeding is not easy and requires a good amount of technical knowledge on the part of the breeder. Selection within a herd involves choosing breeding animals, males and females, which are superior to the average of their age group

In animal breeding improvement can be done by selection, and birth weight is the I[st] observation which can be a criterion to select superior animals. The relation of birth weight in relation to early growth rate has been reported. Birth weight is further influenced by the type of birth as also by sex of the kid. Thus the factors which affect birth weight include heredity, size and age of dam, nutrition, litter size, environment and placental size.

Reproductive rate directly influence the income and profitability for commercial production of meat from goats. Therefore, the economic importance of fecundity should not be abandoned while selecting for performance traits associated with improving meat production.

Lactation length is important because the amount of milk produced varies considerably as a result of variations in lactation length. Several workers have found wide variations in lactation length of animals of the same breed. The lactation length in Indian breeds of goats varies from 140-250 days.The mean lactation length in Surti goats have been reported to be 5.42 months . The average lactation length for Jakhrana breed was 183.04±4.04 days (Mandal *et al.*, 2010).Singh et al (2009) reported average lactation length of 6.52 months in Gohilwadi breed of goats. Several non genetic factors such as year or season of kidding has Breed of goat

Breed of goat	Lactation length	Reference
Jamunapari	106 days	
Jakhrana	183 days	Mandal *et al.*, 2010
Osmanabadi	130-150 days	
Surti	5.4 month or 162 days	
Gohilwadi	6.52 months or 195 days	

Year and season of kidding are found to have significant effect on lactation length of goats. Singh *et al.* (1970) showed that year, season of kidding and lactation length had highly significant effect on milk yield. These factors jointly explained 65% of the total variability of milk yield in first lactation. Lactation length alone accounted for 58% of the total variability. Lactation length is significantly affected by breed, month and year of kidding and number of kids. Lactation length has an obvious effect on milk yield, with greater quantities of milk and milk components for longer lactations.

Mittal (1979) reported that age had significant effect on body weight gain, daily milk yield, lactation yield, total solids and solids not fat. Age, body weight, body length and heart girth affected the daily milk yield and lactation yield. The highest yield was recorded in 4-6 year. Lactation length and dry period were not affected by age.

Singh and Singh (1974) recorded highest milk production in the second lactation in Jamunapari goats. Prakash & Khanna (1972) recorded significant increase in lactation yield and lactation length from Ist to 3rd lactation in Beetal goats. Mittal (1979) recorded highest yield in the 4th lactation and the longest length in 3rd lactation in a flock of Jamunapari goats.

The kidding interval is an economic trait which is inversely related with the reproductive and productive life of the animal and ultimately with the economics of production. Longer kidding intervals are associated with not only loss in milk production but also result in increased cost of replacement, high depreciation and decrease in potential for selection. Usually both kidding interval and age at first kidding vary with breed. Month of kidding is reported to be an important factor affecting kidding intervals. The kidding interval of various breeds of goats ranges from 200 to 350 days. But Black Bengal goats have been reported to have much smaller kidding interval of 151 days (Ali *et al.,* 1973).

Age at first kidding is an important economic trait in goats. Several workers have reported the age at first kidding in various breeds ranging, from 15 to 25 months for most Indian goats and with a lower value of 14 and 12 months for Red Sokoto and West African dwarf goats.Mellado, *et al.* (2000)studied the factors affecting gestation length in goats and the effect of gestation period on kid survival and the study revealed significant effect of breed of dam, litter weight, breeding season and parity on gestation length. Number of kids born and sex of kids were not a significant source of variation affecting this trait. It was concluded that prolonged gestation (152–160 days) in goats was beneficial because it resulted in heavier litters at birth and higher viability of neonatal kids.

Litter size trait is important for goat production. Litter size trait shows low heritability and therefore difficult to be improved by traditional breeding technologies. Molecular breeding has been suggested as one of the possible options to overcome this impediment.

Sex ratio is expressed either as the number of males per 100 females or as the percentage of males. The primary sex ratio is the proportion of males to females at the time of fertilization or conception while secondary sex ratio expresses the proportion of the sexes at the time of birth. Sex ratios deviate from equality frequently and significantly, this deviation may be due to genetic selection, season, and age of dam, parity of dam and frequency of ejaculation by the male. Some published estimates of sex ratio in goats show males to be more numerous than females while others show equal birth rates.

Grading up

The objective of any genetic evaluation program is identification of genetically superior animals so that the germplasm from these animals can be utilized to improve the genetic value of future generations. Grading up is one of the quickest method available for improving the non-descript animal population. In grading up, the first cross shows a marked improvement over the original stock but improvement in successive stock is progressively less.Cumulative genetic improvement by selection and grading up programme is expected to increase the production potential of goats.

Crossbreeding

Crossbreeding is the mating of males and females of different breeds or breed types. Crossbreeding is the systematic use of breed resources to produce offspring of a specific type. Crossbreeding offers two distinct advantages over purebreeding viz. heterosis and breed complementarity. Heterosis or "hybrid vigor" is the superiority of crossbred offspring to their purebred parents.Breeders of crossbred animals rely on the performance of their parents to exploit both the additive and non-additive genetic variances associated with direct and maternal performance. While purebred selection can benefit from the presence of a greater proportion of additive genetic variance in production traits of economic importance to meat goats, crossbred selection based on additive and non-additive genetic variances becomes important as the proportion of additive genetic variance in those traits is exhausted.

Crosses between the established dairy breeds are both feasible and are used to a substantial degree in commercial practice. Crossbreeding should prove useful in reproduction, growth and lactation. Crosses between the tropical breeds with the dairy breeds of the west like Saanen, Toggenburg, Alpine, Anglo-Nubian have been advocated and tried to improve the milk production capabilities of tropical breeds. Though not very successful, Angora has been crossed with other fibre producing breeds time and again, to improve the fibre producing capabilities. Though the tropical breeds have low growth rate, feed conversion efficiency and carcass characteristics, crossbreeding to improve the meat producing capabilities has not been practiced to any extent in any breed. At NDRI Karnal, Beetal breed has been crossed with Saanen and Alpine bucks. At R.B.S. College, Bichpuri, experiments on crossbreeding of four breeds viz Jamunapari, Barbari, Beetal and Black Bengal has been tried for combining the milk and meat producing characteristics of goats.

Heterosis is an important tool of the animal breeders engaged in crossbreeding programmes to exploit commercial benefits. In genetical terms hybrid vigor (heterosis) is measured as the superiority of the means of reciprocal F_1 crosses over the means of two parent breeds. Besides, heterosis not only improves vigour among animals but also produces uniform population of animals, thus increasing consumer acceptability in the marketing of meat and meat products.

Performance studies for milk and meat production of the four important indigenous breeds of goats (Jamunapari, Beetal, Barbari, and Black Bengal) in a 4 x 4 diallele cross under stall feeding and confinement were performed at RBS College, Agra (Singh and Sengar, 1980). In addition, results are available from the AICRP on Goats involving crosses of Beetal and Jamunapari with Black Bengal and of Beetal with Sirohi. The results showed the usefulness of Jamunapari and Beetal as improver breeds for medium and small breeds. Beetal is superior because of its better adaptation and higher reproductive performance.

Marker-assisted selection

Various aspect of goat production has been benefited from the use of different ARTs. However, to achieve directed genetic improvement, the genes controlling the desirable and undesirable traits must be characterized (Basrur and King, 2005). From the available literatures it is found that this has not been accomplished in goat yet. Techniques involving the generation of gene marker (DNA marker) based on the molecular data and the creation and use of genetic maps as selection criteria for breeding i.e., marker-assisted selection (MAS) may help to achieve this goal, especially in cases where pedigree data are not available or the targeted traits are of low heritability (Dentine, 1999). The success of MAS in breeding goats and other livestock has been negligible to date, especially with regard to economically important traits in these animals that are expressed as non-discrete phenotypes (Basrur and King, 2005). Markers are important in screening genetic defects and when genes are introduced from other populations, the markers can be used to track their segregation in the populations (Amoah and Gelaye, 1997). The MAS has little to no risk to the animal donating blood, sperm or embryos for an assay and therefore, imposes no risk to the consumers. Therefore, MAS is expected to be most commonly used techniques in association with other goat ARTs in near future.

Because their high polymorphism, DNA simple sequence repeats (SSRs, microsatellites) are a valuable tool for the study of genetic diversity between populations (Moioli *et al.,* 2001). Takezaki and Nei (1996) and Diez-Táscon *et al.* (2000) have emphasized the importance of microsatellites in the study of evolutionary relationships of closely related populations. However, some problems may arise with the use of these markers for reasons such as irregularities in the mutation pattern and polymorphism differences between populations, because of which caution is required in extending inferences to populations other than those used in a specific study (Takeazaki and Nei, 1996).

Microsatellites are genetic markers highly polymorphic, evenly distributed in the whole genome and easy for genotyping.Goat breeds have evolved in different local environments to fulfill the requirement of the local community in different agro-climatic conditions in India. Genetic drift, as well as selection, has contributed to the differentiation of breeds. Rout *et al.* (2008) carried out studies about the genetic structure and genetic diversity of the several Indian goat breeds using milk protein variability, which can be helpfulfor breed improvement as well as breed conservation decisions.Microsatellite based phylogeny in Indian goats showed the lowest genetic distance between Marwari and Sirohi goats.

Genetics of goat

The characteristics of an animal are determined by its genetic make up as well as by the environmental opportunity that is provided for the expression of its genes. Thus inheritance and environment together are responsible for the final expression of a trait. Genetics is the study of inheritance of characters controlled by units of heredity "genes" and breeding reassort them in various combinations. The basic unit of heredity "gene"is present in the chromosomes. The chromosomes are present in the cell nucleus. There are a characteristic number of chromosome pairs for each animal species. The diploid chromosome number for goats is 60. One pair of chromosome in each cell is related to the sex of the individual and is known as sex chromosome. All the 58 autosomes in goats are acrocentric for each of the sexes. The x- chromosome is also acrocentric while the Y chromosome is small metacentric or sub metacentric in goats (Das and Das, 2011).

Interspecific hybridization in animals including goats appears to occur very rarely in nature. A sheep–goat hybrid is the hybrid offspring of a sheep and a goat. Although sheep and goats seem similar and can be mated, they belong to different genera. Sheep belong to the genus Ovis and have 54 chromosomes, while goats belong to the genus Capra and have 60 chromosomes. The offspring of a sheep-goat pairing is generally stillborn. Despite widespread shared pasturing of goats and sheep, hybrids are poorly attested, indicating the genetic distance between the two species. Mine *et al.* (2000) reported a 5 year old male sheep-goat interspecific hybrid born under natural conditions. The hybrid was castrated at 10 months of age. Karyotype analysis confirmed that the animal was a male and a hybrid with 57 chromosomes, an intermediate number between sheep (2n=54) and goat (2n=60). Morphological characteristics of the animal were compared with those of castrated male Tswana goats of the same age. Interspecific hybridization plays an important role in the evolution and diversification of animal species. It has been suggested that common ancestor of wild goats arose from interspecific hybridization, and that the mitochondrial genome of a species better adapted to life at high altitudes was transferred via this route into the common ancestor of Capra (Ropiquet and Hassanin, 2006)

All inheritance is due to genes but the individual genes are not always identifiable. The genes are located on chromosomes. Each gene is a portion of DNA molecule. Genes controlling such characters as color and variations in structure of animals are usually identifiable. They are qualitative characters identified by Mendel and the genes controlling them are called Mendelian genes. They may be dominant or recessive. Another group of characters controlled by identifiable genes are the polymorphic protein types in blood and milk, including blood groups.

Color in mammals depends on the presence of melanins in skin and hair (Searle, 1968). Melanins reside in cellular organelles called melanosomes, which are produced in melanocytes.. Pigmentation of skin and hair depends on melanocytes being present, and on their relative level of melanogenic and exocytotic activity. The two main mechanisms by which pigmentation is reduced or absent are absence or relative inactivity of melanocytes. Decrease or elimination of pigment by either of these basic mechanisms can be regional, or can involve entire haircoat.Colour in goats is highly inherited but no serious efforts have been made to identify the manner of inheritance. Breeders have had good success in establishing desired color patterns when these attempts have been made. The white colour of the Angora and Saanen goat is known to act largely as a dominant suggesting the action of an inhibitor gene (Lauvergne and Ricordeau, 1973).A complete historic review of the world literature dealing with the loci and alleles affecting color in goats has recently been completed by the Committee on Genetic Nomenclature of Sheep and Goats (COGNOSAG).White has been an important color in many breeds of goats, especially those for fiber production. The expression of whiteness in mammalian hair can come about through a variety of different genetic mechanisms (Searle, 1968).One general mechanism for whiteness in mammals is due to white spotting. White spotting in mammals occurs in regions where skin or hair follicles lack melanocytes, since these regions are incapable for forming melanins. Absence of melanocytes can occur from a variety of mechanisms, including melanoblasts failing to differentiate from the neural crest, or failing to migrate to skin regions, or failing to survive once migration has taken place (Searle, 1968). One of the main determiners of goat color is the Agouti locus (http://www.cagba.org/genetics_goat_clr_20041.pdf.).

Ear length in the goat is inherited in a qualitative manner, as with the long ear of the Jamnapari and the short ear of La Mancha. Horns in goat are inherited as non sex linked simple Mendelian recessive characters.

References

Ali, S.Z. (1981). A repeatability estimate of birth weight of Black Bengal goats. Indian Vet. J. 58: 308-310.

Ali, S.Z., Hoque, M.M. and Hasnath, M.A. (1973). A study on the growth and reproductive performance of Black Bengal goats under farm conditions. Indian Vet. J. 50:438.

Amoah, E.A. and S. Gelaye, (1997). Biotechnological advances in goat reproduction. J. Anim. Sci., 75: 578-585.

Basrur, P.K. and W.A. King, (2005). Genetics then and now: Breeding the best and biotechnology. Rev. Sci. Tech., 24: 31-49.

Das, Bula and Das, Dharmeshwar (2011). Karyotype of Assam local goats (*Capra hircus*) Indian J. Anim.. Res., 45(2):147-149

Dentine, M.R., (1999). Marker-Assisted Selection. In: The Genetics of Cattle, Fries, R. and A. Ruvinsky (Eds.). CABI Publishing, New York, pp: 497-510.

Diez-Tascón, C., Littlejohn, R. P., Almeida, P. A. R. & Crawford, A.M. (2000)Genetic variation within the Merino sheep breed: analysis of closely related populations using microsatellites. Anim. Genet. 31:243–251.

Gall (1969) cited in Gall, C., 1980. Relationship between body conformation and production in dairy goats. J. Dairy Sci. 63, 1768±1781.

Lauvergne, J. J.&Ricordeau, G., (1973) Déterminisme héréditaire de la couleur blanche chez la chèvre Saanen. I el Conf. int. Elev. Capr., Tours 1,971 S.P.E.O., PATRE, Paris, -358-359 (idem 83

Mandal, A., R. Roy, Saket Bhusan, P.K. Rout, M.C. Sharma (2010). Environmental Effects on production traits of Jakhrana Goat. Indian Journal of Animal Sciences, 80:1141-1144.

Mellado, M., J. L. Amaro , J. E. García and L. M. Lara (2000) Factors affecting gestation length in goats and the effect of gestation period on kid survival The Journal of Agricultural Science 135:85-89

Mine, O.M., Kedikilwe, K., Ndebele, R.T., Nsoso, S.J. (2000). Sheep-goat hybrid born under natural conditions. Small Ruminant Research 37:141-145.

Mittal, J.P. (1979). Relationship among traits of growth and milk production in Jamnapari goats India J Dairy Sci 32:379-382.

Moioli, B., Georgoudis, A., Napolitano, F., Catillo, G., Giubilei, E., Ligda, CH., *et al.* (2001). Genetic diversity between Italian, Greek and Egyptian buffalo populations. Livestock Production Science, 70:203-211.

Prakash, C. and Khanna,R.S.(1972) Effect of order of lactation and lactation length on milk production in a closed herd of Beetal goats. Indian J. Anim. Prod. 2:10-13.

Ronningen, K.(1967) Factors affecting body weight and relationship between body weight and milk production in goats. Medl. Norges Landbruk. 46:1-

Ropiquet, Anne and Hassanin, Alexandre (2006) Hybrid origin of the Pliocene ancestor of wild goatsMolecular Phylogenetics and Evolution, 41:395-404

Rout P.K, Joshi MB, Mandal A, Laloe D, Singh L, Thangaraj, K. (2008)Microsatellite-based phylogeny of Indian domestic goats. BMC Genet. 9:11.

Searle, A.G. (1968). Comparative Genetics of Coat-color in Mammals. Logos Press, London, UK.

Shrestha, J.N.B., Fahmy, M.H., (2007). Breeding goats for meat production: a review (2) Crossbreeding and formation of composite population. Small Rumin. Res. 67:93-112.

Shrestha, J.N.B., Fahmy, M.H., (2007). Breeding goats for meat production: a review (3) 3. Selection and breeding strategies. Small Rumin. Res. 67:113-125.

Singh, B.B. and Singh, B.P.(1974) Performance of Jamnapari goats. Indian Vet. J. 51:326-

Singh, M.K., Rai, B., Kumar, Ashok, Sisodiya, H.S. and Singh, N. P. (2009). Production performance of Gohilwadi goats under range conditions. Indian Journal of Animal Sciences, 79:587-593.

Singh, R.N., Acharya, R.M. and Biswas, D.K. (1970). Evaluation of genetic and non-genetic factors affecting some economic traits in goats. Acta. Agric. Scand. 20:10-14.

Singh, S.N. and Sengar, O.P.S. (1980). Studies on the combining ability of desirable characteristics of important goat breeds for meat and milk separately and in combination. P.L.480 Project, R.B.S. College, Bichpuri Agra.

Takezaki N and Nei M, (1996). Genetic distances and reconstruction of phylogenetic trees from microsatellite DNA. Genetics 144:389-399.

4

Goat Anatomy and Physiology

Goat anatomy

Understanding of the basic structure and functioning of goats is required to maintain the health and productivity of goats. Anatomy deals with the form and structure of the animal whereas physiology deals with the mechanism of body functions.

The skeleton of goat is made up of the vertebral column, ribs and skull, the limbs, and the joints. There are 7 neck (cervical) vertebrae, 13 chest (thoracic) vertebrae, 6 or 7 lumbar vertebrae, 4 pelvic (sacral) vertebrae and between 4 and 8 tail (coccygeal) vertebrae.The ribs are elongated, curved bones that form the ribcage, which is the skeleton of the thoracic cavity (chest). There are 13 pairs of ribs attached to each side of the thoracic vertebrae. Most of them are fixed i.e. they are joined to the sternum (breastbone) at the front of the chest but the last two pairs are not attached at the front and are called floating ribs.The skull includes all the bones of the head. It consists of a number of flat bones that form immovable joints, most of which disappear with age; and a lower jaw bone (mandible), which forms movable joints with the other parts of the skull.The limbs include forelegs (thoracic limbs) and hindlegs (pelvic limbs). The forelegs consist of shoulder,forearm and a lower limb made up of carpus,metacarpus and phalanges. The hind legs consist of pelvic girdle, thigh, and a lower limb made up of tarsus, metatarsus and phalanges.

The joints are where two or more bones of cartilages meet. There are two main kinds of joints.Fixed or immovable joints have no joint cavity and are united by fibrous tissue or cartilage. Many of these are temporary joints which become fixed as calcium accumulates in the flexible tissues and turns to bone (calcifies) with age. Examples are the joints in theskull, the joints of ribs to vertebrae, and the pelvic and mandibular symphyses (midline joints).Movable joints have a joint cavity surrounded by ajoint capsule. There are two opposing bone surfaces,which have smooth surfaces of very dense bone.

Movable joints have cartilages between the bones to reduce friction and absorb concussion. The inner lining of the joint capsule is the synovial layer, which produces synovial fluid (joint fluid). Examples include joints of the limbs, such as the shoulder and the hip, and the joint between the skull and the vertebral column.

The goats differ from sheep not only in many conspicuous external characteristics, but also for differences in the bone (structure, presence or absence of certain skin glands characteristics in their behavior and other aspects. Sheep are distinguished from goats by glands in both forefeet and hind feet, by the absence of a true beard and by the absence of the strong goaty odors in the males. There are also marked differences in the skulls and the horns generally spiral it opposite direction.The right horn of the sheep in the right like a cork screw and in the goat to the left. Domestic goat generally carries their tails up, whereas the domestic sheep carry their tails down.

Goats have three groups of teeth: Four pairs of incisors on the lower jaw only, which bite on to a 'dental pad' on the upper jaw.Three premolars and molars on each side of the upper and lower jaws.

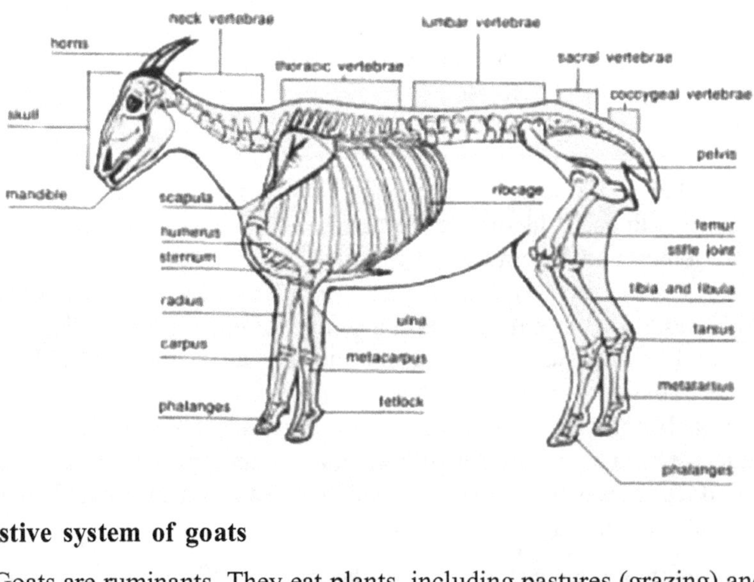

Digestive system of goats

Goats are ruminants. They eat plants, including pastures (grazing) and many weeds, shrubs and trees (browsing). Digestion is the process of breaking down this plant material in the stomach and intestines into components which can be absorbed and used by the goat.Goat needs carbohydrates, fat , protein and wide variety to minerals and vitamins for maintenance, growth and milk production functions.These nutrients are obtained from the feeds and fodders and different parts of the digestive system exerts varying level of action on ingested material to extract these nutrients for host use. The digestive system of goat consists of mouth, esophagus, rumen, reticulum, omasum, abomasum, small intestine and large intestine.

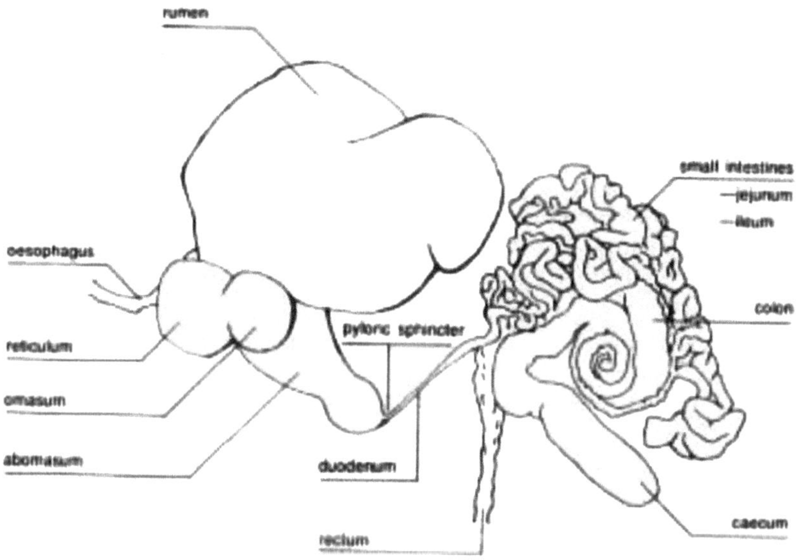

The mouth is the first part of the digestive system. The two main functions of the mouth are to masticate and to wet the feed with saliva. The prehensile tongue enables goat to eatgrowing leaves of short grasses and browse foliage and even thorny vegetations. There are three principal salivary glands in most mammals namely the parotid, sub-maxillary and sub-lingual and same is true for goats. Saliva is about 99% water, the remaining 1 % consisting of mucin, inorganic salts, amylase and lysozyme. Salivation in goats can be reflexly increased considerably by tactile stimulation or the distention of the thoracic portion of the esophagus by fluid, gas or other means (Clark and Weiss, 1952) but the effect can be inhibited by distension of the rumen with gas. Resting secretion rate of kids increases when they are about 7 weeks old, although the stimulated rate of secretion did not reach adult proportions relative to the gland weights until they were 3 months old (Kay, 1960). The rate of salivary secretion at rest and during feeding is greater in goat than in sheep. Saliva plays an important role in buffering the rumen contents against falls in pH.

The esophagus in goats is a small tube connecting the mouth with the stomach.

Stomach of goat comprises four parts viz rumen, reticulum, omasum and abomasum. At birth, the rumen and reticulum are small in comparison to the abomasum but these organs develop relatively more rapidly after birth. The abomasum is like the true stomach of monogastric animals. Although the development of rumen initiates soon after birth but it fully developed at the age of 90 days. The evolution of microbial ecosystem in stomach occurs at the age of 15 days. The process of development can be fastened by introduction of solid food at early age and addition of fermentation end products such as acetate has pronounced effect on reticulo-rumen development. The rapid development of rumen, reticulum and omasum after birth is triggered by the intake of solid foods. The abomasum increase in size at a much slower rate than the rumen and finally, it is found entirely on the right side of the body and in the epigastric region of the abdominal cavity (Benzie and Phillipson, 1957).

The stomach capacity of goats is quite high in the adult. In the pouch of the ruminants, carbohydrates of the diet are converted into fatty acids chiefly VFA. Metabolism in the rumen is dependent on the population of micro-organisms. The contents of the rumen are continually mixed by rhythmic contraction of its walls and during rumination, the material at the anterior end is drawn back into the oesophagus and returned by a wave of contraction to the mouth. The chemical breakdown of food in the reticulorumen is brought out by enzymes secreted by micro-organisms. The total number of bacteria in the rumen and the types which predominate at any time depend on the animal's diet. Cellulose is digested only by ruminant animals; however cellulose is useless for othernon ruminant animals. Monosaccharides generated as a result of degradation of cellulose are metabolised to volatile fatty acids chiefly acetic, propionic and butyric acids. Pyruvic, succinic and lactic acids are important intermediates and lactic acid can be detected in the rumen liquor. Verma *et al.* (1975) reported maximum concentrations of lactic acid at 2-4 hours post feeding which was also accompanied by a high level of TVFA (total volatile fatty acids). Peak production of TVFA was after 2-4 hour in case of goat. The total concentration of TVFA in the rumen is also dependent on the animal's diet. Goats have a higher level of TVFA as compared to sheep and buffalo at maintenance level of feeding. The production of VFA results in lowering of pH and the lowest pH of the rumen fluid was found 4 hours post feeding.

The proportion of various fatty acids as well as TVFA also vary with the nature of the diet. Supplementation of the basal ration with the concentrates increases the TVFA as well as the molar proportion of propionic acid in the rumen. Processing of diet also affect TVFA level and composition. Pelleting favors propionate production compared to mash diets.Higher proportion of propionic acid tends to favour energy retention in the body. The acetate acts as precursors of milk fatty acids. Propionate which makes a net contribution to glucose synthesis is quantitatively the most important precursor of glucose.

Ruminal methane production represents a loss of 2 to 15% dietary energy in ruminant animals and is also a major contributor to greenhouse effect.The estimated CH^4 emission rate per cattle, buffalo, sheep and goat are 150.7, 137, 21.9 and 13.7 (g/animal/day) respectively.Reducing ruminal methane production could improve animal performance and decrease greenhouse effect.Monensin (MO) and other ionophores have been used to effectively manipulate ruminal fermentation and mitigate ruminal methane production.

Food proteins are degraded to amino acids, peptides and ammonia by the rumen micro-organisms which are then used for the synthesis of their own proteins. Goats convert about 50% of the dietary nitrogen to microbial nitrogen. Bacterial and protozoal accounts for about the half of the total N in the rumen of goats. Some of the essential amino acids deficient in the diet can also be synthesized by rumen microbes. Free amino acids and amides present in diet are further degraded by deamination, to organic acids, ammonia and carbon dioxide. The ammonia produced may be absorbed from the rumen into the blood, carried to the liver and converted to urea. Some urea is returned to the rumen via the saliva and also directly through the rumen wall but the greater part is excreted in the urine.

Excessive dietary protein is a wasteful process which also utilizes energy to get excreted from the body after degradation to ammonia which in turn enters urea cycle. Since rumen micro-organisms use only NH_3 as nitrogen source, thus urea could be used by ruminants as protein source. Although urea is used as source of NH_3 for rumen microbes but it gets dissociated rapidly and may be toxic to animal. Hence for faster utilization of this nitrogen source, rapidly fermentable carbohydrate souces are recommended. While sources for slow release of NH_3 such as biuret may provide NH_3 for a large duration and this higher efficiency of utilization. The microbial biomass thus produced gets digested and absorbed in rumen.

Rumen microbial ecosystemconsists of bacteria, ciliate protozoa, anaerobic fungi and bacteriophages. These microbial groups live in a symbiotic relationship with the host, act synergetically for the bioconversion of lignocellulosic feeds into volatile fatty acids which serve as a source of energy for the animals. Rumen bacteria are endowed with the unique ability of synthesizing and secreting the enzyme cellulase. Cellulases are responsible for the degradation of cellulose part of the feed to soluble carbohydrates, which are further fermented to the production of volatile fatty acids. Other fibrinolytic enzymes of rumen microbes are glucosidases and xylanases.The goats feed upon diets rich in tannin and their ruminal microflora are characterized by the presence of tannin resistant bacteria like *Selenomonas ruminantium* (Kamra, 2005). The bacterial population in the rumen is in the range of 10^6-10^9 in each ml of rumen fluid.

It has been established that the microbial population of the rumen fluctuates seasonally and that the variation in the number and proportion of various species of micro-organisms is due to variation in the amount, composition and nutritive value of the diet. Goat rumen microflora is known to contain a greater proportion of Bacteroidetes/lactobacillus species potentially resistant to tannins.The higher diversity of rumen microbial flora is upon supplementation of feed having soluble starch. The diets with R:C : 50:50 seems to be adequate to have great rumen microbial diversity. The major bacteriapresent in goat rumen which collectively form 70-80 % total bacterial population include Ruminococcus flavefaciens, Fibrobacter succinogenes, Bacteroidetes species etc.

The protozoal count is higher in goats fed on green grass and soaked gram as compared to those fed banyan leaves. The population of protozoa ranges from 10^4-10^5/ml of rumen fluid. The value of total protozoa in cattle, buffalo, sheep and goats have been reported to be 2.28, 2.91, 3.44, and 3.69×10^5 g/ml strained rumen liquor, respectively.The total Protozoa population in cattle and buffalo are lower than sheep and goats. Protozoa present in goat rumen include Diplodinium,Dasytricha, Polyplastron, Diploplastron, Enoploplastron, Elytroplastron, Entodinium,Isotricha,Butschlia, Blepharocorys, Blepharozoum, Holophyyoldes, Eodiniuin,Ophisthotrichum etc. The number and type of protozoa are affected by the diet. In one study, increasing the level of soybean hulls in diet of goats caused a reduction in the number of total protozoa and Entodinium, and Entodiniomorphos, and increased the percentage of *Dasytricha*, *Diplodinium*, *Diploplastron* and *Holotricha* subclass.Although protozoa numbers are less but contribute more than 90% fibrolysis of the rumen.

The species *Pichia membranifaciens* was the most prominent yeast (fungi) in goat rumen.The zoospore stage of rumen fungi was once thought to be a flagellated protozoan, and was named *Neocallimastix frontalis*.

Goat is an effective disperser of several legume species. For example ruminal incubation as well as ingestion by goats improved germination in *A. decorticans* (up to 68.0%). Considerable time is spent by feed residues in passing through the alimentary tract and the rate of passage varies with the type and consistency of the diet. The feed particle size affects rate of passage from the rumen. The amount of water in the forage eaten is also known to affect the rate of passage of digesta. Duration of feed in the rumen is longer for goats kept on a dry fodder regimen since large or dry particles will take longer time to be digested and hence retained in the reticulo-rumen for a longer time. Solid food passes through the alimentary tract of young goats slightly more rapidly than in adults. Chopping of grass increases the rate of passage through the digestive tract of goat.

Small intestine in goats is about 18 m in length. The chyme of the abomasum is acted upon by the biliary, pancreatic and intestinal secretions render it absorbable. In goats, bile is secreted continuously (no night variation), the daily quantity varying from 24 to 30 ml per kg body weight but decreasing with fasting and increasing with feeding. Bile salts promote emulsification of lipids and are thus important in the digestion of lipids. Food is considerrably delayed in the large intestine and the movement is by the peristaltic and antiperistaltic movements. The large intestine of goat is approx 5.5 meters long.

Adaptability

Goats are known to exist in a wide variety of habitats. Goats can thrive under conditions where crops and other forms of livestock would die because the climate is too arid or the soil is too poor. Consequently they are particularly valuable in the arid and semi-arid parts of India and world. Goats integrate well with crop farming and livestock production of other species like cattle, buffalo, sheep etc. Goats can survive in very harsh environments because of several adaptation mechanisms, such as the capacity to select the most nutritive plants or plant fractions, the efficient digestion of the less nutritive fractions rich in fibre etc. For goat holders, this species appears to be demanding little in feeds because it can use bushes, shrubs and range vegetation, which cattle and sheep accept poorly.

Adaptation refers to the morphological, anatomical, physiological, biochemical, and behavioral characteristics of the animal which favour their survival and development in a particular environment. Biological productivity is largely a function of the adaptability of the animal to its environment. Density of an animal species in a particular environment is indicative of its adaptability to such environment. The distribution of goats is mostly in the northern hemisphere and its coldest natural habitat is the hill areas of Asia Minor, the home of Angora goats. Goats occupy an important place in the subsistent agriculture of India, the Middle East, Northern Africa, and some countries of Central and South America. Natural distribution of goats is confined to the drier regions of Europe, Africa and Asia Minor. Most goats of northern hemisphere are resident of deserts, semi deserts and scrublands. Goats are quite successful in surviving and proliferation in the extensive grasslands of northern hemispheres. Such grasslands occur in Deccan Plateau (India), Texas (U.S.A.), Mexico and some parts of U.S.S.R.

Goats are generally adapted to environments having lesser precipitation. Thus in drought polygon of north-east Brazil, goats were found everywhere but especially in the regions with less than 500mm of rain where no other agricultural activity is possible. Another advantage of goats is that they have a high reproductive rate which is especially important in an unfavorable environment such as drought. When the environment become favorable after the drought, the number of goats can increase quickly but the number of cattle or buffalo stays low for several years.

Goat's inability to withstand the extremes of wetter climate is documented by the fact that Angora can withstand the extremes of cold but high rainfall is detrimental to them.

Goats generally do not occur at higher altitudes of either hemispheres of the world. In addition to Angora, the other breeds of goats adapted to mountain climate include the Chegu (Kashmiri) in the Himalayas and Altai Mountain in the U.S.S.R. and Mongolia. The higher altitude is conductive to the growth of pashmina fibres in Chegu. Rocky mountain goats are also known to exist in Mt Evans, Colorado (U.S.A.) at a height of 3500-5000 metres.

Thus goats thrive in a variety of climates, but they are more concentrated in the drier tropical and subtropical areas than are sheep. However, the high producing domesticated breeds of goats are distributed in the higher or cooler latitudes of the world and low producing Asia type in the lower and warmer latitudes. Goats are highly adaptable and can adapt to new environments quickly. Goats that were developed in temperate countries, such as Swiss Saanen goat, have been successfully acclimatized to the subtropical environment of countries such as Israel.

Environmental physiology of goats aims at the response and adaptation that allow goats to survive and flourish in these habitats. Although acclimatization is often a slow process, taking a year or longer, the Boer goat has the ability to adapt to almost any climate, from the hottest dry desert climate as in Namibia and Australia, to the snow covered mountains of Germany.

Morphological Adaptations

The ability of goats to maintain a constant body temperature survive and proliferate depends very much on morphological adaptations and behavioral responses. Although breeds have been developed by selecting animals suitably adapted for a particular environment, but more often the characters other than their adaptability have guided the selection. Some of them possess distinct morphological features aiding the maintenance of energy balance of the body. Such goats in temperate areas possess thick and copious hair coat (mohair or pashmina), desert goats tend to have longer legs and ears. The long and thin legs of West- African long-legged goat are adaptations as much to aid in browsing as to aid in heat dissipation mechanism by increasing the surface area. The long legs also protect the body from reflected heat load from the hot soil. The long ears of some breeds are also a part of the thermoregulatory heat dissipation mechanism.

The coat of desert goats tends to be limited to a covering of fine, short and sparsely distributed hair, which provide resistance to the absorption of radiant heat and has good reflecting properties. However, Marwari goat is an exception.The thick copious coat of Angora and Chegu is an adaptation to cold environments. In these goats, long hairs are intermixed with finer fibres to give a greater protective covering. These coats act as good insulators because of the air trapped in them. Skin colour is an important morphological adaptation in thermoregulation. Animals inhabiting warm and humid regions show greater pigmentation than those found in cooler, drier areas. Horns of goats have also been attributed a minor thermoregulatory function.

Goat like most homeotherms is endowed with a constant deep body temperature regardless of the temperature of the surroundings. Homeothermy is mainly ensured by a variety of physiological mechanisms in addition to the morphological and behavioural adaptations.Normal body temperatures of mammals including goats range from 36° to 40° C. Normal temperatures of goats lie between 100- 104°F or 37.7- 40.0° C. The goat, being a small animal requires a greater expenditure of energy. This is achieved by a higher rectal temperature as compared to cattle or buffalo. Higher rectal temperature is an adaptation for higher activity than cattle and buffalo. Cattle is having higher temperature than buffalo, is also reputed to be more active. This also means that animal consumes more feed and spends more time in obtaining it. The feed intake of goats is 3-5% of the body weight which is higher than that of buffalo (2-3%) and cattle (1-2%).

Heat Stress

Heat stress is one of the major factors adversely affecting animal welfare and thus productivity.Feed intake is known to be decreased in response to heat stress but in case of goats, the effects are minimal. Heat stress affects the digestion both directly by disturbing the body functions including those of the digestive tract as well as indirectly by altering the supply of nutrients. The digestibility of nutrients is shown to vary with season in kids.

Goats with production demands are susceptible to heat stress in spite of heat resistant characteristics. Depression of feed intake and reduction in production are commonly observed in heat-stressed goats.

Water Economy

Water intake by goats in hot environment is influenced by the severity of the heat stress. Amount of dry matter eaten also affects the water intake. Heat tolerance is generally associated with a low water consumption and heat sensitivity with higher water consumption. Increase in environmental temperature increases the amount of water intake, in order to dissipate the extra heat by vaporization. Extra water taken in during heat stress is virtually entirely used for the regulation of body temperature through avenues of evaporative water loss.

Water is of high biological importance in arid regions which goats inhabit. It is required for evaporative cooling as well for intake of food. The amount of water passing through an animal in an unit time is the water turnover. Goats use less water than sheep and sheep only about half as much as cattle. McFarlane (1975) has advocated that there exists a hierarchy of function in mammals which emerged during evolution in the pliocene or pleistocene. High rate of water and energy turnover with low salt tolerance are found in animals like cattle, derived from the wet tropics. Low rate of water turnover with high salt tolerance occur in desert animals such as the camel. Sheep and goats are intermediate, with energy and water turnover rate between those of jungle and desert animal.

In most areas goats inhabit, increased water requirements are compounded by a paucity of drinking water and water contained in the feed. Under such conditions of absolute water deprivation, goats loose less amount of body weight as compared to cattle, Merino sheep and camel .

Water restriction is accompanied by a sharp decline in the GFR (Glomerular filtration rate) to a third of its normal value. Thus reduced GFR is an adaptational strategy to meet the threat of body dessication during periods of water insufficiency. During water deprivations goats maintained plasma volume and extracellular fluid volume but lost gut and cell water considerably, indicating that the maintenance of fluidity of the blood has priority over the other body fluid requirements. In another study, during dehydration, goats showed a substantial reduction in rumen and reticulum water content which was not shown by other species and also reduced colonic water content to a greater extent (Maloiy *et al,* 1978). Thus water loss via fecal excretion is reduced when animals are deprived of drinking water. Water is absorbed from the large intestine of goats in large amounts. The absorption of water in the large intestine of goats is much more complete as the DM% reported for cattle in terminal colon is only 12.1% as against 31.6% in goats.

Heat stress was found to have minimal effect on the total urine output although the urine became concentrated. The level of Na, K in urine rose as also their total excretion.

Body maintains a balance between the heat production and heat loss. Animals escape the rigours of heat stress by several mechanisms which include mainly the decrease in heat production or an increase in heat dissipation. The decrease in heat production is brought about by (i) decrease in feed intake (ii) decrease in endocrine function particularly thyroid (iii) by acting on the heat production centre in the hypothalamus. Heat loss from the body occurs by both evaporative as well as by conduction, convection and radiation. Evaporative cooling is particularly important as a means of thermoregulation under heat stress considering a large energy exchange which occurs when one gram of water is vaporized. The moisture evaporated in hot arid environment is derived from two main sources viz sweating and panting. Thermoregulatory sweating is elicited in two ways (i) reflexly by stimulation of the warm receptors in the skin and (ii) by a rise of hypothalamic temperature.

The density of sweat gland in goats is about 200/ cm^2 which is almost equal to that of sheep or camel but half that of buffalo and about one tenth that of zebu cattle. The sweat rate from the side of the head is greater than that from the thorax.

Goat uses less of sweating as compared to other domestic animals. Goats exposed to heat stress showed no signs of visible sweating from any part of the body other than mid dorsal flank region. The use of sweating as a means of heat dissipation varies with different breeds. Some breeds are better sweaters as compared to other. Thus Black Bedouin goats are better sweaters as compared to Somali goats. Goats use panting as a means of heat dissipation as effectively as sweating. Panting in goat is accompained by an increase in the minute volume resulting in net increase in ventilation of the lung and concomitant increase in water loss. Polypnea in response to heat stress has been reported in breeds of goats. Seasonal variation in respiration rates has also been reported.

Heat shock genes are activated when cells are exposed to stress stimuli and form heat shock proteins (Gade *et al.,* 2010). HSP 70 is known to protect cells, tissues and organs from stress by promoting folding of nascent polypeptides and by correcting the misfolding of denatured proteins.

Adaptation to high altitude

Higher altitudes are characterized by a reduction in the partial pressure of oxygen and consequent apnea and respiratory alkalosis. In addition, animals living at high altitude encounter several environmentally induced challenges including increased wind speeds, severe cold temperatures. Adaptation to high altitude is characterized by numerous functional changes which collectively facilitate oxygen transport to body tissues. Goats exposed to high altitude are accompained by changes that improve the supply of oxygen to the cell. Goats exposed to high latitude have their blood volume increased. The increased hematocrit, red blood cells and oxygen capacity in mountain goats is due to increased secretion of hormone erythropoietin. The erythropoietic factor is permeable to the membranes of the mammary cells and is found in the milk of high altitude goats. The problems at high altitude are those of cold conditions, complicated for range animals by a precarious fodder supply and a relative shortage of oxygen. Goats at Leh and Laddakh of India, usually face a shortage of fodder during cold weather conditions and many times the Indian army has pitched in to air drop fodder supplies for the goats living there. The oxygen deficiency, if uncorrected, leads to reduced or faulty metabolic conversion of food, with lowered yield of useful products and perhaps with lowered heat production under conditions where a high rate may be essential. Secondary consequences may be leakage of fluid from anoxic capillaries into the pendulous tissues (brisket disease) and impoverished heart function, both making matters worse for the animal. Reproductive functions are often depressed under those conditions. Mountain goats are known to survive such harsh altititude conditions.

Adaptations to cold

Goats are not as well adapted for cold as are other species of domestic ruminants. Angora goats are very sensitive as death and abortions occur frequently during cold stress. Cold exposure has been known to reduce the milk secretion of goats due to a reduced blood flow to the mammary gland. Cold exposure caused the animals to reduce their water intake which was accompanied by a decrease in total body water and an increase in the osmolality of plasma and milk. There was an increase in the concentration of corticoids. Reduced glucose uptake and lactose synthesis are instrumental in bringing about the decrease in milk secretion during cold exposure.

Normal physiological indices of goats

Blood constituents are good indicators of the physiological status of the animals. The value of blood picture and mineral content of the animals vary from region to region and breed is the most important factor influencing the blood parameters, followed by age and physiological status.

Rectal Temperature	39.1 (37.7-40.0 °C)
Heart Rate	70-80
Respiration rate	12-16
Hemoglobin	8-12 g/dl
Glucose	48-76 mg/dl

References

Benzie, D. and Phillipson, A.T.(1957) The alimentary tract of the ruminant. Oliver & Boyd, London.

Clark, R. and Weiss, K.E.(1952) Reflex salination in sheep and goats initiated by mechanical stimulation of the cardian area of the fore stomachs. Journal of South African Veterinary Medical Association 23:163-165.

Gade, Nitin *et al.* (2010) Molecular characterization of heat shock protein 70-2 gene of goat (Capra hircus). Molecular Biology International 108429, 7 pages

Jindal, S.K.(2011) Introduction to animal physiology, New India Publishing Agency, New Delhi

Kamra, D.N. (2005) Rumen microbial ecosystem. Current Science 89 : 124-135.

Kay, R.N.B. (1960). The rate of flow and composition of various salivary secretions in sheep and calves. Journal of Physiol. 150 : 515.

Macfarlane, W. V. (1975.) Distribution and Dynamics of Body Fluids in Sheep, in BLUNT M. H. (ed.), The Blood of Sheep: Composition and Function. Springer-Verlag, New York: 1-27.

Maloiy, G. M. O., C. R. Taylor and E. T. Clemens (1978). A comparison of gastrointestinal water content and osmolality in East African herbivores during hydration and dehydration. The Journal of Agricultural Science 91 : 249-252

Verma, D.N., Pant, H.C., Rai, G.S. and Rawat, J.S.(1975) Concentration of VFA and lactic acid in rumen of goats. Indian Veterinary Journal 52:442-444.

5

Management

Goat husbandry has been practiced for thousands of years, since the first domestication of goats. Goat rearing for long mainly consisted of "zero input" concept, which suits well under extensive system of management. Major goat management systems in vogue are nomadic (transhumant)/extensive, semi-intensive and intensive, which have evolved on age-old experience and convenience of resource poor farmers under diverse agro-climatic and agro-ecological conditions.

Nomadic/Transhumant/Migratory/Extensive System

Extensive grazing lands cover vast areas of temperate Asia, and are important both environmentally and as a source of livelihood for goat and sheep herders.This practice is strengthened by migratory, free range, pasture cum range grazing options. The goats are compelled to often graze over long distances in search of feed and water. Under nomdic (transhumant) system, both grasslands and browse are important vegetation type. Land tenure problems, or lack of clarity in grazing rights are some of the emerging challenges for the goat herders under nomadic system. Many a times, the conflict of interests between settled farmers and herders is increasing with rising population pressure and intensification of agriculture. Poor pasture condition is one of the major constraint for the goat herders under nomadic system. Some of the measures suggested to improve the situation include better grazing management, reseeding with high-yielding species, and herder training.

Goat and sheep are two species which have been traditionally managed extensively. Mixed flocks of sheep and goats are common, although separate flocks of either species can also be seen. Extensively managed animals have considerably more behavioural freedom compared to intensively managed animals that are always more confined. Goat has an advantage over other species of livestock in that they can live and produce on land unfavourable for other forms of agriculture. Goat has the ability to forage and survive in areas, where cattle and buffaloes would perform poorly. Goat can revert to wild conditions if given the opportunity whereas sheep donot.

The large ruminants in general and the small ruminants in particular are reared under the extensive system, which includes migratory, transhumance, free range, pasture and range grazing management of different livestock species over long distances in search of feed and water. The system is principally one of low resource use; however, the poor nutritional availability results in a low level of productivity: these fluctuates among different regions, years and seasons.

The greatest limitation in Indian range lands and natural pastures is the lack of availability of adequate energy throughout the year and adequate amounts of protein for more than half the year. Although grazing on the range lands is considered to be the cheapest method for livestock production, over-grazing of available lands is causing serious problems of soil erosion and degradation, leading to desertification. Because of long, dry summers, erratic rains and light- textured soils deficient in organic content, the natural potential of these lands falls short of the nutritional requirements of the animals, adversely affecting livestock's adult body weight, reproduction rates, milk production, morbidity and mortality rates. A narrow bone to meat ratio is also found when animals graze solely on degraded lands. There are great prospects for improving these natural rangelands at a low investment cost, for example, through reseeding with nutritious, perennial and high yielding grasses and legumes. Large scale fodder tree plantations should be taken up on pasture lands, waste lands, river banks and road sides and the bunds of ponds, canals and agriculture fields.

Migratory or semi migratory system of goat rearing is practiced in regions where there is scarcity of food for whole or part of the year. Migration of goats is in search of food. Daily movement of goats from home to the grazing fields is recognised as an important aspect of management within the rural goat production system . Nomadism exists since thousands of years. The herds follow the fodder and the herders follow the herds. It is a well-adapted lifestyle for marginal areas (arid and semiarid regions). Nomads are interested in gaining wealth just as most humans, but since they do not have any permanent settlements, it needs to be "movable wealth". Animals are this movable wealth.

Goat in migratory production system depends solely on common grazing resources to fulfill their nutritional requirement. Hence the cost of feed and fodder for goat during migration becomes almost zero. The practice of migration is mostly common in large sheep/goat flocks of arid region especially in Rajasthan,

Gujarat, Jammu & Kashmir and Himachal Pradesh. Migratory goat keepers (nomads) when they reach Uttar Pradesh, Haryana and Punjab usually charge something which can be money or goods like grains, ghee etc for staying their flock in cultivable fallow fields on per night basis. As a result, landowner gets manure in the form of urine and droppings of goats for his field and migratory goat keeper gets something in return. The Phulwani tract in Orissa is another migratory route. The sheep/goat flocks from Ganjam district migrate to Chilka area and Phulwani forest (up to 200 km). Even the small farmers owning 8-10 goats fix a person as grazer who collect around 100 goats from 8-10 farmers and is responsible for grazing and managing the goats during migration. In return the grazer gets cloths and salt from the goat owners and he also retain the income from migrating animals earned in the form of milk and charges for staying the animals during night in the field of other farmers. The goat keepers during migration also get access and opportunities to sell their goats in the animal markets spread along the migratory route. In migratory system, labour is the major cost of rearing goats, which has negligible opportunity cost. Therefore, goat rearing under migratory system becomes more profitable as compared to semi-intensive (traditional flock) and intensive organized flocks.

It has been observed that nomadism and transhumance animal husbandry offers the best productive system from an ecological point of view for the use of fragile ecosystems. That cannot be easily stopped or reversed. Therefore, there is need to improve the productivity of migratory flocks. To get the optimum production from the migratory flocks, the efforts are needed for improved breeding, better management, feeding, effective disease prevention and control and marketing. To begin with, it is essential to map the seasonal movement of nomadic and semi-nomadic and migratory type of shepherds and to obtain information on the class and number of animals and the seasonal fluctuation in stock number. The development and extension activities for small ruminants should be based on 'watering points' on the route of migration of stock instead of revenue district. The state especially Rajasthan, Jammu & Kashmir, Himachal Pradesh, Gujarat and Uttar Pradesh would require surveying the pattern of migration and establishing service centers along the migratory routes, particularly on the watering points. It is economics that suggest that under adverse conditions, migration is a resilient way of life and under optimal conditions, it is productive activity.

Under nomadic conditions, certain skills and adaptation mechanism are requested by the animals. Not every species is suitable for a life under such harsh conditions. Among these specific requirements are the adaptations to water scarcity; whereas cattle and sheep need to drink water every two to three days, goats can cope without water for four to five days. Camels can do so even for up to two weeks. Due to that, the grazing radius of camels and goats around a water source is much larger than that of cattle or sheep. An important system of small ruminant production prevalent in dry and cold arid regions of the country is transhuman (migratory) where the flocks follow well-established migration routes year after year for feed and water. Migration is a way by which every now and then new surroundings and new pastures are introduced to the goat and sheep flocks. Frequent changes in pasture/fodder give the animals an opportunity to fulfill their nutritional requirements and to consume various fodder ingredients, minerals, and vitamins and help them to remain healthy. The compulsions leading to emergence and persistence of transhumance in our country derive from its environment. The precariousness of agricultural practice and low agricultural yield characteristic of arid and semiarid region have entailed the distribution of production risk between two subsistence techniques, agriculture and pastoration. The utilisation of large tract of unareable and marginal land, alongwith the use of seasonally fallow rain crop tracts, as pastures, form the primary basis of the transhumance (migratory) system. Migration in fact is a necessary condition of existing large-scale small ruminant production in arid regions of the country.

The migration in goats is much less as compared to sheep however the large flocks of goats having 80 to 100 goats or more in these regions do follow the transhumance system. The largest migration takes place in the state of Rajasthan, where around 35 lakhs small ruminants mostly sheep migrate every year to M.P., U.P., Punjab and Haryana. These numbers go up to 60 to 70 lakhs during the year of severe droughts. There are two kinds of migratory flocks in Rajasthan: (i) flocks migrating largely from Jaisalmer, Barmer, Jalore, Pali, Nagaur, Ajmer districts leave the village soon after Deepawali (late October – early November) and return with the onset of monsoon. (ii) The flocks (mostly sheep) on permanent migration graze in the forest areas of M.P., U.P., Gujarat, Haryana and Punjab. These flocks traditionally come to the areas of Bundi, Kota, Jhalawar Sawaimadhopur, Chittorgarh and Bhilwara districts during the monsoon season and remain in and around these districts up to October. The flocks in Himalayan region migrate to mountains and highlands in summer months for alpine grazing along with the sheep and return back to foothill and lowland valleys during winter. The migration starts in the month of April, when the flocks move to alpine pastures at high altitude and descending down in the month of October. During the period of April to October, they graze on bushes, shrubs and other ground vegetation. During winters, goats are supplemented with stored dry fodder, tree leaves, and grains to a limited scale. They are penned in closed houses for protection from severe cold.

There are three pastoral groups of Himalayas which inhabit Ladakh, Sikkim and Himachal Pradesh which raise livestock including goats. The Changpas nomads of Changthang raise herds of sheep and Pashmina goats, yaks and horses. The Gaddis of Bharmour are agropastoralists and raise large flocks of sheep and goats. The Bhutias of North Sikkim are agro-pastoralists and raise local cows and ox, yaks, sheep, goats and ponies. These societies use animals as providers of food, fuel, fiber, draught power and transportation. However, nomadic, semi-nomadic and transhumant pastoralist societies have lifestyles that revolve mainly around their livestock. The transhumant pastoral societies inhabiting the high Himalayan areas exploit the seasonal abundance of grazing areas. As social and ecological conditions change, pastoralists adjust accordingly. Pastoralists play an important role in the ecology of India. Their production of organic manure contributes to the maintenance of soil fertility.

Since pastoralists do not own land, their produce is generated by dependence on communally and state-owned grazing land. Currently, the trend towards globalization of the market, with pastoral lands increasingly being commercialised and/or turned in to national parks has created problems for the pastoralists. Due to neglect by officials and policy makers, pastoralists face deprivation from their traditional and customary rights to these grazing areas. Due to changing circumstances, the pastoralists have brought adjustments in many aspects of the traditional pastoral system, including migratory cycle, local economy and social organisation. Many of them left their traditional transhumant way of life and settled along valleys. Some have settled in urban areas; others stick to the pastoral activities by changing the composition of livestock by increasing number of goats and decreasing number of yaks. Natural exigencies-extreme weather conditions, drought, epidemics and predators result in reduction of animals including goats.

Small-scale mixed farming systems, in which crops and animals are integrated on the same farm, are more important than either the grassland-based or industrial livestock systems in terms of their contribution to the total output of animal products in India. Mixed farming is more economical in developing countries in the sense that the waste products (crop residues) of one enterprise (crop production) can be used by another enterprise (animal production), which returns its own waste (manure) back to the first enterprise. Focusing on improving small-scale mixed farming systems and farming systems for the small ruminants can much more beneficial in terms of poverty reduction than working on intensive industrial systems. As semi-arid areas are drought prone areas with a high depletion of natural resources, the adoption of farming systems based on the development and adoption of local innovations and local knowledge will be more suitable. Even if such systems are not highly profitable, they at least allow resource poor farmers to make a living and they contribute to protect environment and natural resources. Bottom up approaches and methods in terms of programs and projects design should be adopted.

Semi-intensive system

A semi intensive system of goat management is a combination of limited free-range grazing and stall feeding. Animals belonging to several owners may be combined for grazing in the morning and evening for 4 to 6 hours. The animals are supplemented with kitchen wastes, concentrate mixtures, crop residues, green and dry fodders and tree leaves according to availability. Thus livestock utilise all available feed resources, including natural grasses, shrubs, bushes, tree leaves, crop residues, stubbles, weeds, cultivated fodders and concentrates etc. under this system. The level of nutrition is just optimum or below but a definite improvement on the extensive system.

Studies show that the natural range/grazing lands in India cannot support livestock for commercial milk and meat production without supplementation of additional energy and protein through concentrates. If the roughage portion of the diet can be made available from grazing, the remaining 50 percent of the diet has to be supplemented through concentrate mixture.

Intensive system

The goats can be kept tethered or under intensive system. The intensive system of goat management includes grazing on developed pastures or complete stall feeding on cultivated fresh or conserved fodders, crop residues and concentrates. This system requires high labour and capital investment and is suitable for only intensive milk and meat production. Stocking rates of 15 to 20 goats/ sheep per hectare are feasible depending on the type of grass, level of fertilisation and the presence and absence of legumes and fodder trees. Increasing agriculture pressure on land resources is making intensive and semi-intensive system of management more popular. In the intensive production system the animals are being pushed towards maximizing productivity, whilst in the extensive and small holder systems in developing countries animal productivity and welfare are compromised by inadequate nutrition. This statement appears to hold forth for goat nutrition too.

Zero grazing: This is the most intensive form of production in which goats are confined or tethered all the time. Tethering is popular with small-holders because of shortage of grazing land in predominantly cropped areas or in cities. This system also reduces labour inputs. Often the grazing orbit of the goat is determined by the length of the tether. This restriction does not permit free selection of feed from natural pasture which matures rapidly and has a low N and mineral content.This type of system is mostly practiced in thickly populated areas of cities where goat are kept on kitchen or industrial wastes, vegetable peelings etc. This type of system is suitable only when small number of goats is maintained. Barbari breed of goats are found to be especially suitable for this type of system in India.

The intensive system is practised in cities where one or few goats are stall fed and taken individual care. While the extensive system involves a large number of animals which are allowed to browse on the range, in the intensive system of management, the animals can be protected from the extremes of environmental influence. This type of management permits the utilization of largely unused resources for animal production under intensive conditions. In the extensive system, the animals are subjected to extremes of environmental conditions. This form of management cannot or only to a limited extent be used by other herbivores. Goats are managed almost semi-extensively and they live on grasses of road side, home yard. They survive mostly on browse obtained from bushes, shrubs and tree leaves. Although recommended concentrate feeds are seldom given to goats in the field conditions, they are being raised in remote place on almost zero input. There is an increasing tendency in livestock farming in the tropics towards intensive and semi-intensive production system. Under intensive and semi-intensive system, greater consideration is given to the health and nutritional needs of goats.

Stall fed goats have certain advantages as compared to open grazed goats but some disadvantages too:

- Conservation of energy, which otherwise the animal would have wasted in hunting after the fodder.
- Better conversion of energy, available from feed and fodder into flesh and milk.
- Prevention of indiscriminate grazing, thereby offering optimum scope for re-growth of fodder.
- Prevention of uncontrolled mating.
- Better collection &utilization of manure.
- Goats and their kids can be sold and encashed anytime. They are like bearer blank cheques.
- Control and reduction of parasitic re-infestation.
- Close supervision and easy management.
- Easy access for record keeping.
- No danger from wild animals.

Some of the so-called features of goat management which have been discussed here are only indicative and the actual practising of the various operations described here may vary with the conditions.

Type of goat management determines the economics of goat enterprise. It also determines the integration of goat production in to the wider farming system. Understanding the importance of goat production system in the context of larger farming and social systems will ensure appropriate management decisions in goat farming. Basic requirements of goat welfare and good management system include the following

- Food and water to sustain health and vitality
- Sufficient space to provide freedom to stand, lie down, stretch, turn around and groom themselves

- Protection from predation
- Protection from disease, including disease that can be exacerbated by management
- Protection from extremes of climate during certain phases of their life and
- Protection from pain, suffering and injury.

Scientific goat management

The economics of goats keeping, however, depends a great deal on scientific management. It involves proper breeding, proper feeding, proper housing as also looking after the herd health, care of the young, care of the common ailments and diseases, cleanliness etc., and a hygienic milking procedure. Stress conditions are known to reduce goat productivity. The management practices that improve animal welfare in goat farms lead to a higher performance. The best management, therefore, is one which leads to higher production and economic return. An array of managemental factors e.g. housing and bedding, restraining systems, space and crowding, transport conditions, stunning and slaughter methods, castration of males and tail docking etc affect welfare of goats.

Some goat facts

Goats produce a distinctive sound called bleating. Normal goat feces are usually voided in piles of individual pellets 0.5 to 1.0 cm in diameter. A daily sweeping of the goat yard keeps the goats clean and free from parasites.

General management guidelines

- In widespread to heavy rainfall areas, goats need to be housed in dry place or kept in elevated area and dry bedding (straw) should be provided to young animals
- In case of warning of floods, the goats should be shifted to higher ground immediately. Animals should be housed at dry places and should have proper ventilation.
- Area should be cleared of water accumulation and disinfected using bleaching powder and lime application.
- Goats should not be allowed to graze in water logged areas.
- Goats to be observed for diseases like pneumonia, nasal discharge, wounds and injuries and services of veterinary doctor be taken for treatment
- Clean drinking water should be ensured round the clock and water troughs / feeders should be regularly cleaned
- Feeds for goats should be protected from fungal contamination and wet

feeds to be dried and fed. Feeds should be protected from exposure to wet conditions

- 10-20g salt for each goat should be provided daily through feed.
- Fortified complete feed blocks to be provided particularly to the pregnant and animals in milk. Requirement of energy may be met by providing crude jaggery or molasses, if available and economic. Dry roughages can be sprayed with 10% molasses or crude jaggery solution and 2% urea for maintenance of animals.
- Top feeds/tree leaves available in the area can be fed to meet the dry matter requirement.
- Damaged grain (not fungus contaminated) to be diverted for livestock feeding
- Sheds constructed for goats should be properly ventilated
- Mangers should be daily cleared off leftover and disinfected once a month.
- Growing and milking animals should be provided with concentrate supplements and green grass to be mixed with dry straws before feeding.
- Goats should be vaccinated against FMD, Brucellosis, Haemorrahagic Septicaemia, PPR and Goat Pox.
- Goats need to be dewormed with suitable anti-helmentic drug and treated for ecto-parasites, if any.
- Carcass of dead goats should be buried deep to avoid spread of diseases to other animals.

Identification of goats

External characteristics of goats have been used to identify the animal. Proper identification system for goats is needed to deliver the requirements for traceability and animal health. The ears in different breeds may be long and pendulous (Jamunapari) or small and erect (Barbari) or medium sized. The ears are used for identification of the animal either by Tattooing or tagging. Ear tagging using metal or plastic have been used at organized goat farms. Tatooing is a time tested, permanent and economical system which is practiced most often. Electronic identification system in developed countries has been advocated for the purpose. However, this is a costly proposition for developing countries.

Judging the age

The goat has about 12 to 15 years of life span under normal conditions. Age of the goat can be judged by dentition. Both the kids and adults have eight teeth on the lower jaw. These are small and sharp in kids. At about 1 year of age the central pair drops out and is replaced by two large permanent teeth, at 2 years of age, 2 more small teeth drop out and are replaced by two larger teeth, one or each side of the first pair, at three years of age, a complete set of permanent teeth. After this the degree of wear and tear gives rough indication of age.

Methods of restraining goats

Goats do not bite, strike or kick but are funny. They vocalize and they may stamp their feet in obvious threat, but once they grabbed they do not strike. They do, however, use their heads for butting; The bucks usually have heavy horns which can inflict serious injury on the unwary. The initial approach to handling a goat is that one arm is placed around the goats chest as the other hand grabs the tail. Goats are far more agile and much better jumpers than sheep. The fences must be more than 6 feet or higher. Although the horn's can be used for initial capture, goats dislike being held by horns or ears. To hold a goat without a collar or a halter, place the open hands on each side of the lower jaw beneath the ears. The beard can be grasped to assist in immobilizing the head. A small goat can be restrained by holding one leg.

Recording Body weight

Knowing the body weight is very useful for good animal management, including understanding medication doses, adjusting feed supply, monitoring growth and choosing replacement males and females. The most intuitive way to assess body mass is weighing animals with a spring balance, a steelyard balance or any suitable scale. However, such devices are too expensive for most of small farmers. Heights and girth measurements can also be used to calculate body weight of goat.

Dehorning of goats

Due to the linkage of polled condition with infertility in certain males, it is now preferred to go far dehorning the male rather than selecting the male for polled condition. In India where most of the breeds are horned, such infertility problems perhaps don't exist but in organised goat dairying, it is preferable to have the animals dehorned. Removing the horn buds from kids is easily done at the age of 5 to 7 days. First, hair from the area of the horn buds are clipped and surrounding area is covered with petroleum jelly to protect it from caustic potash stick. The caustic potash stick is then thoroughly rubbed on the bud until the horn button is well blistered. Mature goats can be dehorned by sawing the horns close to the head with a meat saw. This should be done during cool weather and wounds should be coated with pineter or other disinfectant repellant. To permanently prevent the growth of the horn it is necessary to saw very close to the head to remove the growing layer.

There is a difference in the horn structure of goats which makes advisable the use of the hot iron for dehorning or debudding young kids. The horns of a goat grow from the top of the head rather than the side, as with cattle. Dehorning goats at a late age presents a problem. With the horns removed, the sinuses are open on top allowing direct and debris to collect, but not allowing good drainage. Also, the horns must be sawed off manually with a hacksaw or wire saw. Due to the shape and placement of the horns, electric saws will not fit and because of closeness of the horn bases, neither will manual dehorners. A flexible saw is required so that the contour of the head can be followed.

Record keeping

It is helpful to keep records of flock performance. Records should include inventory of animals, production, reproduction, health and financial accounts records. These records are helpful in culling of animals on age, health or production grounds. The financial records should mention all sales by way of animals, produce (milk, meat, fibre, manure etc) and all purchases such as feed, concentrate, medicines, wages and interest on establishment or capital etc). The profit made by the goat flock is the value of total sales minus the value of total purchase.

Transport

Some times the goats have to be transported long distances such as haat or cattle markets, slaughter houses and sold to far off places. Small number can be transported for short distances by rickshaw, motor cycle, cycle, tempo etc. Large number transport is by truck or train. In India goats are frequently transported from market to slaughterhouse mainly by truck (Das *et al.*, 2001). Transportation can cause emotional and physical stress in goats that can affect their well-being. Transportation stress may lead to increased frequency of aggressive encounters like pushing and fighting. Sick, weak or extremely thin goats should not be transported. The transport stress some times is fatal to the goats, so overcrowding and heat stress should be avoided. Enough space should be allowed to each animal to stand comfortably. Proper feeding and watering should be ensured during long journeys. Stressful transportation can affect the carcass quality and health of goats.

Housing of Goats

Proper housing is required to protect the goats from vagaries of environment and from predation. It is generally believed that goats do not require housing. In fact, like other domestic animals, goats also need shelter for protection from inclement weather such as rains (in particular), extreme cold during winter and excessive heat load during summer. Although goats have adapted to diverse and adverse climates without the aid of man-made shelters and support, maintenance of good health and dairy productivity require minimizing the stresses associated with excessive heat, cold, humidity, and wind. Normally goats do not require elaborate housing facilities, but minimum provisions will definitely increase productivity, especially protection against inclement weather conditions and predation. Often, the flocks are penned in the open during fair weather and some temporary shelters are made use of in monsoon and winter. Housing systems for goats varies considerably. Farmers use different kinds of housing such as brick-walled, earth floored and grass thatched structures whilst some farmers use part of the family house. Under extensive system, farmers use either open or walled enclosures with tin or asbestos roofs. Housing requirements of goats under intensive system depend on climate, level of adaptation, breed and production system. Measures to protect kids from cold during winter are essential.

In the southern states of India where the weather is wet, they are provided with dry housing; therefore, sheds on stilts are erected adjacent to the owner's house with an extension of the roof. The floor is elevated about 1-1.5 m to facilitate cleaning. Another floor underneath the slatted one is provided; it is here that the urine and dung are collected. Palm leaves or tiles are used as roofing materials and bamboo or wooden slates are used for flooring. Facilities for feeding concentrates and roughage are also provided in the goat house. In drier parts of this region, ground level houses are constructed by a few organized farmers. This type of housing is about 2-3 m high at the front and 1-1.5 m high at the back. Usually, a thatched roof with mud flooring is common to these houses.

Housing is required in winter and field shelter is needed in summer. This is particularly important at kidding time and after shearing.

- Construct shed on dry and properly raised ground.
- Avoid water-logging, marshy areas.
- In low lying and heavy rainfall areas, the floors should be preferably elevated.
- In temperate Himalayan region, the floor may be made of wood.
- Bucks should be housed in individual pens.
- Does can be housed in groups upto 60 per pen.
- Provide proper shade and cool drinking water in summer.
- Dispose of dung and urine properly.

Goats may be kept under wide shady trees, where available. But, it is preferable to house them in a shed or small barn which is well lighted and also well ventilated. The shed must be clean and dry. Dampness is dangerous, as goats easily catch cold which may later develop into pneumonia (one of the few diseases to which goats are quite susceptible). Cheap houses with low roofs and large corral, hanging bay tracks, water buckets, concentrate trays, kid boxes and raised platforms with narrow drains are prerequisites for the proper care of the milking does. The ideal width of the shed is 3 m to 3.6 m, with a manger 36 cm wide, running through the centre. Goats are tied on either side and about a square metre of space should be allotted to each goat. The milch goats, specially, should not be allowed to run together in their pens for getting roughages and concentrates. They are preferably fed in separate stalls, or in a group of 8 to 10 does. It is better to house them in groups of 30 to 40. Thus a goat house should provide safety, comfort, cleanliness and convenience for handling the animals.

Where animals are kept stanchioned, a minimum of about 21 feet by 5 feet is required for each animal. This presupposes that the goats will receive adequate exercise in outside pens or range. Where goats are shut in the barn during parts of the day or night, bus not confined to stanchions, from 15 to 20 sq.ft. should be allowed for each goat.

The important features of ideal goat housing are as under:

- Animal Sheds should remain dry and comfortable to the animals.
- There should be provision for sufficient space. The space requirement of various categories of goats is as under:

Category of goats	Per goat space requirement (m^2)	
	Covered space	Open space
Kids up to 3 months of age	0.2-03	0.4-06
3 to 9- month old kids	0.75	1.5
9 to 12- month old kids	1.00	2.00
Adult dry does	1.00	2.00
Pregnant & lactating does	1.5-2.0	3.0-4.0
Breeding bucks	1.5-2.0	3.0-4.0

Source: CIRG

Provide sufficient ventilation ie. 5-10, 25 , 75 and 100 % of floor area during winter, comfortable, hot dry and hot humid seasons, respectively.

- Over turn the soil to ensure soft and comfortable surface
- Use lime @ 10 kg/100 m2 of floor area to avoid excessive dampness in the goat sheds
- Replace old soil once every year after winter season
- Bricks or cement concrete floor need proper washing and disinfection. Do not allow goats on wet surface.

Goat houses can be made up of traditional material such as thatch or modern material like asbestos roof and iron /concrete pillars and walls.

Drinking troughs should be easy to clean and depend on the number of goats in the flock. For small flocks, simple bucket are sufficient. For large flocks, trough made up of cement and bricks with about 1.5 feet high may be constructed. The area around the trough may be brick lined in a slanting way so that water should not accumulate around the trough. Kutcha ground will soon become muddy and can cause foot disorders. The feeding trough should be white washed periodically and lime is used to keep the water clean and sparkling. The goats should not be allowed to get inside the trough.

Goat sanitation or hygiene

Goat hygiene is important to keep the animal healthy, productive and as an aid to control diseases. Livestock hygiene including goat is key to improvement of the environmental management system. Goat farmers can be trained or educated in proper hygienic practices using a process of social mobilization. Proper fencing is the key to goat hygiene. Fencing prevents access to dogs, predators etc. Pests like rodents and birds should be controlled by various means. Foot bath at the entrance of goat houses can be very helpful in reducing infection to the animals. The foot bath solution may be either 5-10 % copper sulphate or 5 % formalin (Formaldehyde). Sprinkling of lime on floor can help in keeping the floor dry as well free from infection. This should be coupled with a proper and efficient method of waste disposal. The droppings can be collected and deposited in a pit for vermicomposting. Vermicomposting is an additional source of income if carried out scientifically. Further, goat houses should provide proper ventilation and hygienic atmosphere inside the goat house. Simple cleaning of the udder before and after milking has been found to reduce the chances of mastitis.

The milking should be done in a clean utensil and all precautions should be taken to keep the milk clean before consumption. Microbiocidal solutions can also be used in goat houses and slaughter houses for disease control. However, the following should be kept strictly in mind.

1. Use biocides safely. Always read the label and product information before use.
2. Keep disease free animals away from infected animals.
3. Raise kids in a disease free environment and prevent them from contacting infected animals or contaminated quarters.
4. Keep the goat yards or houses as clean as possible.

Predation is one of producers' major concerns and certainly represents a threat or constraint to goat producers. Goats on rangeland and wasteland are vulnerable to predation. Many wild animals have traditionally predated on goats grazing in the forests. Predators causing problem with goats include domestic dog, fox, tigers or other wild cats, wild hogs, golden eagles, python (Ajgar) etc., and in the case of the kid, many other small mammals and birds. Lion, Tigers, leopards, Coyotes (Bhediya in Hindi), hyena, wild dogs, foxes and Python (Azgar in hindi)etc. are known for predation of goats. Python snake, also known as Ajgar, is one of the most massively built snakes of the Indian subcontinent which is known to attack goats. In such cases goat generally die because of strangulation and swallowed whole. Domestic dogs (commonly more than one) typically attack the animal in an indiscriminate manner, often leaving multiple injuries on a number of animals.There are numerous approaches to prevent or evade losses to predation, but the persistent nature and seriousness of the problem may be taken as an indication that none of these are totally satisfactory. Animal management can be used to some extent to evade predator losses. Fencing is generally employed to prevent predators from entering the sheds. However, fencing is a costly option. Goat has been a common choice as a bait since times immemorial while going to Shikar for hunting tiger, lion etc.

Goat manure and waste disposal

The droppings of goat increase the fertility of soil. Goat flocks are allowed to be herded overnight in the field and the farmers pay the flock owner in cash or kind. Goat droppings are used as manure for organic farming. Penning of goat herds in harvested fields (goat folding) brings in additional income to the flock owners (Bhat and Khan, 2009). The solid excreta of the goat is several times richer in manurial ingredients than that of cows/buffalo. One adult goat produces around 0.8 to 1.0 tonne per year. Goat droppings from infected animals can carry bacteria such as Salmonella, Campylobacter, and E. coli.

In India, nearly 2000 million tons (MT) of animal wastes, 300 MT of crop wastes, besides huge amount of agro-industrial and domestic sewage waste is produced annually (Mishra, 2001) and therefore there is a tremendous scope for recycling of this waste using vermitechnologies so that quality organic manure is produced. Goats produce about 120 million tones of manure per year in India.

Goat keepers are generally not much aware or interested to know about economic importance of goat faeces. Dumping of goat faeces in an open area for use as manure under natural decomposition is a common practice resulting in loss of nutrients due to direct exposure to sunlight, temperature and rainfall. The practice created foul smell and provides favorable conditions to various insect and pests growth. In this process, decomposition also takes long time to mineralize nutrients for conversion into manure. Commercial goat farms can benefit from vermi composting of goat manure. Goat keepers may enhance their income by making vermicompost from goat faeces. This can be marketed for organic crop, vegetable or ornamental plant productions. Goat producers can also use vermicompost for their own farms, which has better nutrient densities because of reduced nutrient losses due to lowered decomposition time and fasten mineralization process. Plant material *i.e. Saccharum munja, Calitropis sp. Azadirachta indica, Ficus benghalensis* and grasses can be mixed with goat faeces. A special kind of earth worms easily converts these in to vermicompost in a very short time. While sole plant material as such are not ingested by earthworm and took months together for conversions into vermicompost (CIRG technique).There are many species of earthworm which can be used for vermin composting but Eisinia foetida is most popular species of earthworm which is used for vermin composting now a days.

Breed selection

Whenever we talk of sheep/goat raising, the question which breed to keep crops up first among a few other important things. Selection of breed will depend on the purpose of goat keeping. If it is for milk then choose a milch breed and if it is for meat, then the locally available goat meat breed will be most suitable. It may not be advisable to bring a breed from a very far off place. The best would be to use a more available breed, knowing that a careful and proper breeding programme could upgrade any breed and may even give many of the desired qualities of the less-available breed. By adding and using one special ram/buck, at a later stage might help accomplish your breeding goal.

The goats purchased from whatever source need to be transported to the farm. Transport of animals including goats is stressful and some of the animals are not able to sustain this stress and succumb to the stress causing economic loss to the owners. A suitable transport system should be able to reduce the transport stress so that mortality or morbidity is as low as possible. The transport vehicle should not be over crowded. For short distance, the goats are sometimes transported in mini trucks or vans. Individual goats are sometimes transported on a motorcycle, rickshaw, bicycle etc. Long distance transport is some times undertaken by railways or water boats or ships etc. Special care and arrangement must be made for proper food, water etc during long distance transport.The goats after reaching the farm should not be mixed with the existing flock immediately, instead they should be kept under quarantine minimum for four weeks. Some countries need health certificate papers while transporting goats.

When a farmer starts a goat farm, he purchases goats from various sources. It is always best to purchase goats from the breeding tract of the breed selected for the farm. The purchase can be made either directly from the farmers, or from *Haats* or animal markets held in the area. The goats can also be procured from government or private livestock farms who dispose of animals which become surplus from their own requirements.

Normally the goats purchased for breeding stock are of one to two years old (Ek daant or do daant- Single or twin teeth). Animals should not be purchased from areas having known incidence of FMD, PPR or JD, Brucellosis etc.

Management of male goat

Goats attain puberty at an early age which depends on the breed. It is imperative that males be separated from females at an early age. Goats should not be used for semen collection before one year of age. Importance of proper nutrition and exercise in breeding buck management needs to be emphasised although scientific experiments on this aspect are sparse.

To keep the buck in good breeding condition, there should be an opportunity to exercise. The buck should not be overfed and should not be allowed to run with the does. It is best to house the males apart from the does. Cleanliness helps to reduce odors.

What a pedigree breeder needs most is knowledge of both genetics and various desirable strains he could make his choice from. His first consideration evidently will be the vitality and good health enjoyed generally by a breed. The second will be a stock of known capacity for milk production, its inherent milking capacity, feed intake capacity and feed to milk conversion efficiency. A well chosen breeding male can, indeed influence a whole range of succeeding generations.

One buck is required for breeding of 25-30 goats. Selection of breeding buck from the same herd for several generations should not be practiced to avoid inbreeding.

Bucks for breeding should be selected on the basis of 9 or 12 months body weight. Bucks should be provided with extra concentrate @ 300-400 gm/day during the breeding season.

Castration

Castration is the removal or destruction of the testes, epididymis and a portion of each spermatic cord from a buck. Castration is known to increase the growth rate and feed utilization of male goats. Male kids which are not required for breeding can be castrated. Castrated animals are usually less aggressive and easier to manage. Castration of male kids can be done using Burdizzo castrator when they are 10 days to 3 weeks of age. The Burdizzo is an instrument used to crush the spermatic cords and associated blood vessels leading to the testicles, thus destroying the blood supply for the testes. Without this blood supply, the testicles degenerate and atrophy. This method is known as a "bloodless" method since no cutting is done and when done properly even the skin is not broken. While no castration method is completely painless, the least painful is the Burdizzo method. Castration can also be carried out by banding. It is also believed that castration reduces the goaty smell in meat and therefore increases the acceptability of goat meat.

Management of female goat

Care of pregnant and post-parturient goats and new born kids

A normal gestation period for a doe goat is 145-155 days with the average gestation being 150 days. There are generally three stages of labor that may vary in length and intensity, depending on the doe and doe's age. First stage labor may begin 24 hours before delivery. Signs of first stage labor include pawing the bedding, nesting, restlessness, looking back at her sides, white discharge from the vulva, vulva becomes flabby, and doe hollows out, lifts tail and becomes vocal. The doe will become soft around the tail head as the muscles relax to allow delivery. The beginning of second stage labor is signaled by labor pains and pushing. A water bag is normally visible at this time which may break or remain intact. A second bag may appear with darker fluid. Following the presentation of the water bags, the doe will normally get down to business. Doe will usually lay down to strain and may bleat loudly. The doe may stand, turn around several times and paw the bedding, then lay back down again to push. This routine may happen several times. Assuming a normal delivery, the nanny delivers a kid in less than an hour after beginning to push. Sometimes the doe may need a little help to just get the head delivered. Never pull while the doe is resting. Always work with the doe by pulling at the same time she is having a contraction. If there is a need to correct an abnormal position , do the correction during a resting period. When pulling, be sure to pull down toward the doe's feet.

Clear the kid's nose with a clean towel and lay the kid by the doe's nose if she doesn't get up to clean it off. Stage three labor is the delivery of the afterbirth. This takes several hours.

The most important thing after kidding is to make sure that the kids receive colostrum within the first ½ hour to an hour after birth.

The condition of the doe during gestation will have great influence on the quality of kids at birth. The goats should be examined for pregnancy at 3 months of age and if possibly at one month of age with the help of ultrasound. Those goats which are found pregnant should be separated. The pregnant goats should be well fed, allowed liberal exercise and protected from adverse climate. Under-feeding of goats during pregnancy leads to production of weak and under weight kids. Chances of parturitional problems are also more. Mishandling and over excitement during later stage of pregnancy should be avoided.

In case of large herds, a separate kidding shed with a provision of cubicles for keeping goats individually is essentially required.

Preparation for Kidding

The kidding shed should be cleaned and disinfected before the doe's due date.

Do provide a clean pen, well bedded with straw, dry grass or shavings, for your does to kid in cleanliness especially for the first three days is most important to the new arrival. The following supplies are normally required at kidding.

- A good light in the delivery area.
- A clean bucket for water.
- Surgical scrub or a bottle of mild detergent for cleaning hands and the vulva of the doe.
- Obstetrical lubricant (K-Y) and, if possible, disposable obstetrical gloves for assisted births.
- Dry towels for cleaning and rubbing kids.
- Iodine (7% tincture) for dipping navels. A small jar or film canister for individual use is handy. Dip navel immediately after birth, and repeat in 12 hours.
- Scissors for umbilical cord.
- Clean bottle and nipple for feeding colostrum.
- Feeding tube and large syringe (35-60 cc, with catheter tip) for giving colostrum to weak kids.

1. About a week before the expected date of kidding, the doe should not be taken out for grazing and shifted to the kidding shed.
2. It is necessary to protect both mother and young one from both excessive heat and cold.
3. Kids should have colostrum within 15-30 minutes of birth. The longer it takes them to get it, the less effective it is.
4. Paint the navel immediately with 7% iodine (Lugol's iodine) or Betadine .
5. Do not be in too big a hurry to help the doe do her kidding. Going in and pulling the kid should be avoided until you are certain she would not make it otherwise.
6. Provide the doe after kidding with a bucket of clean water.
7. Its mouth and nostrils should be wiped clean, as soon as the kid arrives.
8. The doe should be kept in the same cubicle for 3-4 days after kidding. Thereafter, she may be allowed to go out for grazing with other goats.

Signs of approaching parturition in goat

1. Sunken at tail and hip.
2. Udder has shiny look.

3. Heavy breathing and worried look.
4. Looking back at sides and talking.
5. Restlessness.
6. Great display of affection for keeper.

Silent heat periods

Some dairy goats when at peak of their lactation show only feeble signs of estrus. One has to be a close observer in order to determine when these animals are manifesting signs of heat. They may be so engrossed in milk production that the desire to breed is very faint and of a short duration. When their lactation begins to subside the periods become more marked and noticeable.

The time of parturition is most critical period both for the mother and newly born young one. Inefficiency or negligence at the time of parturition may lead to high rate of neonatal mortality. Therefore, it is advised that in organized goat farms, the workers need to be sensitized that they donot proceed on leave during the kidding season and should be prepared to work overtime during this period.

Major points in breeding management of female goats are

- Knowledge of breeding season-major breeding season are (May-June and Sept-October.
- Knowledge about right time for breeding. The oestrus duration in goats normally varies from 24-36 hrs. Right time for breeding is towards end of estrus when ovulation takes place.
- Tropical goats like Jamunapari or Barbari have short or long cycles. Does coming in heat for the first time during breeding season should not be bred at first estrus. Instead the second heat period is best for insemination.
- First time a female can be bred after it attains 65-70% of adult body weight.
- Avoid inbreeding.
- Number of males to be maintained for breeding should be in proportion to the number of breeding does. It is 1:10 under uncontrolled breeding and 1:20 under controlled breeding system.

Management of lactating goats

Goats should be milked at regular interval after kidding. Once daily milking is common for goats kept by farmers in the field. Once daily milking reduces the quantity of milk produced as compared to twice daily milking but also reduces the labor costs involved in milking . For best results, the goats should be milked twice a day, *ie* morning and evening. Thrice daily milking has been shown to increase the milk yield of goats by 5-11 % and this increase was affected by the stage of lactation (Henderson *et al.,* 1983).Once daily milking resulted in an 18% reduction in the yield of 4% fat-corrected milk compared to twice daily milking in goats (Salama *et al.,* 2003). Goats are generally milked by hand but in advanced countries, machine milking is sometimes practiced. Machine milking though prevalent in advanced western countries, is not economically viable in India. A large round or globular udder is a good indicator of milking ability of goat. A good milk goat should have a good conformation with a well-developed body. A soft shining coat is a good indicator of health. Farmers should wash the udders of the goats prior to milking and should use teat-dips after milking. Mastitis can be a problem, especially on farms where the goats are not kept clean, teat dips are not used, or where goats are overcrowded.

Sound health of the udder is the most important in production of safe and suitable milk for human consumption. Goat mastitis should be considered as the serious condition because of reduction in quality and quantity of milk which can lead to potential zoonotic problem to the consumer. Mastitis is an inflammation of the udder resulting from infection. Mastitis is described as 'clinical' when there are actual signs of infection such as lumps in the milk, discolouration or watery fluid, or when there is swelling, hardness or heat in the udder. 'Subclinical' mastitis has no outward signs.

Precautions for clean milk production

- People who are ill should not milk.
- The milking shed should be cleaned after each milking and disinfected
- Milker keeps himself, his hands and buckets clean. The doe's udder should be carefully cleaned before and after milking. Remove any dust or dirt from the udder and teats by gentle washing the udder with clean water.
- Both teats should be simultaneously milked.
- Milking from left side as well as from rear is practised but the left side is more convenient and cleaner practice.
- Milking should be gentle, quick and thorough.
- Use a clean bucket or bowl to collect the milk.
- Avoid pulling or stretching the teats or using vigorous up and down movements.

Management of meat goats

Goats chosen for slaughter should be healthy. Animal welfare rules should be applied before slaughtering. The animals must be rested from 8 to 10 hours before slaughtering. Slaughtering process must be applied in the slaughter houses and / or at the places that the municipalities allot for slaughtering. After slaughtering and bleeding is completed, skinning must be applied carefully. During the skinning process, the skin must not be damaged and any meat traces should be avoided on. Hygiene should be at maximum levels during the whole slaughtering process particularly after removing the internal organs. The carcass must be cut into the parts properly. Veterinarians must definitely inspect the animals that would be slaughtered before slaughtering processes especially in big cities.

Methods of slaughter of goats

There are several methods of slaughter of goats.In India mostly slaughtering of goats is done either by way of Halal or Jhatka method. Halal is the method preferred by Muslims and Jhatka by the Hindus/Christians/Sikhs, etc. To slaughter the animals in a humane way stunning of the animals is prescribed, but in most of the cases stunning before slaughtering has yet not been adopted due to certain religious feelings. In the organized slaughter houses in the western countries, captive bolt stunning is common. However, Halal is getting popular because of increased demand from Islamic and ethnic population in many western countries. Muslims are mandatorily prohibited from consuming non-Halal meat, which has either come from non-Halal animals like pig or from a Halal animal slaughtered in the non-Halal manner. People from Qureshi or Khatik community are commonly involved in slaughter of goats in India.

Halal method of slaughtering of goats is the method sanctified as per Islamic law. This method of slaughtering animals consists of a swift, deep incision with a sharp knife on the neck, cutting the jugular veins and carotid arteries of both sides but leaving the spinal cord intact. It is believed by Muslims to kill instantly and painlessly. Islamic dietary law states that a Muslim must not consume blood; however traces of blood may remain within the carcass due to the method of slaughter. However, according to Islamic scholars, it is only necessary to remove 'most' of the blood from the animal. As a result meat produced by the halal method is physically indistinguishable from meat produced in most non-halal slaughterhouses, which also allow as much blood as possible to drain from the carcass to prevent the meat going off quickly. The practice of draining blood from slaughtered animals in the hot climate of the Middle East may also originally have been done to prevent rapid decay of meat. With the coming of Islam the practice of blood letting came to symbolise releasing the holy spirit or the spirit of the animal.

In Jhatka the animal is beheaded in one go using a sharp knife or Khukhri (Nepal). This method is common in Nepal and some parts of India. However, meat of goats slaughtered by this method is Haram for the Moslem.

After exsanguination, the carcass is dressed, that is, the head, feet, hide (except hogs and some veal), excess fat, viscera and offal are removed, leaving only bones and edible muscle. Due to lack of means and tools, dehiding of the carcasses is done on the floor itself, which causes contamination of the meat. The hides and skins are spread on the floor of the slaughtering area. Similarly legs, bones, hooves etc. are not removed immediately from the slaughtering area. Goat carcass are not split in half along the mid ventral axis unlike cattle and pig carcass. Subsequently goat carcass is cut into wholesale pieces.

Evisceration: Evisceration is removal of the fecal material from the intestines. This is generally carried out immediately after the slaughter and is the source of maximum waste material during slaughter. The butchers who carry out illegal slaughtering of animals generally throw visceral material at the community bins and wash the small intestines at their shops itself and thus create pollution problem.

While the slaughter houses in India come under the purview of the Animal Husbandry Division of Ministry of Agriculture mainly for the purpose of funding towards expansion and modernization activities, the respective local bodies are mainly responsible for day-to-day operation/maintenance of the slaughter houses. Most of the slaughter houses are more than 50 years old without adequate basic amenities viz. proper flooring, ventilation, water supply, lairage, transport etc. In addition to these deficiencies, slaughter houses suffer from very low hygiene standard posing a major public health and environmental hazards due to discrete disposal of waste and highly polluted effluent discharge. Unauthorised and illicit slaughtering has also increased manifold and thus the related problems. The butchers are not ready to bear the transportation costs for transporting meat from the slaughter houses to the shops.

However, there is an urgent need to modernize the slaughter procedure and facilities. Some of the points which should be kept in mind while slaughtering the animals include

- Slaughter only healthy goats
- Use clean and isolated area away from houses and locality for slaughter
- Hang the carcass up to bleed and bleed within 15 minutes of slaughter
- Separate skins and carcasses without delay.
- Provide an easy to wash slauther slab as far as possible.
- Strong sharp knife which is not rusted should be used for slaughter.

Contaminated meat can be responsible for many meat borne diseases and food-poisoning.

Equipments required for a small slaughter house

Set of knives -For cutting the carcass.

Knives Sharpener -For keeping the knives in good condition.

Wheel barrows -For moving the carcasses into the slaughtering house.

Gas cylinder -For seingeing the animals.

Electric saw -For sharing the carcass into two parts.

Metallic gloves -For protecting the employees while cutting.

Scales -For weighing

Wash basin, toilet paper, soap, shower,water pressure hose -For cleaning the carcasses

Feeding management

Feeding alone costs 65-70% of the total production cost. It needs attention on following points

- The feed requirement of goats is about 3% (dry matter basis) of the body weight. It needs proper monitoring.
- Ensure a minimum 250 g concentrate and 5 g of each common salt and mineral mixture in the daily diet of the goat.
- Use proper feeding and watering devices. The feeder space requirement of individual adults and kids is 30-40 cm and 10-20 cm respectively.
- Pregnant does should be provided additional feed @ 55 g DCP per doe/day (irrespective size and breed) during last 45 days of pregnancy.
- Lactating does be offered additional feed @ 50 g DCP per kg of milk production.
- Ensure colostrum feeding to the new born kids within 30 minutes from births.

Use of improved feeding devices can reduce the wastage of feed. Some improved devices have been designed at Central Institute for Research on Goats, Mathura.

Health Management and Disease prevention

Protection from common disease forms another important area of scientific management. The following ailments are quite frequent among goats-pneumonia tympany, entrotoxaemia, acetonaemia, pregnancy-toxaemia, eye troubles, worms (tapeworms, round worms, lungworm, ringworm etc.), diarrhea, constipation, caked udder lice, foot and mouth rot and sore teat leading to blood in milk and mastitis. Prophylactic measures include routine vaccination of kids at three months of age and routine deworming at three months interval, preferably before and after the monsoon season. Periodic tests of flock against tuberculosis and parasitic worms are recommended. Caked udder or mastitis should be treated by fomentation with Epson salt solution followed by application of iodex . Foot and mouth rot is common mostly in rainy season. Soaking the affected area with saturated solution of copper sulphate and application of pine tar promotes healing after infection has been controlled.

The mortality rate is larger in small breeds probably because of low birth weights and large litter sizes. In general, the mortality rate of goats under range conditions and in and and semi-arid regions with well-drained, sandy soils is lower than that of goats in hot, humid environments. Confinement and stall feeding also result in a higher mortality, possibly because of the greater chances of infection.

Drenching

Drenching an animal entails the oral administration of a liquid. The goal of this procedure is to ensure that the animal swallows the full amount given. Grasp the goat under the jaw to raise its head. Raising the head of the goat will assist in ensuring the liquid is swallowed. A finger or thumb can be put into the mouth where there are no teeth (goats lack canine teeth as do all ruminants) to assist in opening the mouth for the drenching equipment. Generally a bottle with a tube over the end or a drenching gun is used. Liquids should be given slowly to allow time for the animal to swallow. Dewormers must be given using appropriate drenching equipment ensuring that they are given over the back of the tongue and swallowed.

Giving injections

Administering drugs via injection is a common herd health procedure routinely practiced by almost all producers. Following proper guidelines for each type of injection and using proper equipment will ensure that injections are done correctly and inflict minimum stress on an animal. Proper sanitation will ensure that you don't inject bacteria into your goat and cause an infection. In general, 18 to 20 gauge needles are sufficient for goats.

Preventive health care

Preventive health care in goats can greatly reduce mortality and morbidity. The following points form the basic tenets of preventive health care.

- Deworming
- Dipping

- Drenching
- Vaccination

A preventive health care calander is usually recommended to be followed.

Vaccination

Vaccination for following diseases is followed/ recommended in case of goats.

- Peste de peste ruminantis (PPR)
- Enterotoxaemia (ET)
- Goat Pox
- Foot and Mouth Disease (FMD)
- Haemosepticaemia (HS)

In India, FMD vaccination is recommended in January, ET in February, PPR in March and HS in June. In July before the rainy season, the second vaccination for ET and FMD can be carried out.

Routine herd immunisation, improvement of supply chains including management of cold chain facility is needed to improve the vaccination programmes followed by the central and state government agencies.Vaccination kit comprising of syringe, needle, cotton etc, need to be essentially provided for vaccination work.

Most of the vaccines for goat diseases are available from the following sources in India

1. Biological Products Division, Indian Veterinary Research Institute, Izatnagar, U.P.
2. Bio-Med (P) Ltd, Ghaziabad
3. Biological Products Division, Badshah Bagh, Lucknow
4. BAIF- Institute of Animal Health, Brahnagar, Pune.

PPR vaccination should be carried out in goats before the rainy season will help in prevention.

Newer vaccines using biotechnological advances are being developed. For example a vaccine against *Haemonchus contortus* seems to be most promising.

Deworming

Goats as a species are very susceptible to internal parasites. Intestinal parasites cause inefficient feed utilization leading to lowered growth rates in young animals, reduced weaning weights, low milk production, enhanced susceptibility to other diseases, and poor quality products. Animals may succumb as a result of heavy parasitic infection, especially in circumstances where infection is accompanied by malnutrition and general poor management. Increased mortality in goat herds also occurs when parasitism is accompanied by other diseases and serious stressful conditions.

Haemonchus contortus is widely prevalent, causing acute gastritis due to voracious blood feeding and burrowing habits. Main symptoms are diarrhea, anemia and later on oedema of the under jaw. Frequency of deworming depends upon the wetness/dryness of the area, population density in pens and pasture, overall health of the goats, and several other factors. Current diagnostic protocols undertaken by veterinarians for parasites are highly specialized and demand special skills and laboratory equipment. The FAMACHA © system, initially developed in South Africa for sheep, has now been shown to work for goats as well and promises an easy method for diagnosis of heavy parasitic infection. FAMACHA © involves a comparison of the colour of the ocular mucous membrane of the animal to a colour chart that categorizes animals into one of five colour categories ranging from 1 (healthy) to 5 (severely anaemic). The degree of anaemia in the animal reflects the degree of infection by dangerous blood sucking worms, hence the need for drenching. Examination of the inner lower eye membrane for coloration gives an idea about the work load. Red to bright pink membranes indicates a very low worm load, pink to light pink reflects the need to do de-worming, and white means anemia exists and the goat needs immediate medical attention. One of the popular dewormer is 1% Ivermectin injectable given orally at a rate of one cc per 50 pounds bodyweight. Other dewormers which can be used include Benzimidazoles, Imidothiazole, Amino-Acitonitrile Derivatives (AAD). Tetramisole (15 mg/Kg), fenbendazole (7.5mg/Kg), albendazole (8-10 mg/kg), Banminth (10mg//Kg) and closental (10 mg/kg) are effective against nematode infestation. The easiest way to give oral deworming medication to a goat is to draw it into a syringe, remove the needle, straddle the goat (facing the same direction as the goat), lock your legs around its middle and place your feet in front of its back hooves, open the mouth with one hand (watch those back teeth), put the syringe into the side of the mouth and over the back of the tongue, and push the syringe. The cost of the treatment for Fenbendazole is Rs. 100 for 10 goats per year. A local herb (*Mucuna pruriens*) has also been reported to be useful as a dewormer in goats. The trichomes on the pods of the herb were used for treatment @20 mg/kg body weight of the animals. This was roughly equivalent to the trichome of two mature pods for each adult doe (25 kg body weight) (A.L. Joshi, BAIF). In BAIF study using Fenbendazole, it was observed that the mortality of kids was lower in dewormed animals (8%) as compared to untreated animals (18%).

Use of chemical drugs for deworming has been in question because of recent observations appear to indicate that strategic and tactical protocols are in themselves the main cause of widespread development of anthelmintic resistance experienced worldwide. A huge variety of ethnobotanic remedies are used in the treatment of parasitic diseases in farm animals including goats.

It is always recommended to deworm new goats before allowing them to join existing herd of goats. New goats can introduce new parasites and worms to your herd. Use different deworming products each time you deworm your goats as parasites in goats can become immune to de-worming products.

Dipping

Goats commonly get infested with lice, which usually go unnoticed until the infestation becomes extensive and harmful. Dipping in goats is practiced to kill the external parasites *ie* ticks, mites, lice and pests which causes damage to the health of the animal. The dippings needs to carried out on frequent intervals depending on the disease risk. Louse infested animals need not be held in the dip longer than necessary to wet the fleece and skin thoroughly. The following medicines are generally recommended for dipping of goats.

- Cythion/Malathion @ 0.5% in water
- Lindane
- BHC
- Butox @0.1 to 0.4 % in water
- Cypermethrin @ 0.4 to 0.6 in water
- Ectomin@ 0.1 % in water

Zoonotic diseases

A zoonotic disease is an illness that animals pass to humans. An excellent way to manage disease on goat operations is to improve biosecurity, which should be developed in consultation with a veterinarian experienced in goat production. Good biosecurity reduces the likelihood of introducing disease to a herd and also manages disease spread among animals within a flock. The two most commonly used biosecurity measures on dairy goat operations are to park away from the goat area and washing hands before handling goats.

In summary, the following points need to be taken care of

- Routine inspection of flock for detection of sick goats if any.
- Carry out examination of faeces to find out load of gastro-intestinal worms.
- Strictly follow vaccination schedule and other prophylactic measures as per need.
- Ensure proper cleaning and routine disinfection of goat sheds.

- Prevent contamination of feed material with faeces, urine and soil in particular.
- Isolation of sick animals from healthy stock.
- Prompt and suitable disposal of animals suffering from diseases like brucellosis, John's disease etc.

Behavior of goat

Animal behavior is the expression of an effort to adapt, or to adjust to different internal and exteroceptive conditions; that is, behaviour is a response to stimuli. Behavioral characteristics are inherited just as the morphological characters do. Goats are ruminants but don't have a split upper lip like sheep so don't graze as close to the ground as sheep. Goats seem to be less concerned about prickly plants. Goats will also stand on their hind legs to reach up high to browse and will use their front legs to hold branches down. Goats void their faeces and urine indiscriminately. They defecate while standing or walking but urination is usually done in standing posture. Frequency of elimination is affected by the quality and quantity of feed, ambient temperature and relative humidity. The males of all farm animals fight when they meet other strange males of the same species. Male goats stand on their hind feet and swing their heads sideways as a means of striking one another as they come down.

Sexual behaviour is classified into three groups. Precopulatory patterns or courtship, copulatory patterns and post copulatory patterns. The precopulatory behaviour in goats is simple and of very short duration extending only to about 30 seconds. The male generally sniffs the female genitalia and urine and then raises his head with lips curled in the ritualized 'Flehmen' reaction. In goats, the tactile stimulation of the female is made by muzzling and licking the perineal region by the buck. The buck frequently micturates on the forelegs during excitement and emits courting grunts. Receptive goats too emit some non-specific bleatings. Estrous goats tend to mount or stand still while being mounted by other goats, but this behaviour is not as well marked as in cattle. The goats turn their head back when approached by the male. The duration of mating is very short. Goat can ejaculate seven times on an average till exhaustion.

Both humoral and neural factors control and modify the expression of sexual behaviour. When the kids are born, the mother cleans the young by licking them and encourages them to stand and to nurse. Goats appear less likely to reject one of the twins. Tendency for maternal isolation at the time of birth is seen in some goats . Goats establish the identity of their own young immediately after birth.

When a young kid is born it at first shows no fighting behaviour. Its relationship with its mother is peaceful and may remain so after the animal becomes adult. Likewise, the relationship between twins or between kids born at about the same time is also peaceful. However, a kid who approaches an adult female other than the mother is almost sure to be butted away. Older males respond in the same way if kids attempt to compete with them. This establishes an important bias for the dominance hierarchy namely that older animals are usually more dominant over younger ones. Thus a particular bebavioial phenomenon apparent in nearly all gregarious animals is that of a social order within a group, based on their relative aggressiveness. Pugnacious behaviour at the feeding troughs comprises mainly locking with the horns, butting with the head and pushing while biting and pulling of the ears and hair is also seen frequently. Biting and pulling of the ears or hair is characteristic of this species. The dominant animals generally took up the most favourable positions at feeding time, notably at the sides of the trough where competition arises from one side only. Signs of fear were clearly noticeable in submissive animals when approached by a more dominant animal and invariably they tried to evade conflict. The order of dominance is linked with the productivity too and more aggressive animals are most often more productive also.

Vices/abnormal behaviours are faulty habits acquired by goats. These vices affect the performance and health of their own as well as other goats. Milk sucking is one such faulty habit. The udder bags are commonly used by farmers to prevent milk sucking.

References

Bhat , P.N. and Khan, B.U. (2009) Goat Production, Studium Press, New Delhi

Das, K.S., B.B. Srivastava, and N. Das (2001). Standing orientation and behaviour of goats during short-haul road transportation. Small Ruminant Research 41:91-94.

Henderson, A. J., Blatchford, D. R. and Peaker, M. (1983). The effects of milking thrice instead of twice daily on milk secretion in the goat. Quarterly Journal of Experimental Physiology. 68, 645-652.

Mishra, B., (2001), Organic waste recycling in aqua farming, Yojana,Nov. 2001, pp.42-45.

Salama, A.A.K., Such, X., Caja, G., Rovia, M., Casals, R., Albanell, E., Marin, M.P. and Marti, A. (2003). Effects of once versus twice daily milking throughout lactation on milk yield and milk composition in dairy goats. Journal of Dairy Science 86: 1673–1680.

6

Feeds and Feeding

Introduction

Optimum nutrition is one of the fundamental requirement for sustainable and efficient goat production . It involves the judicious selection and use of available feed resources in formulating a palatable, economical and nutritionally balanced ration for goats. In common with cattle, sheep and buffalo, goat is endowed with a pouch in the stomach called rumen and can digest a wide variety of herbage (tree leaves, grasses, weeds, legumes); agro-industrial by-products (Salseed meal, neem seed cake, bagasse, molasses, citrus pulp, oil cakes) and non-protein nitrogen sources such as urea. The rumen ecology of the goat is unique among other ruminants, with an adaptability to rapid changes in dietary components.Goats are reputed to be better utilizers of poor quality roughages. The traditional feeding systems for goats are based on native grasses available in the natural grassland and forests and the main constraints to goat production are lack of feed, particularly in the dry season. Goat production in developing countries is largely dependent on fibrous feeds – mainly crop residues and low quality pasture – that are deficient in nitrogen, minerals and vitamins. Goats diet in the tropics is largely composed of tree leaves and shrubs (browse), which ensure a reliable and steady supply of nutrients all the year around, albeit at a low to medium quality food

Goats are generally maintained on browsing on natural rangelands, community pastures and tree loppings. Goats prefer browsing as compared to grazing. They can digest tree leaves and farm weeds which cattle do not consume. Now the goats are being used as natural weeder. Goat producers in India are primarily located in semi-arid and arid zones where low capability land with shrub vegetation provides the grazing area. Improved pasture or its management for the goat production is naturally considered irrelevant to landless and socio-economically depressed farmers. Due to progressive fall in the forest cover (currently less than 20%), the administrators and planners are highly critical about the development of goats, dependent on extensive grazing in areas defined as fragile zone. On the contrary, the demand for reclamation of low capability soil to more productive agricultural land is ever increasing with the phenomenal growth in human population over the years in India.

Optimum nutrition is the fundamental requirement for all farm animals including goats. Improper nutrition not only affects productivity but also health, behaviour and welfare of an animal. Stress factors, poor welfare and imbalanced nutrition increases susceptibility to diseases, thus increasing the need of veterinary treatments, posing risks to food consumers, decreasing profitability and endangering environmental sustainability of the livestock production systems and of the associated animal food chains. Goat is no exception.

Feed and fodder for goats

Feed and Fodder plays a vital role in animal production and its productivity. Feeding contributes 70% of the production cost of any animal product. Goats are fed concentrates and roughages including green fodder, dry fodder and tree leaves.

Feeding of tree leaves to goats is traditional practice of sustainable goat production system. Some of the tree fodders yielding leaves that provide sufficient biomass are considered dependable resources for goats in arid and semi arid zone. Tree leaves and pods are rich sources of protein and their supplementary feeding in sheep and goats improve growth, production and reproduction.

There are many trees and shrubs that can be used as drought feed of goats, some more suitable than others. But goats are quite choosy in selecting their diets and may get fed up with one type of forage all too soon. Lopped tree fodder is an important component of the dry season diet but its use falls in June before the start of the wet season. Cactus (*Opuntia* sp.), *Zizyphus nummularia*, *Acacia leucophloea*, *Acacia nilotica* and *Prosopis cineraria* are major components of the diet at the end of the dry season, the first two feeds being the most important quantitatively. The major tree leaves consumed by goats are subabool, Neem, Khair, Ber, Umber etc. Ber is a hardy fruit (*Ziziphus mauritiana*) crop whose leaves (as hay) provide staple food for goats especially.Some of the important tree leaves consumed by goats are listed below.

- *Acacia catechu* (Khair)
- *Acacia lecophloea* (Safed Kikar, Reru Rinj, Raunj, Rhea)
- *Acacia nilotica* (Babool)
- *Aegle marmelos* (Bel)

- *Ailanthus excelsa* (Ardu)
- *Albizia lebbek* (Siris)
- *Albizia procera* (Safed Siris, Gurar, Karak)
- *Anogeissus latifolia* (Bakli, Khaura)
- *Anthocephalus chinensis* (Kadam)
- *Artocarpus heterophyllus* (Kathal)
- *Azadirachta indica* (Neem)
- *Bauhina purpurea* (Khairwal, Karar, Koliar, Kaniar)
- *Bauhinia malabarica* (Amli, Amlosa)
- *Bauhinia semla* (Semal, Semul)
- *Diospyros melanoxylon* (Tendu)
- *Ficus glomerata* (Gular)
- *Ficus lacor* (Pakar)
- *Ficus religiosa* (Pipal)
- *Gauga pinnata* (Kharpat, Kaikar)
- *Mangifera indica* (Aam)
- *Melia azedarach* (Bakain)
- *Populas ciliata* (Pahari pilal, Chalaun, Chalni, Safeda, Ban Pipal)
- *Pterocarpus marsupium* (Bija sal, Pia sal)
- *Schleichera oleosa* (Kusum)
- *Shorea robusta* (Sal, Sakhwa)
- *Syzygium cumini* (Jamun)
- *Tamarindus indica* (Imli)
- *Terminalia belerica* (Bahera)
- *Zizyphus mauratiana* (Ber)

Utilization of top feeds or tree leaves was determined by the availability of these leaves in the nearby forests or waste lands. In India, 80–90 percent of community grazing-land is in poor to very poor condition mainly due to over-stocking and year-round grazing without resting the pasture, all of which does not allow vegetation to grow and attain peak yield (Shinde *et al.,* 1998). Goat rumen micflora is capable of utilizing tanniferous feeds efficiently because of the presence of higher quantity of tannin utilizing microbes. Diets containing tannin @ 30 to 40 g/kg can be utilized without any deleterious effects on health and production. Further, strategic use of tanniferous feed can control gastro-intestinal nematodes burden and reduce ruminal methane production.

About 60 % of feed resources available to goat are top feeds ie feed obtained from trees, shrubs and bushes. Goat is labeled as browsers as compared to sheep which are grazers. The most commonly available top feed species in India are Albezia, Ailanthus, Acacia, Azadirachta, Bouhinea, Ficus, Hardwickia, Leucaena, Prosopis, Merus, Sesbania and Zizyphus. The production of leaves from various trees ranges from 20-60 kg DM /tree/year.

Most common tree leaves fed to goats include Ber, Neem and Kikar. Neem tree leaves are not consumed by cattle or buffalo but are relished by goats. Neem leaves contain about 15 % CP and 48% TDN. Kikar or Babul tree is commonly found in Rajasthan, Uttar Pradesh, Madhya Pradesh and Haryana. Babool tree leaves are most commonly consumed by goats and camel but are not consumed by cattle or buffalo. The leaves contain about 10-12 % crude protein. Ber (*Zizyphus mauratiana*) is also found as common tree in several states including Rajasthan, Punjab, Haryana, Madhya Pradesh and Uttar Pradesh. The leaves of Ber tree are also relished by goats and contain about 8 % CP.

Lopping of tree leaves provide feed to goats but standard lopping practices need to be followed for higher biomass yield and good plant health. Lopping of trees is done by means of sickle shaped blade made up of iron tied at the end of a long bamboo pole. Forest department many a times raises objection on over lopping of tree leaves as it may damage the growth of the tree. Lopping should not be carried out in areas prone to erosion. A proper lopping interval needs to be provided. The lopping intensity also varies with the type of tree and various other factors.

Top feed resources generally contain higher concentration of phenolics including tannins, mimosine etc, which render anti-nutritional properties to the feed. By feeding goats with tree leaves containing tannins, there is a shift in the nitrogen excretion from urine to faeces, which is beneficial in terms of preventing environmental pollution and better utilisation of nitrogen through application of manure. Although several methods like alkali treatment, formalin treatment, water treatments etc are suggested for detannification but these are hardly practicable under field conditions. However, judicious use of these feed can promote goat production in the country.Under intensive system complete feed block (CFB) has been recommended for feeding of goats. In CFB for goats , the roughage portion can be straw or tree leaves.The maximum level of tree leaves in goat diets should not exceed 30% because of higher contents of secondary metabolities.

Roughages include hay, legume, hulls, straw, silage and pasture. Roughages contain greater than 18 % crude fibre and less than 20 % crude protein on dry matter basis. Roughages can be broadly classified as green fodder and dry crop residue.

Goats can be fed a variety of browse plants and tree leaves. Goat production is mainly based on grazing and crop residues feeding. Goats under extensive system subsist entirely on open grazing/browsing. Poor-quality crop residues (PQCRs) constitute the bulk of dry matter consumed by the goats under field conditions, but high-lignin, lignocellulose complex and low nitrogen content limit their efficient utilisation. Due to the highly fibrous nature and low nutrient content of crop residues, several physical processing methods have been employed to improve their utilisation in goats. Among the physical processing methods, grinding and blending crop residues with concentrate (in a given ratio) into mash or pellet can be a useful technology for efficient utilization of crop residues in goats.The technology of straw-based Densified Total Mixed Ration (DTMR), also called Densified Complete Feed Block (DCFB) is promising technology for intensive feeding of goats in future.

Goats are very selective in their feeding. Goats are energetic, inquisitive and versatile in the art of food gathering. Standing on their hind limbs, they always like to pluck the tender leafy twigs of herbs, shrubs and small trees. Goats become fed up with one type of diets very soon and seek out new types of fodder etc. They eat only tender leaves of the plants leaving aside the coarser ones. Browsers have less rumen volume relative to body weight than do grazers.

Goats are more highly selective in taking only plant parts palatable to them. The mobile upper lips of goats enable them to select discriminately favoured parts of plants. Goats spent over half their total grazing time eating leaves and shoots of trees and brushes.Goats eat more frequently than sheep. Goats also help in wide dissemination of seeds of several plant species. Goats can consume a wide variety of bitter plants as they are reported to have bitter taste receptors. Goats have a higher threshold for bitter tastes than do camels. The threshold of taste discrimination is partly genetic.

The stall feeding of goats is mainly composed of dry stalks and straws of different crops along with a small quantity of food grains.Sheep and goats have higher DM intake per 100 kg body weight than cattle and buffaloes.

Cultivation of fodder crops is some times replacing the range or free pastures. Areas receiving < 500 mm average annual rainfall are cultivated mostly with pearl millet, cluster bean, mothbean and mung; where there is less than 200 mm rainfall *Lasiurus indicus* has been found adaptable and productive. The area under fodder crops in general is very low in India and the fodders grown are fed only to the large animals as green or hay. The fodder crops should, therefore, be included in the grain/commercial crop rotations to increase production of green and dry fodders. They may also be sown mixed with the grain crops in such a way that they do not adversely affect the production of grains. The leguminous fodder crops may be sown with cereal crops for obtaining optimum production of the two. Perennial grasses like Blue Panic, Elephant, Guinea, and Napier etc. may also be cultivated.

Pasture is a valuable feed resource for goats because it is the cheapest way of supplying the proteins, energy, minerals and vitamins necessary for maintenance and production. Most common cultivated fodders used for goat feeding include berseem, lucerne, maize, cowpea, lobia, oat etc. Some of the common fodder crops which can be fed to goats include berseem, lucerne (alfalfa), maize, cowpea, lobia, oat etc.

- Lucerne (*Medicago sativa*)
- Berseem (*Trifolium alexandrinum*)
- Oat (*Avena Sativa*)
- Tall fescue (*Festuca arundinacea*)
- Rye grass (*Lolium perenne*)
- White clover (*Trifolium repens*)

Forage maize: Harvested at grain dough stage (+ 75 days), is very palatable and a good source of digestible energy for fast growing goats.

Cultivated pastures are used for goat feeding such as *Cenchrus ciliaris. Leucaena leucocephala* is a cultivated fodder tree used for goat feeding. Azolla has also been useful for feeding to goats. Studies have shown that under existing farming system, the major limitation in our rangelands and natural pastures is the non-availability of adequate energy throughout the year and adequate amounts of protein for more than half of the year. During the period from January to June, energy scarcity is very acute and the intake of goat is much less than even their maintenance requirements. The pasture lands should, therefore, be improved by sowing or reseeded with nutritious and perennial grasses and legumes that give considerably increased nutritious forage production. The management of such improved pastures is equally important for protection of pasture from unauthorized grazing, removal of undesirable bushes and weeds, soil and water conservation, application of fertilizers, proper stocking rate and grazing systems. Some of the common grasses that can be sown are ;

- *Brachiaria mutica* (Para grass)
- *Cenchrus ciliaris* (Anjan grass)
- *Chloris gayana* (Rhodes grass)
- *Chrysopogon fulvus* (Dhabloo grass)
- *Cynodon dactylon* (Bermuda grass)
- *Dictylis glomerata* (Orchard grass)
- *Panicum antidotale* (Blue panicum grass)
- *Panicum maximum* (Gunea grass)

- *Pennisetum pedicelatum* (Dinanath grass)
- *Pennisetum purpureum* (Napier grass, Elephant grass)
- *Sorghum sundanenses* (Sudan grass)
- *Stylosanthes hamata* (Stylo grass)
- *Stylosanthes humilis* (Stylo grass)

In the existing practice, the goat and cattle are allowed for grazing in the available pasture land. In some cases, farmers collect grass from the bunds and waste land to feed their animals. The nutritional level of the pasture land is depleting very fast due to over grazing with decreased edible plant population. There is a need to rejunivate and maintain these pasture lands with nutritionally rich improved species having self sowing ability so that the availability of quality pasture for the animals is ensured.

Several alien plant species have been introduced in India in the past and have become a threat to its biodiversity. These species of plants are steadily taking over the forest habitats in India. However, goats provide an alternative to their control and utilization as their leaves can only be consumed by goats but not by other species. These plants include the following

- Lantana (*Lantana camara*)
- Raanmodi (*Eupatorium glandulosum*)
- Congress grass (*Parthenium hysterophorus*)
- Vilayti Babool (*Prosopis juliflora*)
- Water hyacinth (*Eicchornia crassipes*)
- Pink Morning glory or Besharam (*Ipomea carnea*)

Availability of fodder seeds for fodder cultivation at farmer's field is an important issue.The foundation seeds need to be multiplied by the certified seed growers to increase the availability of seeds suitable for different agro-climatic zones.

Salinity is one of the major agricultural problems in India and other developing countries. Goats have the potential to survive on several salt-tolerant plants such as *Acacia ampliceps, Brachiaria mutica, Cynodon dactylon, Desmostachya bipinnata, Echinochloa colona, Eleusine flagellifera, Kochia indica, Sesbania aculeata, Sorghum vulgare, Sporobolus arabicus and Suaeda fruticosa*.The use of salt-tolerant plants can be a tool for poverty alleviation by improving the income of poor small farmers on saline lands.

Dry fodder or agricultural by-products

There are many agricultural by-products which can be used as goat feed.

Crop residues such a wheat straw, rice straw, gram straw and arhar straw are commonly used to supplement the ration of goats in addition to browse and limited quantity of grains. Arhar straw is sometime preferable to wheat straw for feeding to goats if available. In one experiment, average daily gain was significantly higher ($P<0.05$) in goats than in sheep fed gram straw (Gupta and Murdia, 2002)

Due to shortage of conventional feeds it may be desirable to incorporate one or more non convetional feed in the diets of goats. Generally non-conventional feeds used for goat feeding include kitchen waste, banana waste, brewery waste, apple pomace, citrus by-product waste, and sugarcane by products, olive by-products etc. Most of the non –conventional feeds contain one or other kind of anti nutritional factors that have adverse effect on the palatability and nutritional quality. However, these can be safely used 20-30 % in goat diets.

Sugarcane Tops: Used extensively as a forage source to maintain smallholder livestock, the fresh leaves with a dry matter digestibility of + 60% can be used as a roughage source in high performance rations at a rate of up to 25% of the diet (dry matter basis) or about 50% as fed.

Concentrate feed

Concentrates include animal proteins, plant proteins, grains, by-products and liquid supplements.

Grains such as wheat, oat, barley, maize, gram, rye etc are used in goat feeding as supplements during critical physiological stages. The whole grain with or without coarse ground /crushed are used in traditional goat production systems. Stall fed animals fed on whole grain *ad libitum* during fattening periods are known to have higher muscle accretion. Goats may be fed limited quantity of molasses as source of energy with other feed supplements, however, it cannot be fed as sole feed to goats.

Urea is the most common nonprotein nitrogen source fed to ruminants. It reduces the amount of protein required in the diet, thus reducing feed costs to the owner. This synthetic product is specifically manufactured for feed and fertilizer use. A ruminant animal utilizes proteins from feed and urea in exactly the same way, and the cost-savings of using urea may be substantial. Urea can be included in concentrate mixture at 1% or 0.5% in complete diet.

Concentrate mixture composition

For one year old kids

1.	Maize or Oat	42-47%
2.	Groundnut cake /Mustard cake	30%
3.	Wheat bran	20-25%
4.	Mineral mixture	2.0%
5.	Common salt	1.0 %

Concentrate mixture for adult goats

1.	Maize/Oat/Millet	32%
2.	Groundnut cake/Mustard cake	30%
3.	Wheat /Rice bran	20%
4.	Oilseed husk (Dal Chuni)	15%
5.	Mineral mixture	2.0%
6.	Common salt	1.0 %

Another example of concentrate mixture

1.	Gram	15%
2.	Maize	37%
3.	Groundnut cake	25%
4.	Wheat bran	20%
5.	Mineral mixture	2.5%
6.	Salt	0.5 %

Silvi-pasture in goat farming

Silvi-pasture (Latin, silva forest) is the practice of combining forestry and grazing of domesticated animals in a mutually beneficial way. Advantages of a properly managed silvi-pasture operations are enhanced soil protection and increased long-term income due to the simultaneous production of trees and grazing animals. Silvi-pasture is grass farming in forest enclosures. Silvi-pasture farming offers great potential for simultaneous improvement in productivity of goats and degraded lands. Perhaps the oldest agroforestry system used in the world, silvopastoral systems is characterized by integrating trees with forage and livestock production. The integrated silvipastoral system of farming has been recognized as a low-input technology for utilization of marginal, sub-marginal and other waste lands, which comprise about 50 percent of the total land needed to meet the shortage of forage besides fuel wood and timber. It has been observed that 4-8 t/ha/year dry forage could be produced from silvipasture system without much affecting the growth of the associated trees (Patil and Alagundagi, 2005).

Biomass production of the community grazing lands can be improved from 4.0-4.5 to 30-35 quintals dry matter/ha through silvipasture development which would increase the carrying capacity from one to 7-8 goat head per hectare per year. The community grazing lands in arid and semi-arid regions that cannot support cattle and buffalo should, therefore, be identified, developed into two and three tier perennial pastures through reseeding with nutritious, perennial and high yielding grasses, legumes and fodder trees and utilised for small ruminant production. A marked improvement in reproduction and survival rates, milk yield, quantity and quality of meat production can be achieved by grazing goats on developed two and three tier pastures and supplementing with concentrate mixtures and/or cultivated leguminous fodders and tree leaves at appropriate levels. Dutta *et al.* (2009) has reviewed the small ruminant production through silvi pasture system in India.

Some silvi-pasture management practices for goats are as follows:

- Stocking levels should be low enough to allow sufficient plant growth.
- Encourage rotational grazing to give plants a chance to regenerate.
- As another option, goats may be kept in pens and forages brought to them.
- Avoid exposure of the soil surface by overgrazing.
- Periodic but continuous introductions of multi-purpose trees that grow well in the local environment, have forage with high nutrient value, resist diseases and are acceptable culturally.

Trees provide fruits, fuel, shade and animal feed, prevent soil erosion, conserve water, reduce pollution, purify air, fix nitrogen and improve soil fertility. The fodders obtained from trees, bushes and shrubs are called top feeds. Although the top feeds are regarded as emergency fodders for livestock in general, they form integral part of the dietary of goat round the year and throughout the country. The common fodder trees found and may be propagated in arid and semi-arid regions are Khejri (*Prosopis cineraria*), Kankera (*Gymnosporia spinosa*), Babool (*Acacia species*), Neem (*Azadiratcha indica*), Siras (*Albizzia lebbek*), Kala Siras (*Albizzia odoratissima*), Soo Babool (*Leucaena leucocephala*), Anjan (*Hardwickia binata*), Dichrostachys (*Dichrostachys nutans*) and Ardu (*Ailanthus excelsa*) etc. The fodder trees not only provide green fodder throughout the year but also check soil erosion and improve soil texture. They also provide shade to the grazing animals during summer months. Babul (*A. nilotica)* leaves were better utilized by goats compared to sheep.

The top feeds may be best utilised through direct browsing by small ruminants. Several multipurpose trees can supplement the fodder biomass under range land by supply of fodder, fuel, timber and as a soil cover to check soil degradation. Among such trees, Khejri (*Prosopis cineraria*), Neem (*Azadirachta indica*) and Ardu (*Ailanthus exceisa*) are some of the most promising ones. Many kinds of foliages from trees have been studied as supplements for goats. Some of them were offered as sole feeds while others were supplemented with other feeds and most of these foliages had a high feed intake and digestibility and gave a positive nitrogen balance in goats, such as foliage from Acacia, Cassava, Erythrina, Jackfruit, Mulberry, Leucaena. Foliages from trees can improve the feed quality when feeding roughages of low nutritive value to goats.

Table 1: Important fodder trees and shrubs for feeding of goats

English name	Botanical name
Banana	*Musa sp*
Cassava	*Manihot esculenta*
Fig	*Ficus racemosa*
Guava	*Feijoa sellowiana*
Jackfruit	*Artocarpus heterophyllus*
Jujube	*Ziziphus jujuba Mill*
Leucaena	*Leucaena leucocephala*
Mango	*Mangifera indica*
Tamarind	*Pithecellobium dulce*
Water spinach	*Ipomoea aquatic*

The type and variety of foliages that can be used for feeding of goats depend on climatic conditions and the vegetation. Some of these tree leaves may contain anti nutritional factors.

Some of the anti-nutritional factors present in plant resources are mentioned below.

Grasses /Browse forages/Forage legumes

Leucaena	mimosine
Acacia	condensed tannins
Berseem	phytoestrogens
Lucerne	Phytoestrogens
Cenchrus	Oxalates
Grain legumes	
Cotton seed	gossypol
Mahua seed	saponins

Inclusion of fruit trees in farming system is beneficial especially in arid and semi-arid regions. Several plants such as *Ziziphus nummularia* have been recommended in areas under free pastures because the top feed of such species comes to the rescue of farmer's animals even in drought years when the crops fail. Sharma and Diwakar (1987) worked out the economics of the horti-pastoral system and found the returns remunerative. Fruit trees provide green fodder and fuel wood, check soil erosion, improve soil texture and fertility and provide shade to the grazing animals. Trees can be planted under silvi-pasture, agro-forestry, farm forestry and horti-pasture systems.

Fodder Preservation and Conservation

The preservation and conservation of forage and fodder are the technologies of feed processing to maintain the nutritional quality of feed resources and supplement feeds during lean/feed scarcity periods. Hay and silage preparation are proven technologies of green forages and fodder conservation. While staking and balling are technologies for dry feed resources conservation. To have proper availability of feed resources preservation and conservation of feeds is required.Even if much of the unutilized land is brought under developed pastures; the pastures will turn dry during summer months in arid and semi-arid areas and will be covered with snow during winters in temperate and sub-temperate regions. The most economic, simplest and perhaps the most satisfactory method for preserving forage crops or grasses is hay making. The grasses and legumes should be harvested at the pre-flowering stage to maintain their nutritive quality. The hay should be conserved properly without allowing it to sun bleach as good hay should retain its green colour. If it is not possible to conserve as hay due to adverse weather conditions, the fodders should be turned into silage in pits or trenches. Similarly, the tree leaves should be lopped during the period when abundance grazing is available and conserved as hay or silage. The fodders, grasses and tree leaves which have poor nutritive value may be supplemented with, for example, urea, molasses and mineral mixture to improve their feeding value. If grass from the forests is not fully utilized for the animals, it grows very tall and becomes unfit for grazing. If these grasses are harvested during the late summer season before allowing the animals to graze, a substantial amount of hay or silage can be made. In pasture lands green and dry biomass is abundant during monsoon season and there is a scarcity during post monsoon and summer seasons. The need for conservation of fodder is all the more warranted in the drought-prone areas where crop failures are frequent.

Enrichment and Utilization of Agro-Industrial By-Products

As the grazing lands in India are shrinking and the livestock population is increasing day after day, there is acute competition not only between men and animals but also between small and large ruminants for the same area of land. Therefore, goats are largely dependent on meagre community rangeland, low-grade roughages, non-conventional feeds and agro-industrial by-products to harvest their nutrient need. Fortunately, the increase in agricultural production has also resulted in enhanced production of various agro-industrial by-products such as straws, kadbies, beet pulp, sugarcane bagasse, molasses, oil cakes, brans, fruit pulps and fruit peels etc. These sources of energy and protein can be exploited to solve the problem of feed shortage for livestock in general to a very large extent through improvement of their palatability, digestibility and nutritive value by employing modern physical, chemical, biological and biotechnological techniques. Feed compounding plants capable of incorporating tree leaves, seasonal grasses, stovers, straws, dead litters, oil cakes, brans, husks, bagasse, molasses and newer unconventional feed materials in the supplementary and complete feeds could be established in the goat rearing regions of the country to provide economical rations. Studies have shown that the low grade roughages like straws and stovers added with little oil cakes, brans and mineral supplements may be very suitably compounded into Complete Feed Blocks and Pellets for livestock feeding. As compared to the raw material, these have advantages in terms of less storage space, and easier and cheaper transportation. Selectivity of ingredients by the animals from the feed blocks is avoided, and thus the palatability and nutritive value of the ration is improved through synchronized fermentation.

The estimated total available crop residues in India are 523.4 Mt/year. Using minimum feed processing technologies, the crop residues could be improved to have maintenance to production type feeds such as addition of urea, mineral mixture and water. In India, the availability of crop residues is dependent on monsoon rains. The browsing on community land and crop residues based goat production systems have a positive bias towards the small farmers and landless agricultural workers in the sense that large goat farmers cannot be sustained economically, if urban wages levels were paid to the rural workers.

Chemical composition of some common crop residues

Crop residue	Composition (% DM Basis)			
	Organic matter	Crude protein	Crude fibre	Ash
Rice straw	82.0	4.0	37.0	18.0
Wheat straw	92.5	3.5	35.6	7.5
Finger millet straw	90.6	3.7	36.5	7.2
Sorghum stover	90.8	4.2	33.3	7.3
Maize stover	89.0	4.6	32.0	7.1
Sugar cane tops	92.55	5.0	32.0	8.5

Goats are sometimes fed a variety of vegetable crop residues. Chemical composition of some common vegetable crop residues is given below.

Name	Composition (% DM basis)				
	OM	CP	EE	OF	Ash
Cabbage waste	87.60	10.12	2.91	13.82	12.40
Cauliflower waste	89.62	18.12	4.92	14.50	10.38
Brinjal waste	91.74	17.42	3.10	22.55	7.82
Pumpkin waste	94.58	15.12	3.98	14.79	5.42
Bottle gourd waste	92.14	16.05	2.55	15.69	7.59
Reddish	85.70	12.80	2.10	9.98	14.30
Potato skin	90.33	12.75	3.40	9.34	9.67

Goats consume a variety of industrial by products like coffee pulp, citrus by-products, pineapple by products, sugar cane by products and caged layer waste. But off smells and putrification may lead to palatability problems.Citrus pulp is a by product of the processing of oranges and grape fruit for juice. It consists of the peel and residue from the inside portion. Citrus pulp contains very little protein, phosphorus and carotene. It contains a high level of calcium, because lime is added during processing. Goats can efficiently utilise citrus by-products. In cities, goats are often tied near the vegetable or fruit seller and fed on banana peels, left over or unsold vegetables etc. Brewer's grain are fibrous by-products of beer industry containing a significant amount of protein can be fed to goats for growth promotion.

Some by-products contain toxic compounds. Such by-products should be fed in small quantities. Level of toxicity can be reduced by appropriate treatments in some of the instance.

Development and utilization of complete feeds

As protein supplements such as oil cakes are generally not available for feeding of goats or only available at a very high price, this has led to the use of non-protein-nitrogen sources, such as urea, to compensate for the nitrogen deficiency in fibrous feeds, thus enhancing their digestibility, intake and nutrient availability through optimization of rumen fermentation. The use of solid feed supplementation blocks, i.e. urea-molasses blocks or multinutrient blocks, to provide the nitrogen, minerals and vitamins lacking in fibrous feeds offers several advantages: ease of transport, storage and use, and reduced risks compared with other approaches, such as giving a small amount of urea in drinking water, sprinkling of urea solution on fibrous feeds before feeding, or urea-ammonization of crop residues. In this system, all feed ingredients exclusive of roughages are proportioned, processed and mixed in a uniform blend, which is available to the animal to supply adequate nutrients. Feeding ruminants on complete feeds ensures consumption without selective eating and avoiding refusal of unpalatable plant residues. Feeding of complete feeds also stabilizes the rumen fermentation through minimal fermentation losses, better ammonia utilization and stabilizes the propionate to acetate ratio. Molasses is the vital component of complete feeds as it not only increases the palatability, energy value and flavour but also acts as a cheap binding agent. Thus, complete feed concept has a potential for utilizing existing feed resources more efficiently for economical animal production and overcoming the shortage of range grazing.

Feeding of goats during different physiological stages

With only 2.4 percent of the world geographical area, India supports 12 percent of world livestock. India has 13.65, 56.31, 5.79 and 14.87 percent of the total world population of cattle, buffalo, sheep and goats (FAO, 2005). Although the population of all four species has shown an increasing trend since 1951, the buffalo and goat population has increased more rapidly than others and they are considered the animals of the future for the country. Farmers are forced to maintain a large herd of animals to compensate for low livestock productivity. The increasing livestock population provides an opportunity to utilize the biomass from natural resources to produce animal foods for the increasing human population.

Productivity of goats is limited due to acute shortage of livestock feeds and fodders in the country and a large gap exists between the requirement and availability more so in arid and semi-arid regions.The availability of crop residues in India is 231 million tonnes against the estimated requirement of 869 million tonnes annually, based on the present livestock population . To meet the required deficiency of livestock feeds to optimize productivity, the feeds and fodders available in the community grazing land, road sides and forests during rainy season should be preserved and utilized during the scarcity period. The goat production system at present largely consists of extensive system which should be replaced with semi-intensive and intensive systems for commercial milk and meat production. Locally available crop residues and agro-industrial by-products may be enriched with fortification of deficient nutrients and utilized for compounding cheaper complete feeds as feed pellets and feed blocks. Physical form of the diet can affect production and composition of goat milk, although effects appear of smaller magnitude than in dairy cattle.

It is essential that the kids receive colostrum within one hour after birth. Colostrum has to be fed to the new born kid for at least 3 days. Colostrum is rich in nutrients and provides antibodies which protect the kids against disease. Kids could be fed free choice of concentrate and roughage (dry and green) to have optimum growth. A concentrate mixture having 10% DCP and 70% TDN seems optimum for proper nutrient supply to optimize growth.

Age of kids	Milk	Creep feed (g)	Forage Green/dry(g)
1-3 days	Colostrum 300ml	-	-
4-14 days	350 ml, 3 feedings	-	-
15-30 days	350 ml, 3 feedings	A little	A little
31-60 days	400 ml,2 feedings	100-150	Free choice
61-90 days	200 ml,2 feedings	200-250	Ad-lib

Over 75% of the growth of the unborn kids takes place during the last six weeks of pregnancy. This development requires feed nutrients that be transformed into the tissue of a new life. The dry period gives the doe an opportunity to meet this demand upon her nutritional intake, to replenish her body reserves and to build up additional reserves for the following lactation. The body reserves are composed largely of fat, minerals and vitamins. A high producing doe cannot consume, digest and assimilate all the nutrients needed during the period of greatest production.

It is at this time she draws on the reserve nutrients stored in her body. Proper feeding during the dry period is necessary to get the doe in condition to kid easily, to develop the udder without too great an amount of ingestion, to have the doe ready for producing large quantities of milk and to be a more presistent producer during her entire lactation.

Pregnant goats should be provided with leguminous green fodder *ad libitum* and during the last month of pregnancy, does should be fed good quality concentrate at the rate of 500 g/day.

Recurrent droughts in arid and semi arid regions of the country leads to feed scarcity situations affecting livestock production. Goats and sheep are said to be more resistant to drought as compared to cattle and buffaloes. A drought meant lack of feed resources (feed, fodder, grasses) and water scarcity, followed by hunger, malnutrition, disease and finally loss of animal genetic resources. This situation obliges the owners to leave the animals free to forage for themselves. Goats survive on forages resistant to drought such as opuntia, acacia and tree leaves. However, even goats can not withstand long spells of drought. Two important plant species which help goats survive in the deserts during prolonged drought are sevan grass (*Lasirus indicus*) and Khejri (*Prosopis cineraria*). One of the newer approach tested for feeding of goats during drought or scarcity include collection and feeding of pods of *Prosopis juliflora* during the period of feed scarcity. In Rajasthan, this resulted in higher kidding rates in goats.

Fodder banks come in handy when crops fail due to drought and famine situations. Cultivated fodders, natural vegetation, fodder tree leaves and crop residues may be harvested during the period of their abundance and enriched, chaffed and conserved as hay, hay meals, mash, pellets, briquettes and blocks in the fodder banks for feeding during scarcity periods. Feed banks to store feed grade grains, oilcakes and agro-industrial by-products and other ingredients may also be established. Several organizations/agencies have developed mechanized bailing, pellet and block making machines. Cooperatives should also be roped in to provide support to farmers for establishment of feed and fodder banks.

Water scarcity is one of the major issues in Gujarat and some villages in Rajasthan, while feed scarcity is a constraint in goat production in villages in Rajasthan, Maharashtra and Karnataka. Alleviation of feed scarcities during the dry season would improve the livestock production and reduce the mortality, thus generating more income for farmers. The possible interventions include increasing tree fodders, increasing fodder production, improved management of feed resources and improved utilization of feeds.

Breeding buck should be fed at the rate of 3.0-3.5 % dry feed of their live weight and ration having 4.0-6.0 % DCP and 50-60% TDN with sufficient minerals and vitamins to maintain normal health and fertility. Breeding bucks should be fed good quality green fodder and concentrate upto 0.5-0.7 kg/day depending upon breed and size of the buck.

During the non-breeding season, the buck does not require additional grain if good pasture is available. During the breeding season, concentrate mixture may be fed to the does at the rate of 450-900 g (depending on the body weight) daily. Provide roughage free choice along with clean fresh water . Care must be taken not to allow the buck to get too fat. Reduce the intake of energy feeds as needed to prevent this. Make sure the buck gets plenty of exercise.

Nutrient requirements

A well balanced ration containing adequate amounts of protein, energy, vitamins and minerals must be fed in sufficient quantities for optimum production. Classical principles based on "feeding standards" – such as those used with controlled diets based on "good quality" feeds – are sometimes of little help in feeding goats at the farmers flock. The current concepts in feeding of goats are based on the fact that it is essential to take advantage of the rumen's ability to make use of fibrous feeds and of non-protein N (both inexpensive nutrient sources that are not usable by monogastric animals, including humans). For this it is necessary to develop an efficient ruminal ecosystem, ensure efficient fermentation of fibre and increase the production of microbial protein. This preconditions that there should be adequate ammonia supply and minerals (sodium, phosphorus, sulphur) and vitamins.Thus, provided that the animal receives sufficient fibrous feeds, the diet will allow survival or may even cover maintenance requirements. However, if higher production (growth, pregnancy, meat, milk or wool) is expected, supplementary 'bypass' protein and energy will be necessary in addition to the products of fermentative digestion.

Recommendations are available for the nutrient requirements of goats for meat and milk production. However, there is a paucity of information on nutrient requirements (energy, protein, minerals and vitamins) under extensive system of management

Goats require on an average daily dry-matter intake of 3-5 per cent of body weight . For optimal performance dry-matter intake relative to body size is higher in temperate breeds than in tropical goats.

Energy

Energy is used for basal metabolic processes, body heat, physical activity, tissue maintenance and growth, fat deposition, and lactation. Excess energy is stored as fat. Efficient utilization of nutrients depends on an adequate supply of energy, which is of paramount importance in determining the productivity of goats. Energy deficiency retards kid growth, delays puberty, reduces fertility, and depresses milk production. Energy in feedstuffs is contained primarily in the carbohydrate and fat fractions. Energy deficiency is frequently the major cause of retarded growth and lower milk production. Energy requirements are affected by the physiological stage of animals, type and level of production.Maintenance requirement of goats for Energy is 2.34 Kcal/day for 50 kg body weight (NRC, 1981). The energy requirements for weight gain are 4.09 Kcal/kg gain. Goats on an average require less energy per kg metabolic weight than cattle and buffalo but slightly more than sheep.

Pregnancy

No extra energy is apparently required during early pregnancy. It has been found that greatest energy needs are during the last 2 months of pregnancy.

Lacation

The amount of nutrients required for lactation depends mainly on the quantity and composition of milk, which varies not only among species but also within species.

Protein requirement

Proteins are most important structural components of the body, in addition to being part and parcel of such important constituents of the body as enzymes, hormones, antibodies, blood proteins etc. They are needed for the body metabolism, cell repair, nutrient transport and synthetic processes. The fundamental structural unit of proteins is the aminoacid. The proteins are vital for animal maintenance, growth, reproduction and milk production.

The protein requirement for maintenance is 2.82 g digestible protein (DP) or 4.15 g TP/kg metabolic body weight with an average digestibility of 68% for total protein. The protein requirement for pregnancy is 4.79g DP/kg metabolic body weight. For lactation the requirement is 57.20 g DP or 81.71 g TP/kg of milk.

Table 1: Daily Nutrient Requirements of Goats*

Body weight (kg)	Feed Energy		Crude protein		Ca (g)	P (g)	Vitamin A (1000 IU)	Vitamin D IU
	TDN (g)	ME (Mcal)	TP (g)	DP (g)				
Maintenance only (includes stable feeding conditions minimal activity and early pregnancy)								
10	159	0.57	22	15	7	0.7	0.4	84
20	267	0.96	38	26	1	0.7	0.7	144
30	362	1.30	51	35	2	1.4	0.9	195
40	448	1.61	63	43	2	1.4	1.2	243
50	530	1.91	75	51	3	2.1	1.4	285
60	608	2.19	86	59	3	2.1	1.6	327
70	682	2.45	96	66	4	2.8	1.8	369
Maintenance plus low activity (=25%increment ,intensive management ,tropical range and early pregnancy)								
10	199	0.71	27	19	1	0.7	0.5	108
20	334	1.20	46	32	2	1.4	0.9	180
30	452	1.62	62	43	2	1.4	1.2	243
40	560	2.02	77	54	3	2.1	1.5	303
50	662	2.38	91	63	4	2.8	1.8	357
60	760	2.73	105	73	4	2.8	2.8	408
70	852	3.07	118	82	5	3.5	2.3	462

Contd.

Body weight (kg)	Feed Energy		Crude protein		Ca (g)	P (g)	Vitamin A (1000 IU)	Vitamin D IU
	TDN (g)	ME (Mcal)	TP (g)	DP (g)				
Maintenance plus medium activity (=50% increment semi-arid rangeland slightly hilly pastures and early pregnancy)								
10	239	0.86	33	23	1	0.7	0.6	129
20	400	1.44	55	38	2	1.4	1.1	216
30	543	1.95	74	52	3	2.1	1.5	294
40	672	2.42	93	64	4	2.8	1.8	363
50	795	2.86	110	76	4	2.8	2.1	429
60	912	3.28	126	87	5	3.5	2.5	492
70	1023	3.68	141	98	6	4.2	2.8	552
Maintenance plus high activity (=75% increment arid rangeland sparse vegetation mountainous pastures, and early pregnancy)								
10	278	1.00	38	26	2	1.4	0.8	150
20	467	1.68	64	45	2	1.4	1.3	253
30	634	2.28	87	60	3	2.1	1.7	342
40	784	2.82	108	75	4	2.8	2.1	423
50	928	3.34	128	89	5	3.5	2.5	501
60	1064	4.69	146	102	6	4.2	2.9	576
70	1194	4.29	165	114	6	4.2	3.2	642
Additional requirement for late pregnancy (for all goat sizes)								
	397	1.42	82	57	2	1.4	1.1	2.13
Additional requirement for growth –weight gain at 50 g per day (for all goat sizes).								
	100	0.36	14	10	1	0.7	0.5	108
Additional requirement for growth –weight gain at 100 g per day (for all goat sizes).								
	200	0.72	28	20	1	0.7	0.5	108
Additional requirements for milk production per kg at different fat percentages (including requirements for nursing single twin or triplet kids at the respective milk production level (**% Fat**)								
2.5	333	1.20	59	42	2	1.4	3.8	760
3.0	337	1.21	64	45	2	1.4	3.8	760
3.5	342	1.23	68	48	2	1.4	3.8	760
4.0	346	1.25	72	51	3	2.1	3.8	760
4.5	351	1.26	77	54	3	2.1	3.8	760
5.0	356	1.28	82	57	3	2.1	3.8	760
5.5	360	1.29	86	60	3	2.1	3.8	760
6.0	365	1.31	90	63	3	2.1	3.8	760
Additional requirements for mohair production by Angora at different production levels Annual **Fleece yield (kg)**								
2	16	0.06	9	6				
4	34	0.12	17	12				
6	50	0.18	26	18				
8	66	0.24	34	24				

(*) Adopted from NRC 1981

Vitamins

Vitamins are trace organic substances essential in the function of most forms of life which some organisms are unable to synthesise and must obtain from exogenous sources. Vitamins are broadly classified in two groups on the basis of their solubility. Fat soluble vitamins include, A, D, E and K while water soluble vitamins include B-complex and C. The vitamins most likely to be deficient in the diet of goat are vitamin A and D. Vitamin B and K are formed by bacteria found in the rumen of the goat and are not considered dietetically essential. Vitamin C is synthetisd in the body tissues in adequate quantities to meet needs.

Pasture and range plants usually contain adequate levels of vitamins to maintain health in goats. However, during periods of drought, or when the only source of feedstuffs is crop residues, vitamin supplementation requires especially vitamin A which is quite important. Normal grazing conditions also provide vitamins D & E. Other vitamins like K, B complex and C are either adequate in the diet or are synthesized by the micro flora in the rumen in adequate amounts to meet the nutritional requirements of goats. However, young growing kids during pre-ruminant stage must be provided with adequate amounts of essential vitamins in their diet.

Vitamin A is essential for variety of processes of body growth and reproduction. Vitamin A is not contained in forages consumed by goats, but carotene found in green, leafy forages is converted into vitamin A in the body. In addition, vitamin A is stored in the liver and fat of goats during times when intake exceeds requirements. Zinc appears to be required in the conversion of â-carotene to vitamin A. Goats that have had access to good quality green feeds can probably be held on a low carotene diet for a minimum of three months without showing signs of Vitamin A deficiency. Mechanism exists for maintaning vitamin A constant in plasma irrespective of its content in liver. Vitamin A deficiency in goats results in loss of weight, unthrifty appearance, night blindnes and thick nasal discharge. Goats maintained on very low carotene diets for long periods developed signs of acute vitamin A deficiency such as night blindness, denudation of hair and elongation of horns besides extreme emaciation and susceptiblity to cold.

Vitamin D is essential for Ca and P metabolism. Vitamin D is not required as dieatary supplement to goats on range or browse or access to sunlight. Vitamin D deficiency has not been demonstrated in goats, but presumably a deficiency would cause rickets in young goats. Goats do not require a dietary source of Vitamin E.Vitamin K is required as a factor in the clotting of blood. Vitamin K is not a dietary essential for goats as it is synthesised in the rumen as well as pesent in enough quantity in a variety of feedstuffs.

B-complex vitamins are synthesised by rumen micro-organisms, therefore, goats rarely suffer from the deficiency of B-vitamins. Moreover, they are present in enought quantities in a variety of forages. Several metabolites of riboflavin have been reported to be the degradation products of riboflavin by rumen bateria of goats. A folate binding protein (a minor whey protein) has been reported to be present in goat blood which presumably acts as a trapping mechanim to accumulate the vitamin from the plasma into the milk. These binder proteins also facilitate the absorption of folate in the gut both directly and indirectly by preventing uptake by intestinal micro-organisms. Vitamin C is synthesised in the tissue hence not required by goats.

Minerals

Although minerals and vitamins are needed in a very small proportion of dietary nutrients but they are very important in goat nutritional programs for proper animal function, such as bone development, immune function, muscle contractions, and nervous system function. Essentiality of minerals for growth, production and normal functioning of body systems of the animal, soil, plant and human is well recognized. Supply of these essential minerals (macro and micro) depends upon their contents in feeds, fodders, soils and plant grains used for human consumption. Uptake of these elements by the plants is governed by their contents in soil, soil-pH, and concentration of organic matter, soil texture, temperature and rainfall. These factors have led to a great variation in mineral contents in soil, feeds, fodders and grains. Deficiency or toxicity of minerals owing to such variations is causing economic losses. Goats require at least 17 different mineral elements in their diets. Required minerals are classified as either macrominerals (major minerals) or microminerals (trace minerals), based on the quantities required.

Macrominerals are required in larger quantities (g per day) than microminerals (milligrams or micrograms per day). Macrominerals required by goat include calcium, magnesium, phosphorus, potassium, sodium, chlorine, and sulfur. Required microminerals include chromium, cobalt, copper, iodine, iron, manganese, molybdenum, nickel, selenium, and zinc.Requirements of specific mineral elements vary, depending on animal age, weight, stage of production, lactation status, breed, stress, and mineral bioavailability (the degree to which a mineral becomes available to the target tissue after administration) from the diet.

Goats require both macro and micro minerals for optimum growth and reproduction. Balancing diets with trace elements is important for optimum nutrition of small ruminants. Body contains a large number of mineral elements which occur both in combinations with each other and in combination with other organic constituents. Goats when allowed access to browse, supplement their diets with shrubs and tree leaves which are often much higher in mineral content than the forages more commonly used tor cattle and sheep. As such a dietary supplement is not needed for these goats. Under stall fed conditions, salt or mineral lick should be made available. Goats tolerate feeds deficient in certain minerals to a better extent as compared to other species of livestock. Haenlein and Anke (2011) and Haenlein (1980) reviewed the mineral nutrition of goats. In general the deficiency of trace elements resulted in reduced reproductive efficiency, high mortality and abortion rates and decreased weight gains. Mineral deficiency or excess in animals are area-specific problems and influenced to a great extent by contents of minerals and their bioavailability from feeds and fodders. Mineral requirement of animals varies with the type of soil and vegetation on which goats are being maintained. Deficiency /excess of a mineral element affects the bioavailability of other minerals in animal system.Several minerals such as S and Mo, Zn and Cu has inter relationship. Therefore, macro –micro mineral requirement and level of feeding depends on animal physiological stage, level of production and geo meteorological environment.

Appropriate intake of key minerals and vitamins is essential for goat productivity and health. BIS standards for preparing mineral mixture for goats are as follows (BIS 2005)

Mineral mixture is not normally fed or available to goats in the farmer's flock of developing countries. A suggested mineral mixture for goat can typically have the following composition.

Sr. No	Mineral	Amount
1.	Water (maximum percentage)	5
2.	Calcium (Minimum percentage)	30
3.	Phosphorus (Minimum percentage)	14
4.	Iron (Minimum percentage)	0.55
5.	Iodine (Minimum percentage)	0.35
6.	Copper (Minimum percentage)	0.03
7.	Lead (Minimum percentage)	0.20
8.	Manganese (Minimum percentage)	0.08
9.	Magnesium	
10.	Salt	22
11.	Cobalt (Minimum percentage)	0.008
12.	Sulphur (Minimum percentage)	0.13
13.	Fluorine (Maximum percentage)	0.03

Salt	Percentage
Dicalcium phosphate	60
Sodium chloride	20
Sodium sulphate	10
Magnesium sulphate	9
Zinc sulphate	0.5
Copper sulphate	0.09
Magnesium sulphate	0.40
Cobalt sulphate	0.01
Total	100

The marked improvement in performance when goats are given a proper mineral mixture, more than compensates for the cost of minerals. However, if mineral mixture is not possible to be fed or unavailable, common salt at least should be provided to goats as a mineral supplement.

With introduction of high yielding varieties, intensive cultivation and uses of inorganic fertilizers, there is a continuous depletion of all essential plant nutrients from the soils. The soils of Haryana are 92% deficient in N, 70% in P, 5% in K and 28% in sulphur. The deficiency of micronutrients is 54, 2.2, 21.0 and 4.6% for Zn, Cu, Fe and Mn, respectively.In Odisha (Orissa) feeds and fodders have been found deficient in Ca, P, Zn and Cu. Supplementation of deficient minerals in the diet under existing feeding practices is implied (Singh *et al.,* 2011).

A regular monitoring of soil and plant samples for mineral nutrients is essential for providing good quality fodders to the animal and to avoid nutritional disorders. The frequent changes in soil mineral profile, non-supplementation of mineral mixture to animals have affected the economic of animal production .

Various diseases and reproductive disorders, characterized by the deficiency or toxicity of minerals and poor health is very common. Deficiency of some minerals like phosphorus, zinc, copper, manganese, etc in our livestock population including goats may cause infertility, repeat breeding, delayed sexual maturity, sterility, low milk production, weakening of bones, retarded growth, and rough hair coat.

Water

As for most other animals, water is quite important for goats too. The total amount of water in the body remains relatively constant from day to day. Water is gained by ingestion or as an end product of cellular metabolism. Water loss occurs in urine, from the skin, with expired gases and in the faeces. The lactating goat also loses large amount of water in milk. A high milk yield is dependent on an adequate supply of water as also the survival of animals in semi-arid and arid tropics is often threatened by lack of water. The requirement for water is affected by such factors as the amount of dry matter content, the nature of food, individual variations, physiological condition, and temperature of the drinking water, ambient temperature and even frequency of drinking. When ambient temperature is high water is consumed in excess of metabolic needs as it is essential for evaporative cooling. Consumption of free water during the day time was four times than that consumed at night. It is well known that water with very high levels of dissolved salts depresses feed intake and animal performance. However, limited research is available that indicates giving goats high-quality water sources instead of letting them drink from any water source will improve animal's performance. Water available to goats is generally high in total dissolved salts and sometime high in coliform count.

A general recommendation is to provide goats with all the clean water *ad libitum*. Goats are more discriminatory than other species in selection of clean water for drinking.

Extremes in water temperature will increase energy requirements. Taste factors will also affect normal water intake.

Factors affecting the free water intake of goats are lactation level, ambient temperature, water content of forage consumed, amount of exercise, and salt and mineral content of the diet. Therefore, the daily range of free water intake may be from zero to several liters. When feeding on dry forages and when water is lacking, the efficiency of reproduction will suffer. Sub optimum water intake will result initially in reduced feed intake, then reduced performance and gradual starvation. Acute problems result when goats are unable to maintain water balance or control body temperature.

Goats are often more sensitive and reluctant than other species to drink from foul-tasting water sources. If they are forced to drink poor quality water, the result may be infections or undesirable mineral intake.

Goat is among the most efficient domestic animals in the use of water, close to camels with respect to water turn over rate per unit of body weight. They have the ability to conserve water by reducing losses in urine and faeces. In many environments the water intake through forage may be high relative to other species because of their ability or willingness to browse. The result is that goats are less dependent on free water source than other domestic species.

Growth Rate and feed conversion efficiency

Growth of the livestock is of concern to the farmer because of the time that may elapse and the feed that he must provide before he can derive any income in return. The growth rate and the weight of mature goats varies in different breeds, plane of nutrition and management practices. Higher gain in body weight occurs during early phase of growth which goes on decreasing as the kids grow older. Misra and Chawla (1975) reported that the average gain in weights per day ranged from 43 to 51g in case of Beetal kids.

Shalash *et al.* (1970) in Egypt has given the values of 301, 522, 609 and 492 g per day in Nubian, Saanen X Nubian, Saanen and Zwaibi goats respectivly. Fehr *et al.* (1976) report that daily mean gain (g/day) of male Alpine kids receiving milk replacer can reach 250 g /day during the 1st month. The mean gain tended to decrease when the live weight exceeded 16 kg at slaughter. Wilson (1958) studied the growth rate of East African goat kids on two planes of nutrition. The nutrition of the kids during the first stage of experiment was governed by the nutritional status of their dams. When the kids weighed 9 kg, half the kids from each plane were switched to the opposite treatment. Thus four treatments were used after the kids weighted 9 kg : high-high; low-low; high-low and low-high. Differences between the live weight of the kids on the high-high and low-low regime were statistically significant. Kids receiving high-high level of nutrition reached 15 kg live-weight in about 26 weeks while the low-low kids required 48 weeks to reach the same weight. Lindahl (1954, 55, 56) did not find any significant change in the growth rate to Toggenburg doe kids fed with high energy diets in contrast to the doe kids receiving good quality roughage diets. Jindal (1977) found that in Alpine X Beetal goats, the TDN required per kg gain in body weight was 8.44, 7.89 and 14.14 kg in the three groups fed 100, 120 and 140% of the energy requiremets of Morrison's standard . The corresponding values of DM/kg gain were 10.85, 9.28 and 14.43 kg. Johri and Talapatra (1971) have showed that under identical conditions, browsing group of goats recorded 64% higher growth rate than stall fed group. Weight gain of kids after the point of inflection of the growth curve take places at a low rate and apparently it is difficult to alter if high energy and protein diet is given. Weight gain alone is not a suitable criterion of response to different feeding regimes since the chemical composition of the gained tissue may not be identical in all animals. Therefore, the same increment in weight resulting from a different treatment does not mean that there is equivalent effect.

There exists a point in the life of a slaughter animal at which the cumulative TDN required to produce a unit liveweight of saleable meat were minimal. This point represented optimum slaughter weight if biological efficiency alone is considered. Goats are efficient meat producers. From the above duscussion, it is clear that the tropical breeds, although have good carcass characteristics, have slow growth rate and feed conversion efficiency. Thus a considerable scope exists in improving the meat production characteristics of indigenous goats by upgrading with suitable breeds to maintain higher reproductive rates and carcass characteristics but with a marked improvement in growth rate, mature weight and feed conversion efficiency.

Nutrition and reproduction in goats

The profitability of small ruminant breeding is derived from their ability to exploit harsh environments and survive periods of nutritional deficiency. No single nutrients is responsible to ensure optimum reproduction but a host of nutrients work in tandem to ensure optimum reproduction. Several nutrients have direct effect in ensuring reproductive success or failure while others indirectly affect the reproductive ability through their effects on various reproductive hormones, metabolic process etc. Anti nutritional or toxic factors present in the diet pose many a hazards for causing poor reproductive ability of small ruminants as these animals depend on browse or tree leaves of varying composition and many of these fodders are of dubious nutritional ability. Small ruminants have to undergo prolonged underfeeding or malnutrition during periods of drought or natural calamities and such situations affect the reproductive ability besides survival of these livestock.

Nutrition influences ruminant fertility directly by the supply of specific nutrients required for the processes of oocyte and spermatozoa development, ovulation, fertilization, embryo survival and the establishment of pregnancy. It is a well known phenomenon that nutritional flushing in ewes stimulates folliculogenesis and ovulation rate. Nutrition affects reproduction through short (40 days, i.e., "immediate nutrient effect"), and long-term effects ("static", i.e., mediated through body condition; "static and dynamic", i.e., confounded effects of body condition and bodyweight gain). Body condition affects the onset of anoestrus, the resumption of post-weaning if photoperiod is favourable, and ovulation rate.

As goats frequently browse leaves or other parts of trees, shrubs etc rich in tannins, it is not known that to what extent tannin content in feeds affect reproductive ability. Some of the feeds and fodders consumed by goats and sheep are highly unbalanced in minerals, the role of these feeds on reproduction of small ruminants need to be studied in greater details.

Nutritional disorders

One of the nutritional disorder is bloat. Goats are fairly susceptible to bloat, which is the accumulation of gas in the rumen. Bloat is a condition in which the contents of the rumen of goat becomes frothy and the goat is incapable of eructing gases. Gas is a natural by-product of digestive fermentation in the rumen, and it is expelled continuously as the goat belches. Bloat occurs when gas is trapped in the rumen.

References

Dutta, T.K., Prabhat Tripathi, U.B. Chaudhary and M.C. Shrama (2009) Small ruminant production through silvi-pasture system in India, Central Institute for Research on Gaots, Makhdoom, Farah, Mathura

FAO. (2005) Production Yearbook, FAOSTAT, FAO, Rome.

Fehr P.M., Sauvant D., Delage J., Dumont B.L., Roy G. (1976): Effect of feeding methods on performance of entire young male goats. Livest. Prod. Sci., 3, 183-194.

Gupta, Lokesh and Murdia, P.C. (2002) Voluntary intake, nutrient digestibility and rate of passage of gram straw in sheep and goats, Indian Veterinary Journal, 79: 250-252.

Haenlein, G.F.W. (1980) Mineral nutrition in goats. J. Dairy Sci. 63;1729-1748.

Haenlein, G.F.W. and Anke, M. (2011) Mineral and trace elements research in goats: A review Small Ruminant Research 95:2-19

Jindal, S.K. (1977) Studies on the energy metabolism of the goat. Thesis Kurukshetra Univ. Kurukshetra, India.

Johri, C.B. and Talapatra, S.K. (1971) Growth studies with Jamunapari goats. I. Early growth of Jamunapari goats. Indian Vet. J. 48:389

Johri, C.B. and Talapatra, S.K. (1971) Growth studies with Jamunapari goats. II. Goat kids under browsing and stall fed conditions. Indian Vet. J. 48:495

Johri, C.B. and Talapatra, S.K. (1971) Growth studies with Jamunapari goats. III. Goats as a meat producing animal. Indian Vet. J. 48:602

Lindahl, I.L. (1954) Urea as a partiial replacement of protein in the diets for milch goats : Annual Report Ars Usda .

Lindahl, I. L. (1955) Goat feeding investigations : Annual Report Ars Usda

Lindahl, I. L. (1956) Goat feeding investigations : Annual Report ARS, USDA
Misra, R.R. and Chawla, D.S. (1975) Annual Report, NDRI, Karnal
NRC - National Research Council. (1981). Nutrient Requirements of goats: Angora, dairy, and meat goats in temperate and tropical countries. Washington: National Academy Press, 91 p.
Patil, S.A. and Alagundagi, S.C. (2005). Estimates.In P.S. Pathak and S.S. Kundu (eds.), Livestock feeding strategies for dry regions, International Book Distributing Company, New Delhi, India
Rajpoot, R.L. (1978) Energy and protein in goat nutrition. Thesis RBS. College, Bichpuri.
Shalash, M., Mousa, A., Nawito, M., Farrat, H.f. and Ooof, F., Selim, M.K. and Taufik, M.A. (1970) Economics environment evaluation of some goat breds in Egypt. Vet. Med. J., U.A.R. 18:295-312.
Sharma, S.K. and Diwakar, G.D. (1987). Economic evaluation of horti-pastoral systems in arid regions of western Rajasthan. Indian J. Range. Mgmt., 10, 119-122.
Shinde, A.K., Karim, S. A., Sankhyan, S.K. & Bhatta, R. (1998). Seasonal changes in physiological responses and energy expenditure of sheep maintained on semi-arid pasture. J. Agric. Sci., (Camb.). 131: 341-346.
Singh, R.K., Mishra, S K. Swain, R. K. dehuri, P.K. Sahoo, G. (2011) Mineral profile of feeds, fodders and biochemical profile of animals in west- central table land zone of odisha Indian Journal of Animal Sciences, 81: 1148-1153
Wilson, P.N. (1958) Age changes in the carcass composition of female kids. J. Agric. Sci., 51:4-21.

7

Reproduction

Reproductive processes have profound influence on the ultimate economics of livestock production. Regularity in reproductive functions guarantees a profitable return to the farmers. Reproductive efficiency is paramount to the success of goat husbandry. Disruption of one or another of the reproductive processes in male and female results in decreased reproductive efficiency and hence is of concern to the animal production strategies. Reproductive performance or efficiency depends on many hormonal, genotypic and environmental factors. Environmental stress can drastically reduce reproductive efficiency. Goats are the most prolific of all domesticated ruminants under tropical and subtropical conditions. Goats are genetically endowed with good reproductive efficiency in the sense that goats can breed three times in two years and many breeds give birth to twin and triplets.

Age at puberty in male and female goat

Puberty is the time when the reproduction first becomes possible and is characterized by the release of germ cells and sexual maturity. Age at puberty depends primarily on the growth rate of the kid which in turn depends on its quality and quantity of the feed offered.

Age at puberty in males has been variously defined as the age at which the complete separation of the penis occurs from the sheath, or the age of 1st appearance of spermatozoa in the seminiferous tubules or the availability of the first ejaculate. Although animals develop sex play much earlier than their ability to reproduce,considerable variation can exist between the age at puberty determined in different ways as it evident from the study of Elwishy and Elsawaf (1971) in male Damascus goats. The separation of the penis occurs at a mean age of 242.9 days while first ejaculate could be obtained only at the age of 509.2 days. Age at puberty varies with different breeds, plane of nutrition, presence of females etc. The endocrine development usually precedes the testicular development and androgen production is usually high prior to the actual onset of puberty.

Puberty in the female is the age at first estrus followed by ovulation. Age at puberty in the female doe is the time at which oestrous cycles start. The reproductive activities of goats begin with the onset of puberty. This is the time when animal expresses its full reproductive potential for the first time. However, mere attainment of physiological puberty in females in the form of production and liberation of viable ova cannot be taken as granted that the female has developed ability to carry fetuses to term. Attainment of puberty is a complex pituitary hormonal mechanism regulating the synthesis and release of gonadotrophic and gonadal hormones. Levasseur (1979) considers that gonad maturation is not a determining factor in the onset of puberty, since in all the mammals, the injection of gonadotrophic hormones sometimes before the normal age of puberty induces ovulation in the female. Age at puberty is affected by factors such as breed, birth weight and parity, season of kidding, nutrition and environment.The ovaries are essentially inactive from birth until puberty.The ovaries become active as the hypothalamus and anterior pituitary gland begin to produce stimulatory hormones such as the gonadotropin-releasing hormone (GNRH), the follicle-stimulating hormone (FSH), and the luteinizing hormone (LH). Presence of male goat may influence the estrous behavior in does. Photoperiod also affects the onset of puberty in does. Age at puberty differs with the breed. In general the smaller breeds experience puberty at an earlier age.

Age at puberty in different breeds of goats

Breed	Age at Puberty	Reference
Jamunapari	18-20 months	Khan, 1980
Jamunapari	429 days	Singh and Sengar, 1980
Barbari	6-8 months	Prasad, 1969
Barbari	288 days	Singh and Sengar, 1980
Barbari	9 months	Prasad and Bhattacharyya, 1979
Black Bengal	10 ±2.48 months	Ali *et al.*, 1973
Black Bengal	10.2 ± 1.78 months	Rahman *et al.*, 1977
Jakhrana	547.5 days	Tiwari and Rai, 2005
Marwari	370.4 days	Tiwari and Rai, 2005
Kutchi	560 days	Tiwari and Rai, 2005

Once puberty is reached, it is best to breed a goat when she reaches approximately 70 percent of her mature body weight depending on the breed. If a doe becomes pregnant before achieving 70 percent of her estimated mature body weight, growth and development of the kid may not be proper or adequate. In addition, goat could suffer abortion, increased post-partuminterval, and repeat breeding. Female goats come in estrous long before the attainment of mature body weight. It is inferred that although goats come in estrous at the age of 6-8 months, it will be unwise to breed them at this stage because the smaller dimensions of the reproductive tract. In well managed flocks, breeding in not allowed until female is 1 to 1.5 years old.

Reproduction in the male

The major functional parts of the male genital tract of goats include the testis, epididymis, vas deferens, penis and several accessory sex glands including the prostate, seminial vesicles and bulbo-urethral glands.

The testes are suspended outside the body cavity in the scrotum, at a temperature several degree below that of the body. This lower temperature is essential for spermatogenesis. The testes produces the spermatozoa and the male sex hormone testosterone. The differentation of gonad as testis begins in the embryos of 33.5 mm crown rump length (CRL). The leydig cells make their appearance at 78.3 mm stage. The rete tubules develop as cellular cords at 48.8 mm CRL and were luminised at 230 mm CRL. The testes of buck are oval in shape. The average weight of goat testis was found to be 69.13±4.13g. The spermatozoa passes from the testis in to the epididymis where they acquire the capacity for fertilisation and mobility and are stored there until ejaculated. At ejaculation, they are squeezed along the *ductus deferens* into the urethra and are mixed with the secretion of the accessory glands to constitute ejaculated semen.The testosterone production by the testis is controlled by the secretion of LH (ICSH) from the anterior pituitary whose secretion is further regulated by the secretion of releasing factors from the hypothalamus.

Testicular fluid is important in the supply of nutrients to the testis as well as the removal of its end products, both exocrine and endocrine. Goat has similarities in blood supply to the testis with the ram and the bull. It shows the most pronounced coiling in the vascular cone. Gonadal spermatid reserves of goats was 88.25 x 106/gm of testicular parenchyma. It was estimated that an average goat produces 1.85 billion spermatozoa/day (Jindal, 1984).

Epididymis is composed of a single torturous, colied tubule that is essential for the transportation, nutrition, storage and maturation of the spermatozoa. The epididymal weights of goats were found to be 9.08±0.06 g.The proximal or spermatic cord end of the epididymis is more or less flat, broad and V shaped and is called the head of the epididymis (caput). The intermediate narrow part is called the body (corpus) and the distal enlarged end, which acts as a storage site for spermatozoa, is called the tail of the epididymis (cauda). Epididymis of goat is supplied by the epididymal arteries which arise from testicular artery at or close to the apex of vascular cone. The spiral course adopted by the epididymal arteries is responsible for creating congenial environments for post testicular maturation of spermatozoa in the epididymis. Important maturation changes take place in spermatozoa during their transit through the epididymis, acquiring the potential to fertilize eggs.

The number of spermatozoa stored in the epididymis has been said to be related to the rate of sperm production by the testis. The epididymal sperm reserves in the caput, corpus and cauda of mature goats have been found to be 1.90, 0.66 and 6.18 (10^9) respectively which represented 21.7, 7.5 and 70.8% respectively of the sperm reserve on that side (Jindal and Panda 1980). Panda and Jindal (1982) found the reserves in Black Bengal goats to be 1.60, 0.60 and 4.79 billions in caput, corpus and cauda, respectively.

The maturation changes which make the spermatozoa fertile as it traverses the epididymis have been reported in goat. Atreja and Anand (1977) studied the lipid metabolism of epididymal spermatozoa and found that phospholipid content of goat spermatozoa decreased as it moved from the head to the tail region of the epididymis. The intracellular sperm phospholipids were oxidised to the extent of 55-60% while those of droplets were completely oxidized. Jindal (1984) found that more than 90% of fluid gets absorbed from corpus to caude.

The main accessory glands in the male bucks include the seminal vesicles, the prostrate and Cowper's glands (also known as bulbo-urethral glands) all of which produce secretions which contribute to ejaculated semen.

Seminal vesicles in goat are known to elaborate fructose and this is found to be androgen dependent. In goats, the glands of the two sides are generally assymmetrical in size.

The Cowper's or bulbo-urethral glands are associated with the caudal portion of the urethra. Roy (1957) reported the presence of an egg yolk coagulating enzyme which was found to be secreted by Cowper's gland in goat. Major portion of the seminal plasma is secreted by seminal vesicles in the goat.The prostate is a tubulo-alveolar gland which produces a colorless fluid rich in proteolytic enzymes and almost lacking in reducing sugar.

Reproduction in female

Female reproduction is all the more important, because it is the female that conceives and nourishes the young. The female reproductive apparatus consists of the ovaries, oviducts, uterus, cervix, vagina and vulva.

The reproductive tract of the goat resembles that of the sheep in all its main features but differs from it in some minor details. The uterine horns are more coiled than those of the sheep. The cervical canal is characterized by numerous folds arranged in a series of horizontal rings unlike the hard ridges present in the sheep. In the doe, the cervical mucosa contains simple tubular glands, unlike that of ewe.

The ovary of the goat is oval or bean shaped. Goat ovary measures approximately 2 to 3 cm in length, 1 to 2 cm in width and 0.8 to 1.0 cm in thickness. The average weight of goat ovaries is around 1-1.5 gm in tropical goats whereas in temperate goats the weight varies from 2-3 gm.The ovaries that contain many follicles have a spongy appearance. The size, shape and consistency of goat's ovary vary with the presence of follicles or corpus lutea.

The fallopian tubes are relatively long and sinuous. The uterine horns are long and coiled. The formation of a spiral is more marked than in the cow. The caruncles in the uterine horn are very distinct even in nulliparous animals.

The body of the uterus is small, and joins with the cervix which feels firm and fibrous and the consistency is quite different from the rest of the organ. The caruncles in the uterus of goat are arranged in four rows.

The clitoris in the goat does protrude far out of the Fossa clitoris and normally should not be visible between the lips of the vulva.

Estrus and ovulation

Estrus is defined as the period of sexual receptivity in the female, during which ovulation occurs and the corpus luteum begins its formation. Estrous behavior in goats includes sniffing, vocal exchange, courtship, standing heat and mounting. A doe in heat will usually wag her tail from side to side constantly. In an organized flock, aproned buck are used twice a day every 12 h to detect estrus. Thc beginning of estrus is a gradual phenomenon. The detection of the precise time of the onset on estrus is usually based on the period of acceptance of the male. Breed and environmental temperature may influence the duration of estrus.

Duration of estrus in most breeds of goats vary from 24 to 48 hours. Thus goats have a longer duration of estrous as compared to dairy cows (17.8 hrs) or dairy heifers (15.3 hrs). The length of estrus in goats has been reported to be highly variable. Sahni and Roy (1967) observed that the duration of estrus varied from 12-60 hours in Barbari nannies. They found that the duration of estrus in 75% of the female goats ranged between 24 and 36 hrs on the basis of number of detections at 12 hrs intervals.

Silent estrus in goats is not a prominent phenomenon except in Angora where incidence as high as 43.5% has been reported. Silent estrus is generally non ovulatory. Farshad *et al* (2008) indicated that silent heats occurred mostly in the early breeding season in Markhoz (Angora) goats in Iran.

In many breeds of goat, two or more ova are shed during estrus. The ovulation rate is higher in case of smaller breeds like Black Bengal, Assam Hill and Barbari but lower in case of large or medium sized breeds like Jamunapari, Beetal, Marwari, Sirohi and Jakhrana. Among the environmental factors influencing ovulation rate, season and level of nutrition are important. The right ovary appears to be relatively more active than the left. Multiple births are not common in Jakhrana goats and an ovulation rate of 1.33 has been reported (Goel and Agrawal, 2003). Ovulation time varies from 24-48 hrs after the onset of oestrus and depends on breed, season, nutrition and managemental factors. Goel and Agrawal (2003) reported that the Jakhrana goat ovulated towards the end of the oestrus. None of the goat ovulated 20 hrs post-onset of natural oestrus. Ovulation occur 28 hrs post-onset of oestrus (towards the end of the oestrous period) in Jakhrana goats and reach to its peak at 36 h of post-oestrus.

The length of estrous cycle in goats is 21 days, although there is considerable variation due to breed, season, environmental stress etc. Wide variations have been reported in the length of estrous cycle of different breeds of goats. Some workers have reported the occurance of short estrus cycles (4-12 days) and long estrus cycle (29-42 days) in tropical goats. Some of the long estrus cycles are the result of undetected estrus. The abnormally short cycles may be associated with prematurely regressing corpus luteum or anovulation.

The estrous cycle is divided into two very unequal phases, viz. luteal phase which extends from the formation of the corpus luteum after ovaluation until its regression at the end of the cycle and follicular phase which begins when the corpus luteum regresses and ends with estrus and the ovulation of one or more graffian follicles. The follicular phase in goats is short (2-3 days).

Estrous is due to a local effect of estrogens on the central nervous system. Progesterone has an important synergistic action with estradiol in inducing sexual receptivity. Increased level of estrogen during estrus exerts a positive feedback on the hypothalamo-hypo-physial system to bring about the preovulatory surge in LH and an increased secretion of FSH too. The progesterone level is lowest on the day of estrous, starts rising on the days following estrous and the peak value is reached on or near day 12 of the estrous and the peak value is reached on or near day 12 of the estrous, after which there is an acute and continuous fall. Higher corticosteroid values have been reported on the day of estrus which decline suddenly on day 2 of the estrus. After this, there is a gradual and continuous rise, till finally another peak is observed on the day of next estrus.

Striking differences occur in the physical characteristics of cervical secretions during different reproductive stages in the females and are mainly related to the ovarian estrogenic activity. The general smear pattern in the estrus Angora doe was characterised by a copius flow of thin clear mucus which formed distinct fernlike patterns. Following ovulation the cervical secretion become thick white cheesy mass containing large number of cellular elements and debris. The luteal period, as well as anestrous was marked by a scant serous secretion which shows no crystallization patterns. Desquamation of the vaginal epithelium reached a high level during late estrus when large number of cornified cells appeared in the smear. Vaginal secretion in goats is watery in early stage and thicker in later stage of estrus.

Right ovary of goat appears to be more active than the left because of higher rate of ovulations. The fertile zygote have a marked tendency to migrate to the opposite horn as is evident from the fact that 20-40 cross pregnancies occurred trasuterine migration could be due to the peristaltic and antiperistaltic movement of the uterus. Transuterine migration has been reported to be more frequent in goats than sheep.

Breeding season

It is generally established that the tropical breeds are distinctly non seasonal while the temperate breeds are seasonally polyestrous, but there is no clear cut distinction. Thus Jamnapari, a tropical breed, is seasonally polyestrous and breed twice in a year, June-July and September-October. The highest incidence of estrus is usually found in June and October. Rajkonwar and Borgohain (1978) found that in Assamlocal does, the incidence of estrus, though observed throughout the year was maximum in May followed by that in November and October in the given order. Wani *ct al.* (1980) found the incidence of estrus in Jamunapari does to be highest during June followed by October. Under extensive conditions, continuous mating is practiced, and bucks are maintained with the females throughout the year. A gestation length of 150 days presents goats the opportunity to kid twice per year or three times in two years.

Pregnancy and parturition

Pregnancy starts from fertilization and ends at parturition. Fertilization is the fusion of an ovum and a spermatozoa resulting in the formation of a diploid cell called the embryo or zygote. The site of fertilization is ampulla of the oviduct. The embryo remains free floating in the uterus for 10-12 days in goats after which it gets attached to the uterine wall. The developing embryo receives nutrients from the uterine secretions.

Progesterone is essential for maintaining pregnancy in goats. Corpus Luteum in the ovary is the principal source of progesterone during pregnancy and placenta does not secrete progesterone in goats. In goats, the progesterone is produced mainly by corpus luteum, whereas in sheep, the placenta makes the larger contribution towards the progesterone status. Stress which upsets the function of the corpus luteum will cause abortion.

The progesterone value in pregnant goats increases from the 45th day and reach maximal values between 90 and 120 days after which the levels decline until term.

Oxytocin is known to help in parturition, sperm transport and milk ejection. Fetal and maternal plasma concentration of estrogen rises before and during labour and increases markedly just prior to fetal delivery. In certain Angora goat populations is South Africa, the incidence of abortions is quite high thereby affecting the economic viability of the mohair industry there. Several investigations have indicated of luteal insufficiency in aborters.

Proteins secreted by the placenta, when detected in the peripheral circulation of the mother, can be useful indicators of both pregnancy and of fetal well-being. Antigen(s) immunologically related to pregnancy-associated glycoproteins (PAGs) have also been detected in the serum of pregnant goats. Garbayo *et al.* (1998) isolated and partially characterized a pregnancy associated glycoprotein from pregnant goat serum.

The parturition consists of processes by which the living fetus along with the placental membranes comes out of the pregnant uterus. Most of the kids are born in an anterior longitudinal presentation. The front feet of the fetus emerge first with its nose between them; the head is extended and the dorsum of the fetus is in contact with the sacrum of the dam. This presentation coordinated the natural curvature of the birth canal and the curvature of the fetus. The posterior presentation in the goat per se predisposes them to dystocias and obstetrical disorders.

A complex interaction of endocrine, neutral and mechanical factors bring about the process of parturition. A preliminary luteolysis acts as a triggering factor in parturition. PGF_2 alpha secretion is known to bring about this luteolysis and subsequent decline in progesterone.

The interval between parturition and the first post partum estrus is an important component of overall breeding efficiency of domestic animals. An early post partum estrus reduces the kidding interval and thus has a direct bearing on the economics of livestock rearing. The post partum estrus is dependent on the regression of the corpus luteum of pregnancy.

Postpartum oestrus interval is of comparatively longer duration in Indian goat breeds (Goel and Kharche, 2009). Post partum oestrus is affected by season of kidding. The average post partum estrus values were 143.31, 192.93, 76.25 and 64.21 days in Jamunapari, Beetal, Barbari and Black Bengal goats. Interval to first post-partum oestrus in Black Bengal goats was 68.3±6.4 and 52.1±3.3 days under intensive and semi-intensive systems respectively (Miah and Alim, 2009).In 69 Jakhrana goats, the interval between kidding and oestrus averaged 129.8±9.2 days (range, 6-263) (Goel and Agrawal, 1989). Goel *et al.* (2009) showed the possibility of augmentation in kidding rate in Jakhrana goats during early postpartum anoestrus period by hormonal interventions.

Induction of parturition

Induction of parturition has been found usefulin several conditions such as toxaemia of pregnancy, hydro allantois, and cardiovascular diseases in late pregnancy, to solve the calving problem when there is foetus dam size disparity etc. Mainly glucocorticoids (Short acting-dexamethasone, flumethasone, long acting-Dexamethasone phenyl propionate) and prostaglandins have been used for induction of parturition in goats.

Detection and synchronisation of estrus

Signs of estrus in goats include restlessness, noisy bleatings, frequent twitching of tail, flabby and swollen external genitalia, moist appearance and redness of vulvathe tendency to cluster around the buck and allowing him to tease and tendency to bleat. Estrus does actively seek the presence of the male. The most dependable sign of estrus is the doe's response to the buck . A doe will stand to be mounted by a buck only when she is in estrus and she will actively seek the presence of the male at this time. Signs of estrus in does also include tail wagging, bleating and urination near the bucks. There is some swelling of the vulva and mucus discharge also. The reaction of the buck to the doe being teased is an indication of the estrus in the does. The buck may exhibit and strike the doe with a forelimb. Vocalisations and shorting are common at this time. Some does show few signs of estrus other than limited tail wagging and standing for mounting by the buck and these signs are only present after teasing. The odor of the buck seems to have a stimulating effect on the expression of estrus by does. Mounting by does in estrus on other does is generally not observed. Does will occasionally stand for mounting by other does, but the level of homosexual activity in goats is low in reproductively normal females. The use of homosexual activity as an index of estrus is not reliable since serum progesterone was not detected in does which stood for female early in the breeding season.The initiation of the estrus is followed by hyperemia in the cervix and vaginal wall. The cervix becomes oedomatous, increases in size and the cervical canal extends. Detection of estrus in does is best accomplished with the use of aproned buck or vasectomized bucks.

Estrus was observed to appear in both the morning and afternoon with greater number of cases in the afternoon. Ott *et al.* (1980) studied the effect of the male goat on initiaion of estrous cycle activity in dairy goats. Introduction of the male to a herd of 17 does late in seasonal anestrus resulted in estrus behaviour in 16 of the does with a mean (±SE) of 5.5±1.3 day.

Synchronization of oestrous is an effective management tool to bring a group of goats into oestrous at predetermined time enabling kidding at a desired period. The control of oestrus and ovulation in farm animals remains the basis and a prerequisite for the success of controlled breeding. Oestrus synchronization in does is achieved either by reducing the length of the luteal phase of the oestrous cycle with prostaglandin $F_{2\,alpha}$ ($PGF_{2\,alpha}$) and or its analogues, such as cloprostenol (Estrumate. Coopers UK) or extend it artificially with exogenous progesterone or more potent progestagens. Oestrous synchronization in goats, using progestagen combined with PMSG administration 48 hrs before or at progestagen withdrawal, has been extensively applied achieving an acceptable oestrous response. The objective of estrus synchronisation is to manipulate the reproductive process so that females may be bred during a short predefined interval with normal fertility. It may involve inhibition of ovulation and/or induction of ovulation as well as induction of or delay of corpus luteum regression.

Several luteolytic substances like progestational compounds and prostaglandin F2β has been used for estrus synchonisation in goats. Progesterone can be administered by several means. They can be fed daily, implanted, injected intramuscularly, or inserted in the doe in the form of a vaginal pessary or sponge. Medroxyprogesterone acetate (MAP) and fluorogestone acetate (FGA) sponges are normally used for oestrous synchronisation and are efficient in controlling oestrus and ovulation in goat. Controlled internal drug release (CIDR) devices serve as an alternative method of administering exogenous progesterone for oestrous synchronization. However, the use of intra vaginal sponges has been the method of choice for effective synchronization of oestrous in goat during the breeding as well as non breeding season. Intra vaginal sponges are inserted in the vagina of the animal for a period of 9-14 days in conjunction with a low dose of eCG. Any naturally occurring corpus luteum on the ovaries will regress during this period, leaving the exogenous progesterone as the only progesterone source. At pessary removal , the doe are given a intramuscular injection of PMSG. PMSG causes a closer synchronization and increases ovulation rate. In another protocol, Lutalyse and Cyclix are administrered @ 7.5 mg/goat each time in double dose schedule at an interval of 10-11 days. Under these regimes, 70-80 % animals exhibit oestrous within 24-72 hours after the withdrawal of sponges/prostaglandin treatment and fertility ranges 70-75 % after mating. Effect of synchronisation agent on fertility at synchronised estrus is important.

Pregnancy diagnosis in goats

The early and precise pregnancy diagnosis is an economically important tool for maximizing reproductive efficiency in a goat flock.. The inability to detect early pregnancy results in loss in milk production due to longer kidding interval.Various methods of pregnancy diagnosis in goats have been described.

1. Non-return rate : This is the most commonly used method of pregnancy diagnosis.
2. Rectal abdominal palpation : Rectal abdominal palpation involves the overnight fasted goats placed on their backs . A hollow plastic 1.5 X 50 cm rod with a rounded tip is lubricated and inserted into the rectum 30 to 35 cm. The

rod is moved up and down and from side to side until an obstruction is encountered ora decision reached that the goat is not pregnant. Accuracy at 60 or more days after mating has been reported to be more than 90% .

3. Palpation of the abdomen : Movements of the fetuses can often be palpated between 3½ to 4 months. Put the doe on a stanchion. Place your hands just in front of the udder with your fingers extending into the flanks. Press upward into the belly and hold for a few seconds. You may feel one or more kids moving.

4. Doppler method : In this method does are sedated with xylaxine (0.11 ng) prior to examination by Intra rectal doppler device. The probe is inserted into the doe's rectum and the pub of the fetus is audible in the pregnant does.

5. Progesterone assay– After the discovery that progesterone is excreted in milk in much higher concentratration than in the blood and availability of sensitive radio-immuno assay to measure it, opened the possibility of detecting pregnancy early in the gestation. Studies have been reported in goats using this method (Jain, *et al.,* 1980). The percentage accuracy on days 19, 21, 25 was reported to be 93.33, 93.33 and 92.30% respectively while it was 100% on day 27 post-mating. The animals were classed as pregnant if their milk progesterone concentration was 7.25 ng/ml or above on days 19-27. Milk progesterone can be used to provide an early indication of the pregnancy status of does.

6. Pregnancy specific proteins : *eg* pregnancy specific protein B and pregnancy associated glycoprotein

7. Radiography : The cost of the equipment and potential health hazard to the operator has limited its use.The pregnancy in goats can be diagnosed from about 38 days after covering with this method.

8. Ultrasonography : Ultrasonography is a diagnostic technique that involves directing high frequency sound waves at tissues in the body to generate images of anatomical structures. Ultrasonography is also called sonography, diagnostic sonography, and echocardiography when it is used to image the heart. Ultrasonography has become immensely popular and useful in reproductive biomedicine. Advantages of ultrasonographic imaging techniques are,

    - The high reliability of the results that are generated by ultrasonography
    - Pregnancy diagnosis may be conducted relatively early after insemination (i.e., as early as 27 days after insemination).
    - Ultrasonography techniques are non invasive and are therefore painless.

- There is no need for sedating the animal.
- Another advantage of ultrasonographic imaging over the existing X-ray technology is that it is useful for examination of soft tissues of the bodies where X- rays failed.

The basic principle of ultrasonography is that it uses high frequency sound waves produced by transducer to produce images of soft tissues and internal organs. The internal organs and tissues have inherent abilities either to transmit or reflect the sound waves to varying degrees.

The portion of the sound waves that is reflected is received by a transducer, converted to electrical impulses and displayed on the ultrasound screen as a series of dots. The characteristics of the particular tissue determine what portion of the sound beam will be reflected. Liquids donot reflect sound waves, therefore the image of a liquid containing structure appears black on the screen (eg follicle filled with follicular fluid will appear as a black dot). On the other hand, dense tissue like bone, cervix etc reflect much of the sound beam and appear white on the screen. Other tissues appear in various shades of grey depending upon their echogenicity or ability to reflect the sound waves.

A-mode ultrasound : (amplitude modulation) that in which on the ca-thode-ray tube (CRT) display one axis represents the time required for the return of the echo and the other corresponds to the strength of the echo, as in echoencephalography. Recently ultrasonography has replaced the A-mode ultrasound non imaging system used in the past (Goel and Agrawal, 1992 ; Ishwar, 1995).

B-mode ultrasound — (brightness modulation) that in which the position of a spot on the CRT display corresponds to the time elapsed (and thus to the position of the echogenic surface) and the brightness of the spot to the strength of the echo; movement of the transducer produces a sweep of the ultrasound beam and a tomographic scan of a cross-section of the body.

Presently, real time B-mode ultrasonography is used for the determination of early pregnancy in livestock (Goel *et al.,* 2009). In case of goats, B-mode real time transrectal ultrasonography using frequency of 5-7 mHz can be effectively used for early pregnancy diagnosis (4 week of gestation) and to study early embryonic and foetal development in goats. Real-time ultrasound evaluation of small ruminants offers an unparalleled range of information regarding pregnancy status, number of fetuses, and gestational age. The advantages of real-time ultrasonography are its sensitivity and accuracy of various diagnosis, its speed, and its safety.

Ultrasonography in small ruminants is very popular as a method of pregnancy diagnosis. Like large animals, rectal palpation in small ruminants is not possible due to small sized pelvis (Goel and Kharche, 2009). By using real time B-mode ultrasonography pregnancy can be detected 30 days post insemination using a modified human probe to make it suitable for goats (Goel *et.al.,* 2009). Authors used a modification of the probe used for human ultrasonography to make it suitable for goats. The microconvex transducer in real time ultrasonography is known to cause less discomfort to the animal, allowed faster visualization of the ovaries and produced higher quality images, compared to the linear transducer. Diagnosis other than pregnancy, such as pyometra, hydrometra, fetal resorption, and fetal mummification also can be made using real-time ultrasonography

Reproductive biotechnologies in goat

Reproductive biotechnologies are playing an increasingly important role in the production and management of goats. Examples of current animal biotechnologies include artificial insemination using fresh, frozen or sexed semen, embryo transfer using fresh or frozen in vivo or in vitro produced embryos, cloning using somatic cell nuclear transfer procedures and production of transgenic animals.The evaluation of animal breeds, followed by frozen semen and embryos of the best animals can improve goat production and productivity considerably.

Artificial insemination

Artificial insemination (AI) involves collection of semen from a buck and transfer of the semen to the reproductive tract of the doe. Does can be inseminated with either fresh semen or with frozen goat semen. Artificial insemination is an important technique devised for the rapid spread of superior genetic potential to a large number of animals in a population. Artificial insemination has been successfully exploited for large scale genetic improvement of cattle. However, AI in goats is not practiced on a large scale in the field. Artificial insemination techniques in goats involve collection, evaluation, dilution and storage of semen in addition to inseminating the diluted semen. Satisfactory fertility to artificial insemination requires attention to each step of the procedures for semen storage. The careful management of males that produce semen is the first step toward achieving acceptable fertility after artificial insemination (Leboeuf *et al.,* 2000).

There are several advantages of artificial insemination in goats, which include

- Eliminate or reduce the cost of maintaining bucks.
- Increase the rate of genetic improvement.
- Increase the number of does to which a buck could be bred.
- Breed several does the same day through estrous synchronization and fixed time AI.

Artificial vagina is the most commonly used method for collection of semen from bucks for artificial insemination although semen can also be collected by electroejaculation. Electroejaculation yields a greater volume of semen but a lower concentration of spermatozoa as compared to semen collected by artificial vagina. Collection of semen from the vagina after natural mating has yielded variable results and semen collected is also of poor quality and contaminated with vaginal secretions. Temperature inside the A.V. for goats has been recommended to be 40-42° C.

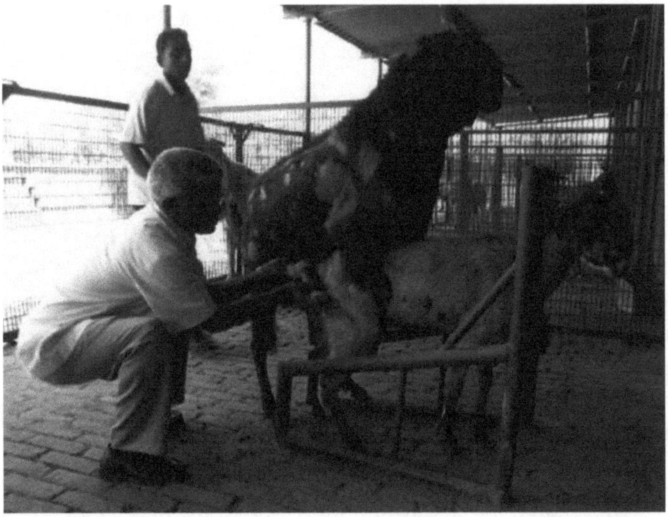

AI includes semen collection, evaluation, dilution, cryopreservation and insemination

Semen production, composition and evaluation

Goat semen is composed of two components-spermatozoa and seminal plasma-each of which performs specific functions towards the ultimate goal of conception or fertilisation. The seminal plasma functions as a medium for the transport of male gametes to the female reproductive tract. This function is accomplished by providing a buffering medium that contains nutrients for the spermatozoa and maintains an optimum concentration of spermatozoa required for fertilisation in a suitable volume.

Sperms produced by the testis are infertile and undergo a series of maturation changes in the epididymis before confirmed with the ability to fertilize. During its transit through the vas deferens and ejaculatory ducts of the penis, spermatozoa gets mixed with the secretions of the accessory sex glands which from the bulk of the seminal plasma. The sperm production as well as the secretory function of epididymis and other accessory glands is under androgenic control whose production is further regulated by the hypothalamo-hypophyseal system. Successful artificial insemination necessitates the use of good quality semen. Poor quality semen does not keep as well as semen of good quality and the fertilizing capacity of a semen sample is fairly correlated with various semen characteristics. Unlike stallion and boar, goat semen has a small volume and a higher sperm density. Goat semen has a small volume and a higher sperm density. Goat semen is ejaculated very rapidly and these appears to be a function of the seminal plasma which is to act as a vehicle for conveying sperm to the female reproductive tract.

The three measures of semen quality are sperm concentration, sperm morphology and sperm motility. They are correlated with each other and with fertility. Attention to the bulk seminal values of these characteristics is based upon the sufficient number of normal spermatozoa.

Sperm concentration can be determined visually using a hemocytometer or automatically using an electronic particle counter. Accurate dilution pipettes and replicate counts are necessary to ensure the accuracy and precision of the visual method. The confounding influence of seminal debris with low sperm concentration is a potential problem with automatic counters. Addition of lytic enzymes to the semen prior to counting,by dissolving the debris can help alleviate this difficulty.

Sperm motility is the most useful single criterion for semen evaluation. Motility is evaluated by examining a drop of semen at body temperature under the microscope and is expressed empirically from + to +++++, depending upon the percentage of motile spermatozoa and the type of wave motion.

Microscopic studies of semen can also determine the percentage of abnormal spermatozoa, percentage of live and dead spermatozoa and bacterial contamination. Excessively higher percentage of abnormal spermatozoa is an indication of osmotic pressure, ionic equilibrium, resistance to thermal shock, electrical impedance and optical properties are also used for evaluation of semen.

Goat semen is white or cream colored. The viscosity varies from thin to thick, depending, on the concentration of spermatozoa. Semen should be free from dirt, blood, leukocytes and other contamination observable either by gross examination or by simple microscopic techniques.

Volume and spermatozoa concentration of semen are required to calculate the total number of spermatozoa per ejaculate. This measurement of spermatozoa output, when ejaculates of semen are produced frequently, is excellent simple measurement of the quantitative aspects of spermatogenesis. In addition, this number determines how many inseminations can be performed from each ejaculate. The volume of ejaculate in goats normally ranges from 0.3 to 1.5 ml. Young males produce smaller quantities of semen than older animals.

Concentration of spermatozoa per ml is probably the most important single characteristic measured. Average sperm counts of goat semen are 3600 x 10^6/ml. Spermatozoa must be alive to be fertile and live spermatozoa usually are motile. It is essential for obtaining good conception rate that at least 60-70% of the spermatozoa show good motility.

Goat sperm possesses the typical filiform structure which can be distinguished in three regions viz., sperm-head, middle piece and tail, the latter two constituting the flagellum. Goat sperm length is similar to that of rabbit, ram bull, boar and human sperm (about 50μ). The head of goat spermatozoa is usually ovoid in common with bull, boar and rabbit, but unlike the hook like shape in the mouse and rabbit.

Sperm motility and proportion of abnormal sperm are measures of the quality of spermatozoa. A sperm to be fertile needs to be motile, but all motile sperms are not fertile. Abnormalities of acrosome are most important for reduced fertility besides various other forms of sperm abnormalities. Number of abnormal spermatozoa in goat bucks that fertilize satisfactorily should be less than 10%.

Most important component of spermatozoa is the surface membranes. The surface has several components known as sperm coating antigen (SCA). Membrane changes have been reported to take place in the spermatozoa, as it matures in the epididymis. The sperm acrosome is of particular significance as it contains enzymes essential for fertilization. Bovine Seminal Plasma proteins have been isolated from goat seminal plasma and these proteins interact with choline phospholipids on the sperm surface and play a role in the membrane stabilization (decapacitation) and destabilization (capacitation) process (La Falci *et al.,* 2002).

Fructose is the major carbohydrate in the goat semen. In addition, glucose and sialic acid have also been reported to be present. Glucose was present as free sugar in goat semen in addition to fructose. No evidence for the presence of a polysaccharide of any sugar (Mannose, glucose and galactose) was obtained. A large variation in fructose values in goat semen (465 to 1294.50 mg/100 ml) has been reported by various workers.

Lipids and phospholipids constitute the important structural components of sperm membrane and acrosome which are utmost importance for their integrity and permeability. It has been suggested that various phospholipids, present in the spermatozoa, combine with the protein molecules to form a lipoprotein complex, which is an integral part of cell membrane. In addition, phospholipids have been suggested to provide an endogenous source of energy to the spermatozoa when the exogenous source is not available. Citric acid in semen binds calcium ions and is important in maintaining the osmotic equilibrium. It is exclusively produced in the prostate. Citric acid content of goat semen has been reported to be 641.74±40.15 mg/100 ml (Patil and Raja, 1973) and 665.60±99.1 mg (Varshney, 1977).

Other tests of semen quality include motility of spermatozoa following refreezing, loss of enzymes from the spermatozoa such as glutamic oxaloacetic transaminase (GOT), acrosin etc. and metabolic changes. Lot of research effort has gone into probing suitable biochemical indices to forecast the fertilizing capacity of semen. Among other which has been tried at one or other time include rate of respiration and glycolysis, fructolysis index and methylene blue reduction time.

Fructose is the glycolysable sugar present in semen. Fructolysis rate can be measured in two ways; either by measuring the amount of fructose which is used up in the course of fructolysis or alternately by the determination of lactic acid, which is formed as the end product. Under aerobic conditions, lactic acid formed as a final product of sperm glycolysis, undergoes further oxidation to provide metabolic energy for spermatozoa. Addition of glucose, fructose and mannose increase respiration as well as motility.

High quality semen is crucial for successful insemination and artificial insemination. Nutrition, environment and chemical agents, management factors etc are some of factors which affect the quantity and quantity of goat semen. There are seasonal as well as climatic variations in the quantity and quality of semen produced by goat. Nutrition has a profound influence on the quantity and quality of semen produced. Specific deficiencies of vitamins and minerals and other nutrients may bring about changes in the activity and functioning of male reproductive system. Nutrition and feeding practices can have a profound effect on fertility. Lipids are important molecules that serve as a source of energy and are critical components of the physical and functional structure of cells. Omega-3 fatty acids, in particular Docosahexaenoic acid (DHA), are important for sperm membrane integrity, sperm motility and viability. Fish oil supplementation with excess vitamin E and omega-3 fattt acids have a beneficial effect on the semen quality and fertility in the Markhoz bucks (Dolatpanah *et al.,* 2008).

Seasonal variation in reaction time, semen quantity, motility of the diluted semen, viability duration and number of spermatozoa per unit volume, testicular histology and spermatogenic activity of goat semen have been reported.Twice weekly collection is normally recommended for buck in AI programme. Studies on the effect of frequency of semen collection on seminal attribute and fertility indicated that goats can donate semen of good quality without ill effects on their health when used continuously for 5-8 weeks on once-daily collection schedule.

Cryopreservation and insemination of goat spermatozoa

Frozen semen of goats has not been used as successfully as in cattle. Most of the procedures developed for cryopreservation and insemination of cattle semen has been extrapolated for use with goat semen. However, the efficacy of several of them, for goat spermatozoa has not been proved beyond doubt.The biggest obstacle to the exploitation of frozen semen is that the freeze–thawing process of goat sperm generally leads to a decrease in the percentage of motile and viable sperm cells after thawing as a result of damage to membrane integrity and ultrastructure (Watson, 2000).

The ability to cryopreserve spermatozoa from all of the domestic species is challenging. Semen from most species must be extended with a medium for its successful preservation and this applies to goats as well. Successful preservation should result in a fertilised viable egg after artificial insemination. There are many acceptable methods for cryopreserving goat semen. Most semen is preserved at sub-zero temperatures; cryoprotectants have to be used in dilutors to prevent the spermatozoa from cold shock. Glycerol is the most commonly used cryoprotectant although ethlene glycol and dimethyl sulfoxide are also considered good. In case of bull semen, 7% (v/v) glycerol is included in the final extendor. Available data provide insufficient indications as to this regard also individual differences in semen preservability by freezing and thawing are quite high. Low fertility observed with certain bucks could be due to a high incidence of ejaculates with low freezability. Important factors in semen cryopreservation include cooling, freezing, thawing, and the addition of cryoprotectants. Spermatozoa subjected to cryopreservation are very sensitive to a rapid reduction in temperature from 25 to 5 °C. Prompt processing of semen after collection is important to avoid accumulation of products of metabolism, to maintain sperm motility and to prevent possible harzardous effects of exposure to light. Addition of protective media to protect sperm against prefreeze cold shock and refrigeration are the first steps. For freezing semen, glycerol is included in the final extendor. Removal of seminal plasma prior to freezing spermatozoa in an extender containing egg yolk had an unfavorable effect on their post-thaw motility and integrity (Tuli and Holtz, 1994)

Egg yolk is known to protect bull spermatozoa against cold shock and the low-density lipoprotein fraction (LDF) is well-established as the active constituent. Roy (1957) reported the presence of a egg yolk coagulating enzyme in goat semen. Several investigators have successfully used egg yolk dilutors for the dilution of goat semen. Aboagla and Terada (2004) concluded that the inclusion of egg yolk significantly improved sperm motility, indicating its beneficial effects during the freezing step of cryopreservation in goat and trehalose appeared to synergistically increase its cryoprotective effects. Ranjan *et al.* (2009) found that Marwari buck semen extended in the diluents having 10% egg yolk level could be stored upto 72h at refrigeration temperature for further use as liquid semen for artificial insemination. It seems that the best goat sperm extender is Tris, citric acid, fructose, egg yolk, and glycerol. Freezing of goat semen in straws is better than pellet freezing, therefore it is recommended that goat semen should be frozen in straws. It is possible to successfully utilize frozen-thawed goat sperm for artificial insemination, IVF and embryo production.

Temperature has an important effect on the preservation ability of the semen. Goat spermotozoa can possibly be stored for 4-7 days at room temprature. Goat's sperm can also be stored more successfully by freezing in liquid nitrogen although the fertility is generally lower than that of fresh semen. The success of AI technology is based on both semen quality and freezing process.

Productivity potential of goats can be augmented through use of sire testing and artificial insemination. Artificial insemination (AI) can play an important role in goat breeding, especially in intensive systems of production, to control reproduction and, in conjunction with accurate progeny testing, to improve the production of milk, hair and meat. Other advantages of AI include more efficient genetic selection schemes, and the manipulation and storage of the genetic material. Spermatozoa are usually inseminated with the aid of an insemination gun. When cows are artificially bred, an insemination pipette is inserted through the vagina and threaded through the rings of the cervix. The operator inserts his hand into the cow's rectum and uses his thumb and fingers to help guide the pipette through the cervical canal. Semen is deposited into the body of the uterus. In small ruminants, especially goat, this procedure is difficult, due to the smaller body size and, a more complicated anatomy of the reproductive tract in the goat. Goat has a longer and more complex cervix than other ruminant livestock. It is approximately 12 centimeters in length and has 6 or 7 offset rings which make passage of AI gun entry even through the first cervical ring difficult. Efforts are being made to overcome these obstacles and improve the conception rate in future so that the technology can be adopted on a large scale throughout the country.

In goats, frozen semen is used with good fertility, provided it is deposited through the cervix into the uterus. Apparently, frozen thawed spermatozoa do not penetrate the cervix as easily as do fresh (unfrozen) sperm cells. Spermatozoa survival time is reduced following freezing and thawing and so time of insemination may be more critical with frozen semen. The following equipment is needed for artificial insemination in goats

Equipment needed to inseminate does

1. Liquid nitrogen tank
2. Speculum (25 x 175 mm for doelings or 25 x 200mm for does)
3. AI light or headlight
4. Straw tweezers
5. Sterile lubricant (non-spermicidal)
6. Insemination gun (for straws)
7. Breeding stand or facilities to restrain the doe
8. Thaw box
9. Paper towels
10. Straw cutter
11. Thermometer

Thawing of semen

For thawing frozen goat semen, remove the frozen straw from the liquid nitrogen tank with the straw tweezers and place it in a thaw box filled with warm water (95°F) for 30 seconds. After thawing, wipe the straw thoroughly with a paper towel.

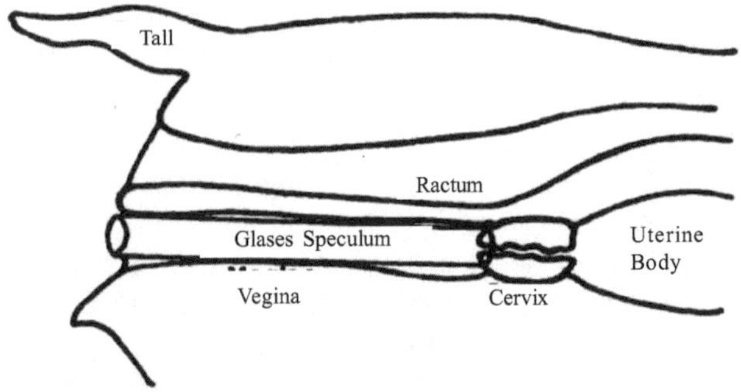

Procedure for locating the os cervix with a vagnial speculum and light source.

Three types of insemination techniques e.g., vaginal, cervical and intrauterine, are currently used in goats. Cervical insemination involves deposition of sperm on the uterine side of the cervix.The intrauterine method is Laparoscopic insemination, which involves the use of laparoscope and manipulating probe to aid in depositing fresh or frozen-thawed sperm directly into the uterine horns.

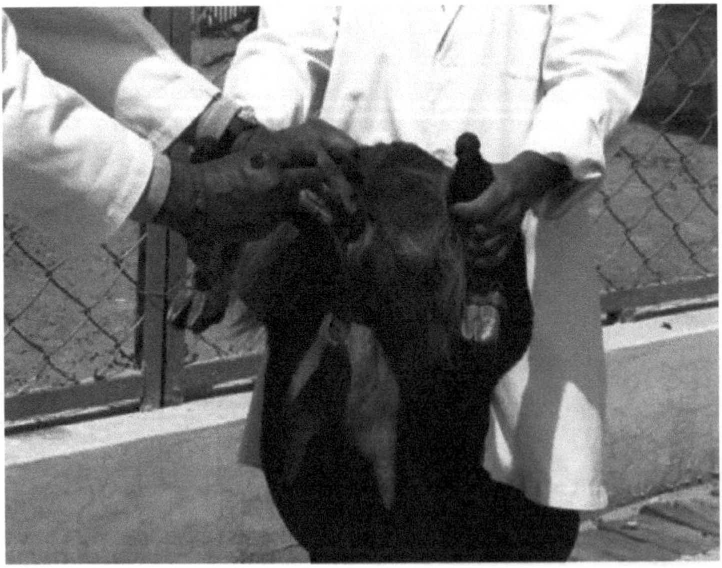

Conception rate

An approximately 62% kidding rate was achieved by using hormones to induce and inseminate 17,438 Alpine and Saanen goats using semen doses stored from 0.5 to 3 yr (Leboeuf, 1989).

In the field of semen technology, attempts were made to freeze-thaw Cashmere buck semen in pellet form at high densities (1:0.5 to 1:2; semen:diluent). However, under these conditions, fertility after cervical AI remained low when compared to that obtained after laparoscopic AI of 1:23 diluted semen (33 YS 43% of kiddings; Ritar and Ball 1993). Although significant progress has been made in the last five years regarding the control of goat reproduction, in the field of semen production and processing and of AI, progress remains to be done for improving the efficiency of deep-freezing technique.

Embryo transfer, IVF and associated reproductive technologies

Embryo transfer involves superovulation of the donor, egg recovery, manipulation of eggs, synchronisation of both donor and recipient and technique of transfer. The application of MOET has generally been sluggish, when it comes to the genetic improvement programmes of small ruminants over the years. This is mainly due to the implication of surgical intervention in the recovery and transfer of the embryos and the high costs per embryo (Gordon, 1997).The inherent risks involved in the procedure of MOET in small stock include the healing of wounds, the formation of the post-operation adhesions leading to subsequent infertility of donor animals and a reduced response to exogenous gonadotrophins over time.The birth of kid from embryo transfer was reported in 1949 for the first time. However, it was not until mid-1980s when ET emerged as an industry in cattle, the development of ET technology in small ruminants was begun. Reproductive efficiency in goats may be increased by induction of superovulation to harvest a large number of embryos followed by their transfer into synchronized recipient. The response of does to exogenous gonadotropin are highly variable. The commonly used gonadotropins are pregnant Mares Serum Gonadotropin, porcine FSH-P and ovine FSH-P. Pregnant mares serum gonadotropin is administered as single injection of 750 to 1000 IU during mid luleal phase, followed by 7.5 mg of prostaglandin $F_{2á}$ (Lutalyse) 48 hr after PMSG injection. Embryos are commonly recovered either from oviduct or uterus at laparotomy.Three methods of ET, namely, laparoscopic ET, surgical ET and transcervical ET have been reported in small ruminants of which laparoscopic ET is more successful (Ishwar and Memon, 1996).

Detrimental effects of repeated surgical embryo-recoveries cause adhesions and reduce fertility of donor females, limiting the usefulness of the embryotransfer technique for genetic improvement. Two effective methods of embryo recoveries that require less surgical trauma are laparoscopic and other nonsurgical procedures

(Amoah and Gelaye, 1997). Ovulation profile in Jamunapari goats indicated that ovulation occurred in this breed during 32-36 hours following estrus (Goel et al CIRG). Multiple ovulation and embryo transfer (MOET) in goats has not become widely used due to its unpredictability.

Jamunapari goats started cycling from May and their oestrous activity reached peak in September through December. Oestrous activity started declining from January and complete cessation in March-April. Oestrous duration ranged between 24-48 hours. Incidence of short cycles and long cycles also has been observed in goats. The goats and sheep embryo transfer has to be surgical because of the small reproductive organs which cannot be manipulated per rectum as in case of cattle and buffaloes. Using Surgical methods for embryo transfer at CIRG it was found that the superovulatory respone in Jamunapari goats averaged 6.80 ovulations /goats, embryo/ova recovery 4.50/goat and transferable embryos 4.0/goat (Goel *et al.,* 2003-2004 annual report CIRG).

Agrawal *et al.* (1979) using surgical technique reported 62% recovery of eggs from the fallopian tubes of which 84.6% exhibited normal cleavage. Upon transfer 75% of recipient goats conceived and carried 54.5% of embryos to full term.

Goel and Agrawal (2005) reported that Jakhrana goats can be superovulated for embryo production using FSH to augment productivity. This is the first report of superovulation in Jakhrana goats, a large size breed of the tropics. No optimal superovulatory protocol has been established for goats because of ovarian variation (Greyling *et al.,* 2002). Embryo production and recovery is affected by factors such as age, breed, source and dose of exogenous hormone used for superovulation. Better superovulatory response has been reported in exotic breeds of goats as compared to Indian or tropical breeds.The success of ET depends on several factors including management of donor and recipient does, estrus synchronization in donors and recipients, superovulation of donors, breeding (natural or AI), embryo collection and evaluation, transfer of embryos and factors affecting survival of transferred embryos.

Embryo cryopreservation is a means of long-term storage of valuable strains, breeds or animals. Embryos are preserved in a cryoprotectant then slowly frozen. Embryos are then transferred to liquid nitrogen tanks for long-term storage. Cryopreservation of gametes has provided a extremely useful tool for improvement of livestock at a much faster rate. Cryopreserved semen and embryos offer a unique tool for improving the genetic potential of livestock including cattle, buffalo, sheep, goat, pig, horses, camel and other species useful to human being. The present day breeds of livestock are a result of continued and sustained selection of superior animals over a period of several thousand of years. For faster genetic improvement cryopreserved gametes have excellent opportunities.

Bilton and Moore (1976) reported the first successful cryopreservation of goats embryos. Since then several workers have succeeded in cryopreservation and transfer of goat embryos. However, it soon became clear that techniques in permeability, cryopreservation and freezing characteristics of embryo cells of one species cannot be extrapolated to another (Amoah and Gelaya, 1997). Factors affecting cryoprotection of embryos are discussed (Kumar *et al.,* 1998). It is concluded from the literature that application of cryobiological principles can result in high survival rates for morulae and blastocysts in several livestock species; however, an optimal method for one species is not always applicable to embryos of any other species. Vitrification of goat embryos has been attempted and kids were produced (Yuswiati and Holtz, 1990). Vitrification involves the exposure of goat embryos to high concentration of cryoprotectants followed by direct immersion in liquid nitrogen.

Recent progress made in the field of oocyte maturation and in vitro fertilization of farm animals has provided a new dimension for exploitation of animal reproductive set up. This technology has great potential for application on genetically superior animals to have progeny from it in numbers many fold than numbers it would produce in its life time, if left to reproduce normally. Breifly this technique involves collection of oocytes from the ovary, in vitro maturation of oocytes, in vitro capacitation, fertilization and culture of the embryos so produced.

A number of studies have been conducted to investigate IVM competency of goat oocytes, from both adult and prepubertal goats. Studies were carried out with oocytes derived from abattoir ovaries, laparoscopic guided ovum pickup, laparotomy or ovariectomy using untreated or hormonally treated goats. TCM-199 is the main base medium for IVF in goats which is supplemented with hormones, serum, carbohydrates and other components as required. Generally, selected oocytes are cultured in presence of CO2 (5%) in air and humidity (95%) at 38 to 39 °C. IVM oocytes are less competent than oocytes matured in vivo. Future researches should be directed towards finding factors affecting maturational competence of goat oocytes in vitro. Successfully production of an in vitro fertilized (IVF) goat kid has been reported by Kharche *et al.,* 2008, 2011.

Embryo transfer technology has become a tool for enhancing lifetime productivity of livestock. A large number of embryos are required for the success of Embryo Transfer programme under field condition. With variable superovulation response, reduced embryo recovery rates and the interruption of the normal reproductive cycle of the donor, *in-vitro* maturation and *in-vitro* fertilization procedure is an attractive alternative for the production of large number of embryos required for the rapid multiplication of superior germplasm of goats with lowered fertility and conservation of endangered breeds of goat. Laparoscopic ovum pick-up is of importance in the production and early propagation of such goats.

A large number of early and late stages of embryos are required for the biotechnological experiments such as micromanipulation and micro-injection for the production of identical twin, sexed offspring, cloning and transgenic goat.

However, the number of embryo obtained by superovulation is limited and expensive due to unpredictable superovulatory response; reduce embryo recovery rate and limitations of repeated surgical embryo collection in small ruminants. Therefore the use of ovaries collected from slaughter house material as a source of oocytes for IVM, IVF and embryo development is an attractive alternative for large scale economical production of early and late stages of embryos that can be used in the development of new biotechnologies.

Goat embryos seem to be more difficult to bisect than other livestock embryos. Hatched blastocyst was more suitable for bisection of goat embryos (Amaoh and Gelaye, 1997). Sexing of embryos prior to transfer has commercial application, especially in dairy goats. In a study, after transferring 12-sexed blastocysts to recipient does 8 (67%) were carried to term (El Gayar and Holtz, 2005).

Infertility in goats

Infertility in goats is not a major problem with goat keepers. Incidence of infertility in goats is of moderate degree in comparison to large animal species like cattle and buffalo. Goel and Sinha (2005) reported an incidence of infertility in goats as 11.50%. Anoestrus and abortion were recognized as major causes leading to lowered fertility followed by repeat breeding and still birth. However, the infertility can occur because of anatomical, hormonal as well as infectious reasons. Infections like brucellosis can cause abortion in goats. The cases of dystocia etc are seldom encountered.

Infertility problem in goats is caused due to various reasons. Deficiency of some minerals like phosphorus, zinc, copper, manganese, etc in goats may cause infertility, repeat breeding, delayed sexual maturity, sterility, low milk production, weakening of bones, retarded growth, and rough hair coat.

Due to the linkage of polled condition with infertility in certain males, it is now preferred to go for dehorning the male rather than selecting the male for polled condition. In India where most of the breeds are horned, such infertility problems perhaps don't exist.

Genital tract of goat can get infection with bacterial, viral, mycotic and chlamydial agents. Some of them are potential pathogens and infection with them results in abortion in pregnant animals and may subsequently lead to infertility. These infectious diseases are common like: Brucellosis, Vibriosis, Chlamydial abortion.

Therefore, goats under field conditions also require proper management and hygienic practices before, during and after kidding to minimize lowered fertility.

Fertility and reproductive efficiency

Reproduction is the most important production parameter. The number of offspring born and the number that are weaned and survive to market readiness determine to a large extent the economic viability of the production system. Fertility is both a heritable trait and one that can be managed and improved through nutrition and health management programs.

Fertility is difficult to measure exactly, but is indicated by the number of services required per conception and for the male by the percentage of services resulting in conception. Since each depends on the fertility of the other sex, measures of fertility are only useful as a comparative index for large number of animals. Prolificacy of the female goat is expressed as the number of kids born per doe per year or as kids per birth (litter size). The number of services per conception has been reported to vary from 1.14 to 2.3 for various breeds of goats. Black Bengal goats have been reported to have especially high litter size as compared to other breeds of goats. Among Indian goat breeds, Black Bengal is reputed to have the highested fecundity. In this breed about 20 % of triplets and 0.5% of quadruplet births have been reported. Twins are common in most breeds like Jamunapari, Beetal, Barbari and Black Bengaletc.

References

Aboagla, E. M. And Terada, T. (2004). Effects of egg yolk during the freezing step preservativ on the viability of goat spermatozoa. Theriogenology 62 : 1160- 1172.

Agrawal, K.P., Mongha, I.V. and Bhattacharyya, N.K. (1979) Success in embryo trnasfer in indigenous goats. Curr. Sci. 48:792

Ali, S.Z., Hoque, M.M. and Hasnath, M.A. (1973) A study on the growth and reproductive performance of Black Bengal goats under farm conditions. Indian vet. J. 50:438.

Amoah, E.A. and Gelaye, S .1997. Biotechnological advances in goat reproduction. Journal of Animal Science 75:578-585.

Atreja, P.P. and Anand, S.R. (1977) Studies on epididymal lipid metabolism by epididymal spermatozoa of goats. Annual Report, NDRI, Karnal, pp 93.

Bilton, R.J. and Moore, N.W. (1976) In vitro culture storage and transfer of goat embryos. Aust. J. Biol. Sci. 29:125-129.

Dolatpanah MB, Towhidi A, Farshad A, Rashidi A, Rezayazdi. (2008) Effect of fish oil on semen quality of goats. Asian Aust Anim Sci., 21:29-34.

El Gayar, M. and Holtz, W. (2005). Transfer of sexed caprine blastocysts freshly collected or derived from cultured morulae. Small Rum. Res., 57:151-156.

Elwishi, A.B. and Elsawaf, S.A. (1971) Development of sexual activity in male Damascus goats. Indian J. Anim. Sci. 41:350-356.

Farshad, A., Akhondzadeh, S., Zamiri, M.J., Sadeghi, Gh. (2008). The Estrous Cycle of the Markhoz Goat in Iran Asian-australasian journal of animal sciences 2008, 21(10):1411-1415.

Garbayo, J.M., Remy B, Alabart, J.L., Folch, J., Wattiez, R., Falmagne, P., Beckers, J.F. (1998I) solation and partial characterization of a pregnancy-associated glycoprotein family from the goat placenta. Biol Reprod 58:109-115.

Goel, A.K. and Agrawal, K.P. (1989) Post-partum oestrous interval in Jakhrana goats. Indian Journal of Animal Reproduction, 1989, 10(2):175,

Goel, A.K. and Agrawal, K. P. (1992) A review of pregnancy diagnosis techniques in sheep and goats. Small Rum Res 9:255-264.

Goel, A.K. and Agrawal, K.P. (2003) Ovulation in Jakhrana goats native to tropical climates. Small Ruminant Research 50:509-512.

Goel, A.K. and Agrawal, K.P. (2005)Ovulatory response and embryo yield in Jakhrana goats following treatments with PMSG and FSH Tropical Animal Health and Production. 37: 549-558.

Goel, A.K. and Sinha, N.K. (2005). Studies on the incidence and causes of infertility in goats reared under fields conditions. Indian Journal of Animal Reproduction 26(1): 64-65.

Goel, A.K. and S. D. Kharche (2009) Advances in reproductive techniques in goats- A review The Indian journal of small ruminants 15(1)1-34.

Goel A.K., Kharche, S.D. and Jindal, S.K. (2009) Determination of Early Pregnancy and Embryonic Development by Trans rectal Ultrasonography. Indian Journal of Animal Sciences 79(5): 476 - 478.

Goel, A.K., Kharche, S.D. and Jindal, S.K. (2009). Efficacy of Progestin Implant – eCG to increase kidding rate in post- partum anoestrus Jakhrana goats. Indian Journal of Animal Sciences, 79: 473-475.

Gordon, I., (1997). Controlled Reproduction in Sheep and Goats. Cambridge University Press, Wallingford, UK.

Greyling, J.P.C., NestVander, M., Schwalbach, L.M.J. and Muller, T. (2002) Superovulation and embryo transfer in South African Boer and indigenous Feral goats. Small Ruminant Research 43: 45-51.

Ishwar A.K., Memon, M.A. (1996)Embryo transfer in sheep and goats: a review. Small Rumin Res;19:35–43.

Ishwar, A.K. (1995) Pregnancy diagnosis in sheep and goats: A review. Small Rum Res;17:37-44.

Jain, G.C., Arora, R.C. and Pandey, R.S. (1980) Milk progesterone content and pregnancy diagnosis in goats. Zbl. Vet. Med. A. 27:103-108.

Jindal, S.K. (1984). Sperm concentration in different segments of the goat epididymis. Theriogenology. 22:511-513

Jindal, S.K. (1984). Testicular sperm reserves of goats. Indian Journal of Animal Science 54 (5), 511-513.

Jindal, S.K. and Panda, J.N. (1980). Maturation changes of goat spermatozoa during transist through the epididymis. Andrologia. 12, 328-331.

Jindal, S.K. and Panda, J.N. (1989). Epididymal sperm reserves of the goat (Capra hircus), Journal of Reproduction & Fertility (Cambridge) 59:469-471.

Khan, B.U. (1980) Goat breeding in India-A Review. Agric. Rev. 1(2):133-140.

Kharche, S.D., Goel, A.K., Jindal, S.K., Goel, Puja and Jha, Vipul Kumar (2011) Birth of twin kids following transfer of in-vitro produced goat embryos Indian Journal of Animal Sciences 81 (11): 1132-1134

Kharche, S.D., Goel, A.K., Jindal, S.K. and Sinha, N.K. (2008) Birth of a female kid from in-vitro matured and fertilized caprine oocytesIndian Journal of Animal Sciences 78 (7): 680–685

Kumar, A., Saini, A. Jindal, S.K. & Punj, M.L. (1998). Cryopreservation of embryos of various domestic animals. Indian Dairyman 50 (5) 5-10.

La Falci, V.S., H. Tortorella, J.L. Rodrigues and A. Brandelli,(2002) Seasonal variation of goat seminal plasma proteins, Theriogenology 57 pp. 1035-1048.

Leboeuf, B. Restall Salamon, B.S. (2000) Production and storage of goat semen for artificial insemination. Anim Reprod Sci 62:113-141

Leboeuf, B., (1989). L'inse'mination artificielle caprine en France, e'tat actuel et perpectives d'avenir. Sympo-sium International sur la Reproduction chez les petits Ruminants. In: Greppi, G.F.Ed.., La reproduzione nei Piccoli Ruminanti, Camera di commercio industria artigianto agricoltura di Varese, pp. 87–113,Varese

Levasseur, Par Marie-Claire (1979) Thoughts on puberty . The gonads. Ann. Biol. Anim. Bioch. Biophys. 19(2ª) 321-325.

Miah, G. And Alim, M.A. (2009) Performance of Black Bengal goats under intensive and semi intensive farming systems. SAARC J. Agri., 7(2):15-24.

Ott, R.S., Nelson, D.R., Hixon, J.E. (1980) Effect of presence of male on the initiation of estrus activity of goats. Theriogeneology 13:183-190.

Panda, J.N. and Jindal, S.K. (1982). Effect of chronic use of cyproterone acetate on the epididymis of goats. Andrologia. 4, 397-402.

Patil, R.V. and Raja, C.K.S.V. (1973) The fructose, citric acid and ascorbic acid content in the semen of Malabari buck. Kerala J. Vet. Sci. 4:94-95.

Prasad, S.P. and Bhattacharyya, N.K. (1979) A note on the characteristics of puberal oestrus and oestrous cycle in Barbari nannies. Indian J. Anim. Sci. 49:969-970.

Prasad, S.P. (1969) Studies on some productive traits of Barbari goats. M.V.Sc. Thesis, Agra Univ. Agra.

Rahman, A., Hussain, A., Ahmed, M.U. and Sen, M.M. (1977) Studies on some reproductive performances and biometry of the female genital organs of Black Bengal goats. Indian J. Anim. Sci. 47:724-725.

Rajkonwar, C.K. and Boragohain, B.N. (1978) A note on the incidence and signs of oestrus in local does (Capra hircus) of Assam. Indian J. Anim. Sci. 48:758-759.

Ranjan R, Ramachandran, N., Jindal, S.K., Sinha, N.K., Goel, A.K., Kharche, S.D. and Sikarwar, A.K.S. (2009) Effect of Egg Yolk Levels on Keeping Quality of Marwari Buck Semen at Refrigeration Temperature.. Indian Journal of Animal Sciences 79(7): 662–664.

Ritar, A.J., Ball, P.D. (1993). The effect of freeze thawing of goat and sheep semen at a high density of spermatozoa on cell viability and fertility after insemination. Anim. Reprod. Sci. 31, 249–262.

Roy, A. (1957) Egg yolk coagulating enzyme in the semen and cowpers glands of goat. Nature 179:318-319.

Sahni, K.L. and Roy, A. (1967) A study on the sexual activity of the Barbari goat and conception rate through artificial insemination. Indian J. Vet. Sci. & A.H. 37:269-276.

Singh, S.N. and Sengar, O.P.S. (1980) Studies on the combining ability of desirable characteristics of important goat breeds for meat and milk separately and in combination. P.L.480 Project, R.B.S. College, Bichpuri Agra.

Tiwari, S.B., B.Rai, (2005)Bharat Me Bakri Palan, In Hindi, Saroj Prakashan, Allahabad

Tuli, R.K., Holtz, W., (1994). Effect of glycerolization procedure and removal of seminal plasma on post-thawsurvival and got-release from Boer goat spermatozoa. Theriogenology 42, 547–555.

Varshney, V.P. (1977) Studies on the endocrine aspect of production and reproduction in ruminants. Thesis Agra Univ. Agra.

Wani, G.M., Sinha, N.K. and Sahni, K.L. (1980) Note on the seasonality of breeding behaviour in Jamunapari does under tropical conditions. Indian J. Anim. Sci. 50:1153-1155.

Watson, P.F. (2000). The causes of reduced fertility with cryopreserved semen. Anim. Reprod. Sci., 60–61 , pp. 481–492

Yuswiati, E., and Holtz, W. (1990) Successful transfer of vitrified goat embryos. Theriogenology 34:629–632

8

Meat Production

Meat is animal flesh that is used as food. Most often, this means the skeletal muscle and associated fat, but it may also describe other edible tissues such as organs, liver, brain, bone marrow, kidney, or lung. Meat is a nutrient dense food. Meat contains protein, fat, enzymes, vitamins and minerals for proper human nutrition. Goats are important producer of meat besides milk, fiber and skin. Goat meat is lower in calories, total fat, saturated fat and cholesterol, than traditional meats.Goat have number of characteristics , such as high reproductive potential , short generation interval , ability to thrive on shrubs, bushes and tree leaves, high digestive efficiency for cellulose and less susceptibility to infectious diseases, that make them suitable as meat producing livestock. Since these animals are more concentrated in the developing part of the world, they play a major role in subsistence agriculture of developing economies of poor and marginal farmers inhabiting such countries. More than 95 % of goats are concentrated in dry tropical and subtropical areas of poor agricultural potential and even on marginal lands of the world (Morand Fehr and Boyazoglu, 1999). Goat has several other advantages as producer of meat which make it predominant and preferred animal for meat production. Often because of the above mentioned reason, goat meat is sold two to three times costlier as compared to pork in India. Beef is unavailable in India with the exception of Kerala and West Bengal. Goat meat has an edge over mutton too, as the number of goats slaughtered for meat purposes (40%) far exceeds the number of sheep slaughtered for similar purposes. The slaughter rate of goat is at the level of 39.7 % as compared to 31.8% for sheep and 11% for buffaloes, respectively. Sheep and goat meat are both called "mutton" in India. Goats convert the poor quality roughage, browse tree leaves, which would have otherwise gone waste, into valuable source of protein in several desert or hostile areas of the world where other classes of livestock like cattle and buffalo will starve to death. Goat meat production and consumption has an important place in the economy of Asian and African countries. Goats have been recognized as an important source of meat in the rural areas of these countries. Commercial meat-goat enterprises account for majority of the meat-goat production systems and herd sizes range from five to several thousand does. Prolificacy, milk production and pre-weaning growth are important in achieving good productivity of commercial meat production enterprises.

Whereas, beef is taboo with Hindus, Pork is not consumed by the Muslim. Goat meat has the advantage of being preferred by all the communities and therefore, the demand invariably exceeds the supply. Goat meat is especially prepared during festivals like Eid when goats are slaughtered in large numbers. People of all the old cultures (Chinese, Mayan, African, Middle Eastern and Greek) used to eat goat meat in indicative of the fact that goat meat has been used and important since times immemorial.

The world production of sheep meat was 8.89 million tones and goat meat was 5.14 million tones in 2007. India ranks second in goat meat production in the world. China,India, Nigeria, and Iran are among the top countries of the world goat meat production. India's export of sheep/goat meat has been increased from Rs. 65.87 Crores in 2006-07 to Rs.134.10 Crores in 2007-08. Major Export Destinations (2007-08) for goat meat were: Saudi Arabia, UAE, Qatar, Germany, and Oman. Goat meat contributes almost 10 -12 % of the total meat production in India. In India about 6% cattle, 11% buffaloes, 33% sheep, 38% goats and 84% pigs are slaughtered each year. The share of bovine meat in the total meat production in India is about 60% as against small ruminants (15%), pigs (10%) and poultry (12%). Export of goat meat and goats in India is regulated by the statutory body i.e. APEDA which came into existence videthe Agricultural & Processed Food Products Export Development Authority Act 1985 and this is in operation w.e.f. 13th February, 1986.

There are several factors which affect the extent and pattern of small ruminant meat consumption such as regional differences, system and intensity of production, ownership, affluence, ethnology and religion. Meat quality can be defined strictly in terms of its physical and chemical properties, or in terms of consumers' perceptions. A general definition of meat quality is that of eating quality that comprises palatability, wholesomeness and being free of pathogens and toxins. Palatability includes tenderness, flavour, residue-free and succulence. Meat quality of goats can sometimes leave much to be desired. Possible reasons are many and a few are discussed below.

There are about 3,600 licensed slaughter houses in India. These are primary meat processing houses and are administered by local authorities. Most of them are outdated and use primitive technologies for the production of meat. There are very few modern facilities, although a few such do exist for pork and bacon processing, for the integrated slaughter and processing of buffalo, sheep and goat meat and for the processing of poultry meat. In addition to this, a large proportion of meat production is slaughtered in houses or small unlicensed establishments.

Most goat meat is sold in the domestic market without proper sanitary inspection by the veterinarians. Most of the slaughter houses for goat are outdated and use primitive technologies for the production of meat. A large proportion of goats are slaughtered in backyard of houses or small unlicensed establishments by the individual butchers and meat is sold fresh on the same day. Production of meat and meat products in India (in thousand tones) Ministry of Food Processing Industry website 2002.

For improvement of goat profitability as a meat producer in India the following measures are recommended.

- Government intervention to regulate the animal market to some extent.
- The under-age animals should not be slaughtered.
- The economic age of slaughter is 8 - 12 months in different breeds.
- The animals should be sold on a live-weight basis instead of on a unit basis.
- The facilities for modern slaughter, cold storage and processing needs to be strengthened.

However, more important in the modern context is to slaughter goats in a hygienic way. Clean and hygienic meat production in goats is a much debated subject especially in the Indian context especially when the prevailing slaughter and meat handling procedures in the field leave much to be desired. Clean animals, good hygiene practice, skilled and healthy operators and stringent hygiene under slaughtering process are essentially required to keep the bacterial load on carcasses at low levels. However; these practices are a far cry under the Indian and South East Asian conditions. Use of plastic bags during evisceration and improvement of slaughter lines will no doubt reduce the number of *E.coli* in meat but difficult to implement. Decontamination using hot water, steam etc can also reduce the microbial load on goat meat. Using some superior breeds with fast growth rates, especially those from South Africa, have revolutionized meat goat production. Meat importing countries may ask for certification regarding herds to be free from *T.gondii* , *Salmonella* etc. Such certification will need elaborate tests to be carried out on herds which are being used for meat exports. Small ruminant meat ranks second in export earnings after buffalo meat in India.

Meat production traits

Meat production traits mainly include body weight at slaughter, efficiency of feed conversion, dressed carcass weight and dressing percentage. Increase in dressing percentage at higher body weight is largely attributed to disproportionate increase in fat % at the cost of lean meat. Every breed has a standard carcass weight at which proportion of muscles, fat and bone is optimum. Disproportionate increase in fat reduces the quality of meat. Thus the optimum body weight for slaughter is an important factor for consideration, while developing a breeding strategy for improving the mutton production. For indigenous breeds, the optimum ideal body weight for slaughter is 20kg for optimum meat yield without compromising its quality. Male carcasses had more muscles and bone while female carcasses had more fat and trimmings (El Muola *et al.,* 1999).

The breeds of western region, e.g., Sirohi, Marwari, Kutchi, Jakhrana and Beetal are larger in size and attained an average body weight ranging between 19.2 and 23.4 kg at 6 months of age. It is difficult to find out the dressing percentage of live animals. Pre-slaughter body weight at 6 months of age is the simplest criterion for selection of future breeding population. Goat meat is a product of many different production systems from widely varying environments, nutritional regimes and genotypes.

Processing of goat meat

Carcasses are normally cut into wholesale cuts and then into retail cut. However, the meat can be processed into high value products. Most of these products are utilizing fresh meat in ready meal packets or pre-cooking products that traditionally have taken a long time to prepare. Traditionally, meat processing is a means of extending shelf life (preserving) and producing a convenient item for use later and elsewhere. Processing is aimed at reducing the enzyme activity in the meat, retarding oxidation of the fat, and preventing spoilage by microorganisms. These aims have been achieved through drying, curing with salts, or smoking meat.

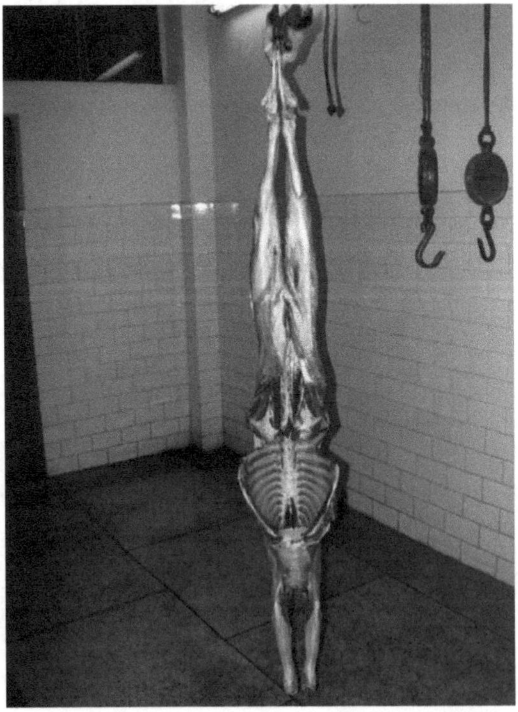

Goat meat compostion and quality

Goat meat is highly nutritious meat, with a distinct characteristic. Goat meat has more moisture and less fat than mutton. Goats deposit more internal fat and less subcutaneous and intramuscular fat compared with sheep. The normal composition of goat meat is : moisture 74.2%, protein 21.4%, fat 3.6%, minerals 1.1%, calcium 12 mg/100gm, phosphorus 193 mg/100gm. Goat meat have a high proportion of muscle and a low proportion of fat therefore considered as healthier. Despite being classified as red meat, goat is leaner and contains less cholesterol and fat than both lamb and beef. Fat is the most variable component of the goat carcass. Among body fat depots, intramuscular fat contributes the highest proportion in empty body weight.

Meat quality is based on appearance and palatability. Palatability includes attributes like tenderness and flavor. Fresh goat meat should have good color and little excess fat. Many factors influence the tenderness of meat including the grain of the meat, the amount of connective tissue, and the amount of fat. Meat is most tender immediately after slaughter while still in pre-rigor state, then reaches maximum toughness in full rigor. Aging of the meat then results in further improvement of tenderness. The palatability of meat can be influenced appreciably by altering time temperature combinations, as well as by the method of cooking. Different muscles in the same cut respond differently to heat, apparently because of variations in the connective tissue content and composition. Kid meat appears to be less tender than lamb meat.

Regardless of species, the goal in meat animal production is a carcass that contains a high proportion of good quality lean or muscle. It is certainly desirable to have some degree of marbling within the muscle, but excess quantities of external fat or heavy seems of fat between muscle group are not desired. Therefore, a major task in evaluated slaughter livestock is to appraise meatiness-the proportion of lean meat. There are three major kinds of tissue in goat carcasses-lean, fat and bone. If there is leaner, there must be less fat and/or bone. The most variable tissue in the carcass of meat animals is fat and this can be affected by many factors including species, breed, age, sex and management. Proportion of bone in the carcass of goats is known to decrease whereas fat percentage increases with increasing liveweight. The percentage of bone in adult goat varies from 15-20% but the values in young goats can be as high as 40 %. Evaluations of the proportion and location of fat, muscle and bone in carcasses of meat animals is important because it indicates the quality of the carcass. The highest proportion of fat in the body is deposited intramuscularly and omentum constitutes the highest non-carcass fat proportion. Muscle groups towards the rear of the body decrease with increasing slaughter weight. Males generally have higher lean content in their carcass.

Grading of goat carcasses is not practiced to a great extent but it is an important prerequisite for recommending precise cooking method for better palatability and utilization. Variation in subcutaneous fat thickness between goats of different ages, sex and types is extremely limited, which makes it difficult to use fat thickness for purposes of carcass classification or grading. Newer methods of cooking alongwith traditional methods need to be evaluated for recommending suitable methods for goat meat cuts/muscles produced in India. Slaughtering at 9 months of age yield more meaty carcasses. Castration also affects the muscle to fat ratio in goats. The proportion of bone in a dairy breed (Alpine) carcass decreased with increasing liveweight. Srivastava *et al.*(1968) reported that bones in Jamunapari type of animals were significantly more than in Barbari and varied from 19.5 - 20.7% in the former and 16.6-17.6% in latter.

The low appeal of goat meat to some consumers may be due to its lack of tenderness, particularly in meat from older animals. Tenderness should not be a problem for comminuted meat products (e.g., patties) or products that undergo slow cooking or pressure cooking/retorting (e.g., curries and stews). The relatively tough meat of goats may be tenderised by injecting an enzyme called papain into the blood stream of the animal just prior to slaughter. Meat from older animals may be similarly tenderised. Papain does not act on the meat while the meat is chilled, but when the meat becomes warm, this enzyme acts on the myofibrillar proteins in such a way that more tender meat results. Cooking temperatures destroy papain's activity. Blade tenderisation has been suggested to enhance the tenderness of goat meat.

The flavor of meat has a profound effect on its acceptability.Meat from entire males have a stronger flavor. Generally meat from intact male animals possesses a characteristic goaty taint. Castration can reduce the strong male odor of bucks kept and sold for meat when they are more than one year old (Steele, 1996). Age at slaughter can be used to segment goat carcasses into expected palatability groups.

Dressing out percentage is carcass weight as a percentage of live weight. The dressing out percentage has long been used as an estimate of food value of meat animals; however, this parameter is greatly influenced by the extent of gut fill. It is considered that the dressing out percentage is of little use as an indicator of carcass yield unless it is estimated on an empty gut basis. Estimates of this parameter are considered unreliable even when the animals have been starved for 24 hours before slaughter. Dressing out percentage of meat animals depends on species, level of nutrition, breed, sex, season and live weight.

The goat has a lower dressing percentage than cattle. Sheep has lesser dressing percentage than goats, probably due to extra weight of skin having wool and comparatively heavier weight of head. Goat has a lower dressing out percentage as compared to pig and cattle because of the greater amount of skin etc and greater amount of digesta fill. Goats have proportionately more muscles along the spinal cord and proximal thoracic limb, and less in the proximal pelvic limb as compared to cattle. Leg is a major component of dressed carcass followed by shoulder. Akinsoyinu *et al.,* (1975) reported that the leg and lion cuts for West African dwarf goats fed GN Cake gave mean values of 34.25 and 16.19% of the carcass. The values for animals maintained on urea based ration were 32.93 and 15.39 respectively. It is generally assumed that meat from older animals is less tender. As the percentage of fat in the carcass increase, the percentage of moisture declines. This means less weight lost during cooking. Dressing rends to decrease with live weight because of increasing volume of visceral mass (Fore stomach and intestine).

Dressing out percentage is reported to be higher in mature female than in mature male. Males have higher dressing percentage than female. This may be due to extra weight in the female carcass which do not account towards dressed carcass weight, viz., undetected pregnancy and mammary glands.

Plane of nutrition also affects the dressing out percentage. Dressing out precentage increases with higher plane of nutrition. Dressing out percentage of goats increased with increase in age. The stomach contents in per cent of body weight decreased significantly (18.9 to 6.4%) as a result of fattening for 80 days. Fehr *et al.* (1976) stated that young kids for meat production in France are slaughtered at the age of about 2 to 5 weeks and about 6 to 12 kg liveweight. Kids generally have a thin and shallow carcass (Gall, 1980).

Gut contents determine the completely waste percentage of the body. The gut content in goats varies from 12 to 19 %. Edible by-products of carcass include liver, heart, kidney, testes, spleen and lung while blood, hide, head, horns, feet tail, digestive tract, fat, fascia and bones include the inedible by-products. Except the skin and hoof, the utilisation of other byproducts is exploited in India. Several preservation methods like smoking are used to prevent the meat from deterioration. Chilling and freezing are also used for short term preservation of goat meat.

Wholesome meat is produced hygienically, is pathogen free, retains its natural state and nutritive value, has optimum fat and is unconditionally acceptable to the consumer. India is a tropical country, with ambient temperatures conducive to the growth of microorganisms, which can rapidly render the meat unsafe for human consumption. It has been reported that physio-chemical changes brought about in the goat meat at different temperatures and periods of storage are directly related to microbial load and flora of meat present therein. Ahmed *et al.* (2003) reported that the shelf-life of meats from freshly slaughtered sheep and goat carcasses at 5-7 °C was extended after spraying (pressure 3 kg/ cm2) the carcasses with solution containing potassium sorbate, sodium acetate, sodium citrate, sodium lactate each at 2.5% and sodium chloride at 5% (prepared w/v in potable water. The treatment inhibited Bacillus spp. to minimum which were not detected up to sixth day. It extended the lag phase of all organisms including psychrotrophes (pseudomonads) and reduction of differential counts in sheep and goat meat were noted throughout the refrigerated storage.

Identification of meat of goat with different species is relatively simple when carcass is intact but becomes difficult if it has been heat processed. Immunological and DNA based methods are suitable approaches employed for identification of such meats. Satish *et al.* (2009) has described a cytochrome-b gene based PCR method for identification of cooked meat of sheep, goat, cattle, pig and poultry.Such technique offers a promising alterative for meat inspection programmes where species identification of meat after cooking is required.

Goat meat products

Goat meat can be prepared in a variety of ways including stewed, curried, baked, grilled, barbecued, minced, canned, fried, or made into sausage. In the south-western United States, goat's meat is considered superior over mutton for sausage manufacture. In Texas (USA), over 90% of the goat meat processed is used for sausage manufacture.In India, the rice-preparation of mutton biryani uses goat meat as its primary ingredients to produce a rich taste. Several goat and sheep meat products like Kebab, biryani, Rogan Josh, Tikka, Kofta etc are quite popular with the consumers.

Shelf stable meat products like, canned and cured meat products, meat and snack type meat products, meat pickles, intermediate moisture meat products can be prepared from goat meat.

Goat meat pickle

Pickling is an age-old traditional method for preservation of vegetables and fruits. Pickled products are common in Indian diets and are much relished by consumers. Meat pickles are traditional shelf stable ready to eat products. Goat meat pickle can be prepared with indigenous taste and high acceptability (Padda and Sharma, 1982). A very good quality chevon pickle from old buck meat could be prepared with a shelf life of 60 days at ambient temperature (Pal and Agnihotri, 1994). Total viable counts, halophiles, yeast and mould counts remained in the range of 3 log cycle throughout the period of 60 days.Highly acceptable low acid goat meat pickle was evaluated for its storage stability at 32±0.5°C. The pickle was acceptable upto 60 days at ambient storage (Das *et al.*, 2007) suggesting that a highly acceptable low acid goat meat pickle can be prepared using spent goat meat and can safely be stored on shelf for 60 days even during summer season.

Dried goat meat

In India dried meat is processed by mixing salt and turmeric powder and such meat is used and prepared during scarcity due to their long shelf life at ambient temperature. Dried meat has some inherent disadvantages like colour darkening, tough texture, case hardening, lower yields and poor rehydration. Babji, (1993) developed a technique for processing of dried goat meat chunks wherein chunks are dipped in 1%EDTA at 60°C for 1 min. and drained for 30 min. and treated with 5% salt, 1% agar, 50 ppm nitrite and spice mix and oven dried for 20 h at 50°C. The dried chunks are packed in polyethylene pouches and wrapped in aluminium foil and stored at 30°C. EDTA pre-treatment resulted in persistence of pink colour throughout the 60 days storage period of dried meat. The use of agar in preparation improved the textural properties of dried meats.

Meat balls

Meat balls can be prepared from goat meat using traditional methods. Padda (1989) developed processing methods for preparation of goat meat balls. Meat batter is manually rolled into balls, steam cooked, fried and served warm.

Medicinal value of goat meat

Each and every individual part in the goat meat has certain medical value. Goat brain increases the memory power and it also cools down the eye temperature. Semen production is increased by eating goat brain. While boiling goat legs, it leaves some essence. This essence helps to cure throat related problems and it also provides sufficient strength to the bones and muscles. Mental ability can be increased by eating goat heart. Chest of the goat helps to reduces phlegm troubles. Goat head heals the heart related problems. Body temperature can be reduced by feeding goat tongue (http://www.chemungvalleyrhs.com/?p=21). Goat testicles have been used in Ayurvedic medicine to enhance male sexuality in human beings (http://www.toddcaldecott.com/index.php/healing/conditions/220-male-infertility).

Future prospects

It is estimated by the Ministry of Food Processing that only about 0.2% of total meat production in India is processed any further. However, this could be an under-estimate since a very large proportion of meat processing takes place in unregistered cottage industry meat processing units and in very small establishments which cater solely for local needs. Such output would not appear in the official figures. Although most goat and sheep are slaughtered in the backyard and unhygienic conditions, the situation is improving slowly. Less time lapse between slaughter and consumption prevents the development of harmful bacteria but more hygienic practices are needed for storage and transport of meat. Use of spent animals for meat purposes is one of the constraints which sometime reduces the quality and acceptability of goat meat products. Central Institute for Research on Goats, Makhdoom has developed technologies which permit preparation of goat meat products of acceptable quality from spent animals. Meat tenderization is another area where use of papain and other enzymes have been advocated for improving the quality of goat meat. Large scale application of such technologies needs to be taken at field level. Preparation of value added products from goat and sheep meat, cold chain transport of goat /sheep meat and improved hygienic practices during slaughter and storage can greatly improve the value of small ruminants as meat producer of future. Increasing demand for lean meat for a variety of reasons will shift the focus on more preference/development of goat meat as compared to sheep meat. Sheep meat is disadvantaged because of relatively high fat content and lower palatability of lamb fat.

Demand for goat meat in United States has exceeded domestic supply in recent years. In 2004, United States imported 2400 metric tons of goat meat, mostly from Australia (Smith and Sherman, 2009 pp 4). In US, the increasing number of people from Africa, Asia, Middle-East and Hispanic origin increase the demand for goat meat consumption. Australian goat meat is frozen and exported as whole carcass of various types of animals.

The fact that goats are widely adaptable to and productive in a wide range of environments means that goat meat will remain one of the staple red meats of the world. However, there are public health concersn which need to be addressed.Foodborne diseases, in particular those related to meat and meat products, have recently become a matter of great public concern. Sheep and goat meat can transmit infections and diseases either through handling during preparation procedures or as a result of ingestion by the consumer. The association of foodborne diseases with mutton and goat meat is less frequent than with the meat of other animal species partly because of the essential boiling or cooking processes followed in Asian countries.

References

Ahmed, S.N., Chattopadhyay, U.K., Sherikar, A.T., Waskar, V.S., Paturkar, A.M., Latha, C., *et al.* (2003). Chemical sprays as a method for improvement in microbiological quality and shelf-life of fresh sheep and goat meats during refrigeration storage (5–7 °C). Meat Science, 63:339-344.

Akinsoyinu, A.O. , Mba, A.U. and Olubajo, F.O. (1975) Studies on comparative utilization of urea and groundnut cake rations by young growing West African Dwarf goats. 11. Effect on carcass quality and chemical composition of the organs and muscle . Nigerian J. Anim Prod. 2: 81-88.

Casey, N.H., Webb, E.C., (2010) Managing goat production for meat quality. Small Ruminant Res. doi:10.1016/j.smallrumres. 2009.12.047

Das, A.K., Sharma, R.P. and Singh, N.P. (2007). Quality and storage stability of low acid goat meat pickle. American Journal of Food Technology 2:550-554.

EL Moula, I.H.A.; Babiker, S.A.; EL Khidir, O.A.; Ibrahim, S.E. (1999) Meat production from female goat kids compared with males. J. Agric. Sei, Cambridge 133:223-226

Fehr, P.M., Sauvant, D., Delage, J. and Dumont, B.L. (1976) Growth and quality of prime kid carcasses. Journees de la Res. ovine et Caprine Dec.

Gall, C. (1980) Relationship between body conformation and production in dairy goats. J. Dairy Sci. 63:1768-1781.

Morand-Fehr, P. and Boyazoglu, J. (1999). Present state and future outlook of the small ruminant sector. Small Rumin. Res. 34:175-188.

Padda, G.S. and Sharma, N. (1982) Processing and preservation of meat pickle (Meat Achar). Indian Food Packer 36:51-54.
Padda, G.S., Sharma, N. And Bisht, G.S. (1989) Effect of some vegetative extenders on organoleptic and physico-chemical properties of goat meat balls. Indian J. Meat Sci. & Tech. 2:116-122
Pal, U.K. and Agnihotri, M.K. (1994) Storage stability of chevon pickle at room temperature. Journal of Applied Animal Research, 5:89-93.
Satish, Ashwani Kumar, Y. Singh, Minakshi and Prasad, G. (2009) Cytochrome-b gene based PCR for identification and differentiation of cooked meat of sheep, goat, cattle, pig and poultry Haryana Vet. 48:53-57.
Smith, M.C. and Sherman, D.M. (2009) Goat Medicine, Second Edition, Wiley-Blackwell, Oxford, UK.
Srivastava, V.K., Raizada, B.C. and Kulkarni, V.S. (1968) Carcass quality of Barbari and Jamunapari type goats. Indian Veterinary Journal 45: 219 (Fide Animal Breeding Abstract 36:3791.
Steele, Mike (1996) Goats, Macmillan Education Ltd, London,. viii + 152pp.

9

Milk Production

The goat milk has several peculiarities, being a food of high digestibility and high nutritional value.Goats can hardly compete with cattle or buffalo in milk production ability. Goats produce approximately 2% of the world's total annual milk supply. Neverthless, goat is an important source of animal protein for the landless and marginal farmers of tropical countreis, in areas where other classes of livestook cannot possibly survive and for several classes of people allergic to cow milk. Goats contribute about 4 % of the total milk produced in India. Goats and sheep producing milk for people start with the beginnings of domestication. For thousands of years they have provided sustainance for the people. During the last 150 years genetic selection and better feeding conditions led to several superior goat and sheep breeds in some countries in terms of milk and solids productivity, proving a great potential for evolution in both species, and responding to an increasing market demand and popularity. Some sheep breeds can produce more than 1000 kg milk in one lactation and several goat breeds more than 2000 kg milk, but in physiologically comparable terms of 4% fat-corrected milk both species can be equal. Goat milk production leaders have been capable of producing 10 kg milk per day of lactation.

Goat has been referred to as the Poor mans cow or wet nurse in Europe. Goat provides the cheapest source of milk to the poor both in rural and urban areas. The milk of goats is sweet, nourishing and medicinal. Goat milk is white in colour. Goat milk is whiter than whole cow milk. Butter and cheese made from goat milk are also white, but may be colored during processing. Exploitation of goats as a source of milk for human beings dates back from antiquity. Goat milk has been acknowledged as an ideal food for the aged, the sick and convalescent as well as for infants and growing children. Ever since Cleopatra filled her bathtub with goat milk , fresh goat's milk has been revered for its superior moisturizing properties.

Milk is a white liquid produced by the mammary glands of mammals. It is the primary source of nutrition for young mammals before they are able to digest other types of food. Milk is an important source of all basic nutrients required for mammals including human beings. Milk from various mammals such as cow, buffalo, goat, sheep, camel, etc. is used for different nutritional purposes, e.g., feeding to young ones and preparation of some nutritional products such as milk cream, butter, yogurt, ghee, sour milk, etc. Nutrient content of goat milk is slightly less than cow milk but goat milk is more digestible because the fat molecules are one-fifth the size of those from cow milk — making it easily tolerated by those with compromised digestive systems. Goat milk is naturally emulsified. Cream does not rise readily, but can be obtained with a mechanical separator.Goat milk differs from cow or human milk by having higher digestibility, distinct alkalinity, higher buffering capacity, and certain therapeutic values in human medicine and nutrition. Goat's milk can replace sheep's milk or cow's milk in diets of those who are allergic. Goat milk is easily digestible due to the presence of smaller fat globules than the cow's milk.

The mammary gland of goat consists of two functional teats which are situated in the inguinal region. Some goats have in addition to two teats, a number of supernumerary teats, each of which is associated with a small gland. Rudimentary teats are also found in the male.

Goat's milk is also used to make cheeses such as Rocamadour and Feta. Most of the milk breeds of goats are in Europe, which has about one seventh of the goat population of India, has twice as much production of milk as compared to India. The milk production ability of European goat exceeds that of the cow. Dairy goats are almost equipotential in milk production with cattle and sheep. Milk producing abilities of Asian and African goats in general are similar. African countries have about twice the number of goats as compared to Indian; also have almost twice milk production. Indian goats vis-a-vis goats from other Asian countries are poor milk producers when we see that approximately 160 million (excluding 70 million in India produced about 0.71 million tons only. This is partly because of the introduction of dairy genetic potential from European breeds in some Asian countries.

Goat's milk is a common ingredient in soap. Goat milk adds creaminess, vitamins, minerals and proteins to soap.

Goats contribute about 9% of the total milk produced in Africa, while it is only 2% of the total milk produced by cattle buffalo, sheep and goats in Asia. The value for Europe is even less than 1%. This again is a clear indicator of the goat's contribution to the economy and survival of the people in the developing and third world countries of Asia and Africa. However, because of the lack of development programmes, there is hardly any improvement of milk production potential of goats in these countries and there is no breed which can compete with the European breeds in milk production.

Another interesting point to be noted is that although North and Central America has about equal number of goats as that of Europe, the milk production in the latter by goats is about five times as compared to the former. This is because the most prominent dairy breeds of goats originated and are to be found in Europe. The main goat owning countries of Europe are Greece, Spain, France, Italy, Portugal and Ramania in that order. In cournties like Cyprus, Libya, Iran, etc., the contribution by goats to the total milk production exceeds 50%.

The shelf life of goat milk is 6 hr during summer, 12 hour during winter. Shelf life of goat milk can be increased by addition of biocarbonate powder @0.2%.

Goat Milk Composition

The major chemical components of milk include water, fats, proteins, carbohydrates, minerals, organic acids, enzymes and vitamins. Goat's milk composition is basically similar to that of cow's or buffalo milk. However, there are significant differences in physic-chemical characteristics among cow, buffalo, sheep and goat milk. Information on composition and physic-chemical characteristics of goat milk is essential for development of dairy goat industry and marketing of products. The average proportion of the various constitutents is also almost similar to that of cow's milk, though there are variations between breeds and species. The components of milk may be influenced by species, breed, nutrition, health, and environment etc. Goat milk differs from cow, buffalo, buffalo milk in having better digestibility, alkalinity, buffering capacity and therapeutic value.

Table:

		Cow's milk	Goat's milk	Buffalo's milk
Fat (%)		3.8	4.2	7.65
Protein (%)		3.2	3.5	4.37
Carbohydrate (%)	4.8		4.5	4.82
Minerals (%)		0.7	0.8	0.94
Water	87.5	87.0	82.22	

The above table is oversimplified picture of goat's milk. For example, milk contains a large number of trace organic substances, some that pass through the mammary gland directly from the blood and others that result from the synthesis of milk in the mammary tissue. Goats' milk proteins are similar to cows 'major milk proteins in their general classifications of caseins (αs1-CN, αs2-CN, β-CN, and κ-CN) and whey proteins, α-lactalbumin, β-lactoglobulin, serum albumin, and immunoglobulins, but they differ in genetic polymorphism and their frequency in goat populations. Also, goats' milk fat differs significantly in the profile of its fatty acids (FAs) from cows' milk fat.

The goat milk composition of different breeds is given in table below.

Breed	Fat	SNF	Total Solids	Mineral/Ash
Jakhrana	4.39	7.69	12.06	0.76
Sirohi	3.89	7.75	11.60	0.89
Marwari	3.38	7.84	11.35	0.81
Kutchi	3.61	7.60	11.17	1.11

(Adpated from Agnihotri and Rajkumar, 2007)

Milk fat affects nutritional value and physical and sensory characteristics, that all in turn affect product quality and acceptability. The milk fat, or lipid, content of goat milk ranges from 3% to 6%, with the variations due to factors such as breed, feed and lactation stage.The average fat percentage in goat milk is around four. The milk of temperate dairy goats contain less fat (3.8%) which may be due to their higher milk yields. There are district breed differences in fat composition. In genral the Indian breeds of goats (Jamunapari, Barbari etc.) have higher fat content than their European counterparts. Mean fat contents of Jamunapari goat milk was 4.88 %. Fat is the most variable component of milk. Fat is the most important constituent of milk. Among the European breeds, Anglo-Nubian has highest fat percentage. The African breeds also have higher fat percent.

Milk fat is present in the form of minute droplets or globules. Each fat globule is surrounded by a membrane consisting of phospholipids and proteins; these emulsifiers keep the individual globules from joining together into noticeable grains of butterfat and also protect the globules from the fat-digesting activity of enzymes found in the fluid portion of the milk. Fat globules in goat milk are smaller than in cow's milk.

Milk fat from the goat does not cream quickly. This slow creaming was attributed to the belief fat globules in goat milkfat are very much smaller than those found milk. Goat milk is devoid of agglutinin (agglutenating euglobulins), a protein that causes fat molecules to clump together, and which is present in cow's milk. Smaller fat globule size, combined with the fact that the globules do not clump together as in cow's milk, contribute to the higher digestibility of goat milk, and the better tolerance of it for individuals with certain digestive disorders.

The lipid composition of sheep and goat milk includes simple and complex lipids (mono-, di-, tri-acylglycerols, cholesterols, phospholipids and sterols) (Park *et al.,* 2007). Triglycerides constitute about 98% of the total milk fat. Goat milk fat contains significantly greater contents of short and medium chain length fatty acids (C4:0- C12:0) than cow milk fat. Average goat milk fat differs in contents of its fatty acid profile significantly from the average cow milk fat, being much higher in butyric,caproic, caprylic, capric, lauric, myristic, palmitic, linoleic and oleic acid.

Cholesterol content of goat milk is 11 grams/100 grams of milk, which is slightly higher than the 10 grams found in cow's milk. The percentage of saturated fats for goat milk is also analogous to that for cow's milk. Goat milk has higher content of monounsaturated, polyunsaturated fatty acids and medium chain triglycerides than cow milk. Goat milk contains more essential fatty acids (linoleic and arachidonic) than cow milk. Both belong to omega-6 series. Similarly, goat milk has 30-35% medium-chain fatty acids (C6-C14) MCT, while cow milk has only 15-20%. These fatty acids are a quick source of energy and are not stored as body fat.

Fat present in goat milk is distributed in the form of minute droplets or chylomicrons. The size of fat droplets in goat milk is much smaller than in the case of buffalo or cow and this is the reason for better digestibility of goat milk as compared to cow or buffalo milk.

In addition, goat milk's fat reduces total cholesterol levels and maintains adequate levels of triglycerides and transaminases (GOT and GPT). This makes goat milk a food of choice for the prevention of heart diseases. The fat-soluble vitamins A, D, E, and K are found within the milk fat portion of the milk.

The largest changes in milk fatty acid (FA) composition have been obtained either by changing the amounts and the nature of forages in the diets of ruminants, particularly pasture. Recent studies have suggested that the genetic improvement of the nutritional quality of milk based on Fatty Acids profile may be possible.

Cholesterol and phosphlipid content in the milk has been used as a marker for fat globule membrane, as these components are basic to membrane structure. Thecholesterol content of goat's milk has been recorded as ranging form 17 to 39 mg/ 100 ml. Cow milk normally contains 7-10 mg/litre. Patton *et al.* (1980) found a substantial increase in cholesterol and phospholipid in skim milk of goats due to aging. Their studies indicated a speciesdifference between cow and goat in stability of milk fat globule membrane. Perhaps greater fragility of the goat globule membrane explains the ease with which goat milk develops off flavours related to lipolytic rancidity.

Glycerol ethers are a group of substance reported to stimulate the formation of erythrocytes, thrombocytes and granulocytes. Ahrne *et al.* (1980) reported that goat colostrum is richer than milk, in respect of glycerol ethers (0.15% Vs. 0.1%).

Total protein content may vary from 2.6 g/l to 4.1 g/l for goat milk. Average goat milk protein content is about 3.5 % which is similar to that of cow milk.

Protein conmcentration in goat milk is relatively constant within breeds as the selection process at no time laid much emphasis on protein content of milk. The main non-individual factors of protein content variation are the stage of lactation, season, age and feeding. Biological value of products processed from caprine milk may be slightly higher than encountered in those made from bovine milk.

In the early studies on milk, casein was recognised as the principal characteristic milk protein and the major protein present ingoat milkis casein. Casein occurs in four distinct types called alpha, beta, gamma and kappa, respectively, representing 50, 30, 5 and 15 percent of this protein. In addition to casein, another protein which is present in the whey portion of milk is b-lactoglobulin.Casein concentration (76.22%) in goat milk was higher than the cow milk (70.15%). The whey protein likewise was lower in goat milk as compared to cow milk. Most of the major milk proteins present in milk are synthesised in the mammary gland. Generally, goat milk contains less s1 casein than other ruminants' milk.

Besides casein and b-lactoglobulin, a number of enzymes which are of course proteins, too, are present in milk but they account for a very small portion of the total protein content of milk. Enzymes are proteins specialised to catalyse biochemical reactions. Some enzymes act independently while others require one or more non-protein components called cofactors. The enzymes present in milk may be because of cytoplasmic fragments lost in milk by the mammary cells during the process of milk secretion or because of unfinished metabolic reactions and/or because be bacterial contamination.

The enzymes of the milk of the goat are similar to those of the cow, although some specific differences have been described. The principal enzymes whch are found in goats milk include catalase, peroxidase, zanthine oxidase, protease, acid phosphatase, alkaline phosphatase, lipase etc. Peroxidase activity in the milk of both species is the same in all respects, while the xanthine oxidase level is lower in the milk of the goat. Some enzymes are important for milk processing technology, such as lipases which produce hydrolytic rancidity. Lipase activity in goat milk is significantly correlated with spontaneous lipolysis, which may be attributed to its specific lipolytic system. This enzyme acts on fats, freeing the fatty acids from their union with glycerol. It is the cause of rancidity in dairy products, the flavour being due mainly to the highly volatile butyric acid that is liberated. Chandan *et al.* (1968) has reported the lipase activity of goat milk.

Xanthine oxidase is an oxidative enzyme of which the primary function is control of the last stage of purine catabolism by converting hypoxanthine and xanthine to uric acid. Xanthine oxidase is reported to be absent from human milk and is proposed to be a factor in development of atherosclerosis in human consuming dairy products. The xanthine oxidase activity of goat milk is generally considered less than in cow milk. Low content of xanthine oxidase in goat milk does not appear from lack of molybdenum. Goat's milk contains lower alkaline phosphatase compared to cow, buffalo or ewes milk. Heat treatment (Pasteurisation) destroys the alkaline phosphatase activity.

Low levels of several other enzymes like peroxidase, ribonuclease (Prakash and Jenness, 1968), lysozyme (Chandan *et al.,* 1968), Carbonic anhydrase, rhodanese, acid phosphatase have also been reported in goat's milk.

It is convenient to designate the milk proteins other than caseinsimply as 'non-casein' proteins. There are also referred to as 'whey proteins' which included non-casein proteins as well as casein fraction soluble in whey. Heat causes aggregation of whey proteins. Goat milk is reported to be low in lactoferrin content, as compared to cow and buffalo milk.

Colostrum is a good source of passive transfer of immunoglobulins to young kids. Failure of passive transfer of maternal antibodies to kids via colostrum at birth leads to increased morbidity and mortality from infectious disease in young kids.

In goat milk and colostrum the principle immunoglobulins are IgG and IgA. Unique immunoglobulin are absent from lacteal secretions. Those occurring in colostrum or milk are either serum derived or synthesised locally. Goat milk is less immunogenic than cow milk. In goats, the subclass IgGl is selectively transferred from serum to colostrum and eventually to the offspring. Detection of colostrum in bovine and caprine milks is sometimes useful for dairy industries for economic reasons. One of the best markers of the presence of colostrum is immunoglobulin G (IgG). Several methods are available for quantification of Immunoglobulin G in goatmilk including surface plasmon resonance (SPR) spectroscopy and a binding rate method. Milking frequency is known to affect the goat milk immune status which has consequences in susceptibility of goats to mastitis with changes in milking frequency.

Milk allergy and goat milk: Cow's milk contains over 25 different molecules, which have the potential to elicit an allergic reaction. Milk allergy is caused when the immune system (IS) reacts against one or more of the proteins found in milk. Milk allergy is often confused with Lactose Intolerance. Most common symptoms in children are gastro-intestinal symptoms (vomiting, diarrhoea), accompanied by respiratory symptoms such as wheezing. Sometimes, a milk allergic person is advised to use goat's milk. Many people allergic to cow's milk are also allergic to goat's milk.

The substance responsible for the sweet taste of milk is lactose, a carbohydrate. Chemically lactose is a disaccharide consisting of glucose and glactose. Lactose is found exclusively in the milk and mammary gland is the only tissue having the unique capacity for its synthesis. Usually the lactose content of goat milk varies from 4 to 5%. The lactose content of goat milk is approximatly same or a little lower than in cow's milk. The exotic breeds are reputed to have a lower level of lactose than the indigenous breeds (Mba *et al.,* 1975).

In addition to lactose, only other carbohydrate reported from goat milk is inositol. Prakash and Jenness (1968) have reported inositol value in goat milk to be about 7 mg/100 ml. Glucose and galactose were found to be completely absent in goat milk though reported to be present in cow milk (Prakash and Jenness, 1968).

Goat milk has recently been studied as a good source of oligosaccharides, with a much higher content than that of bovine milk (25–30 mg/100 ml vs 2–3 mg/100 ml). Less is known about the role of other nondigestible carbohydrates, such as oligosaccharides, in intestinal inflammation. However, oligosaccharides from human milk seem to play an important role in the development and differentiation of the intestinal epithelium in newborns. Goat milk oligosaccharides reduce intestinal inflammation and contribute to the recovery of damaged colonic mucosa.

The total ash content in sheep milk is higher than in goat milk. Mineral contents in goat milk are much higher than cow and human milk but similar to that of buffalo milk.

Compared with human milk, cow and goat milk are relatively low in iron and copper. Because the synthesis of red blood cells depends on these two nutrients, consuming cow milk or goat milk without supplementation can lead to infant anemia. In addition, cow milk and goat milk may contain too much calcium and phosphorous for the baby's kidneys to handle. (http://www.livestrong.com/article/339040-comparison-of-human-milk-to-goat-milk-cow-milk-nutrition/#ixzz1Yj12mhhM).

The ash content of goat milk ranges from 0.7 to 0.85% and 0.70 to 0.90 % in case of buffalo milk. Goat milk contains about 134 mg Ca and 121 mg P/100 gm, while human milk has only one fourth and one sixth of these two major minerals. It will be noted that goat's milk contains less sodium but more potassium and chlorine than cow's milk. The calcium and phosphorus content of goat milk is almost similar to that of cow milk although goat milk contains less calcium as compared to buffalo milk.

In a recent study from Hungary , the authors did not find significant difference in mineral and fatty acid profile of goat and cow milk. Ash (0.82%), iron (Fe) (0.64 mg/kg) and copper (Cu) (0.19 mg/kg) content was higher in goat milk compared to cow milk (0.74%; 0.39 mg/kg and 0.07 mg/kg.

The principal cations of milk are sodium, potassium, calcium and magnesium and the principal anions are phosphate, chloride and citrate. These help in maintenance of osmotic balance between milk and blood. Potassium is much higher in milk than is sodium as is characteristinc of intracellular fluids. Sodium, potassium and chloride are undoubtely present nearly entirely as free ions. A negative correlation exists between K and lactose for milks of cows, goats, sheep and swine. Chloride is correlated positively with K and negatively with lactose, but Na is not correlated significantly with C1, K or lactose. The chloride content of goat milk has been reported to be 830 mg/100 gm .

Calcium forms one of the most important elements present in the structure of skeletal tissue, which includes bone and teeth. The other two factors required for synthesis of skeletal tissue are phosphorus and vitamin-D. Goat colostrumis high incalcium, obviously to provide additional calcium required for rapid development of bone in the young. However, it declines in the second month and increases until it reaches its highest value during the last month of gestation. Calcium from goat milk has a greater bioavailability than calcium from certain vegetables, such as spinach, that contain high levels of calcium-chelating agents.

The levels of trace elements in goats milk are subject to very wide variations (Prakash and Jenness, 1968). The concentration of trace elements in goats milk is similar to that of cow's milk. Jenness (1980) reports that colostrum is much higher in Fe, Cu, Mn and Zn composition that the normal milk. The concentration of these trace elements is affected by a large measure to concentration in the diet. Akinsoyinu *et al.* (1979) reported that colostrum contained much higher Fe, Cu, Mn, Zn and Iodine than the mature milk. Goat milk contains less Nickel as compared to cow or ewe milk .

Selenium content of milk varies a lot depending upon the dietary intake. Selenium content of cow milk is lower than that of either human or goat milk. Milk or proprietary formulas are the exclusive sources of nourishment for infants for periods of up to 6 mo following birth. Therefore selenium deficiency is most suspected in the young infants. Selenium is an essential trace element and deficiencies have been reported to be correlated to abnormal cardiac function in patients on total parenteral nutrition. Keshan disease (a fatal cardiomyopathy) has been virtually eliminated by supplementation with sodium selenite.Various selenoproteins have been identified in tissues and fluids of mammals.

Citrate is of primary significance in the milk and milk products because it forms complexes with calcium and magnesium which contribute to the stabiliy of milk proteins and it is a precursor of flavour and aroma compounds in cultured dairy products. Citrate is a sort of harbinger of lactogenesis in goats. The total citric acid content of goat's milk has been reported to be lower than the cow of buffalo milk (Lal and Gupta, 1981) although the pattern of its distribution between the colloidal and dissolved state is almost similar inthe three species. Of the total citrate 20.69% is found to be distributed inthe colloidal phase and the remainder 79.13%in dissolved phase (Lal and Gupta, 1981).

Somatic cell counts

Somatic cell count in goat milk is an important quality index. Somatic cell count (SCC) in goat milk increases as lactation advances. SCC in dairy goats is affected by IMI , parity number, stage of lactation , breed, level of milk production, nutritional status and milking method and estrus.Gomes *et al.* (2006) reported that SCC increased from 2.6×10^5/ml in the first month of lactationto 6.5×10^5/ml in the eighth month.

Since milk is used for feeding human beings, often asa sole source of nutrients for the infants, its role in providing adequate quantities of these dietary essential factors has been the pivotal one. Often, milk is considered to be a rich and adequate source of vitamins for the children. However, the adequacy of goat milk as regards its vitamin content for the human infants has been much debated. It is not uncommon to find references in literature about the development of anemia in children fed on goat's milk diets. However, quite often the results were confounded by a concomitant Fe and Cu deficiency. Goat's milk is reputed to contain much lower content of vitamin B_6 and B_{12} compared to cow's milk.

Goat milk has higher amounts of Vitamin A than cow milk. Vitamin A activity in milk is due either to the presence of vitamin A as such (Retinol) or by certain carotenoids. The carotenes have no intrinsic vitamin A activity per se but are converted into vitamin A by reactions in intestinal mucosa and liver. Goat is a more efficient convertor of dietry carotene into vitamin A. Available reports on goat milk indicate that the goat milk contains only negligible quantities of carotenoids. However, goat milk is reputed to have higher content of Vitamin A (retinol) as compared to cow or buffalo milk. Owen and Proudfoot (1959) found abundant b-carotene in the colostrum of British Saanen goats. However, normal goats milk is colorless, which is due to the almost complete converion of carotene into vitamin A. Carotenoids and vitamin A status of milk products is affected by nutrition. The amount found in milk maybe several times as great on feeds high in carotene as on feeds which contain very little. One litre of goat's milk contains about 2074 IU vitamin A. The estimated dietary requirement of vitamin A for adult men is around 2000 to 2500 IU per day. This bears out that a man exclusively taking goat milk will need only one litre of it daily to meet its whole requirements of vitamin A. Vitamin A deficiency in the body causes night blindness, xeropthalmia, among other symptoms. Colostrum contains higher vitamin A potency than normal milk.

Most of the B vitamins act as essential constituents of cofactors for a variety of enzyme systems which explains the vital importance of these compounds to body function. The members of B-complex group include (Thiamine (B_1), Riboflavin, B_6 (Pyridoxine, Pyridoxal, Pyridoxamine), Nicotinic acid, Pantothenic acid, Biotin, Folix acid, Cyanocobalamin, (B_{12}). Goat milk contains much lower contents f vitamin B_6 and B_{12} than the cow's milk (Prakash and Jenness, 1968). However, actual symptoms of deficiency have not been reported (Jenness 1980). Several studies have pointed out the folate deficiency in goat milk. Folate is required for the synthesis of haemoglobin.

Goat milk like cow milk is deficient in its content of vitamin C&D. Pasteurisation of milk is known to further reduce the content of vitamin C. Comparatively human milk is a much better source of vitamin C.

Physical properties

The pH of goat's milk ranges from 6.3 to 6.7 as is also the case with buffalo milk. The pH of normal fresh cow's milk also falls between 6.5 and 6.7. Thus the fresh milk of both cow and goat is slightly acidic. Energy value of goat milk is about 60 kcal/100 g. Goat, cow and human milks are almost isocaloric, with fat, protein and lactose accounting for 50,25 and 25% of the energy.

The reducing capacity of milk is due to the sulphydryl content in milk and is responsible for cooked flavour in heated milk. Cooked flavour is less in goat's milk as compared to cow's milk.This has been corroborated by lower value of total reducing capacity in goat's milk as compared to cow and buffalo milk.

The curd tension of goat's milk is much lower than that of cow's milk. This may account for the said better digestibility of goat's milk as compared to cow's milk. Ultra-high temperature sterilisation produced a less pronounced cooked flavor in goat milk than in cow's milk.

Utilization of goat milk

In tropical countries, goat milk is produced under very unhygienic conditions. Goat milk, most commonly, is used for adulteration in cow or buffalo milk. Hansa test developed by NDRI can be used to detect adulteration of buffalo milk by goat milk. Goat milk has advantages over bovine milk as baby food because it imparts greater resistance against diseases and it has very little allergic reaction to human body. Several trials on the nutritive value of goat milk for human beings indicate the goat milk is as good as or even better than cow milk in infant feeding. Goat milk can cure the allergies caused by feeding cow milk.

In many countries goat milk powder based infant milk formulations are much in demand. The major problem in embarking on powder production is in securing supply of the quantity of milk, on a regular basis. Flavour is an important issue with goats milk and products.

Medicinal value of goat milk

The medicinal property of goat is known by folklore of our country. Use of goat milk for medicinal purpose has been age old practice in our country. The Jewish sources, mainly the Mishna (1st–3rd centuries CE) and the Talmud (4th – 5th centuries CE), that is, the literature of the Jewish Sages, mention several animals and their medical uses: honey was used to treat bulimia and goat's milk to cure coughing.

Nutritional and therapeutic evaluation of goat milk has been investigated mostly in laboratory animal model or human studies. Researchers have carried out a comparative study on the properties of goats' milk compared to those of cows' milk (Science Daily, July 31, 2007). They found reason to believe that goats' milk could help prevent diseases such as anemia and bone demineralization. Goats' milk was found to help with the digestive and metabolic utilization of minerals such as iron, calcium, phosphorus and magnesium. Results obtained in this study revealed that ferropenic anaemia and bone demineralisation have a better recovery with goat milk due to the higher bioavailability of iron, calcium, phosphorus and magnesium, the restoration of altered haematological parameters and the better levels of parathyroid hormone (PTH), a hormone that regulates the calcium balance in the organism was found in the rats that consumed goat milk. One study showed the beneficial effect of goat milk, with respect to cow milk, on the metabolism of iron and copper in control rats, especially those with mal absorption syndrome. Study carried out by one the group (Toit and Weinberg) reported that the potential of goat milk to induce cross reactions and anaphylaxis in human infants with Ig_E-mediated cow's milk allergy (CMA). Goat milk can be an excellent natural food in cases of malabsorption syndrome, as an alternative to bovine milk.

Prevention of Food Adulteration (PFA) Standards of goat milk

Milk, according to the PFA Rules, is the normal mammary secretion derived from the complete milking of healthy milch animal without either addition thereto or extraction therefrom. It shall be free from colostrum.It shall conform to both the parameters for milk fat and milk solids-not-fat (SNF), independently.

PFA standards for different classes and designations of milk in India

Class of Milk	Designations	Minimum percentage	
		Milk fat	Milk solids -not-fat (SNF)
Buffalo milk	Raw,pasteurized,boiled, flavoured and sterilized	5.0	9.0
Cow milk	-do-	3.5	8.5
Goat orsheep milk	-do-	3.0	9.0

Value addition of goat milk products

Use of goat milk for preparation of various dairy products is an age old practice throughout the world. Goat milk either singly or admixed with cow or buffalo milk, can be utilized for conversion into value-added products such as Ghee (clarified butter fat), Khoa (heat-desiccated milk product), Chhana (acid and heat coagulated milk product), Dahi (curd), yogurt, cheese (Paneer, cheddar, mozzarella and gouda) and dried milk products. Some of the products are exclusively prepared from goat milk, for instance cheeses in Europe and Kefir in Russia. Some of the important value added products made from goat milk are described below.

Cheese is primarily a concentrated form of milk with the benefit of a prolonged shelf life. The high content of fat and protein in cheese make it an energy-rich and nutritious food. Cheese can be characterized as a product made from milk in which the protein is coagulated and concentrated. The collection of protein is accompanied by recovery of most of the fat in the milk by its entrapment in the curd. Other constituents in milk remain in the curd or are removed with the whey depending on their solubility (fat soluble vitamins and minerals associated with protein are retained in the curd; water soluble vitamins and minerals are passed off in the whey).

Goat cheese has been made for thousands of years, and was probably one of the earliest made dairy products. In the simplest form, goat cheese is made by allowing raw milk to naturally curdle, and then draining and pressing the curds. Other techniques use an acid (such as vinegar or lemon juice) or rennet to coagulate the milk. Soft goat cheeses are made in kitchens all over the world, with cooks hanging bundles of cheesecloth filled with curds in the warm kitchen for several days to drain and cure. If the cheese is to be aged, it is often brined so it will form a rind, and then stored in a cool cheese cave for several months to cure.

Goat cheese softens when exposed to heat, although it does not melt in the same way many cow cheeses do. Firmer goat cheeses with rinds are sometimes baked in an oven to form a gooey, warm cheese, which is ideal for spreading on bread with roasted garlic, or alone. Because goat cheese is often made in areas where refrigeration is limited, aged goat cheeses are often heavily treated with salt to prevent decay. As a result, salt has become associated with the flavor of goat cheese, especially in the case of the heavily brined feta.

Paneer is an Indian acid and heat coagulated fresh cheece.Goat milk can be successfully used for the preparation of paneer. Freshly prepared paneer from goat milk is creamy white in colour and has no goaty smell and salty taste. Freshly prepared paneer packed in LDPE pouches could safely be stored at $4\pm1^{0}C$ for 3 days. Citric acid is the most commonly used coagulant for paneer manufacture. Paneer yield from Barbari Jamunapari, Jakhrana, Marwari, Sirohi and Kutchi milk was respectively 16.50, 14.59, 13.27, 12.85, 11.88 and 9.88 % being lowest in Kutchi.

All you need to make goat milk paneer is fresh goat milk, a lemon and a clean muslin cloth. Gently warm the milk and squeeze a little lemon juice in it. Not too much, all you want is for the milk to curdle. Gently mix with a wooden spatula and add more lemon juice (or vinegar) until the milk has split into a transparent liquid and little lumps of soft white matter. Strain the paneer using a clean muslin cloth. Let the butter milk or chacch drain and paneer will be left in the muslin cloth. The resulting paneer is dipped in chilled water for 2–3 hours to give it a good texture and appearance.

Paneer is used for preparation of paneer pakoras, vegetable curries like Mattar Paneer, Palak Paneer, Paneer kadhai, Shahi Paneer and Paneer Tikka etc.

Mattar Paneer dish alongwith Roti or Indian bread

Khoa (also khoya) is a milk food widely used in the Indian cuisine, made of either dried whole milk or milk thickened by heating in an open iron pan. The yield of khoa from goat milk is less as compared to cow or buffalo milk. Khoa is used as the base for a wide variety of Indian sweets. Khoa is made by simmering milk in an iron karahi for several hours, over a medium fire. The gradual vaporization of its water content leaves coagulated solids in milk, which is khoa. Khoa is used in various types of sweets like Gulab Jamun, Peda, Barfi, Gujia and Halwa.

Goat milk can be used for the preparation of dahi or curd. The goat milk dahi lack the texture and compactness of cow dahi but is highly digestible and tasty.

This is a dehydrated product from milk which is used in the preparation of sweets. Although buffalo milk is most commonly used, goat milk is sometimes used depending upon availability.

Ghee prepared from goat milk has a goaty flavor and a greasy and weak texture. Most people blend goat milk with cow or buffalo milk and prepare ghee. Goat milk is not considered suitable for the manufacture of ghee (Arora and Singh, 1986), the main reason being its relatively small fat globules which present problems during cream separation and its typical odour and flavor.

Other value added products like Ice Cream, Shrikhand, Kheer, Channa, flavoured or herbal milk or whey drink, Yogurt etc have also been prepared from goat milk with varying degree of success.

References

Ahrne, L., Bjorck, L., Raznikiewicz, T. and Claesson, O. (1980). Glycerol ethers in colostrum and milk from cow, goat, pig and sheep. J. Dairy Sci. 63:741-745.

Agnihotri, M.K. and Rajkumar, V. (2007). Effect of Breed, Parity and Stage of Lactation on Milk Composition of Western Region Goats of India. International Journal of Dairy Science, 2:172-177.

Akinsoyinu, A.O., Tewe, O.O. and Mba, A.U. (1979). Concentration of trace elements in milk of West African Dwarf goats affected by stage of lactation. J. Dairy Sci. 62:921.

Arora, L. and Singh, S. (1986). Effect of blended goat and buffalo milk on sensory characteristics of ghee. Indian Journal of Dairy Sci., 39:488-490.

Chandan, R.C., Parry, R.M.J. and Sahani, K.M.(1968). Lysozyme, lipase and ribonuclease in milk of various species. J. Dairy Sci. 51:606.

Gomes, V.A.M. Libera, M.P.D. Paiva, M. Madureira, K.M. and Araujo, W.P. (2006). Effect of the stage of lactation on somatic cell counts in healthy goats (Capme hircus) breed in Brazil. Small Rumin. Res. 64:30-34.

Jenness, R., (1980). Composition and characteristics of goat milk: review 1968–1979. J. Dairy Sci. 63:1605-1630.

Lal, Munna and Gupta, M.P. (1981). Status of citric acid in goat milk. Indian J. Dairy Sci., 34:93-95.

Lara-Villoslada F., Debras E., Nieto, A., Concha, A., Galvez, J., Lopez-Huertas, E., Boza, J., Obled, C., Xaus, J. (2006). Oligosaccharides isolated from goat milk reduce intestinal inflammation in a rat model of dextran sodium sulfate-induced colitis. Clin Nutr., 25:477-488

Mba, A.U., Boyo, B.S. Oyenuga, V.A. (1975). Studies on the milk composition of west African Dwarf, Red Sokoto and Seanen goats at different stages of lactation : 1 Total solids, butterfat Solid not fat , protein lactese and energy content of milk J Dairy Res 42:217-

Owen, F.C. and Proud Foot, R. (1959). The effect of tungstate ingestion on xanthine oxidase in goats milk. Proc. Nutr. Soc. 18:1-11.

Park, Y.W., Ju´arez, M. Ramosc, M. Haenlein, G.F.W. (2007). Physico-chemical characteristics of goat and sheep milk Small Ruminant Research 68:88-113

Parkash, S., Jenness, R. (1968). The composition and characteristics of goat's milk: a review. Dairy Sci. Abstr., 30:67-75.

Patton, S., Long, C. and Sobba, T. (1980). Effect of sterilizing milk on cholesterol and phospholopid of skim milk. J. Dairy Sci. 63:697-700.

10

Leather, Skin and Hair

Goats are used primarily for milk and meat production, but their skin is also a valuable by- product. Goats are an important source of hides and skin . The term hide is used to denote the outer covering of large animals such as cows, buffaloes, horses ,sheep, camel etc. The term "Skin" is applied to that of smaller animals such as sheep, goats , calves etc. Raw hides and skins are used mainly for the manufacture of leather.Goat skin is in great demand for making leather gloves , shoes , luggage, book covers etc.Goat skin was also used in many of the musical instruments .Goat skin has been used since time immemorial as water-containers. The water containers from goat skin were called "Mushk" and the person carrying such containers as "Bhisti".Pelt is undressed skin of sheep & goats. To prevent putrefication, the skin is treated as well as preserved by dry salting and are graded according to curled type quality of the skin.

The Leather Industry holds a prominent place in the Indian economy. India produces 13.14% of the goat skin production of the world.This sector is known for its consistency in high export earnings and it is among the top ten foreign exchange earners for the country. With an annual turnover of over US$ 7 billion, the export of leather and leather products increased manifold over the past decades and touched US$ 3.40 billion in 2009-10; recording a cumulative annual growth rate of about 5.43% (5 years).It is estimaed that 72.3 million goat skins were produced in India in 2008 (FAOSTAT). India ranks second among the goat skin producing countries of the world, second only to China. India produced 130 thousand tones of goat skin in 2008 (FAOSTAT) against China producing 351.7 thousand tones and Pakistan 94 thousand tonnes (FAO Stat).

The major production centers for leather and leather products are located in Tamil Nadu - Chennai, Ambur, Ranipet, Vaniyambadi, Trichy, Dindigul ; West Bengal – Kolkata ; Uttar Pradesh – Kanpur, Agra & Noida ; Maharashtra – Mumbai ; Punjab – Jallandhar ; Karnataka – Bangalore ; Andhra Pradesh - Hyderabad ; Haryana - Ambala, Gurgaon, Panchkula and Karnal; Delhi. India is the second largest producer of leather footwear and garments in the world.

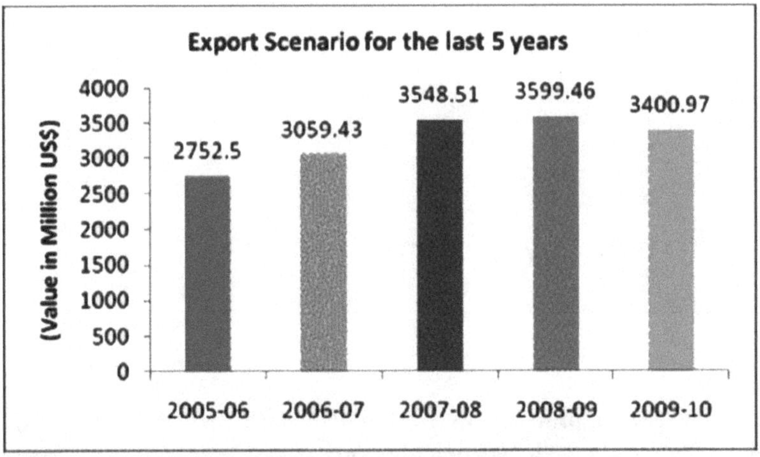

India's export of leather and leather products for five years

Goat skin

In India, Kolkata and Amritsar used to be the two major centres for goat skin trade and likewise, skins are known as Calcuttias and Amritsari. In recent times, Chennai is the hub of tanneries with more than 2000 tanneries. West Bengal is the finest goat skin producing state. Chhatisgarh is also a major supplier of goat skin. The skins are ultimately taken to Chennai and then processed. First, it is dipped in a chemical solution to remove the hair of outer skin (eastern chrome). Then, the colouring of skin is done. The Calcuttias, which come mostly from the Bengal breed of goat, are considered superior to the Amritsari. The Amritsari are inferior in quality and therefore, used as lining for shoes, while the Calcuttias are used for shoe uppers. Goat skins are graded in six classes according to thickness , each class includes five grades of skin quality. The demand for shoe linings remains stable, whereas it fluctuates for the shoe-uppers with the vagaries of fashion. Some of the most valuable goat skins come from Sokoto goats in Nigeria and Morocco. The leather from Red Sokoto breed of goat is known as Morocco leather. Indian goat and kid skins are mostly exported to USA, where they get utilised in the shoe industry. In present times, goat skin leather is losing out because of competition from Italian synthetic leather. Skins decompose very rapidly, so cleaning and salting must be done immediately. The skin must be cleaned, that is, removal of any piece of flesh or connective tissue, before salting. Cut off any tag ends of skin, and spread a layer of salt over the skin, fold the sides to the middle, then roll up loosely.

Goat skin is in great demand for use as leather gloves ,shoes, luggage, book covers etc. Non-tanned goat skin is used for parchment or for drumheads or sounding boards of some musical instruments, e.g., mišnice in medieval Europe, bodhrán in Ireland, esraj in India, and for instrumental drum skin named bedug in Indonesia.

Goatskin leather is very soft and supple. Soft goat leather is comfortable as well as durable. The soft goat leather contains a pleasing pebble grain which enhance its beauty. It colors beautifully, and is identified by a distinctive texture of ridges and furrows in the grain.

Usually there are two types of goat skin leather such as straight-grained and crushed. Straight-grained goatskin leather is produced by rolling a damp skin, so that all the grains run in the same direction. Crushed goatskin leather is produced by flattening the ridges with ironing, rolling or plating.

Tanned leather from goat skin is considered extremely durable, and is commonly used to make rugs *eg* in Indonesia and carpet binding. It is often used for gloves, boots, and other products that require a soft skin. Kid gloves, popular in Victorian times, are still made from goat skin. It is used for a traditional Spanish container for wine called bota bag . Traditional kefir was made in bags from goat skin. Untanned goat skins are used for making musical instruments like Dhol, Majira, Nagada etc. The untanned raw goat hide is used for making drum heads because it is stiffer and more brittle and does not need to flex significantly. Goat skin when used as drum cover, produce a crisper and high sound. The skin after tanning process become soft and useful for making a variety of products like football shoes, golf gloves, bags etc. The goat hide is used for the manufacture of silver foil. Small pieces of silver or aluminium are placed between leaves prepared from goat skin and beaten with the help of a hammer. This trade is flourishing in Aligarh, Moradabad, Kanpur, Lucknow and other cities of Uttar Pradesh. The goat hide was used for transport of water in olden times. The water container made of whole goat carcass was called "Mashk" and the person carrying water in these containers, used to be called "Bhisti".These containers were highly useful for ceremonies and transport of water for construction purposes.The skins are usually obtained as slaughter house by-products or inedible offals, after slaughtering the animals for meat or other purposes, but also from fallen or dead animals. Glands and fat cells, responsible for sponginess in sheep leather, are less abundant in goat skins. The thermostat layer occupies less than one half of the total thickness of the skin. In Asia and Africa, where goats are slaughtered in large number for meat, considerable export market exists for the skins so obtained. Both in weight and value, goat skins are the second most important constituent of the Indian trade in hides and skins, ranking next to cow/buffalo hides only. In trade of hides, the great bulk of the export consists of the raw products.

Tamil Nadu accounts for about 40% of India's exports and has about 60% of tanning capacity of all types of leather including goat leather.

In addition to India, several other countries like Nigeria, Morocco, Somalia, Uganda and Pakistan are important producers of goat skins. Careless or unskilled handling, skin diseases and insect damage reduce the value of goat skins enormously. Any form of indiscriminate branding on such parts of the body as flank, which scars it, considerably reduces the value of the skin in the market. To avoid this, branding should be confined to areas such as ear, cheek or the fore of hind feet below the shoulder and stifle, respectively. Scratches etc. from barbed wires, wounds, mechanical injuries and diseases also reduce the value of skin. Animal rights groups such as PETA have called for boycott of leather products. Their contention is that we should encourage the use of alternative materials such as synthetic leathers.

Goat skin provides the raw material for many of the top quality products of leather industry. In any shoe, the upper materials are one of the most important and expensive components. The new hummel 2006 football boots use a variety of natural and man made materials for ultimate performance and quality. One of the key materials, as used in the 4.2 Concept and 8.2 Concept is Pittards WR Premiership Goat Skin leather.

The skins from the male animal are characterised by a strong smell which does not disappear even after some finishes of the leather, but if the males have been castrated, their skins are said to be free from this drawback and command a higher price in consequence. The average weight per hide is about 1100 gms. The cold weather skins are considered better than hot weather skins. Goat skin has characteristics between calf and sheep and the reticular fibres run straight. Goat's skin tends to be 'grainy' during the cold months due to heavier growth of hair.

Skin diseases are an important cause of huge losses for leather industry. The skin diseases like goat pox, ecto parasitism etc. can be controlled by proper and timely health management and vaccination programme. In 1974, there was a great controversy in America surrounding goat skin products originating in Haiti. The Center for Disease Control discovered that some of these products contained deadly anthrax spores. All Haitian goat skin products in America were recalled.

Excessive fat is known to reduce the quality of goat skins. It is recommended avoiding excessive feeding to goats to avoid deposition of undesirable fat in the skin. At the same time under-feeding would tend to increase the follicular density by restricting skin expansions, and might also reduce the connective tissue layers, providing thinner and weaker leather. A normal plane of nutrition will thus be adequate for the healthy growth and development of the body and at the same time to produce the right quality of leather from their skins. The best leather is likely to be produced from young animals fed sufficiently well to enable them to reach full growth by about a year.

The skin is sold raw and the skin traders treat it with salt. The raw skin sells at Rs. 50 per skin. The skin of smaller size sells at Rs. 25-30 and the discarded ones at Rs. 10 (cuts/ sore) etc.The raw skin is collected and salt is put onto it with in 24 hrs, if the salt is not put the skin, it will get damaged. For one skin, approximately 2 kgs of salt is required(http://www.downtoearth.org.in/dte/userfiles/images/Goat_meat_sub_sector_report.pdf).

Goat hair

Goats, in addition to providing milk and meat, are a valuable source of fibers which can be used for various purposes. Though not as important as sheep, a few breeds of goats have been selectively bred to provide much finer and superior quality hairs than sheep.The economically important hair/fibres obtained from goats are of two major types which include Mohair and Pashmina. Ordinary goat hair is used in the manufacture of ropes, rugs, poor quality carpets and gunny bags as it is not suitable for textile manufacture.

Breeds of goats reputed to produce goat hair

Breed	Place of origin	Fibre produced
Angora	Turkey, USA, South Africa	Mohair
Chegu	India	Pashmina
Changthangi	India	Pashmina
Don	Russia	
Altai Mountain	Russia	
Soviet Mohair	Russia	
Orenburg	Russia	
Raeini	Iran	Cashmere/Pashmina

Mohair

Mohair is the long, lustrous fleece of the Angora goats. The Angora goat is the only breed of goat utilized for the production of mohair. The origins of the Angora breed can be traced to the Himalayan Mountains of Asia. Angora goats are a native of Turkey and are presently found in South Africa, USA, Australia and New Zealand. In India, Angoras have been introduced years back and have stabilised well in the state of Himachal Pradesh. Attempts have been also made to use Angora for crossbreeding with the locals in hilly areas of UP or semi-arid areas of Maharashtra.

Mohair is known worldwide as the "noble fibre" or "the diamond Fibre".Its exclusive qualities are the lustre, resilience and colour reflection that have been its success. The quantity of mohair production from Angora goats is larger in quantity as compared to Pashmina. Mohair has certain unique qualities which make it quite desirable by various people around the world. Mohair is the strongest textile fibre. Mohair fiber is approximately 25-45 microns in diameter.It is one of the oldest textile fibers in use. It is both durable and resilient. It is notable for its high luster and sheen, and is often used in fiber blends to add these qualities to a textile . Mohair also takes dye exceptionally well. Mohair is also warm, as it has great insulating properties. It is durable and resistant to moisture-wicking, stretch, flame and creases. Angora goats are maintained primarily for the production of this quality luxury fibre, as opposed to the basic use of the ruminant animals, in general for meat, milk and wool production. This distinctive breed hybridizes readily with any type of goat, yet it has retained its essential fleece characteristics. This survival has been attributed to careful selection in order to maintain the highly cherished quality of the fleece. The production of mohair is also limited by the fact that the Angora is a creature of the environment which will not thrive or survive except under the geographically and climatic conditions exactly suited to its needs. Only limited regions of the surface of the earth are suitable for this animal and the fact that there is no substitute for it, is the reason why it commands better prices than wool. Mohair is considered a luxury fibre which is soft, light and hard wearing. The characteristics of mohair that make it a sought-after fibre are its lustre, soft handle, strength, elasticity and low felting properties. Mohair is also very durable, easy to clean, flame resistant, has a very high affinity for dyes and possesses both insulating and sound absorbance properties. The factors which influence price are primarily fibre diameter (fineness) and length, and to a lesser extent style, lustre, character, colour, medullated fibre and fault (contamination).During the cleaning process, grease, vegetable matter, dust, contaminants and short/broken fibres are removed, thus reducing the fleece weight.Mohair is useful in the manufacture of blankets, fabrics, linings, rugs, braids, nets, shoes laces, hats, shoe wigs, curtains and bed spreads. Superior quality mohair is useful for manufacture of knitwears, sweaters and shawls.Mohair is blended with wool, polyster and acrylic fibres for producing hosiery goods and shawls.

Mohair is unique in the fact that it cannot be reproduced synthetically. Thus mohair has a constant market undisturbed by competition from artificial substitutes. The market for mohair, is however, affected by the fashion industry and world prices are subject to large fluctuations.The demand for cashmere garments is strong, particularly in Western Europe, USA and Japan and is less affected by fashion trends. Consequently, the price for cashmere is more stable than mohair. Today, South Africa is by far the largest mohair-producing nation, accounting for over sixty percent of the world's mohair clip. Port Elizabeth in South Africa is known as the Mohair capital of the world as 95% of the world's mohair passes through its ports. The United States of America is also a significant producer of mohair. Australia is contributing less than 5% of the world total. Currently, Britain processes 60% of the world mohair, almost all of which is imported. UK production is currently around 25 tonnes, of which approximately 10 tonnes is used by producers or sold to home spinners. Scotland processes over 1000 tonnes of imported cashmere (60% of world production) each year.

Mohair production and quality is affected by several factors like age, season, sex, plane of nutrition etc. Quality of mohair depends on several attributes viz., fineness, length, medullated fibre percentage, freedom from pigmented fibres & contamination such as vegetable matter. Medullated fibres are undersirable and a good quality mohair contains least medullated fibres. The coarse kemp hair fibres have a strongly developed medulla with some of the finer fibres showing a varying degree of medullation.

Mohair in the market is generally classified into two categories on the basis of the age of the animals, that is, kid and adult. The real basis for the two categories is a difference in fibre diameters since an Angora goat under normal feed conditions will produce a much coarser fleece with each shearing. Mohair value is generally determined not only by fibre diameter, which is related to, but not entirely determined by age of the animal, but also fibre length, yield, strength, vegetable matter defect, kemp and other factors.

Mohair is generally classified as normal, light defect, medium defect and heavy defect. Excess vegetable matter contamination in mohair leads to discounted price in the market. Vegetable matter in the grease mohair reduces value by decreasing the yield of products at various stages in processing and/or reducing quality of the product if the vegetable matter is not completely removed.

Several attempts have been made in various countries to cross Angora goats with other goats to increase their fibre production with limited success. Several authors have reported negative correlation between mohair fibre diameter and Angora blood level in the progeny.

Pashmina (Cashmere)

Pashmina refers to a type of fine cashmere wool and the textiles made from it. Pashmina, the "King of Fibres" is known all over the world for its fineness, warmth, softness, desirable aesthetic value, elegance and timelessness in fashion. It has occupied a unique position among the fibres of animal origin due to its fineness, warmth, softness and its ability to absorb dyes and moisture. It has derived its name from the Persian word "pashm" which means "soft gold".Pashmina is the hairy undercoat of several breeds of Pashmina goats. Pashmina shawls are hand spun, woven and embroidered in Kashmir. India, Nepal, USSR and China, are famous for the production of Pashmina. In addition Mangolia, Iran and Afganistan also produce substantial quantities of Pashmina. Vatani and Asmari are the important breeds of goat of Afghanistan and produce fibre from the undercoat.China continues to be the major supplier with more than 50 % of the world cashmere production.In India, Kashmiri (Chanthangi) and Chegu are the two breeds of Pashmina goats found at altitudes above 14,500 feet (4,500 meters) in a few restricted hilly tracts of Kashmir, Ladakh, Lahaul and Spiti in Himachal Pradesh and Chini valleys and the neighbouring areas of Himachal Pradesh and Tehri and Garhwal district of Uttrakhand. The habitat of Pashmina goat is very harsh with extremely cold climate and scarce vegetation. Pashmina goats grow the under coat/Pashmina during winter season, when the temperature reaches below zero degree centigrade, to protect themselves from severe cold. As the temperature start rising from early spring, they start moulting/shedding of this under coat. In India, collection/ harvesting of Pashmina is done by combing. Pashmina is one of the finest natural fibers. These goats are constantly on risk of extinction because of shortage of fodder during extreme winter conditions. The Changthang area of Kashmir bordering China frequently gets cut off from mainland due to heavy snowfall and fodder has to be air dropped during emergency. The principal Pashmina breeds of USSR are Orenburg, Kirghiz, Don and Prodomskay or Gornoaltaskaya. Almost 90% of the population of the Changthang area survives on the income from goats and sheep, which is nearly $ 8.4 million annually.

Pashmina goat

Cashmere shawls have been manufactured in Nepal and Kashmir for thousands of years. The test for a quality pashmina is warmth and feel. Pashmina is used for making the famous ring shawls of Kashmir. Although ring shawls are made from Shahtoosh made from delicate hair (9-11 micrometers) of Chiru or Tibetan Antelope. The woollen shawls made from wool in Kashmir find written mention in Indian texts between 3rd century BC and the 11th century AD. One woven Pashmina shawl requires the wool from three goats.Pashmina is a delicate product woven with very fine fibers; hence very special care should be taken for your shawl. Most manufacturers recommend that 100% Pashmina shawl should always be dry-cleaned.

There is a difference between Cashmere and Pashmina wool. Cashmere is defined as any wool under 19 microns thick from the Angora or mountain goat. Most Cashmere wool is found in the 16-18 micron range. Pashmina wool has the finest and thinnest fibers and is only 12-14 microns thick. Compare this to a human hair which is about 75 microns thick.

On an average, Indian Pashmina goats produce 112 gm of pashmina. Orenburg goats are known to produce 357 gm of Pashmina. The annual production of Pashmina from goats in Ladakh is estimated at 136.2 tonnes, out of which 40.86 tonnes is fine undercoat useful for the manufacture of fabrics. Almost 90% of the population of the Changthang area survives on the income from goats and sheep, which is nearly $ 8.4 million annually. The hair clipped from Kirghiz goats is about 1.6 kg with about 82.5% of the clean fibre yield. Better quality of pashmina is obtained from goats raised on comparatively high altitudes. The kid pashmina is finer and softer. Pashmina production is affected by feed intake, conversion efficiency and the rate of nitrogen retention. By virtue of metabolic priority, lactation and reproduction generally depress the pashmina production.

Females produce significantly more pashmina than males and castrated animals produce more pashmina than non-castrated ones.

To meet the demand, the goats are now commercially reared in the Gobi Desert area in Inner and Outer Mongolia. The region has identical harsh weather conditions to those of the Himalayan region which is suitable for the goats to grow pashmina, but also has acres of grazing ground to produce cashmere economically and commercially. During spring (the moulting season) the goats shed this inner wool, which regrows in winter. The inner wool is collected and spun to produce cashmere. The quality of the cashmere produced in the Gobi Desert is just as high as that produced in the Himalayas, while the cost is less. Biswas *et al.* (1995) reviewed the performance of Indian Pashmina goats and concluded that Indian Pashmina goats have a restricted distribution in higher altitudes of Himalayas and represent unique genetic material.

Pashmina is utilized for the development of knitwears and woven products including jumpers, gloves, jackets, pants, pajama, scarves, blankets and other items. In India, majority of Pashmina is being utilized for production of shawls especially in Jammu and Kashmir State. Pashmina accessories are available in a range of sizes, from "scarf" (12" × 60") to "wrap" or "stole" (28" x 80") to full sized shawl (36" × 80"). Pure Pashmina is a rather gauzy, open weave, as the fibre cannot tolerate high tension. The most popular Pashmina fabric is a 70% Pashmina/30% silk blend, but 50/50 is also common. The 70/30 is tightly woven, has an elegant sheen and drapes nicely, but is still quite soft and light-weight.

References

Biswas, J.C., Deb, S.M. and Kaul, G.L. (1995) Overview of performance of Indian Pashmina (Cashmere) goats International Journal of Animal Sciences 10: 65-68

11

Diseases

A disease is any process which disrupts an animals's normal function. Occurrence of diseases causes heavy economic loss in terms of livestock health and production. Presence and accumulation of infectious agents in the environment lead to reduction in quality and quantity of animal products. Strategic control and eradication of economically important diseases will result in enhancing goat production in the country. Goat suffer from many diseases although the susceptibility of goats to diseases is less as compared to sheep or cattle. Goat diseases can be bacterial, viral or parasitic. Viral diseases are more common in herds and are responsible for large scale mortality at one time. With a good hygiene in the barn and if the goats are kept in a way appropriate to their species, most of the diseases can be avoided.

Much attention has not been paid for prevention and control of goat diseases since most of the goats are reared by poor people and prevention and control is generally considered uneconomical. However, this is not true, as small investment in disease prevention and control can bring enormous gains in goat productivity. Simple preventive measures like deworming and vaccination alone can save the herds from heavy mortality and can increase production considerably. Serious and early efforts on diagnosis and prevention of goat diseases are essential in order to improve the health and production. A wide range of bacterial, viral, parasitic infections, causing heavy mortality and morbidity result in huge economic loss to different goat farming systems. Metabolic and nutritional disorders in goats also affect their production performance. Metabolic disorders are of great importance in pregnant goats, especially those carrying multiple foetuses. Deficiencies of essential minerals, metabolites and amino acids below the critical level also adversely affect the production. Therefore, it is necessary to avert these imbalances (calcium, magnesium, Co, Cu, Zinc, Iodine) in the ration. Provision for extra energy and protein in late pregnancy are necessary to avoid parturient paresis due to low blood sugar and high ketones and hepatic insufficiency of glycogen. Soil-plant- animal interactions in relation to the incidence of chronic deficiency diseases of goats are often being observed.

In one study on Osmanabadi goats from three districts *viz* Ahmednagar, Solapur and Osmanabad, 30.94 goats were infected with worm infestation, 18.01 % by diarrhea, 17.88 % by enterotoxaemia, 15.82 % by contagious ecthyma, 6.86 % by haemorrhagic septicaemia, 6.20 % by Foot and Mouth disease and 0.72 % by bronchitis.The diseases which cause rapid death in goats include anthrax, bacillary haemoglobinuria, black quarter, cyanide poisoning and enterotaxaemia.

In many countries eg USA, there is a restriction on many drugs for treatment of goat diseases because the problem of drug residues is of great concern in species consumed for food. Because of adverse reactions in humans who consumed contaminated animal products, FDA (US) has banned ten drugs from use in any food animal under any circumstances. These products include chloramphenicol, clenbuterol, diethylstilbestrol, dimetridazole, dipyrone, fluoroquinolones, glycopeptide antibiotics, ipronidazole, nitroimadazoles, and nitrofurans.

The production of safe and wholesome goat meat and milk for human consumption is a primary goal of goat farmers. Veterinarians should work to develop effective management programs combined with the use of vaccines, parasiticides, and nutrition to reduce the incidence of disease. Prudent use of antimicrobial drugs is a necessary tool to treat livestock, reduce suffering, and decrease shedding of zoonotic bacteria into the environment and food chain. Antibiotics should only be used with due caution to minimize the residue and resistance concerns.

Some of the important goat diseases are given as follows.

Bacterial and viral infections

Johne's disease (Paratuberculosis)

Mycobacterium paratuberculosis or *M. paratuberculosis* – a bacterium that infects the last part of the small intestine and causes an inflammation called granulomatous inflammation. This disease is found only in adult goats. The symptoms of this disease include debility of the animal combined with diarrhea. The goat gets weak day after day and they become skin and bone before they die. While Johne's disease is found in sheep, goats, elk, deer, bison, llamas and wild ruminants, there is debate whether this is contagious to human (called in human as Crohn's Disease). Johne's disease usually enters a herd when an infected, but healthy-looking, animal is purchased. Since symptoms take years to manifest, the owners are normally unaware of the problem. Johne's disease causes diarrhea and rapid weight loss although not all goats have signs of diarrhea. Young animals are most susceptible to infection, catching the disease by nursing teats that have been in contact with contaminated manure/soil. A doe with later stages of the disease may pass it through her milk. Tests for this disease are unreliable; a positive animal may test negative simply because it is not "shedding" the bacterium at the time of the test. Johne's disease in goats is under diagnosed and can cause weight loss despite a good appetite. Clinical signs common in cattle with Johne's disease are often not present in goats, and laboratory tests for Johne's disease are not as sensitive in goats as they are for cattle.

It has not been considered economically prudent to treat animals with Johne's disease. The chances of curing the animal are low, the cost of the drugs is high and the meat and milk derived from animals treated with potent drugs required are not suitable for human consumption.

Peste des petits ruminants (PPR)

Peste des petits ruminants (PPR) is an acute febrile viral disease of goats and sheep. Clinical symptoms include mucopurulent nasal and ocular discharge, stomatitis, enteritis and pneumonia. The disease is caused by PPR virus (PPRV), a ribonucleic acid virus belonging to the genus Morbillivirus and family Paramyxoviridae. In India, although PPR was believed to have been present in southern India prior to the late 1980s , the disease was not officially recorded in this region until 1987. Economic losses due to PPRV have been estimated to be 1,800 million Indian Rupees(US$ 39 million)annually (Bandyopadhyay, 2002)

Brucellosis

Brucellosis is an endemic disease in small ruminant flocks in many developing countries of the world. The number of cases of *B. melitensis* is relatively high among aborted animals. It is considered as an important cause of abortion in these species. Control measures are based on strict hygiene and vaccination programs. Vaccination is regarded as a measure for reducing the prevalence of the disease to a level where eradication by test and slaughter can be implemented.

Serological test, identification of the agent by culture and Polymerase chain reaction (PCR) test are the most common techniques that are used for brucellosis diagnosis.

Humans become infected by coming in contact with animals or animal products that are contaminated with these bacteria. In humans brucellosis can cause a range of symptoms that are similar to the flu and may include fever, sweats, headaches, back pains, and physical weakness. Severe infections of the central nervous systems or lining of the heart may occur. Brucellosis can also cause long-lasting or chronic symptoms that include recurrent fevers, joint pain, and fatigue. Humans are generally infected in one of three ways: eating or drinking something that is contaminated with Brucella, breathing in the organism (inhalation), or having the bacteria enter the body through skin wounds.

Calfhood vaccination with *B. melitensis* Rev-1 is recommended to prevent infection. In China, oral vaccination with *B. suis* is used to control the disease. Infected animals should be segregated from healthy flock, euthanized and buried in lime. Since it infects human beings also the disease should be controlled and eradicated by repeated sero-screening program in goat herd. Breeding bucks should be screened before the breeding season starts, whereas, female goats should be screened after the kidding season is over, serologically. Strict and proper disinfection of contaminated area and proper disposal of placenta and other secretions by burning, and fumigation or sprinkling of lime should be taken up in the pens where abortions occurs. Kidding pens should not be located within the sheds of healthy animals and should be away from main farm. Sero positive should be immediately segregated from healthy group and removal of such animals should be implemented. Control and eradication methods (test and slaughter or vaccination) depend on level of infection in the herds. Treatment can be difficult. Doctors can prescribe effective antibiotics. Usually, doxycycline, streptomycin, oxytetracycline and rifampin are used in combination for 6 weeks to prevent reoccurrence. Prolonged antibiotic therapy may help but is not cost effective. Depending on the timing of treatment and severity of illness, recovery may take a few weeks to several months.

Enterotoxaemia

This is one of the most important disease of goats.Enterotoxaemia is caused by *Clostridium perfringens*. Goat upto 5-6 months of age are more susceptible. Infection spread through contaminated faeces and soil. E.T. is characterized by sudden abdominal pain, distress, loss of appetite, constipation followed by blackish color diarrhea. E.T. vaccination needs to be carried out at 3 months of age and a booster dose is s/c injected after 21 days. The vaccination schedule needs to be repeated every year. Preventive measures include proper sanitation of the shed and timely sprinkling of lime.

Foot and Mouth Disease

Foot and mouth disease (FMD) is highly infectious disease of cloven-hoofed animals including goats. Also, it is the most important animal pathogen on the global scale because of the potential for rapid and extensive spread through susceptible animal populations. Outbreak can lead to formidable economic consequence for domestic livestock production and international trade. FMD is caused by FMD virus which is a small, non-enveloped, positive-sense RNA virus belonging to the genus Aphthovirus within the family Picornaviridae. There are seven immunologically distinct serotypes; O, A, C, SAT (Southern African Territories) 1, SAT 2, SAT 3 and Asia 1 and a diverse antigenic spectrum of virus strains within each serotype. Characteristic lesion of FMD is the formation of vesicles in the mucosal membranes of mouth, muzzle, foot, and teats. Nowadays, many developed countries have maintained themselves FMD-free as a result of eradication efforts. Culling of infected animals, movement control, and vaccination are the major control measures of FMD.

Foot-and-mouth disease (FMD) is a highly contagious and economically devastating disease. The disease affects all the ruminants and pigs including many wild life species (Sutmoller *et al.,* 2003) and is characterized by fever, lameness, salivation and vesicular lesions on tongue, feet, snout and teats. The disease has debilitating effects including weight loss, decrease in milk production and loss of drought power resulting in loss of productivity of affected animals for a considerable time. The outbreaks of the disease have occurred in every livestock containing region of the world with the exception of New Zealand and the FMD is currently enzootic in all continents except Australia and North-America. FMD is a notifiable disease (formerly List "A" disease) of Office Des International Epizootics (OIE). It has serious impact on international trade of animals and animal products. To protect the countries which are traditionally free of FMD, the OIE has developed certain recommendations for the affected countries to acquire FMD free status for participation in international trade.

The causative agents of FMD are small icosahedral viruses of the Aphthovirus group within the family Picornaviridae. The FMD virus (FMDV) particle is a non-segmented, positive stranded RNA genome of about 8.5 Kb, enclosed within a protein capsid. The genome encodes a single polyprotein from which four different structural proteins (i.e. VP1, VP2, VP3 and VP4) and eight different non-structural proteins (i.e. L, 2A, 2B, 2C, 3A, 3B, 3C and 3D) are cleaved by viral proteases. There are seven immunologically distinct serotypes of FMDV, namely O, A, C, Asia1, SAT1, SAT2 and SAT3. The animals that have recovered from infection or have received vaccine with a single strain of one serotype remain fully susceptible to infection with strains of the other six serotypes. Like other RNA viruses, the FMD virus has also very high genome plasticity and new strains within serotypes evolutes frequently.

Clinical symptoms: This disease show mild effect in adult goats. Vesicles on the tongue, lips, checks, gums, dental pad and on the skin between claws, occasional blisters on teats and under. Lameness is also seen in adult goats, Deaths have been observed in young goat kids.

Preventive care: Isolate the sick goats and vaccinate the herd to prevent outbreak. Wash the mouth of infected goat with mild disinfectants like Alum, Potassium permanganate. Apply boroglycerine on the ulcers.

Goat pox

Goat pox, which is listed in Group A diseases of the OIE (World Animal Health, 1997), is a highly contagious viral disease of goats, characterized by fever, ocular and nasal discharges. Pox lesions appear on the skin and on the respiratory and gastrointestinal mucosa. The disease was described in detail about 200 AD in ancient veterinary medical texts, and has been widespread since early times. Hansen reported goat pox in 1879 from Norway (Rafyi and Ramyar, 1959). Later on it was observed during the First World War in Macedonia and became enzootic during 1926 with a mortality rate of 15% . The disease is caused mainly by goat poxvirus (GPV) and occasionally by sheep poxvirus (SPV), which are enveloped double stranded DNA viruses, classified in the genus Capripoxvirus of the family Poxviridae (Murphy *et al.,* 1995). The disease inflicts substantial losses in terms of reduced productivity and lower quality of wool and leather. It poses a major obstacle in the intensive rearing of goats and also greatly hampers international trade. Goat pox is the most important of all pox diseases of domestic animals causing high mortality in kids and significant economic losses . Scabs around the mouth, feet, or udder may be a sign of pox-virus infection, a cause ofcontagious ecthyma, also known as sore mouth. Since the virus is capable of infecting people, precautions should be taken while handling goats with scabs to prevent transmission of the virus to people.

Goat pox is a contagious viral disease of goats, which result from infection by sheep pox virus (SPV) or goat-pox virus (GPV). The two viruses belong to the Capripoxvirus genus, Poxviridae family, which includes a third virus, causing lumpy skin disease (LSD) in cattle. In sheep and goats, the clinical signs vary from mild to severe clinical disease, normally beginning with the onset of fever followed by erythematous macules that develop into papules . Lesions may also develop on the mucous membrane and on internal organs, causing systemic signs (respiratory signs, diarrhoea, depression, emaciation, abortion and sometimes death). Sheep pox and goat pox is notifiable to the World Organisation for Animal Health (OIE) in accordance with the requirements on notification of diseases set out in Chapter 1.1. of the OIE Terrestrial Animal Health Code. The relevance of this disease for OIE notification is related to the consequences of its spread within the animal population, the resulting economic impact and international trade restrictions.

Sheep pox and goat pox causes considerable production losses in endemic areas as a result of reduced milk yields, decreased weight gain, abortion, poor quality wool and hides, increased susceptibility to pneumonia and fly strike, and mortality. Morbidity and mortality rates may be very high, reaching 100% in naive animals. A study in India calculated that it took approximately 6 years for a flock to recover from an outbreak causing 49.5% mortality. Sheep pox and goat pox prevents also importation of new breeds of small ruminants into endemic regions. The most relevant strategy for controlling sheep pox and goat pox in endemic areas is mass immunisation of the susceptible population. All strains of capripoxvirus of ovine, caprine or bovine origin, such as sheep and goat pox and LSD for cattle, share a major neutralising site, so that animals recovered from infection with one strain are resistant to infection with any other strain. It is recommended to vaccinate annually all sheep and goats regardless of their age. Although some young animals will have maternal derived antibodies, other will not, depending on the immune status of their mother, and considering the low cost of vaccines all young animals should be vaccinated to ensure optimal protection coverage. Those that did not generate immunity due to maternal antibodies will be vaccinated the following year.

Clinical symptoms: Slight fever, congested area and vesicles, appear on ear, nose and udder. After vesicles containing pus, dry crust are formed. In goat kids, high temperature is seen , but death occurs before development of skin lesions.

Preventive care: Isolate the sick goat and daily washing the lesions with hydrogen peroxide dilute with equal part of warm water followed by antibiotic cream. Milkers hand scrubbed in non-irritant antiseptic solution.

Maedi-visna

Maedi-visna is an economically important viral disease of sheep that occasionally affects goats. The maedi-visna virus (MVV), a lentivirus; infects its hosts for life. Although most infections are subclinical, a minority of animals develops progressive, untreatable disease syndromes including dyspnea (maedi) or neurologic signs (visna). Both maedi and visna are eventually fatal. Additional economic costs may include marketing and export restrictions, premature culling, and losses from poor milk production due to indurative mastitis. Economic losses can vary considerably between flocks.

Rift Valley fever (RVF)

Rift Valley fever (RVF) is a peracute or acute zoonotic disease of domestic ruminants in Africa. It is caused by a single serotype of a mosquito-borne bunyavirus of the genus Phlebovirus. The disease occurs in climatic conditions favouring the breeding of mosquito vectors and is characterised by liver damage. The disease is most severe in sheep, goats and cattle, in which it produces abortions in pregnant animals and a high mortality rate in the newborn. Older nonpregnant animals, although susceptible to infection, are more resistant to clinical disease. There is considerable variation in the susceptibility to RVF of animals of different breeds. Those breeds or strains that are exotic to Africa or are from areas where RVF is not endemic tend to be more susceptible. Camels suffer an inapparent infection with RVF, but abortion rates can be as high as in cattle. Among ruminant game, buffalo also abort during an inapparent RVF infection.

Aujeszky's disease

Aujeszky's disease, also known as pseudorabies, is caused by an alphaherpesvirus that infects the central nervous system and other organs, such as the respiratory tract, in a variety of mammals except humans and the tailless apes. It is associated primarily with pigs, the natural host, which remain latently infected following clinical recovery (except piglets under 2 weeks old, which die from encephalitis). The disease is controlled by containment of infected herds and by the use of vaccines and/or removal of latently infected animals.

Border disease (BD)

Border disease (BD) is a viral disease of sheep and goats first reported in sheep in 1959 from the border region of England and Wales, and since recorded world-wide. Distribution of the virus is world-wide. Prevalence rates vary in sheep from 5% to 50% between countries and from region to region within countries. Clinical signs include barren ewes, abortions, stillbirths and the birth of small weak lambs. Affected lambs can show tremor, abnormal body conformation and hairy fleeces (so-called 'hairy-shaker' or 'fuzzy' lambs) and the disease has been referred to as 'hairy shaker disease'. Vertical transmission plays an important role in the epidemiology of the disease. Infection of fetuses can result in the birth of persistently infected (PI) lambs. These PI lambs are viraemic, antibody negative and constantly excrete virus. The virus spreads from sheep to sheep, with PI animals being the most potent source of infection. Infection in goats is less common with abortion being the main presenting sign. In many regions the commonest cause of BD is the pestivirus border disease virus (BDV), but in some parts of the world, bovine viral diarrhoea virus (BVDV) may be a more common cause of BD. The source of BVDV for sheep often is close contact with cattle.

Rinderpest

This disease used to be very common in cattle and buffalo. This disease is characterized by diarrhea followed by death after a few days. Diarrhea leads to deficiency of water in the body. The disease was less common in goats but recently it has become more prevalent in some states.

For prevention of this disease, vaccine used for cow or buffalo can also be used for goats. Movement of animals from infected states to non infected areas is one of the most important sources of infection.

Scrapie

Scrapie is a naturally occurring, infectious, neurodegenerative disease of sheep and goats characterised by vacuolar or spongy changes in the central nervous system (CNS). It has been recognised as a clinical disorder for more than 250 years, and is now classified as a transmissible spongiform encephalopathy (TSE), or prion disease, defined by the accumulation of an abnormal form (referred to as PrPSc) of a host membrane glycoprotein (prion protein or PrP), in the CNS. In some animals, PrPSc accumulation is also detectable in lymphoreticular tissues. Polymorphisms of the sheep PrP gene are associated with susceptibility to scrapie. PrP genotyping has been used as a tool in the control of classical scrapie, but no genotype appears to be completely resistant to infection, and the recently identified variant – atypical scrapie – has been reported in sheep of PrP genotypes that are apparently resistant to classical scrapie. Classical scrapie is endemic in many parts of the world, where it has often been introduced by importation. Australia and New Zealand have maintained freedom by use of strict restrictions on imports and other measures. The infection in sheep may be passed from ewe to lamb in the period from parturition to weaning. Infection can also pass horizontally to unrelated sheep or goats, especially when parturition occurs in confined areas. Fetal membranes are known to be a source of infection, and sheep milk from clinically affected animals has been demonstrated to transmit disease. The incubation time between primary infection and clinical disease is nearly always longer than 1 year and may sometimes exceed the commercial lifespan of the sheep. The majority of cases occur in sheep between 2 and 5 years of age. Clinical disease only develops if the infection enters the CNS. Atypical scrapie, when it presents clinically, appears to affect older animals predominantly, and occurs with a geographical distribution suggestive of a spontaneous disease, although it can be transmitted experiment.

Parasitic infestations

Animals often get infected with a number of parasites, which causes major economic losses in production and health status of animals. They produce diarrhea, blood loss and un-thriftiness. The infected animals exhibit poor growth, weight loss, decreased milk production and mortality. Hence the control of gastrointestinal parasitic infection is of utmost importance due to their ill effects on the livestock profitability and health status. Most of the anthelmintics that are available in the market at present target specific sites on the parasites but they have many limitations. Usage of these synthetic anthelmintics results in toxic manifestation in animals, concern over human safety and environmental hazards and the development of resistance by the parasites.

Diseases of the Kids

There are many diseases which can cause kid to die during their first several weeks of life. Kid mortality is one of the major problems in goat breeding farms, particularly in intensively managed flocks. Kid mortality greatly influences the economic returns from goat farming. Kid mortality rate < 10% is considered normal in an organized flock. Poonia and Mailik (2011) reported an average of 18.88 percent kid mortality in Beetal goat. Kid mortality can be caused by several reasons such as starvation, trauma, pneumonia, collibacillosis, coccidiosis and contagious ecthyma. Collibacillosis is one of the most important diseases that affects the survival of kids. Outbreaks of collibacillosis occur mainly during the first fortnight of life. Vihan *et al.* (1992) and Vihan (2010) reported that mortality was highest with larger litter size or with lower birth weight. There was higher mortality in the Barbari than in the Jamunapari breed.

Pneumonia

Pneumonia is the common term for a range of respiratory infections that kill goats quickly - especially kids. There are many types of pneumonia: bacterial, mycoplasmal, viral, and inhalation pneumonia to name a few. Common symptoms include fever, labored breathing, runny nose discharging yellowish-green mucous, and sometimes a hacking cough - along with generalized listlessness and off feed behavior. The same medications and treatment regimen are used for most forms of pneumonia. The first task with any sick goat is to take its rectal temperature. If fever exists (above 103.5°F), administer Banamine or kid aspirin. One of the few vaccines made specifically for goats is Colorado Serum's pasteurella pneumonia vaccine.

Contagious ecthyma

Contagious Ecthyma (CE), also known as orf, contagious pustular dermatitis, or sore mouth, is perhaps the most commonly encountered skin disease in goats.

CE is caused by a virus from the pox family. Within two to three days of contacting the virus, the first signs of the disease can be seen. By eleven days, scabs are evident which may stay for a week or two. The virus may be passed directly between animals or indirectly by objects that animals contact. The virus is very hardy and live virus has been found in dried scabs up to twelve years after they have been shed.

CE is most commonly seen on the lips and mouth of infected animals, but lesions may also occur on the udder and between the toes. The disease begins with water filled blebs that eventually become pustules. When the pustules break, raised brown scabs form over the resulting wounds. If a number of pustules are found close to each other, large scabs result. It is usually at this stage of the disease that farmers notice that they have a problem. If there is no further infection of the lesions, the disease will clear up in one to four weeks. Animals that carry the disease usually develop a strong immunity and will not be re-infected for at least one year.

It is important to realize that like all diseases caused by viruses; CE cannot be treated with antibiotics. If infected animals are kept clean, the disease will clear up in one to four weeks without treatment.

Ticks and Mites

Goats suffer from ticks and mites which are common ectoparasites who feed on goat's blood. Extensive infestation leads to itching, anaemia and debility. They cause reduction in body weight and milk production by the animals. A herbal drug named "Alquit" developed by CIRG can be used as a spray to get rid of ticks and mites.

Gastro intestinal parasitism in goats has adverse effect of productivity of these animals. Although treatment of goat flocks for parasitic infections has been accepted as a standard practice in organized flocks however, in field flocks this still needs greater push on emphasis. Use of various anthihelminthics has brought the following newer concern to the forefront.

Anthelmintic resistance- reduced efficacy of anthelmintic drugs is being commonly observed. Repeated anthelmintic treatments will not be sustainable alternative as it will be expensive. An alternative for this in the future could be the selection of goats resistant to parasitic diseases.

International trade of meat has been blamed for outbreaks of Foot and Mouth Disease and Swine Fever. However, a qualitative assessment of the risks posed by sheep and goat meat indicate that with the possible exception of foot and mouth disease there is little likelihood that Office International des Epizooties List A or List B diseases would be spread through trade in adequately matured meat obtained from animals which have passed veterinary ante-mortem and post-mortem inspections (MacDiarmid and Thompson 1997).

Diarrhea (scours)

Diarrhea is defined as an increased frequency, fluidity, or volume of fecal excretion. The feces may contain blood or mucous and be smelly. There are many causes of diarrhea: bacterial, viral, parasites, and diet. Despite improvements in management practices and prevention and treatment strategies, diarrhea is still the most common and costly disease affecting neonatal small ruminants. The four major causes of diarrhea in kids during the first month of life are E. Coli, rotavirus, Cryposporidum sp. and Salmonella sp. E. coli scours are most common.

Neonatal Diarrhea Complex is the name applied to hard-to-identify or unidentified causes of diarrhea in newborns and very young kids.

Selenium Deficiency (aka White Muscle Disease) can cause weak rear legs in newborn and young kids and can keep the kid from swallowing.

Mineral and Vitamin Deficiencies can affect newborns and young kids in ways similar to selenium deficiency. Copper is essential to the goat's body. Loss of hair color and inability to breed or ability to carry fetuses to term are indicators of copper deficiency.

Coccidiosis

Coccidiosis is an economically important disease of livestock. It can be a very devastating disease in goats, as it is known to cause mortality and morbidity in a large number of herds every year (Matthews, 2009). Clinical coccidiosis of goats occurs mainly in young goats and has a higher prevalence under conditions of intensive husbandry. The disease may occur under stress factors such as weaning, dietary changes, inclement weather, or travel and regrouping .

Coccidiosis is a managemental disease caused by overstocking and lack of cleanliness. Adult goats can develop coccidiosis if they are stressed or if they are moved into an environment that is heavily infested with oocysts. It can be a very devastating disease in goat herds. Coccidiosis is caused by coccidia, a group of protozoan (single celled) parasites. Goats become infected after ingesting the oocyst from the environment. Seventeen species of Eimeria are known to infect goats, but two species are particularly troublesome: Eimeria ninakohlyakimovae and Eimeria arlongi. Regular deworming and other measures like clean bedding are important. Coccidiosis is more common during rainy season.

If a goat is exhibiting clinical signs of coccidiosis (diarrhea being the most common sign) there are some treatment options. These include sulfa drugs, such as sulfamethazine, sulfadimethoxine and sulfaguanidine, tetracycline and amprolium. These drugs are called coccidiostats. Coccidiostats do not kill coccidia. However, they slow it down. With a heavily infected goat, treatment may not be successful, but it will help reduce the number of oocysts that are being passed into the environment.The best preventive measure a goat producer can take is to use a feed with a coccidiostat added or use a growth promotor. With careful management and sound preventive measures, the losses associated with this disease can be reduced to minimal levels. Prevent Coccidiosis by keeping pens and bedding clean, water fresh, goats uncrowded, and areas dry. Wet and dirty conditions are incubators of Coccidiosis for both kids and adults. Don't forget the absolute necessity of rotating pastures.

The overall prevalence rates for coccidial infections manifested as singles or concurrent states were 42.86 % in Jakhrana goats (Sharma *et al.,* 2009).

Good management practices go a long way towards preventing illnesses. Sufficient space to avoid over-crowding, clean and dry pens, fresh water, quality hay, and sanitary conditions are minimum requirements. Filth and crowding breed sickness.

Mastitis in goats

Mastitis is an important disease in several farm animals including goats. Goats affected by clinical or subclinical mastitis suffer with negative effects on animal welfare, milk production, milk quality and farmer economy. Antimicrobials are often used in treatment of mastitis. Most cases of mastitis are associated with bacterial infections, but mastitis is a multi-factorial disease with a large number of predisposing factors complicating its control. Such factors can be found in the management, (e.g. milking routines), and environment (e.g. hygiene) of the goat, but factors related to the animal itself (e.g. udder conformation) are also important. Predisposing factors resulting in bacterial contamination of udder and teats, and/or negative impact on the local and general immune systems of the goats are most important.

Reproductive disorders

Reproductive disorders can lead to economic losses in terms of reduced fertility, low life time production, longer calving interval and increased expenses on medication in livestock. Reproductive disorders can cause complete or partial reproductive failure. Goats can suffer from many reproductive aberrations and disorders. It has been reported that of all the disorders or infestations, 10 per cent are caused by reproductive disorders. In one study in goats prevalence of 45.8% was recorded for dystocia followed by abortions (23.0%), retention of foetal membranes (10.6%), uterine infection (9.3%), vaginal/uterine prolapse (3.6%), reported anoestrus (2.3%), vaginal infection (2.1%) and vaginal bleeding (1.7%) (Durrani and Kamal, 2009).Reproductive disorders may include dystocia or difficult birth which is one of the most common in goats especially in goats bearing twins or triplets.The different causes of dystocia include incomplete dilatation of the cervix, uterine inertia and abnormal foetal presentation, position and posture. Retention of foetal membrane is common in animals with a previous history of abortion. Major predisposing factors include genital infections, uterine inertia, premature birth and managemental factors. High prolificacy has also been implicated in cases of pregnancy toxaemia. Intersexuality is a rare congenital abnormality in domestic animals, but has been reported in goats. Gynaecomastia with significant augmentation of the mammary glands although not very common has been reported in few cases of goats which impairs locomotion. Ultrasound can be a useful tool in diagnosing the female reproductive tract disorders in goats such as hydrometra and pyometra.

Herbal drugs for goat diseases

A large number of goat diseases have been treated using herbal remedies in many countries of the world since times immemorial. India and China are known for such ITKs. India is known for its rich biodiversity as of today about 1.26 lakhs plant species have been catalogued. A large number of them are used by local people for bio-control of pests or as medicines, industrial raw material, nutritional sources etc.

Vedas, Skand Puran, Devi Puran written by Palikapya (1000 BC) and Salihotra (2350 BC) and script of great phophets Charak and Sushruta (2500 BC – 600 BC) have documented the treatment of animal diseases by using medicinal plants. Ayurveda is in fact the very foundation stone of the ancient medical science, in which an entire section has been deveted to animal therapeutics. The Charak and Sushruta describe a large number of crude drugs and a large part of them has origin in plants. Phytomedicine has been used by farmers and traditional healers to treat parasitism and improve performance of livestock, and many modern commercial medicines are derived from plants.

Some of the important plants having medicinal importance to animals including goats includes satavari, safed musli, kali musli, Bael, Amaltas, Palas, Ashwagandha, Aak, Gokru, Bada Gokru, Isabgol, Imli, Neem, Bapchii, Kalmegh, Dathura, Arka, Dudhi etc. Extract of male fern from Dryopteris fixmas has been used against tapeworms and flukes. Nicotiana tabacumas nicotine sulphate is used against Monizia, Ascaridia and several species of gastrointestinal nematodes. Ripe fruit of Mallotus philippinensis is reported to have anthelmintic activity against thread and roundworm. Leaves of Azadirachta indica and fruit of Embelia ribes are reported to have cercaricidal property. Neem tree containing azadirachtin, vepaol, isovepaol, nimbin, nimidin and vanillic acid and oil from the seed is used as anthelmintic. Further, efficacy of Neem seed against natural gastrointestinal nematodes was observed to be 40-50 % in goats . Seed of Carica papaya, Sapindus trifoliatus and Mimordia charantia have been used as anthelmintic agent against Ascaridia galli. Butea frondosa seeds were reported to be effective against Ascaridia galli in poultry and 80-100% effective against Oxyuris in mice. Berberis aristats has been reported to have anthelmintic activity while extract of Holorrhena have been found effective against mixed coccidiosis. Garlic chips and garlic pearls have been found effective against caecal coccidiosis in chicken.

Although allopathic drugs are often highly potent and work fast, but they are costly and difficult to assess in remote areas by the goat keepers. In addition to this, allopathic treatments may have side effects, cause environmental pollution and develop resistance to treatment. Ayurvedic medicinal plants donot act as fast as allopathic drugs, but stimulate the immune response and improve the inner strength of the body as a whole.

Advances in animal health are expected to play a major role in the progress of livestock industry. Control of animal diseases assumes prime importance in the crucial time of shifting of animal agriculture from extensive to intensive and commercial system of management. In the field there is a great reliance on use of herbal medicine for treatment of goats.

Poisoning

Poisonous chemicals and plants can cause sickness and death in goats. Poisoning is often suspected as the cause of illness when a number of previously healthy goats show similar signs at the same time. The sudden onset of illness soon after goats have had access to unfamiliar feeds, after medication or spraying, or after a change to a new pasture often points to a poison as the cause of illness.

Goats suffer from hydrocyanic poisoning on consumption of Remza or raunza (Acacia leocophea). HCN content in such plants generally increases during drought conditions and animals are forced to eat such plants. Main clinical symptoms are sudden illness, tympany, respiration distress, red eyes, and death may occur within 2-10 hours. Oral administration of sodium thiosulphate at the dose of 4-6 g or the same amount by intravenous route is effective.

Ipomoea carnea is a toxic plant that grows in tropical areas, and is readily consumed by grazing goats. The plant contains toxic alkaloids which inhibit cellular enzymes and cause systematic cell death. This plant was found to grow along roadside in Bundelkhand area and is a threat to goats.

In certain parts of Tamil Nadu, specifically Nilgiris, toxic pasture weeds are thought to seriously affect the health of sheep and goats. Hepatitis, gastroenteritis, and nervous disorders are the complaints commonly attributed to toxic weeds, which include Echium plantagineum, Cycas spp., Euphorbia, Delphinium, Lobelia inflata, and Oxalis cernua. Thorny weeds, such as Ulex europueus, Rubus moulueanus, and Rubus racemousus, pose health risks too. Another group of weeds called "killer weeds," including Juncas, Erogrostis curivella, and Cyprus spp., are fatal when their tender shoots are eaten. In Nilgiris, Bracken fern, canary grasses, perennial rye grasses, panic grasses, and Kikiyu grasses cause various kinds of disorders in the animal.

Vitamin and mineral deficiency diseases

Proper vitamin and mineral levels are essential to the good health of goats. Although no single mineral can be singled out as more important than others, copper, zinc, and selenium levels are especially critical.

Selenium deficiency and Vitamin E deficiency, can cause white muscle disease (nutritional muscular dystrophy), causing the goat to have difficulty controlling its muscles. Newborns with weak rear legs may be selenium-deficient. Kids may be too weak to nurse their dams. Pneumonia may result from weakness in muscles that control breathing.

References

Bandyopadhyay, S.K. (2002). The economic appraisal of a PPR control programme in India. In 14th annual conference and national seminar on management of viral diseases with emphasis on global trade and WTO regime, Indian Virological Society, 18-20 January, Hebbal Bangalore.Indian Virological Society, Hisar.

Durrani, A.Z. and Kamal, N. (2009) Prevalence of genital tract problems in clinical cases of various species of animals The Journal of Animal & Plant Sciences 19(3): 160-162

MacDiarmid, S.C., Thompson, E.J. (1997) The potential risks to animal health from imported sheep and goat meat Rev Sci Tech. Apr;16(1):45-56

Matthews, John, G. (2009) Diseases of the Goat, 3rd Edition Wiley-Blackwell, Oxford, UK.

Murphy, F.A., Faquet, C.M., Bishop, D.H.L., Ghabrial, S.A., Jarvis. A.W., Martelli, G.P., Mayo, M.A. and Summers, M.D. (eds) (1995) "Virus taxonomy." 6th report of the International Committ-ee on Taxonomy of Viruses. Arch. Virol. Suppl., 10:85-86.

Poonia, J.S. and Malik, B.S. (2011) Non Genetic Factors Affecting Mortality of Beetal Kids Indian Journal of Small Ruminants, 17(1):115-117.

Rafyi, A. and Ramyar, R. (1959). Goat pox in Iran. Serial passage in goats and the developing egg and relationship with sheep pox. Journal of Comparative Pathology 69:141-9.

Sharma, D., Agrawal, N., Mandal, A., Nigam, P. and Bhushan, S. (2009). Coccidia and gastrointestinal nematode infections in semi- intensively managed jakhrana goats of semi- arid region of India. Tropical and Subtropical Agroecosystems, 11(1):135-139.

Sutmoller, P., Barteling, S. S., Olascoaga, R.C. & Sumption, K.J. (2003). Control and eradication of foot-and-mouth disease. Virus Res., 91:101-144.

Vihan, V.S. (2010) Diseases of the small ruminant, Satish Serial Publishing House, New Delhi

Vihan, V.S., Kala, S.N. and Singh, V.P. (1992) Epidemiological investigation of neonatal kid mortality due to enteropathogenic colibacillosis. Preventive Veterinary Medicine, 13:179-183.

12

Economics and Marketing

Livestock economics and marketing plays an important role in the economy of farmers in the country. Marketing of goats and goat products suffers from many drawbacks such as involvement of middlemen, avoidable marketing cost, and unnecessary transportation, mortality of animals during transit leading to exploitation of both producers and the consumers. Goat keeping and marketing is fraught with risks. Risks in goat keeping can be managed or reduced but cannot be completely eliminated. Some of the precautions needed include following the recommended systems of management and health care, use good feeding and vaccination schedules and master the art of marketing. Marketing of goat is under the hand of unorganized sector and middleman oriented. Goat producers themselves are most often involved in informal market systems which lead to underestimation of goats' contribution to the rural and national economy. Goats from villages are sold to middleman or butcher or in the local goat market that go to the slaughterhouses of organized or unorganized sector. Male goat is sold at the age of 12-15 months and at higher prices. However, farmer grows the male goat to sell in festive season for more profit. Market Goat price is highly variable. It differs from region to region. In area where good breeds of goat found, the prices are more for these animals. It also depends on health, body status, production potential and market demand for meat/milk of animals. Infact, male goat is sacrificed before God in many places. Goat market price gets higher during the festive season of Bakrid. "Bakra bech rahe ho ya sona," a customer was heard exclaiming at Nai Sadak Mandi, considered the biggest goat market in Kanpur. During Bakri Id, male goat is sold even at the cost of Rs 30-35 thousand. Similar stories are commonplace in most other goat markets. Lame and ailing goats are not purchased by customers for sacrificial purpose. For this purpose goats which are at least a year old are purchased. They are recognised by their two teeth.If animal is young one (1-2 yrs old & or pregnant), then price is higher than old animal. Female goats are sold to market for slaughter at the end of their productive life (Spent goat. Normally goats are sold on lot basis and not on body weight basis. With advancing knowledge, the farmers are now demanding price on body weight basis.

Goats are traditional sacrificial animal. Muslims celebrate Eid Al-adha as the day when the patriarch Abraham offered his only son Ishmael in sacrifice to Allah the God. Allah accepted his offering and ordered the Rooh-ul-quds (The Holy Ghost) Arc Angel Gabriel to save Ishmael and substitute a lamb in his place. For all Muslims who can afford, pilgrimage to Mecca is mandatory on that day which is called the Hajj. Those who cannot afford to go to Mecca celebrate the festival back at home by offering prayers and sacrificing an animal - a goat or a sheep or a lamb, to honor Abraham's sacrifice of his son. The Muslim koranic tradition differs from the biblical Jewish Christian tradition, where it is said that Isaac was offered. Muslims honor Isaac as a prophet but not as that son of Abraham who was offered in sacrifice.

Goats are a major under-exploited food and capital resource in many developing economies of the world. Unlike many industrial enterprises which are owned by a select few, goat enterprises are owned by a large proportion of the rural population. Goats are mostly owned by individual men or women or households who manage these animals and not by large proxy owners as has been the case many other enterprises. Goat production is generally one of a number of farm enterprises that lend a measure of diversity to the larger farm economy.

Now private companies are coming forward in many states like West Bengal and Jharkhand to promote and market goat meat by establishing goat meat processing unit. Responding to the market signals, the goat production system in India has been slowly moving from extensive to intensive system of management for commercial production. However, inadequate marketing facilities are one of the fundamental constraints faced by the people engaged in goat keeping. Most of the goat rearers (> 90%) sell their animals at their village to the butcher or middleman whereas only few (< 10%)goat rearers sold them to the nearest mandi. Goat rearers retain their female kids as replacement stock and males are sold for meat purpose.

The role of goats in developing countries is changing rapidly. Increasingly, goats and their products are being sold for cash. This is driven by the growing urban demand for goat products, based on increased urban populations with higher incomes and associated dietary changes. Small-scale goat keepers in India and Asia can benefit from greater participation in the market economy, achieving higher incomes and improved food security.

Socio-economics of goat farming

Goats are reared by more than 70 % landless, marginal and small farmers of the rural India.When kept on free range grazing/browsing on highly degraded grazing land in semi-arid ecology, indigenous goats were 2.5times more economical than indigenous sheep (Swain, 1984).Veeranna *et al.* (2004) in their study on economic structure of goat farming in selected district of North Karnataka revealed that more number of farmers preferred goat farming with a combination of cow. Singh *et al.* (2006) studied the socio-economic aspects of sheep and goat flock owners during 2001-02 in Himachal Pradesh. Their study revealed that about 46 per cent were small and 54 per cent were large, maintaining 34 and 66 per cent of the total animal,respectively. The share of goats was higher on small (35%) than large flocks. The average family size and land holding varied widely according to flock-size. The average size oflandholding was 0.30 ha for small and 0.77 ha for large flock-owners.

Rath (1992) studied the economics of sheep and goat rearing in Maharashtra state. He observed for 2 years that doe goat costs Rs. 450; the total capital cost of 5 does was Rs.2250 and the return Rs. 700 from sale of kids in the first year and Rs. 1,150 from the sale of kids in the second year.Deoghare and Bhattacharya (1993) studied the costs and returns of goat keeping (in 1990-91). Data were collected from 80 goat-rearing households in Mathura, UP. The income from milk, sale of animals, value of manure and stock acceleration was analyzed. Large flocks (>10 goats), medium flocks (6-10 goats) were better managed than small flocks (2-5 goat). Capital investment per goat was Rs. 813, Rs. 732 and Rs.780 for small, medium and large flocks respectively. The net income from small, medium and large flock was Rs 146, Rs 296 and Rs 616 respectively. Francis (1994) studied the goat rearing challenges and opportunities at the state bank institute of rural development, Hyderabad. Goat rearing under stalled conditions may be encouraged as it is not only sustainable in nature but also provides income and self employment.

Prabaharan and Thirunavakkarasu (1995) conducted a study in Tamil Nadu to assess the income and employment potential of goat rearing enterprise. They observed that the cost of production per herd per annum was Rs.1,909, Rs.4,130 and Rs.6,457 for small (1-8 goats), medium (9-16 goats) and large (above 16 goats) respectively, of which labour cost accounted for 74 per cent, 66 per cent 59 per cent respectively. Annual net income was Rs.1,200, Rs.1879 and Rs.6,800 for small, medium and large herds, respectively.

Shinde *et al.* (2003) studied the economics of goat rearing in Rajasthan. Cost of animal constituted 80.64 per cent and equipment 3.87 per cent of total investments in initiation of the goat rearing ventures. Total cost incurred in goat rearing was Rs.1,425.95 and Rs. 683.45/goat/year. The income from sale of milk, surplus animals and manure constituted 50.64, 39.42 and 9.92 per cent of total receipts. The gross income obtained per goat per year was Rs.911.30 and net income per goat per year was Rs. 277.85. The B:C ratio was found to be 1:1.34. It was concluded, that goat rearing is reasonably remunerative providing Rs.1.34 against every rupee invested.

Jitender *et al.* (2005) studied the costs and returns from sheep and goat farming in Mahendergarh and Gurgaon district of Haryana in 2001-02. The annual average total cost per sheep farm was worked out to be Rs. 26,674 while on goat farm it was Rs.12,169. The average net returns from sheep and goat rearing were Rs. 4,983 and Rs. 16,605 respectively.

Goats are reported to be more economical than cattle and sheep under natural grazing browsing (Sharma and Jindal, 2008). Cost and return of goat farming vary among different breeds and different areas. Goat farming is more economical than cattle and buffaloes because the capital investment is relatively low, land requirements are small, reproductive rates are higher both due to shorter breeding interval and high prolificacy and they can be managed by spare family labour and do not require any serious housing facilities and management skills. There is much less risk in goat farming in drought prone areas where large mortality occurs due to frequent droughts.

The total expenditure of goat farming can be divided into various components like value of existing stock, cost of feed, cost of labour, value of shed, miscellaneous cost & veterinary expenses and interest on total expenditure.Returns in the goat farming include value of milk, sale of kids & goats and value of manure.Goat farming with improved breed of prevalent species and larger herd size is highly remunerative enterprise. The emerging favourable market conditions and easy accessibility to improved goat technologies are also catching the attention of entrepreneurs. High demand for goat and its products with potential of good economic returns have been deriving many progressive farmers, businessmen, professionals, ex-servicemen and educated youths to take up the goat enterprise on a commercial scale. Kumar (2007) reported that a majority of commercial goat farms have been found operating with positive net returns.Use of improved technologies, particularly prophylaxis, superior germ plasm, low cost feeds and fodders and innovative marketing of the produce are the essential pre-conditions for successful commercial goat production.

Singh *et al.* (2011) carried out studies on economics of goat keeping under extensive conditions and found that the overall average net income was Rs. 1183.66 in case of barbari breed and Rs. 894.06 in case of local breed. Relatively lower cost of goats farming was mainly due to higher production of milk and very short breeding interval and fast multiplication and early maturity of kids in case of barbari breed as compared to local breed. Gupta *et al.* (2011) in their studies on economics of goat rearing in Rajasthan indicated that major return to the goat breeder was from milk (59.7%), followed by sale of animals (33.5%) and manure

(6.8%). The net return per goat was 606 Rs with benefit-cost ratio of 2.8 which was better as compared to sheep.

Model Goat project

(Jindal 2003)

1. Title: Running a Goat Farm
2. Objectives:

To rear goats for milk and meat production

- To raise kids for market.
- To improve production and productivity of milk
- To generate income from goat rearing business

Local Area

The project may be located in rural areas or in the outer frings of urban areas. Project Components

- 50 goats and 2 bucks
- Shed
- Feed (green & dry fodder) and concentrates
- Utensils and equipments (Feeding and watering devices, Buckets, cans, etc.)

Assumptions

- Land is available for construction of shed
- Constant breeding stock of 50 breeding goats is maintained. Breeding is about 90% in the female parents.
- Death in the breeder stock will be compensated by insurance claim.
- Project is assumed for 5 years and 7 crops of kids will be sold in 60 months.
- Kids are weaned from mothers after two months, reared as yearling upto 10 months , average weight male -24kg, Female 22kg, @ Rs 60/kg live weight
- During normal season and Rs 80/- kg during festive season.
- Milk = 75 liter/doe/lactation @ Rs 7/ litre.

Project Cost

a. Capital cost	: Rs. 120900
b. Recurring cost (for 5 year)	: Rs. 565101
Income (5years)	: Rs. 908075
Profit	
i. Per annum	: Rs. 68595
ii. Per month	: Rs. 5716

Detailed Project Proposal

1. Steps for Launching the Programme

- Undergo training at CIRG, Makhdoom, Farah, Mathura on 'Commercial goat farming'.
- Visit to a nearby goat farm or organized farm like CIRG, Makhdoom, Farah
- Select project as per viability and availability of resources.
- Prepare an appropriate project report
- Approach concerned department for a loan under PMRY or any other scheme in which funds are available for agriculture/animal husbandry enterprises.
- Make necessary preparation at the site and for launching the enterprise
- On receipt of the loan amount procure the inputs/purchase of raw material
- If possible undertake On-the-Job-Training at the nearby dairy farm running successfully
- Launch and operationalise the project/enterprise
- Maintain the daily record of activities and inputs and accounts

2. Assumption

- Land is available for construction of shed
- Constant breeding stock of 50 breeding goats is maintained. Breeding is about 90% in the female parents.
- Death in the breeder stock will be compensated by insurance claim.
- Project is assumed for 5 years and 7 crops of kids will be sold in 60 months.

- Kids are weaned from mothers after two months, reared as yearling upto 10 months, average weight male -24kg, Female 22kg, @ Rs 60/kg live weight
- During normal season and Rs 80/- kg during festive season.
- Milk = 75 liter/doe/lactation @ Rs 7/ litre.

3. Project Components

- 50 goats and 2 bucks
- Shed
- Feed and fodder
- Equipment /Utensils – Feeding/watering devises/buckets etc.

4. Project cost

A. Capital Investment

a. Land area required for shed : Covered		170^2m
Open		340^2m
b. Shed construction	:	Rs. 39,900/-
c. Cost of animals (50 goats and 2 buck)	:	Rs. 74,000 (70,000+4,000)
d. Utensils and Equipment (Feeder/waterer etc (Buckets, cans, etc.)	:	Rs. 7,000/-
Total Capital Investment	:	Rs. 120,900/-
B. Fixed Expenses		
Interest on capital (@ 12%/ annum)	:	Rs. 15468/-
Depreciation of animals (@ 15%/annum)	:	Rs. 11100/-
Depreciation on shed (@ 10%/annum)	:	Rs. 3990/-
Depreciation on utensils & equipment (@ 10%/annum)	:	Rs. 700/-
Total (Ist year)	:	Rs. 31258/-
Total (5 years)	:	Rs 116342/-
C. Recurring expanses		
Cost of feed and fodder		Rs 38825/-

Cost of veterinary care @ Rs 25/- adult		Rs 1410/-
		@Rs 15/kid
Salary and Wages@ Rs. 1000/month/person	:	Rs. 14400/-
Miscelleneous Expenses including power, fuel, insurance etc	:	Rs. 9760/-
Total recurring Cost	:	Rs 65396/-
Total recurring cost (5years)	:	Rs 4,48,759/-
Total Expenses (B+C) in five year	:	Rs. 565101/-

D. INCOME

Sale of Milk

(i) Income from milk, manure, skin in I year	Rs 29,085/-
Income in IInd Year	Rs 159,596/-
Income in IIInd Year	Rs 2,63,022
Income in IV th Year	Rs 2,53,032
Income in Vth Year	Rs 2,03,340
Total income in 5 years	Rs 9,08,075

E. Repayment in II year	:	Rs 30,000/-
III year	:	Rs 30,000/-
IV year	:	Rs 30,000/-
V year	:	Rs 30,900/-
Total Repayment	:	Rs 120900/-

F. PROFIT + Net Income – Total Expenditure

Net Income	=	Rs. 908075
Total Expenditure	=	Rs. 565101/-
Profit/Annum	=	Rs. 68,595/-
Profit/Month	=	Rs. 5716

Marketing of live goats

Goats are mostly sold in lots in livestock fairs, periodical markets and daily markets. Each goat is assessed individually by the buyer. Factors affecting the price are meat, milk yield, breed, age, sex, quality, locality and season. Majority of goat owners in India prefer to sell their goats in the village itself. Flock owners sell goats to reduce flock size and due to reproductive problems, agalactia, diseases, weakness and old age. Male kids are sold toreduce flock size for profits or to avoid mortality risk. Other reasons for selling goats are to fulfill family needs, repay loans, purchase seeds and fertilizers, for social obligations, replace goats, unforseen expenses and home repair. Government of India provides support for theregulation of the existing markets and to organize co-operative markets to facilitate marketing of products, to make market surveys, to collect and disseminate market news, and to advise better marketing methods and adoption of grading procedures through various schemes.

In Delhi, about two lakh goats are sold during the hold festival of Bakrid. The major market for these goats is Jama Masjid Area. Goats are brought for sale from Meerut, Badaun, Shahjahanpur, Bijnor, Etawah, Aligarh in UP, Bharatpur, Dausa in Rajasthan and Mewat area in Haryana. The goats considered appropriate for slaughter during Bakrid must be Do Daant (Two teeth).

Goat generally donot get sold on the basis of liveweight and there is, every likelihood that the goat farmers get under paid for their goats. Standardisation of live goat sale, based on live body weight is required, so that the farmers don't get under paid for their product. The meat rates does not fluctuate on day today basis and is rising steadily in long run, but the farmers in absence of any standard valuation of their product is under a risk of getting under paid.

Srivastava and Saraswat (2006) studied the marketing of Jaunpuri goats in Jaunpur district of eastern Uttar Pradesh in 2001-02. They concluded that goat keepers frequently sold their goats for slaughter and goat owner carry their goats for sale in the nearby weekly market. On an average, the marketing cost per goat was Rs.66.80. It was indicated the marketing cost per goat was negatively correlated with the size of flock.

Marketing of goat meat

There is no efficient marketing system because production is on a small scale and is scattered throughout the country. Moreover, there is no processing industry and almost all goat meat is sold fresh in the market. For long time meat industry has remained confined to a very small section of people in our country. These people had little knowledge of clean meat production and effective utilization of valued slaughterhouse byproducts. Majority of goat meat in India is marketed through butchers who slaughter one or two animals daily in the backyard of their shop. This is a totally unacceptable situation as far as the hygiene is concerned. The equipment used for slaughtering is sometimes rusted and not sharp enough. The place where the slaughter takes place is usually not clean enough. However the positive point in this whole business is that the time gap between the slaughter and sale is not very long. Moreover, the meat in India is consumed after heating which ensures a more healthy meat as many pathogens gets destroyed during this process. Although in big cities, a large number of goats are slaughtered in big slaughter house or areas but there also the situation is not upto the mark. The conditions at Idgarh slaughter house of Delhi have a large scope for improvement as far as clean and hygienic meat production is concerned. Most of the butchers in cities as well as villages are illiterate and are not aware of the need of proper cleanliness during slaughter.

The first levels of traders in the marketing of goats for meat in many parts of Chattisgarh or nearby states, are called locally as Kuchias (Itinerant traders). These kuchias move from door to door in village and buy goats from the farmers, collects them and then transport and sell to the butchers cum meat retailers at their door steps, or in turn sells to a bigger kuchia. Kuchias form the bulk of sellers in the haat.

Demand for goat meat is more during festivals like Id, Bakrid, Muhharam, Holi, Dusshera and on Sundays. Demand for goat meat is highest around Muslim holidays. In order to appeal to Muslims, goat meat must be slaughtered and processed in accordance to Muslim dietary guidelines (Halal). Several firms in India and abroad sell quality frozen bone and boneless meat to five star hotel and domestic restaurants. Several entrepreneurs are selling goat meat and meat products to Restaurants, Mega marts run by multinational companies,super markets etc. It is essential to ensure that importance is given to international hygiene & safety standards. The U.S. is a big importer of goat products, primarily from Australia and New Zealand. Imported meat is mostly frozen. If we can increase our capacity for transport of quality frozen goat meat under cold chain we can hope to export large volume of goat meat to countries such as US. Demand for goat meat in America is primarily because of their Hispanic and Muslim community who prefer goat meat. The demand for goat meat is increasing. Muslim consumers in some countries are reputed to prefer meat from grass fed goats as compared to grain fed goats.

Despite recent developments of research on goats, the scientific investment in goats remains very low compared to large ruminants. Some of the factors restraining in adoption of scientific goat farming include lack of grazing land, lack of veterinary services, non-availability of improved breeding bucks, non-availability of medicines, lack of drinking water, non-availability of vaccination facility against contagious diseases, lack of institutional credit, insurance and poor marketing infrastructure and distant market.

Marketing of goat milk

In most parts of the world, dairy goat farms are widely scattered, making the pooling of milk for processing or transport to market costly. Marketing of goat milk and its products is still in its infancy. So far, there have been no marketing efforts attempted on a broad scale. As reported by Dubeuf and Boyazoglu (2009), less than 5% of the total milk produced by goats in the world is marketed. Majority of goat rearers use goat milk for home consumption while the remaining sell them as such or by mixing goat milk with the milk of other farm animals. In the last decade, there has been an increased interest for goat milk production and conversion to value added products. As the goat farmers are mostly unorganized and scattered and belong to the lower strata of the society, it is imperative to streamline the goat milk collection by establishing milk sheds in the home tract regions of the different milch breeds of goats especially in the states of Uttar Pradesh, Rajasthan and Kutch Region of Gujarat. This can be achieved through establishment of goat producers/breeders co-operative societies in the line of milk producer's co-operative societies under operation flood projects. Such efforts will ensure supply of goat milk in bulk for industrial use and also augment the production of healthy goat milk and milk products.The development of a professional marketing system is part of the challenge to benefit from the fact that many people consuming dairy products prefer products from goats. Recently few attempts have been made in India to market goat milk commercially eg at Bangalore under the brand name of Nadur goat farm.

Goat development strategies

Goat development sector necessitates a judicious mix of credit and subsidy as most of the stake holders are small holders, many of them living below the poverty line. Many a times, acquisition of credit through livestock development policies has been administered in a top down manner which has in many cases led to further indebtedness of these households. This has to change. Poor farmers depend upon diverse and complex livelihood systems of which agriculture and livestock keeping including goat keeping are important sub-systems. In this the goat, sheep, cattle and crop livelihood system is more sustainable. The input and service delivery mechanism of the government must be geared to deliver the services at the doorstep of the farmers especially in tribal areas where the presence of government functionaries is inadequate and the human settlements are geographically scattered.

Improvement of livestock productivity per unit animal remains the primary concern of research and development efforts. If the present course is followed, the only breeds of livestock that will survive will be those that are particularly useful in the scenario of increasingly modernized farming systems. Thus, there is a real danger that many of the breeds may effectively become extinct unless some conservation or breed utilization programme is put in place.

The poor and landless farmers predominantly keep goats for sustenance. However, at its prevalent scale of production, its potential for providing income and employment remain low. To make significant increase in the income and employment generation potential of goat farmers, it would require a substantial scaling up. This scaling up will go a long way in reducing poverty level among these farmers. Goat rearing has received good support from central and state governments under various rural development programmes. One of the most popular programme for goat farmers is Swarnajayanthi Gram Swarozgar Yojna. Apart from this, there are many programmes /schemes sponsored by various state governments to support the poor goat farmers to enhance their sustainability eg ATMA, AFPRO etc. Various institutions like commercial banks, regional rural banks, cooperative banks and NABARD etc are providing credit to goat husbandry. Credit is extended for commercial goat production, fodder production, slaughter house, processing and marketing. It has been estimated that during XI plan period 5700 crore is required for goat development activities out of which 3740 crore has been estimated under institutional credit.

Under the Community Insurance Scheme, the farmer will receive 75% of the pre determined market value of the animal for death. For example, if the market value of the goat is Rs.1000, the sum assured for the farmer will be fixed as Rs.750. Thus the premium payable in a year is Rs.75/- or an amount equivalent to 7.5% of the market value of the goat insured. If the goat dies during the insurance period, the compensation assured for the farmer is Rs.750 or 75% of the pre determined market value of the goat. Such a scheme is proposed or in practice in some of the states but there is an urgent need to intensify it.

The establishment of self help groups among goat farmers will help to overcome the shortcomings of formal and informal credit channels. Women need to be included on a larger scale in the development process through self help groups. Women need to be involved in decision-making process and all women goat farmers self help groups can be a major breakthrough in this process. Capacity building of poor goat farmers needs to be taken up on a giant scale under a mission mode programme.Indigenous traditional knowledge (ITK) plays an important role in management of goats but the same has not been documented yet. Quantitative information on disease resistance capabilities and draft capacity of many breeds of goats is also not available. Research on these aspects needs to be intensified. The critical intervention in small ruminant farming is availability of quality breeding male which needs to be ensured in future breeding programmes. Farm incomes in the goat sectors are amongst the lowest in the agricultural industry and the financial support received falls well behind that of other more profitable agricultural sectors. Although not being given at present, subsidy for goat production systems is an urgent requirement of improving the livelihood and food security of poor goat farmers. Urgent measures need to be taken at government level to preserve goat farming on an economically sustainable basis.

Support services: The major concern for economic small animal rearing by the farmers is high mortality at different ages. It is observed that high mortality rate among the small animals can be reduced by rendering proper health care measures like de-worming, preventive vaccination and proper treatment to affected animals.The value of goats is also very significant in the wider context of massive agro forestry programmes in India. Production and consumption of balanced goat feed mixtures based on maximum use of by products from these programmes should be developed in a coordinated manner. There is a need to identify pockets and flocks of better germplasm goats of indigenous breeds and then launch programmes of purchasing of breedable males and distributing them to low performance flocks to upgrade indigenous germplasm all over the country.

Effective marketing systems including cooperatives and an assured stable price are essential. A number of attractive markets are generally untapped because of the potential hazards of disease being introduced from the exporting country. Export of prime quality and prime category carcasses to earn foreign exchange is possible if the exporting countries can ensure disease free status of their animals and also International standards of packing, processing and transport of meat is ensured.

References

Deoghare, P.R. and Bhattacharya, N.K., (1993). Economic analysis of Goat rearing in Mathura district of Uttar Pradesh. Indian J. Agric. Econ., 63(4):439-444.

Dubeuf, J-P., Boyazoglu, J. (2009). An international panorama of goat selection and breeds. Livestock Science, 120:225–231

Francis, O.H. (1994) Goat rearing: Challenges and Opportunities. Fin. Agric., 26: 20-25.

Gupta, D.C., Suresh, A. and Sethi, D. (2011). Economics of sheep and goat rearing in semi-arid region of Rajasthan Indian Journal of Small Ruminants, 17:215-2221.

Jindal, S.K. (2003). In Compendium of projects for establishing small enterprises in Agriculture,Vol 1, Edited by A.K.Sacheti et al, PSS Central Institute for Vocational Education, Bhopal pp 48-51

Jitender, B., Pandey, U.K. and Suhag, K.S. (2005). Small ruminant's economy of semi-arid region in Haryana. Indian J. Agric. Econ., 60(2):163-183

Kumar Shalander, (2007). Commercial Goat Farming in India: An Emerging Agri-Business Opportunity Agricultural Economics Research Review 20 (Conference Issue) :503-520

Prabaharan, R. and Thirunavakkarasu, N. (1995). Income and employment dynamics of goat farms in different agroclimatic zones of Tamil Nadu. Indian J. Animal Prod. Mgnt., 11(1): 14-26.

Rath, N., (1992). Economics of sheep and goat in Maharashtra. Indian J. Agric. Econ., 47(1): 62-78.

Sharma, M.C. and Jindal, S.K. (2008). Prospects of goat production in India. Compendium of lectures, ICAR sponsored winter school November 25 to December 15, 2008 on Recent advances in improvement of productive and reproductive efficiency of goats through physiological and nutritional interventions, CIRG, Farah, Mathura , U. P. pp 13-18.

Shinde, A.K., Raghavendra, Bhatta, Sankhyan, S.K., Singh, N.P. and Verma, D.L., (2003). Economics of goat rearing in an organized farm. Indian J. Small Ruminants., 9(1):32-34.

Singh, D.R., Sushila Kaur and Sivaramane, N., (2006). Migratory sheep and goat production system : the mainstay of tribal hill economy in Himachal Pradesh. Agric. Econ. Res. Rev., 19:387-398.

Singh, Satyendra Pal, A.K. Singh and R. Prasad (2011). Economics of Goat Farming in Agra District of Uttar Pradesh Indian Res. J. Ext. Edu. 11 (3):37-40.

Srivastava, S.P. and Saraswat, B.L. (2006). Marketing of Jamunapuri goats in its native tract. Indian J. Ani. Res., 40(2):127-130.

Swain, N., 1984. Performance of sheep and goat in semi-and region under free range grazing anagement. Ph.D. thesis, Bidhan Chandra Krishi Vishvavidya laya, Mohanpur, India.

Veerana, K.C., Singh, D.P. and Shivakumar, M.C. (2004). Economical structure of goat farming in North Karnataka Karnataka J. Agric. Sci. 17(2):303-305.

Appendix

Books on Goats

Acharya, R.M. (1982) Sheep and goat breeds of India. F.A.O.Animal Health and Production Paper No 30,F.A.O., Rome

Ahuja, Kanta, and M.S. Rathore. (1987). Goats and Goatkeepers: A Socio-economic Study. Jaipur: Rupa.

Bhat, P.N. and Khan, B.U. (2009) Goat Production, Studium Press, New Delhi

Bonface K. Kaberia, Mr. Patrick Mutia, Mr. Camillus Ahuya (2003) Farmers dairy goat production handbook (http://www.smallstock.info/reference/index.htm),

Coop, I.E. (1982) Sheep and Goat Production, Elsevier

Copeland, J.W. (1984) Goat production and research in the tropics. ACIAR, Australia

Devendra, C. & Burns, M. (1970) Goat production in the tropics. Common Wealth Agricultural Bureaux, Farnham Royal Bucks. England.

Devendra, C. & McLeroy, G.B. (1982). Goat and sheep production in the tropics. Longman Scientific and Technical.

Ensminger, M.E. and Parker, R.O. (1986) Sheep and Goat Science, Fifth Edition. Danville, Illinois: The Interstate Printers and Publishers Inc.

Gall, C. (1981) Goat Production, Academic Press, New York

Gall, C. (1996) Goat breeds around the world. CTA, Margraf/FAO. Weikersheim, Germany, 186 pp.

Hanumantha Rao, C. (2004) Handbook on sheep and goat production, A.P.Veterinary Council, Hyderabad

Jindal, S.K. (1984) Goat Production, Cosmo Publications, New Delhi

MacKenzie, David and Goodwin, Ruth (1993) Goat Husbandry, 5th Revised Edition, Faber and Faber,

Mathews, John, G. (2009) Diseases of the goat. Wiley Blackwell

Mahgoub, O. Kadim, I.T. and Webb, E. (Ed)(2012) Goat Meat production and Quality, CABI, pp 384

Mathur, P.B. and Dubey, S.C. (1994) Sheep and goat diseases, ICAR, New Delhi

Mishra, R.R. (1978) Management practices for goats, NDRI, Karnal

Peacock, C.P. (1996): Improving Goat Production in the Tropics. A manual for development workers. FARM-Africa/Oxfam,Oxford.

Prasad, Jagdish (2004) Goat, sheep and pig production and management, Kalyani, Ludhiana

Rathore, M.S. (1993). Marketing of goats in Rajasthan, Classic Pub. House, Jaipur.

Sharma, Kusumakar and Bhattacharyya, N.K.(2000) Bakri Palan (in Hindi), DIPA, ICAR, New Delhi

Smith, M.C. and Sherman, David, M. (2009) Goat Medicine, 2nd Edition, Wiley Blackwell,

Solaiman, Sandra Golpashini (2010) Goat Science and Production. Wiley Blackwell

Somvanshi, R. And Chatopadhyay, S.K. (2000) Goat diseases of tropics, Jaypee Brothers, New Delhi

Speedy, Andrew (Ed) (1992) Progress in sheep and goat research, CAB International, Oxon

Steele, Mike (1996) Goats, Macmillan Education Ltd, London,. viii + 152pp.

Tewari, S.B., B.Rai, (2003) Bakri Evam Bhed Me Nasal Sudhar (In Hindi), DIPA, ICAR, New Delhi

Tewari, S.B., Rai, B. (2005)Bharat Me Bakri Palan, In Hindi, Saroj Prakashan, Allahabad

Tu, Y. 1989. Sheep and Goat Breeding in China. Shanghai Scientific & Technology Publishers, Shanghai, P. R. China.

Vidya Sagar, and Kanta Ahuja. (1993). Economics of Goat Keeping in Rajasthan. Jaipur: Classic.

Vihan, V.S. (2010) Diseases of the small ruminant, Satish Serial Publishing House, New Delhi

Wilson, R.T. (1991) Small ruminant production and the small ruminant genetic resosurce in tropical Africa, FAO, Rome

Internet resources on Goats

CIRG : Central Institute for Research on Goats
www.cirg.res.in/
ISSGPU- Indian society for sheep and goat production and utilization
www.issgpu.org/
Small Ruminant Research - Elsevier
www.elsevier.com/wps/find/journaldescription.cws.../description
Langston University Goat & Research Extension
www.luresext.edu/goats/index.htm
www.goatworld.com
www.goatweb.com
Welcome to the American Dairy Goat Association
www.adga.org/
www.allgoats.com/
Maryland Small Ruminant Page (*www.sheepandgoat.com*)
www.sheepandgoat.com/
Dairy Goat Journal. Information, ideas, and insights for everyone ...
www.dairygoatjournal.com/linktous.html
http://www.nabard.org/
http://www.dahd.nic.in/dahd/default.aspx
http://www.tanuvas.tn.nic.in/
Indian Veterinary Research Institute (IVRI)
ivri.nic.in/
http://goat-link.com/
International Goat Association
www.iga-goatworld.com/
FAO: FAO Home
www.fao.org/
www.goat.genome.org
http://www.goatwala.com/
http://www.icar.org.in/

Goat breeds of the world

1. Aardi
2. Abergelle
3. Afar
4. Agrigento
5. Alan Tejo
6. Alpine
7. Altai Mountain
8. American Cashmere
9. Anatolian Black
10. Anglo-Nubian (Nubian)
11. Angora
12. Appenzell
13. Apulian
14. Arapawa Island
15. Arsi Bale
16. Askanian Mohair
17. Asmari (Afganistan)
18. Assam Hill
19. Attapady black
20. Australian Goat
21. Azerbaijan
22. Bach Thao
23. Bagot
24. Bakharwal
25. Baladi
26. Baltistani
27. Baluchi
28. Barbari
29. Bari
30. Beetal
31. Begait
32. Begayit
33. Belgian Fawn
34. Belgian white
35. Benadir
36. Berari
37. Bhuj
38. Bionda dell'Adamello
39. Black Bengal
40. Boer
41. Booted Goat
42. Boran
43. British Alpine
44. Brown Shorthair Goat
45. Bugri
46. Bundelkhandi
47. Campine
48. Canary Island
49. Canindé
50. Carpathian
51. Central Highland
52. Chamois Colored
53. Changthangi
54. Chaper
55. Chappar
56. Charnequeira
57. Chegu
58. Chengde Polled
59. Chengdu Brown
60. Congo dwarf
61. Corsican
62. Criollo
63. Crissons striped
64. Daera Din Panah
65. Damani
66. Damascus
67. Dazu Black
68. Danish Landrace
69. Dera Din Panah
70. Dhofari
71. Djelab
72. Diougry
73. Djelab
74. Dole
75. Don
76. Dorangi
77. Duan
78. Dutch Landrace
79. Dutch Toggenburg
80. Dutch white
81. East African
82. Eghoria
83. Erzgebirg
84. Etawah
85. Feral
86. Fiji
87. Finnish Landrace
88. Fouta Djallon
89. Gaddi (White Himalayan)
90. Galla
91. Ganjam
92. German Improved fawn

Contd.

Goat Breeds of the world			
93.	German Improved white	139.	Khasi
94.	Girgenti	140.	Kigezi
95.	Girgentana	141.	Kiko
96.	Gohilwadi	142.	Kilis
97.	Goingeget	143.	Kinder
98.	Golden Guernsey	144.	Kirghiz
99.	Granada	145.	Kodi Adu
100.	Grisons Striped	146.	Koraput Hill
101.	Gua Chelli	147.	Kosi
102.	Guinean	148.	Kottukachchiya
103.	Guinean dwarf	149.	Kutchi
104.	Hailun	150.	Ladhakhi Pashmina
105.	Haimen	151.	LaMancha
106.	Hararghe Highland	152.	Landim
107.	Hasi	153.	Leri
108.	Hejazi	154.	Loashan
109.	Hexi Cashmere	155.	Maabite
110.	Hipsi	156.	Mahabubnagar
111.	Hkway Seik	157.	Malabari
112.	Hongtong	158.	Malawi
113.	Huaipi	159.	Malkangiri
114.	Huaitoutala	160.	Malaga
115.	Hungarian Improved	161.	Maltese
116.	Iberian	162.	Mamber
117.	Iraqi	163.	Maradi
118.	Irish Goat	164.	Markhoz
119.	Jabali	165.	Marota
120.	Jade Ni	166.	Marwari
121.	Jakhrana	167.	Masai
122.	Jamunapari	168.	Mat'ou
123.	Jattan	169.	Mehsana
124.	Jining Grey	170.	Mingrelian
125.	Kacang	171.	Moroccan Black (Yahyaouia)
126.	Kaghani	172.	Moxotó
127.	Kajli	173.	Mubende
128.	Kambing Gembrong	174.	Mudugh
129.	Kambing Katjang	175.	Murcia-Granada
130.	Kamori	176.	Myotonic (Wooden Leg)
131.	Kangra/Chamba/Kangan	177.	Nachi
132.	Kanni Adu	178.	Narayanapatna
133.	Karamoja	179.	Nigerian Dwarf
134.	Kashmir	180.	Nilotic dwarf
135.	Katjang	181.	North Russian
136.	Kazakhstan	182.	Norwegian
137.	Keffa	183.	Nyaung Oo
138.	Khari (Hill)	184.	Oberhasli

Contd.

Goat Breeds of the world			
185.	Omani Batina	228.	Sudanese Nubian
186.	Orenburg	229.	Sukria
187.	Osmanabadi	230.	Surti
188.	Paggaio	231.	Swedish Landrace
189.	Palestinian	232.	Swiss Alpine
190.	Parbatsar	233.	Syrian Mountain
191.	Pateri	234.	Tapri
192.	Peacock Goat	235.	Tara Bakari
193.	Peranakan Etawah	236.	Tarai (South Nepal)
194.	Philippine	237.	Tauernsheck
195.	Phulbani	238.	Teddy
196.	Poitou	239.	Tegri
197.	Pygmy	240.	Telemark
198.	Pyrenean	241.	Tellichery
199.	Qinshan	242.	Tennessee Fainting
200.	Raeini (Iran)	243.	Tharki
201.	Raighar	244.	Thori
202.	Ramdan	245.	Thuringian
203.	Red Bosnian	246.	Toggenburg
204.	Red Sokoto (Red Skin)	247.	Tswana
205.	Repartida	248.	Turkish Native
206.	Russian White	249.	Uzbek Black
207.	Saanen	250.	Valais Blackneck
208.	Sable	251.	Vatani (Afganistan)
209.	Sahelian	252.	Verata
210.	Salt Range	253.	Verzasea
211.	San Clemente	254.	Vlahiki
212.	Sangamneri	255.	West African Dwarf
213.	Shami	256.	West African Long legged
214.	Sinhal	257.	White Shorthaired Goat
215.	Sirli	258.	Wooden Leg Goat
216.	Sirohi	259.	Woyto-Guji
217.	Skopelos	260.	Xinjiang
218.	Small East African	261.	Xuhai
219.	Sojat	262.	Yemen Mountain
220.	Somali	263	Zairibi
221.	South caucasian	264	Zalawadi (Surendranagar, Rajkot, Gujarat)
222.	South China Dwarf	265	Zhiwulin Black
223.	S.Sudan	266	Zhongwei
224.	Soviet Mohair	267	Zomri (Native goat of Saudi Arabia)
225.	Spanish	268	Zulu
226.	SRD	269	Zumri
227.	Sudan desert		

Glossary

Abomasum	:	The fourth chamber of the stomach in a ruminant which has the functions of stomach of non-ruminant.
Abortion	:	Premature termination of pregnancy
Acaricide	:	A chemical which kills ticks and mites
Acetic acid	:	One of the volatile fatty acids produced in the rumen
Aerobic bacteria	:	Bacteria which survive in the presence of oxygen
Alfalfa	:	A pasture legume crop also known as Lucerne
AI	:	Artificial Insemination
Anaerobic bacteria	:	Bacteria which can survive in an atmosphere devoid of oxygen eg rumen bacteria
Anoestrus	:	Time when the doe does not show oestrous cycle
Anthelmintic	:	Drugs used to kill helminthic parasites
Antibody	:	Serum protein (immunoglobulin) produced by the immune system of body against an antigen
Antigen	:	A molecule capable of eliciting synthesis of a specific antibody in vertebrates.
Antinutritional factor	:	A factor present in the feed which restricts the animals ability to use some desirable nutrients eg tannins
Antiseptic	:	Chemical agent which inhibits micro-organisms and is suitable for treatment of wounds etc
Arid	:	Having a very low rainfall
ART	:	Assisted Reproductive Technologies
AV	:	Artificial Vagina
Bacteria		Single-celled rigid walled micro-organisms which may cause diseases.
Bagasse	:	Dry pulp remaining after the extraction of juice from sugar cane
Bleating		Sound produced by a goat
Breed	:	A breed is a group of domestic animals with a homogeneous appearance,

		behavior, and other characteristics that distinguish it from other animals
Carrying capacity	:	The number of animals that can live on an area of land
CASA	:	Computer Assisted Semen Analyser
Casein	:	Major protein found in milk
Castration	:	Removal of the testicles or making them non functional
Cellulose	:	A polysaccharide made up of long chains of glucose molecules
Chromosome	:	A single large DNA molecule containing many genes and functioning to store and transmit genetic information.
Chronic	:	Lasting a long time
CIDR	:	Controlled internal drug releasing device
Clone	:	An exact replica of all or part of a macromolecule (e.g. DNA)
Colostrum		First or early milk of a freshly kidded goat
Compound feed	:	An animal food made up of a number of separate ingredients which have been ground-up and pelleted.
Concentrate feed	:	A feed which contains a high concentration of nutrients, is low in fibre and highly digestible
Cryptorchidism	:	Failure of one or both testicles to descend into the scrotum.
Culling	:	Removal of animal from the flock on grounds of being chronically sick, old or unproductive
Cytoplasm	:	The portion of a cell's contents outside the nucleus.
Dairy breed	:	Breed kept for milk production
DNA	:	Deoxyribonucleic acid
Diarrhoea	:	The frequent passage of loose, fluid faeces.
Dressing percentage	:	Percentage of animals body sold as meat , the weight of the carcass expressed as a percentage of liveweight at slaughter.
Dwarf	:	Small
Dystocia	:	Difficulty in kidding
eCG	:	Equine chorionic gonadotropin
Enzyme	:	A protein specialized to catalyze a specific metabolic reaction
ET	:	Embryo Transfer
Fat	:	Lipid present in feed, fodder, milk etc
FDA	:	Food and Drug Administration (US)
Fertility	:	Ability to produce kids
Fever	:	Elevated body temperature
FMD	:	Foot and Mouth Disease
Forage	:	Fibrous food for ruminants: mainly grasses and some legumes
FSH	:	Follicle Stimulating Hormone
Gene	:	A chromosomal segment that codes for a single polypeptide chain.
Genetic map	:	A diagram showing the relative sequence and position of specific genes along a chromosome molecule.
Genome		The genome is an organism's complete set of DNA components.
Genotype	:	Genetic make-up of an animal
GH	:	Growth Hormone
GHG	:	Green House Gases
GnRH	:	Gonadotrophin Release Hormone
Hormone	:	Hormone is a chemical substance that is secreted in trace amounts by an endocrine gland or tissue and acts as a messenger to regulate the function of another tissue or organ. *eg* growth hormone, insulin, thyroid hormone.
HOST	:	Hyper Osmomolality Swelling Test

Hybrid : The result of a cross between pure-bred animals
IGF-1 : Insulin like Growth Factor-1
Immunity : The ability to resist and overcome infection.
Immunoglobulin : An antibody protein generated in response to specific antigen
Inbreeding : Mating of animals that are related
Incisors : Front teeth
IVF : *In vitro* fertilization
IVM : *In vitro* maturation
IVP : *In vitro* production of embryos
JD : Johne's Disease
Kid : Young one of goat
Lactation : The period when the animal is producing milk for her young.
Lactose : Milk sugar, a disaccharide found in milk
Large intestine : The final part of the gut
Legume : Family of plants rich in nitrogen, which use bacteria to fix nitrogen in their roots.
LH : Luteinizing Hormone
LH-RH : Luteinizing Release Hormone
Libido : Sexual drive and energy
MAb : Monoclonal antibody
Methane : An inflammable gas produced in the rumen during digestion of feedstuffs
Molasses : Thick brown syrup made from sugarcane juice
Nomadism : Migratory way of life in which people have no permanant house
Notifiable disease ; A disease which must by law be reported to the Government Veterinary Authorities
Oestrus : Time when the doe will stand to be mated
Palatable Pleasant to eat
Parturition : The process of giving birth
Pashmina : Fine undercoat of fibre producing goats
Pastoralists : People who keep herds and flocks in arid and semi-arid areas
Pathogenic : Disease causing
PGF$_2$alpha : Prostaglandin F$_2$alpha
PMSG : Pregnant Mare Serum Gonadotrophin
PPR : *Peste de Pestes* ruminantis
Prepartum : Before birth.
Prolific : Producing more kids per litter
QTL : Quantitative Trait Loci
Roughage : Coarse, bulky feed high in fiber such as wheat straw
Rumen : First stomach of a ruminant responsible for digestion of cellulose present in feeds and production of volatile fatty acids
SCP : Single Cell Protein
Semi-arid : Area with a low rainfall
Silage : Preserved and fermented Green fodder
SOET : Single Ovulation Embryo Transfer
Straw : The dried stalks of grain crops used for feeding livestock
Sub-cutaneous : Underneath the skin
Tethering : A system of tying up a goat with a rope around the neck to restrict its grazing area.
Thiamine : One of the "B" complex vitamins
Toxic : Poisonous

Traditional	: Something which has been done for many years
Transhumance	: The seasonal practice of moving animals between two areas of different climatic conditions.
Urea	: A nitrogen containing compound mixed with molasses in feed to supplement nitrogen in the diet.
Vaccine	: A vaccine is a biological preparation that improves immunity to a particular disease.
Vitamin	: A vitamin is an organic compound required as a vital nutrient in tiny amounts by an organism
Volatile fatty acids	: Fatty acids produced in the rumen , mainly include acetic, propionic and butyric acids.
Wattles	: Appendages of flesh usually hang from the throat neck area. Serve no purpose except cosmetic.
Weaning	: The act of separating the young kids from their mother
Wethers	: Wethers are castrated young male goats.
Yearling	: Goats between one and two years old
Zoonosis	: Diseases of animals that can be transmitted to humans

Index

A

B

"N"

O

P

R

S

FSC
www.fsc.org
MIX
Papier | Fördert
gute Waldnutzung
FSC® C083411

Kolibri 360 GmbH
Ferdinand-Jühlke-Straße 7
99095 Erfurt, Deutschland
produktsicherheit@kolibri360.de